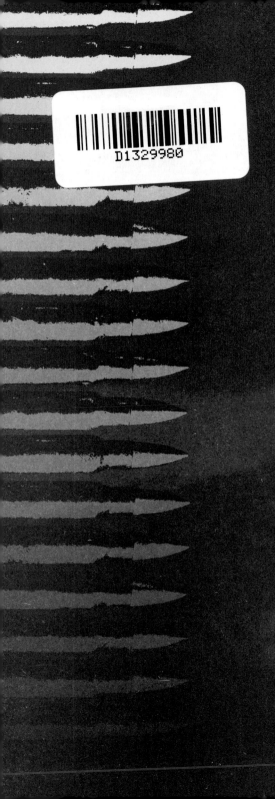

Keitaro Takahashi

Here we are at volume 7.
I've been writing this for
three years now. That's
hard to believe.

JORMUNGAND VOL. 7
VIZ SIGNATURE EDITION

STORY AND ART BY KEITAROU TAKAHASHI

Ⓒ 2006 KEITAROU TAKAHASHI/SHOGAKUKAN
ALL RIGHTS RESERVED.
ORIGINAL JAPANESE EDITION "JORMUNGAND" PUBLISHED BY SHOGAKUKAN INC.

PHOTO BY MIKIYO KOBAYASHI + BAY BRIDGE STUDIO

TRANSLATION/JOE YAMAZAKI
ENGLISH ADAPTATION/STAN!
TOUCH-UP ART & LETTERING/JOHN HUNT, PRIMARY GRAPHIX
DESIGN/SEAN LEE, SAM ELZWAY
EDITOR/MIKE MONTESA

PRINTED IN THE U.S.A.

PUBLISHED BY VIZ MEDIA, LLC
P.O. BOX 77010
SAN FRANCISCO, CA 94107

10 9 8 7 6 5 4 3 2 1
FIRST PRINTING, MAY 2011

www.viz.com

VIZ SIGNATURE
www.vizsignature.com

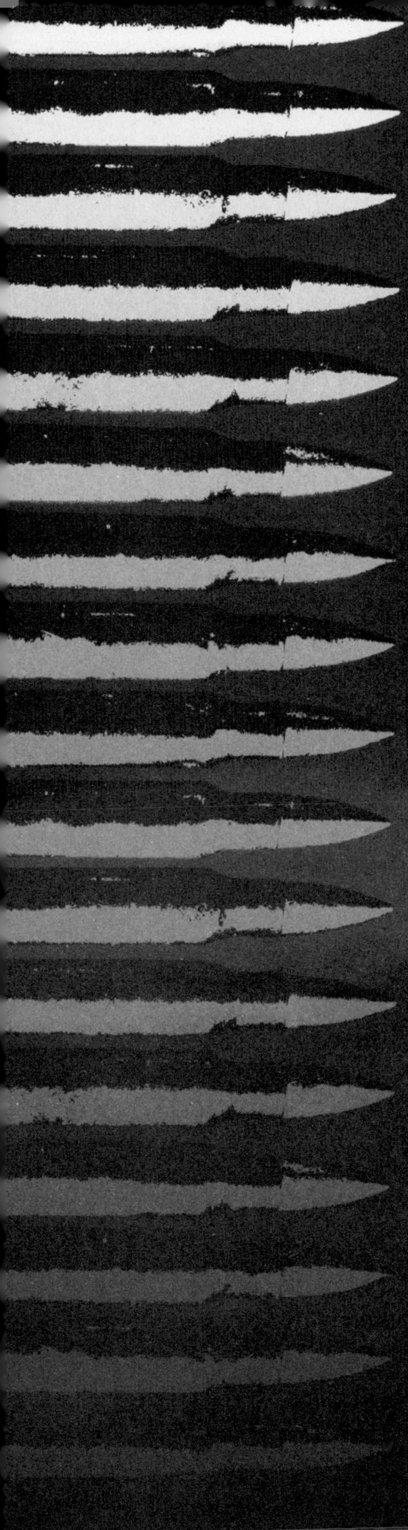

I DEVOURED THE FIVE LANDS
I DRAINED THE THREE SEAS
BUT I COULD NOT REACH THE SKY
IN THIS BODY WITH NO WINGS
NO ARMS AND NO LEGS.

I AM THE WORLD SERPENT.
I AM JORMUNGAND.

Jormungand

7

STORY AND ART BY KEITARO TAKAHASHI

Koko's Squad

Koko Hekmatyar
A young arms dealer whose father is a global shipping magnate. She belongs to HCLI's Europe/Africa Weapons Transport Division.

Lehm
A veteran mercenary with strong leadership skills.

Wiley

utz
he squad's marksman
nd expert sniper.

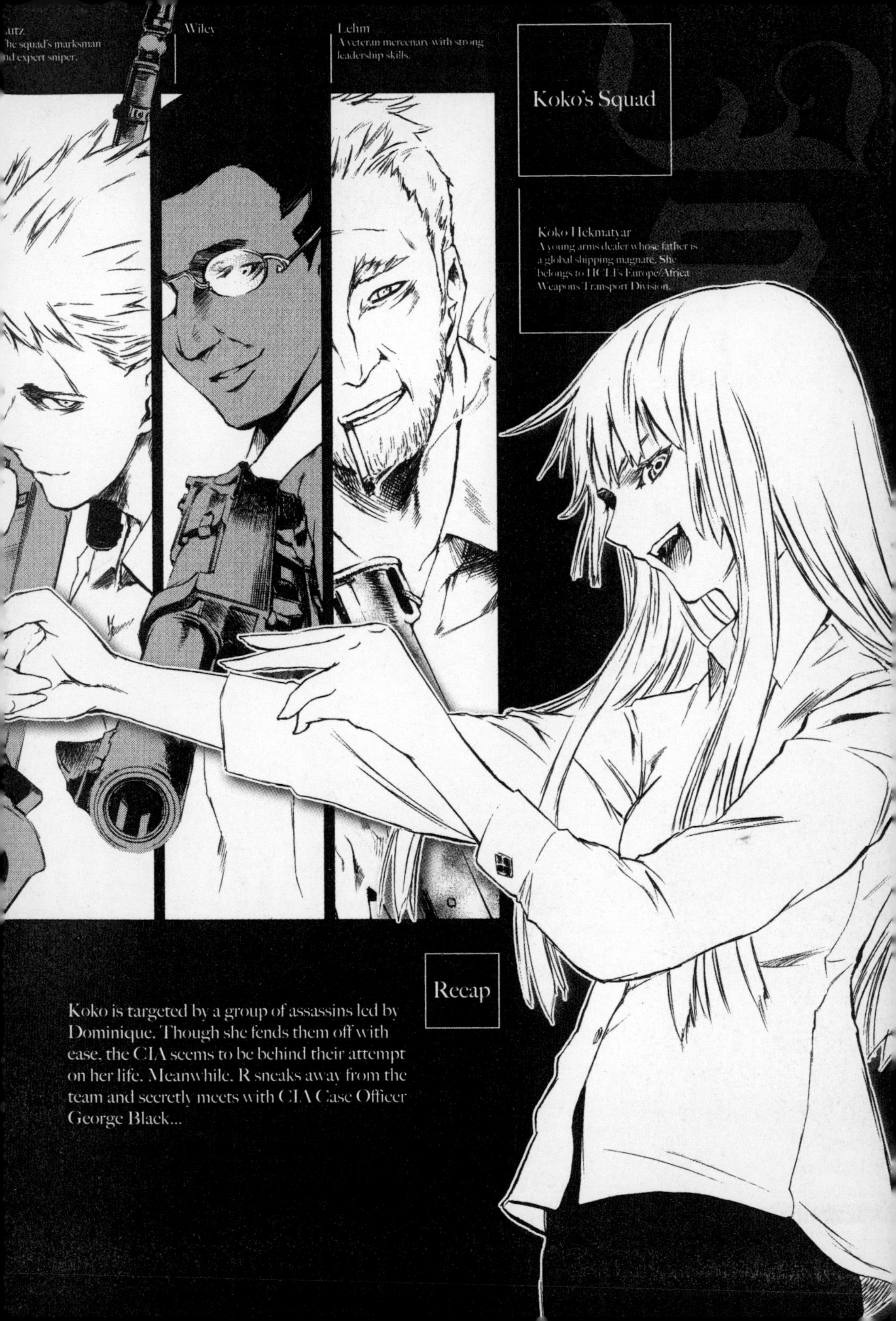

Recap

Koko is targeted by a group of assassins led by Dominique. Though she fends them off with ease, the CIA seems to be behind their attempt on her life. Meanwhile, R sneaks away from the team and secretly meets with CIA Case Officer George Black...

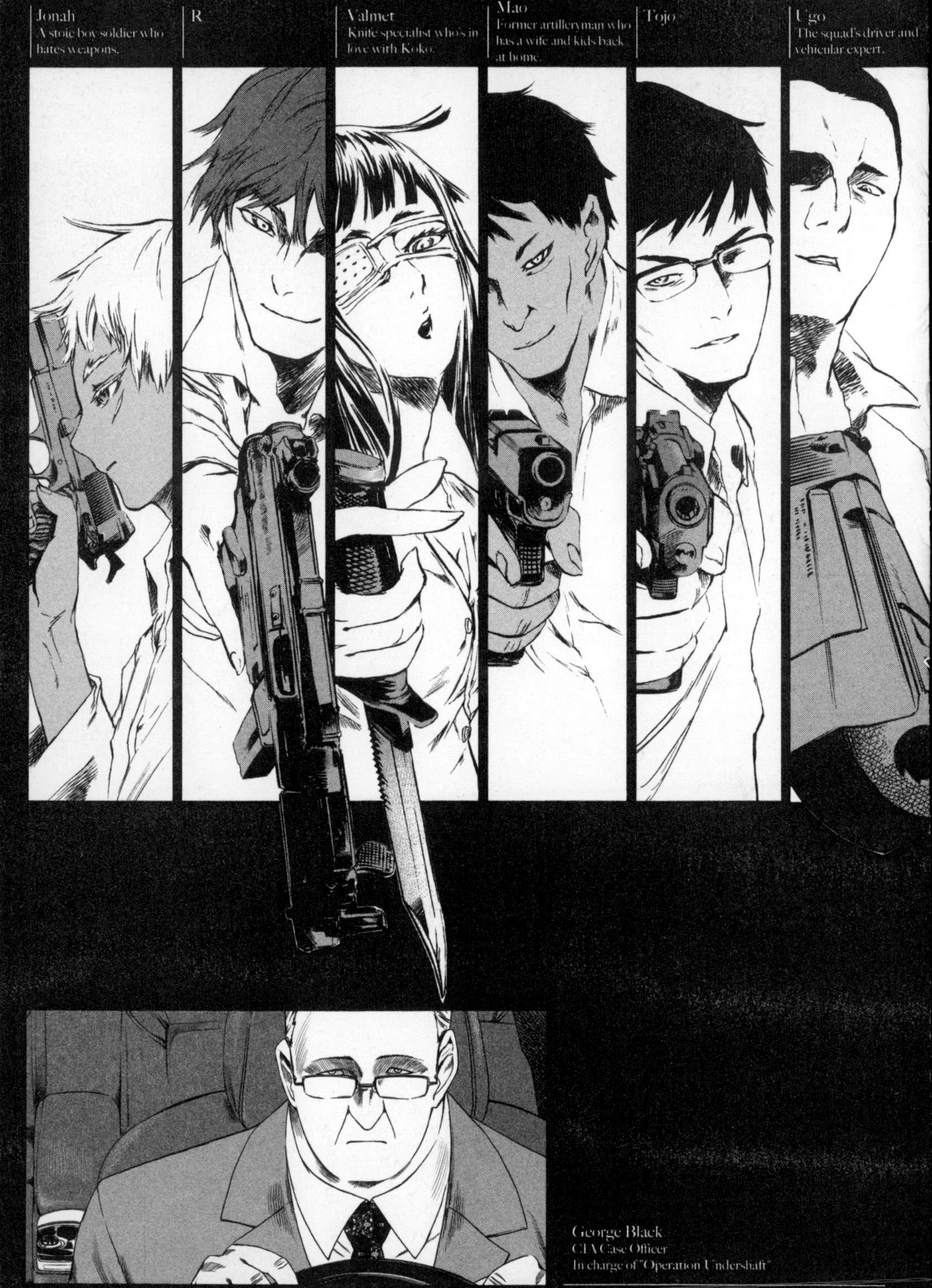
Ugo
The squad's driver and vehicular expert.
Tojo
Mao
Former artilleryman who has a wife and kids back at home.
Valmet
Knife specialist who's in love with Koko.
R
Jonah
A stoic boy soldier who hates weapons.
George Black
CIA Case Officer
In charge of "Operation Undershaft"

CONTENTS

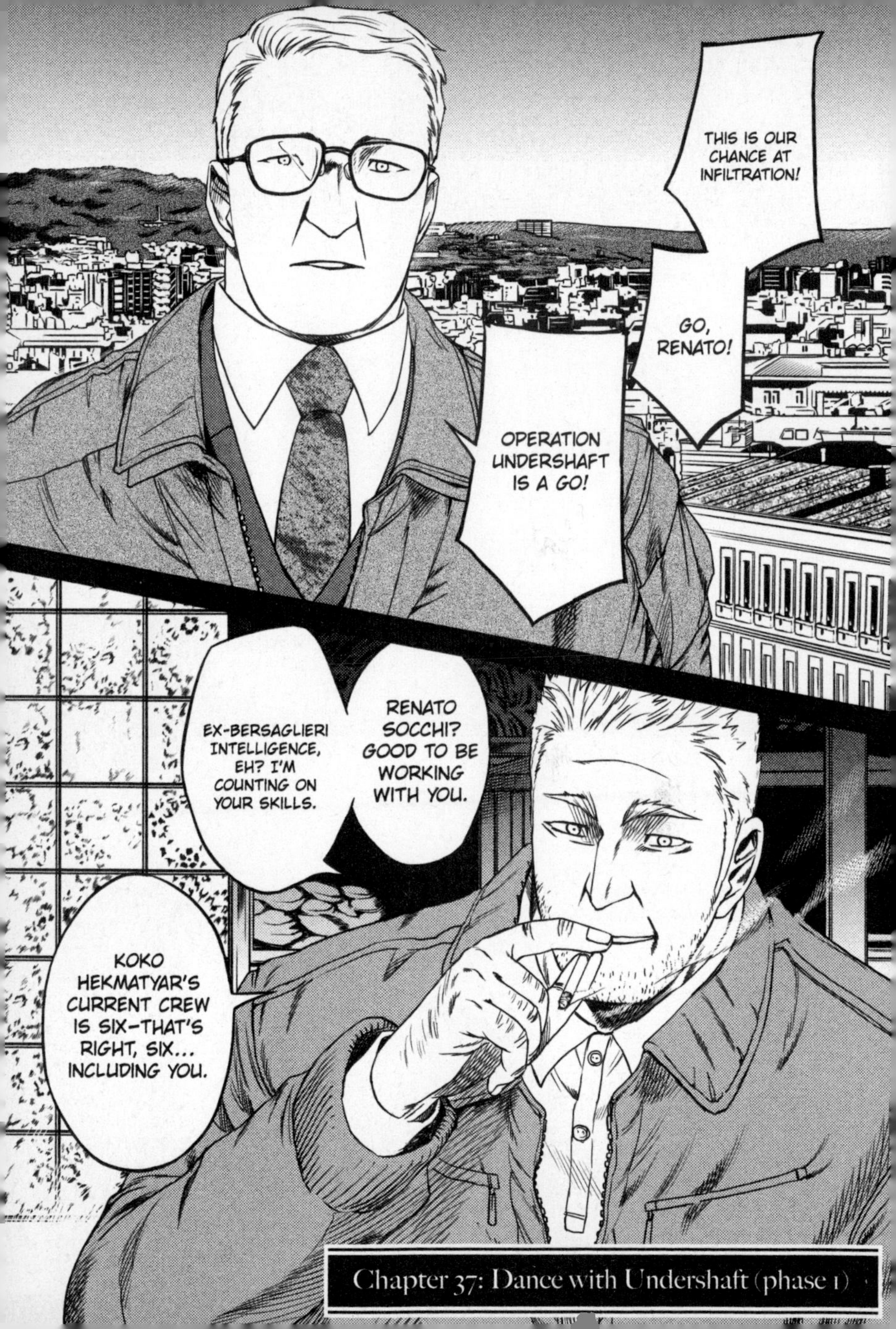
THIS IS OUR CHANCE AT INFILTRATION!
GO, RENATO!
OPERATION UNDERSHAFT IS A GO!
RENATO SOCCHI? GOOD TO BE WORKING WITH YOU.
EX-BERSAGLIERI INTELLIGENCE, EH? I'M COUNTING ON YOUR SKILLS.
KOKO HEKMATYAR'S CURRENT CREW IS SIX—THAT'S RIGHT, SIX... INCLUDING YOU.

Chapter 37: Dance with Undershaft (phase 1)

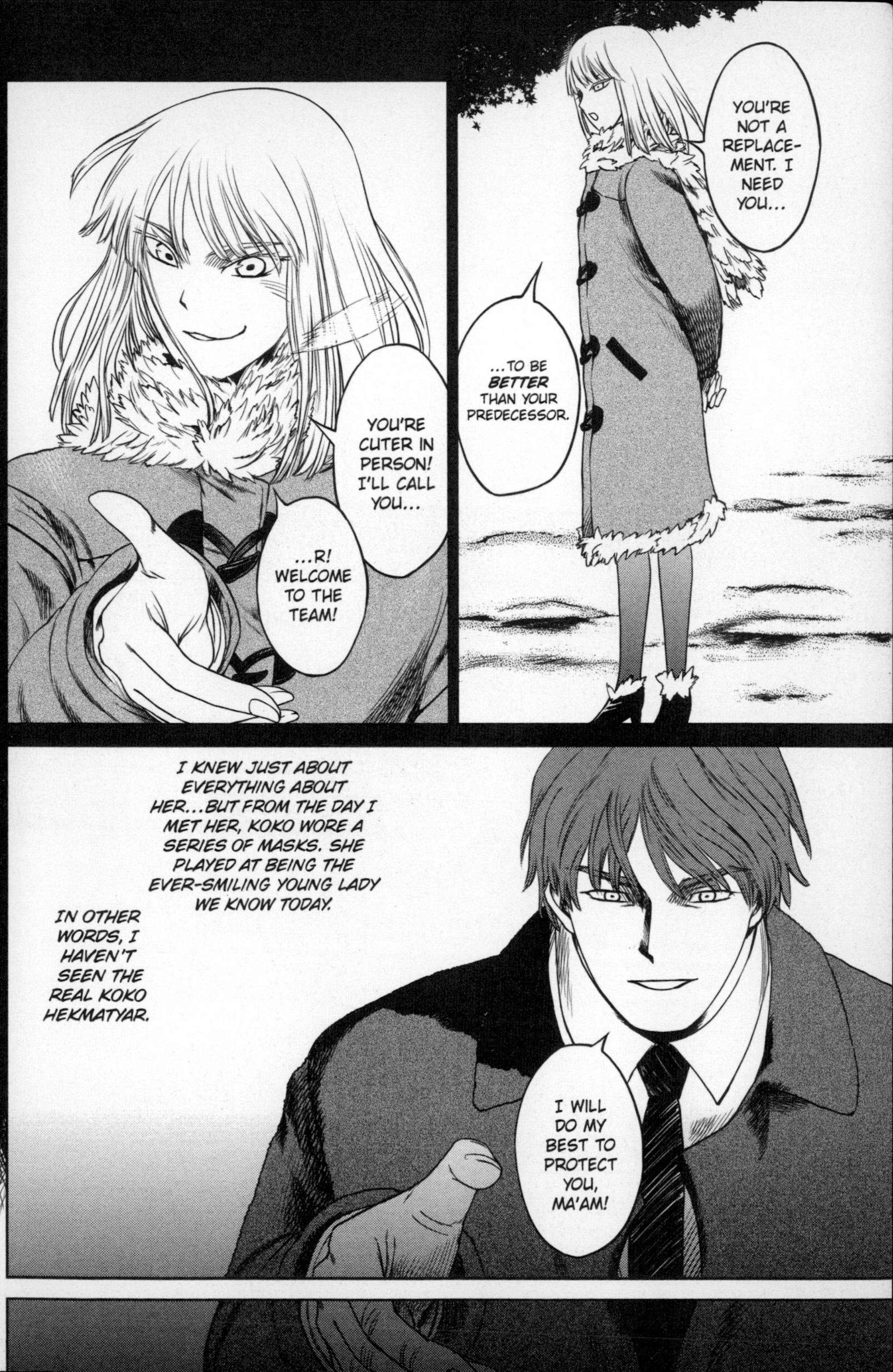
YOU'RE NOT A REPLACEMENT. I NEED YOU...
...TO BE BETTER THAN YOUR PREDECESSOR.
YOU'RE CUTER IN PERSON! I'LL CALL YOU...
...R! WELCOME TO THE TEAM!
I KNEW JUST ABOUT EVERYTHING ABOUT HER...BUT FROM THE DAY I MET HER, KOKO WORE A SERIES OF MASKS. SHE PLAYED AT BEING THE EVER-SMILING YOUNG LADY WE KNOW TODAY.
IN OTHER WORDS, I HAVEN'T SEEN THE REAL KOKO HEKMATYAR.
I WILL DO MY BEST TO PROTECT YOU, MA'AM!

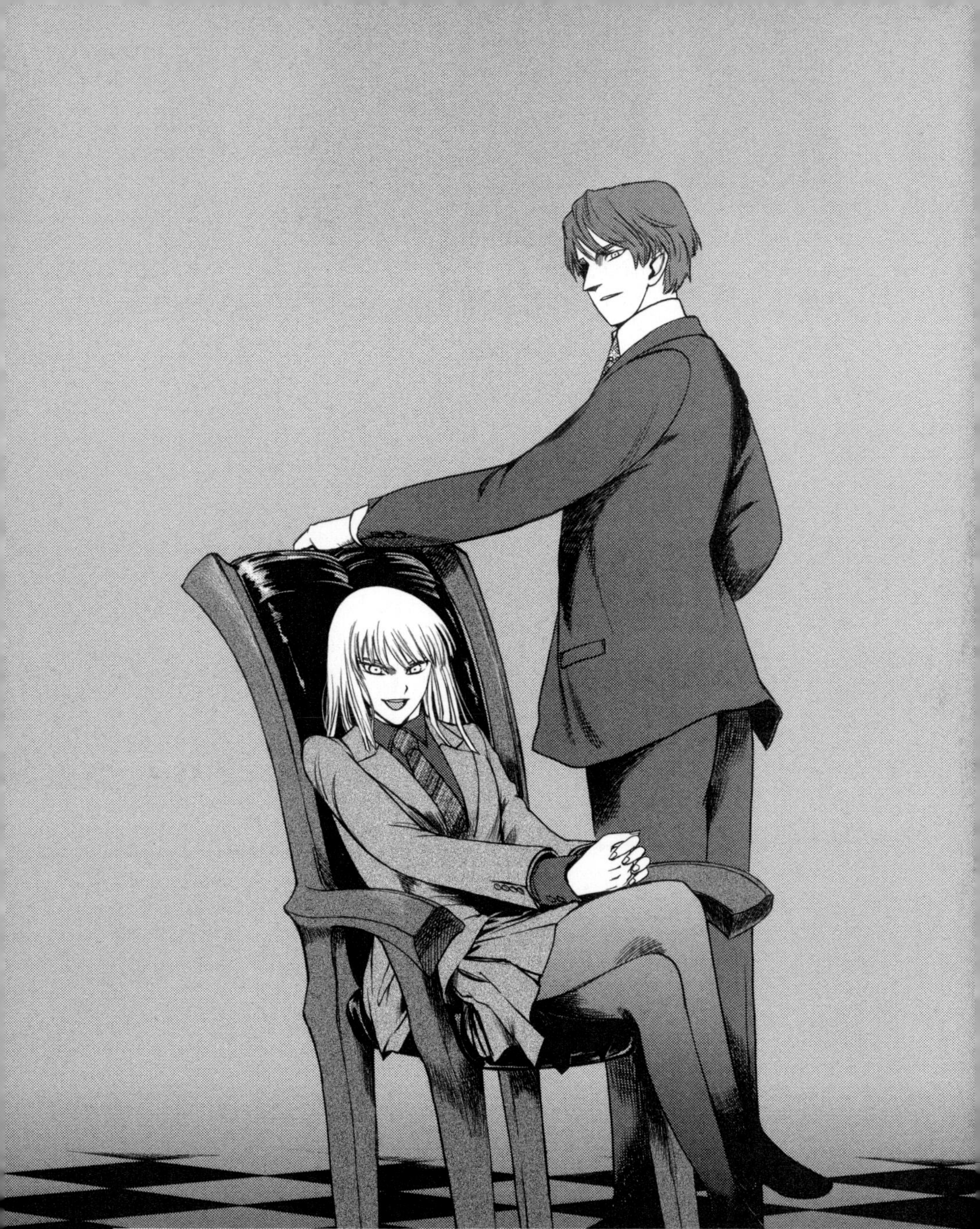

Chapter 37: Dance with Undershaft (phase 1)

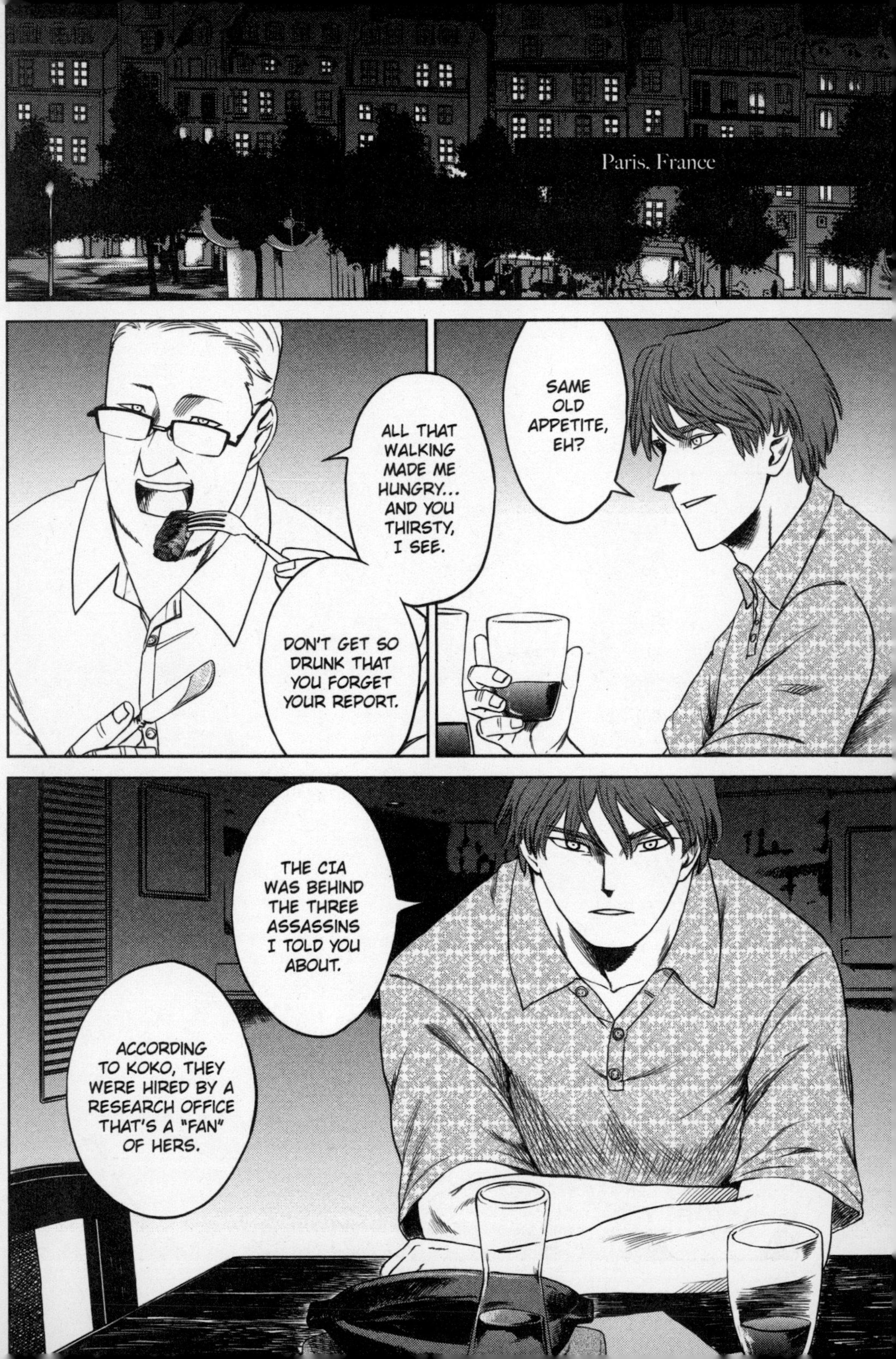
Paris, France
SAME OLD APPETITE, EH?
ALL THAT WALKING MADE ME HUNGRY... AND YOU THIRSTY, I SEE.
DON'T GET SO DRUNK THAT YOU FORGET YOUR REPORT.
THE CIA WAS BEHIND THE THREE ASSASSINS I TOLD YOU ABOUT.
ACCORDING TO KOKO, THEY WERE HIRED BY A RESEARCH OFFICE THAT'S A "FAN" OF HERS.

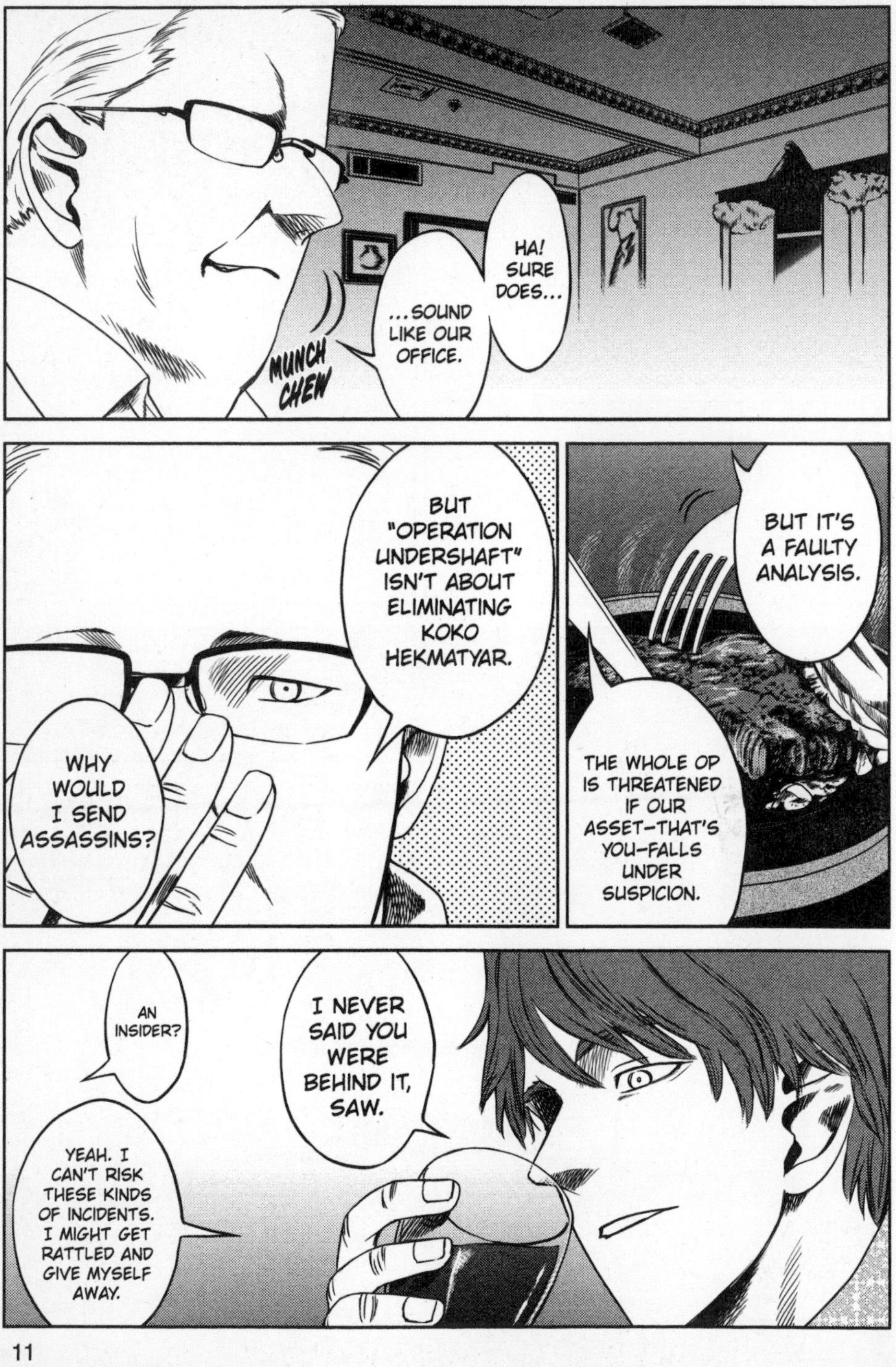
HA! SURE DOES...
...SOUND LIKE OUR OFFICE.
MUNCH CHEW
BUT IT'S A FAULTY ANALYSIS.
THE WHOLE OP IS THREATENED IF OUR ASSET—THAT'S YOU—FALLS UNDER SUSPICION.
BUT "OPERATION UNDERSHAFT" ISN'T ABOUT ELIMINATING KOKO HEKMATYAR.
WHY WOULD I SEND ASSASSINS?
I NEVER SAID YOU WERE BEHIND IT, SAW.
AN INSIDER?
YEAH. I CAN'T RISK THESE KINDS OF INCIDENTS. I MIGHT GET RATTLED AND GIVE MYSELF AWAY.

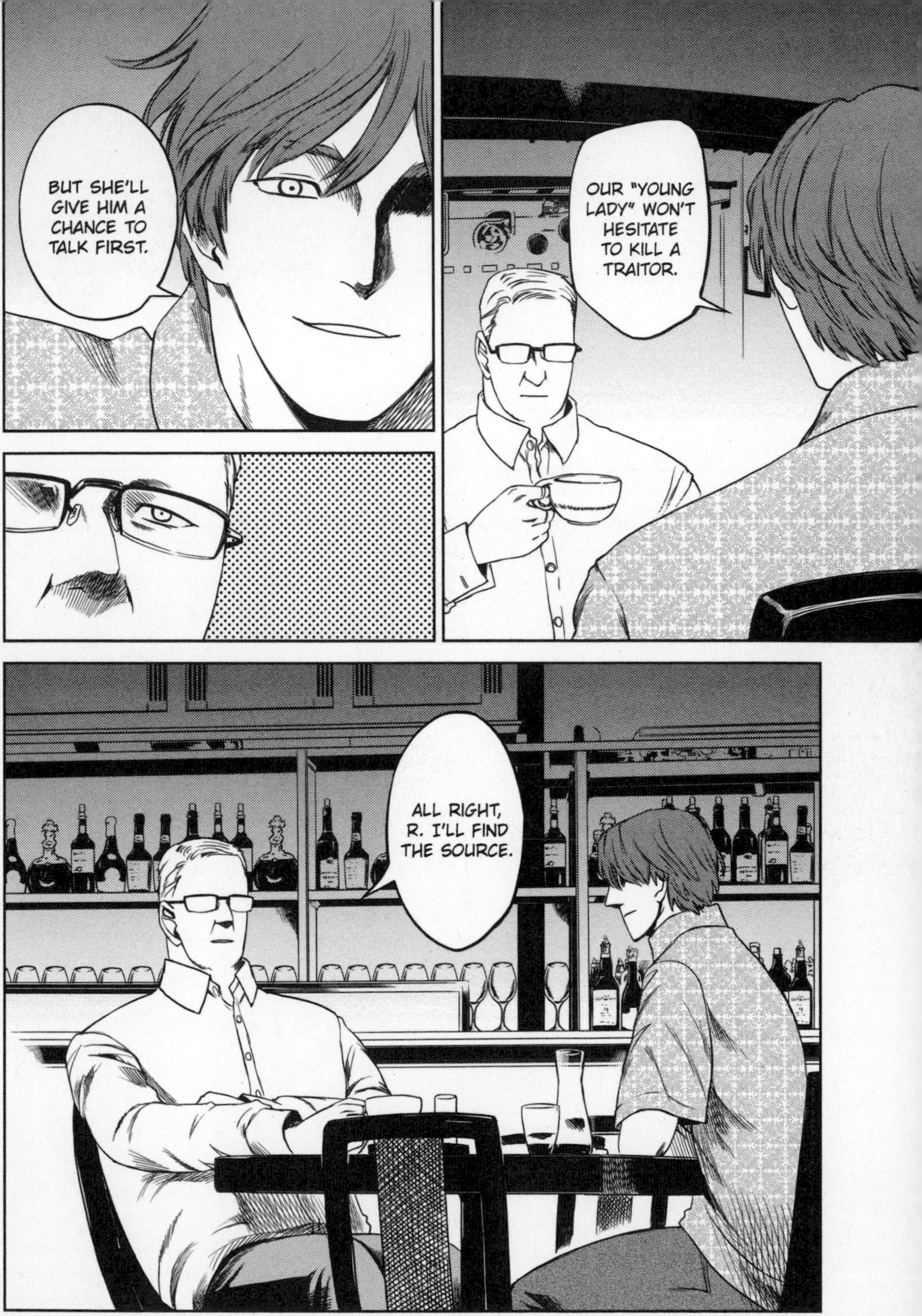
OUR "YOUNG LADY" WON'T HESITATE TO KILL A TRAITOR.
BUT SHE'LL GIVE HIM A CHANCE TO TALK FIRST.
ALL RIGHT, R. I'LL FIND THE SOURCE.

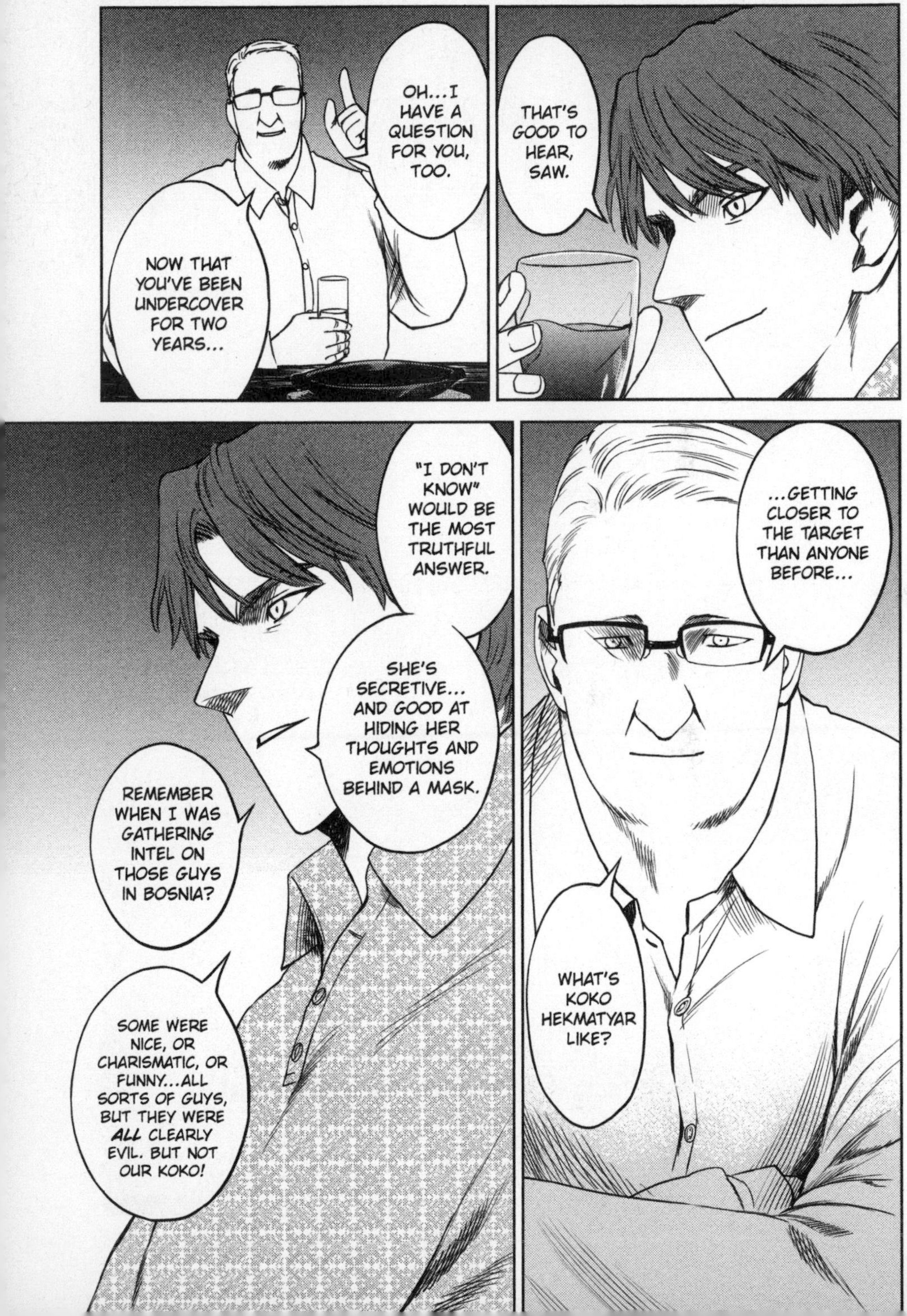
THAT'S GOOD TO HEAR, SAW.
OH...I HAVE A QUESTION FOR YOU, TOO.
NOW THAT YOU'VE BEEN UNDERCOVER FOR TWO YEARS...
...GETTING CLOSER TO THE TARGET THAN ANYONE BEFORE...
WHAT'S KOKO HEKMATYAR LIKE?
"I DON'T KNOW" WOULD BE THE MOST TRUTHFUL ANSWER.
SHE'S SECRETIVE... AND GOOD AT HIDING HER THOUGHTS AND EMOTIONS BEHIND A MASK.
REMEMBER WHEN I WAS GATHERING INTEL ON THOSE GUYS IN BOSNIA?
SOME WERE NICE, OR CHARISMATIC, OR FUNNY...ALL SORTS OF GUYS, BUT THEY WERE *ALL* CLEARLY EVIL. BUT NOT OUR KOKO!

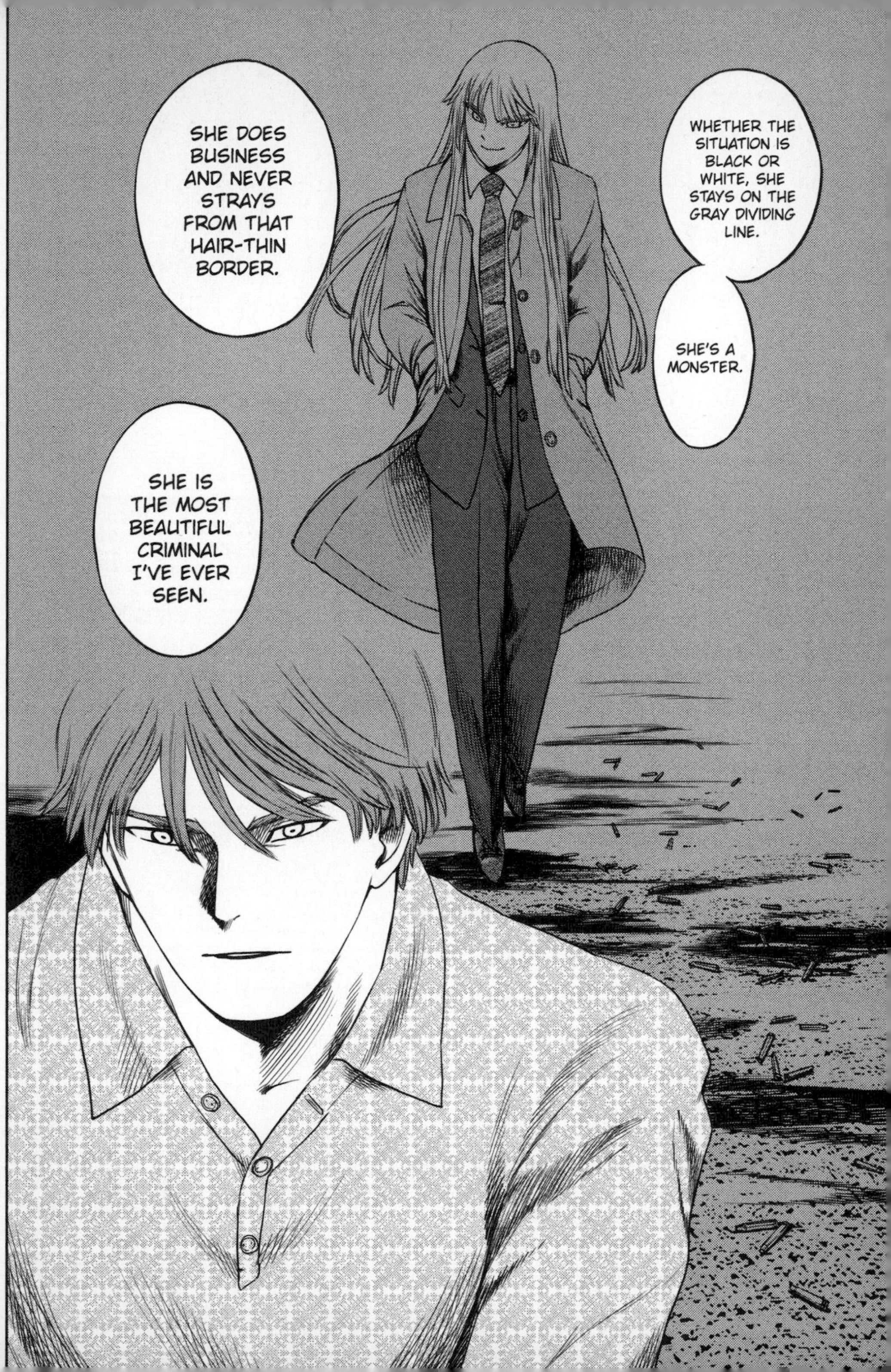
WHETHER THE SITUATION IS BLACK OR WHITE, SHE STAYS ON THE GRAY DIVIDING LINE.
SHE DOES BUSINESS AND NEVER STRAYS FROM THAT HAIR-THIN BORDER.
SHE'S A MONSTER.
SHE IS THE MOST BEAUTIFUL CRIMINAL I'VE EVER SEEN.

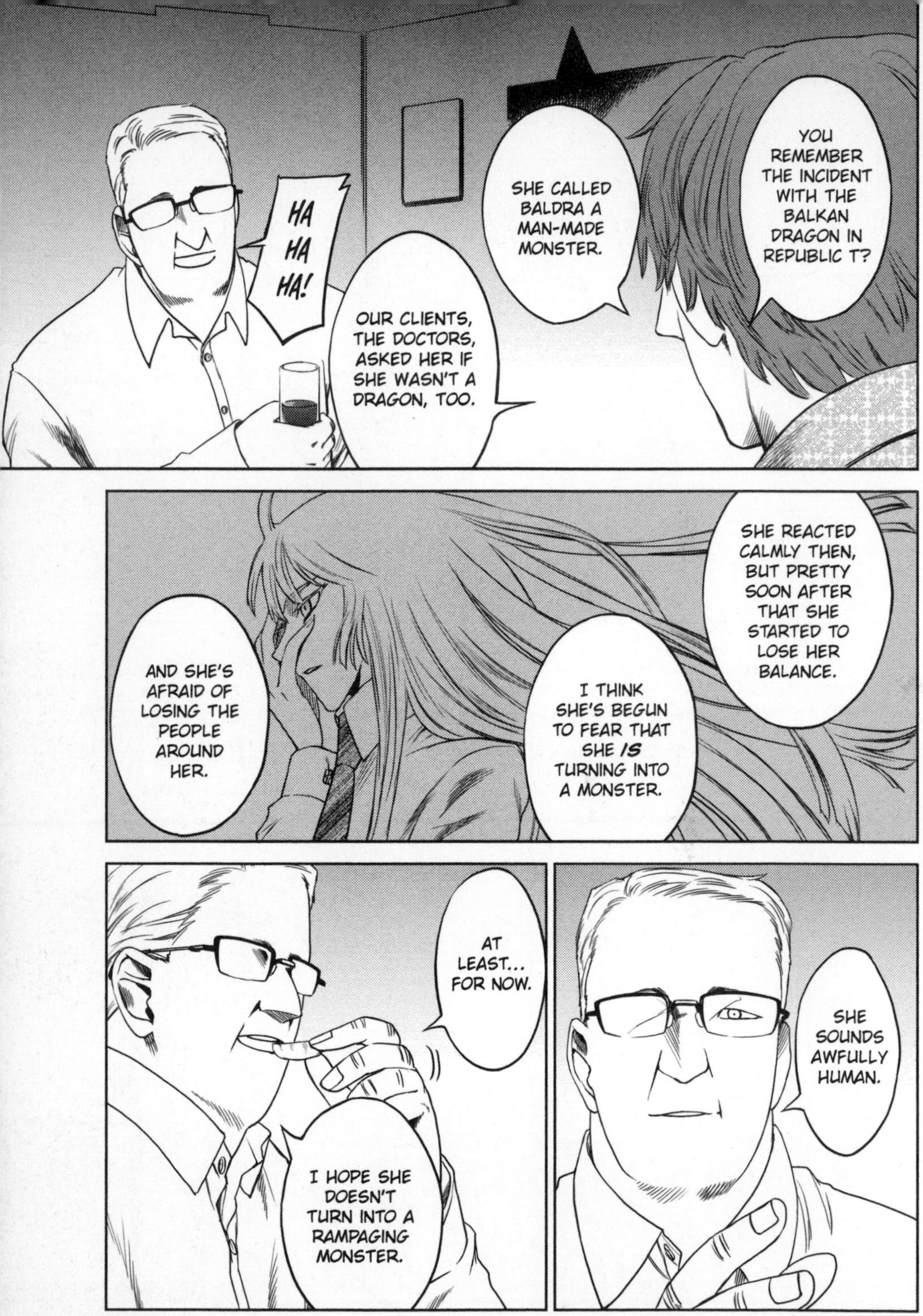
YOU REMEMBER THE INCIDENT WITH THE BALKAN DRAGON IN REPUBLIC T?
SHE CALLED BALDRA A MAN-MADE MONSTER.
OUR CLIENTS, THE DOCTORS, ASKED HER IF SHE WASN'T A DRAGON, TOO.
HA HA HA!
SHE REACTED CALMLY THEN, BUT PRETTY SOON AFTER THAT SHE STARTED TO LOSE HER BALANCE.
I THINK SHE'S BEGUN TO FEAR THAT SHE *IS* TURNING INTO A MONSTER.
AND SHE'S AFRAID OF LOSING THE PEOPLE AROUND HER.
SHE SOUNDS AWFULLY HUMAN.
AT LEAST... FOR NOW.
I HOPE SHE DOESN'T TURN INTO A RAMPAGING MONSTER.

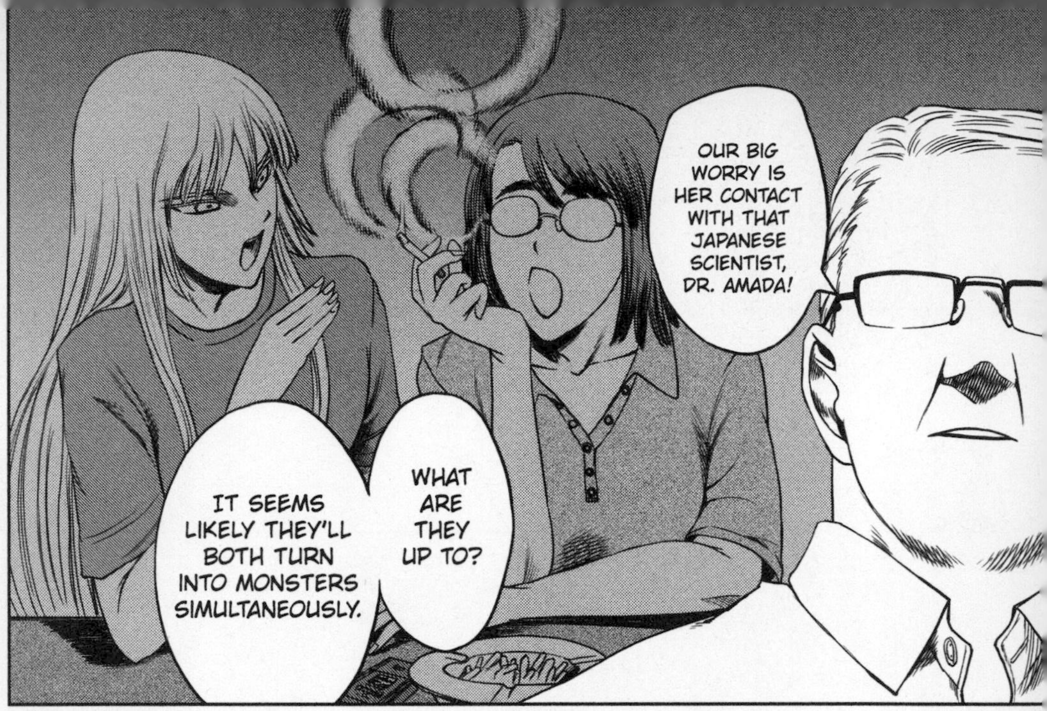
OUR BIG WORRY IS HER CONTACT WITH THAT JAPANESE SCIENTIST, DR. AMADA!
WHAT ARE THEY UP TO?
IT SEEMS LIKELY THEY'LL BOTH TURN INTO MONSTERS SIMULTANEOUSLY.

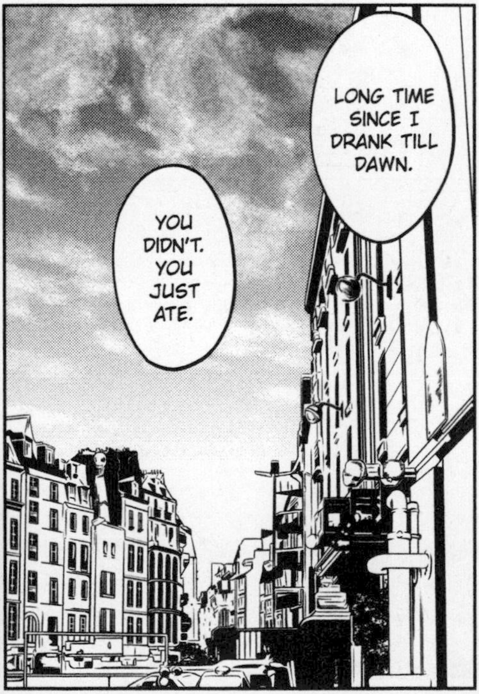
LONG TIME SINCE I DRANK TILL DAWN.
YOU DIDN'T. YOU JUST ATE.

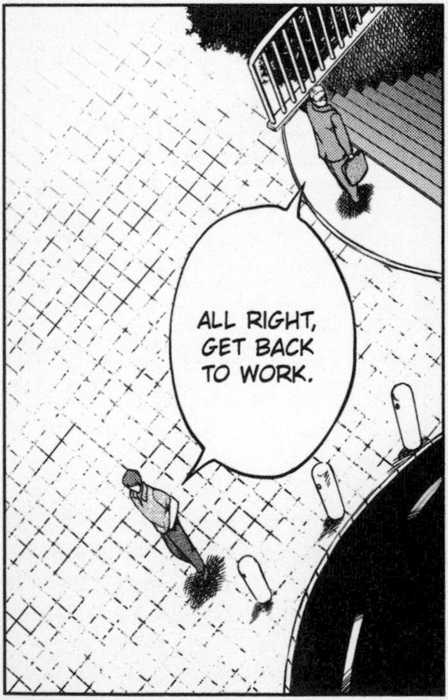
ALL RIGHT, GET BACK TO WORK.

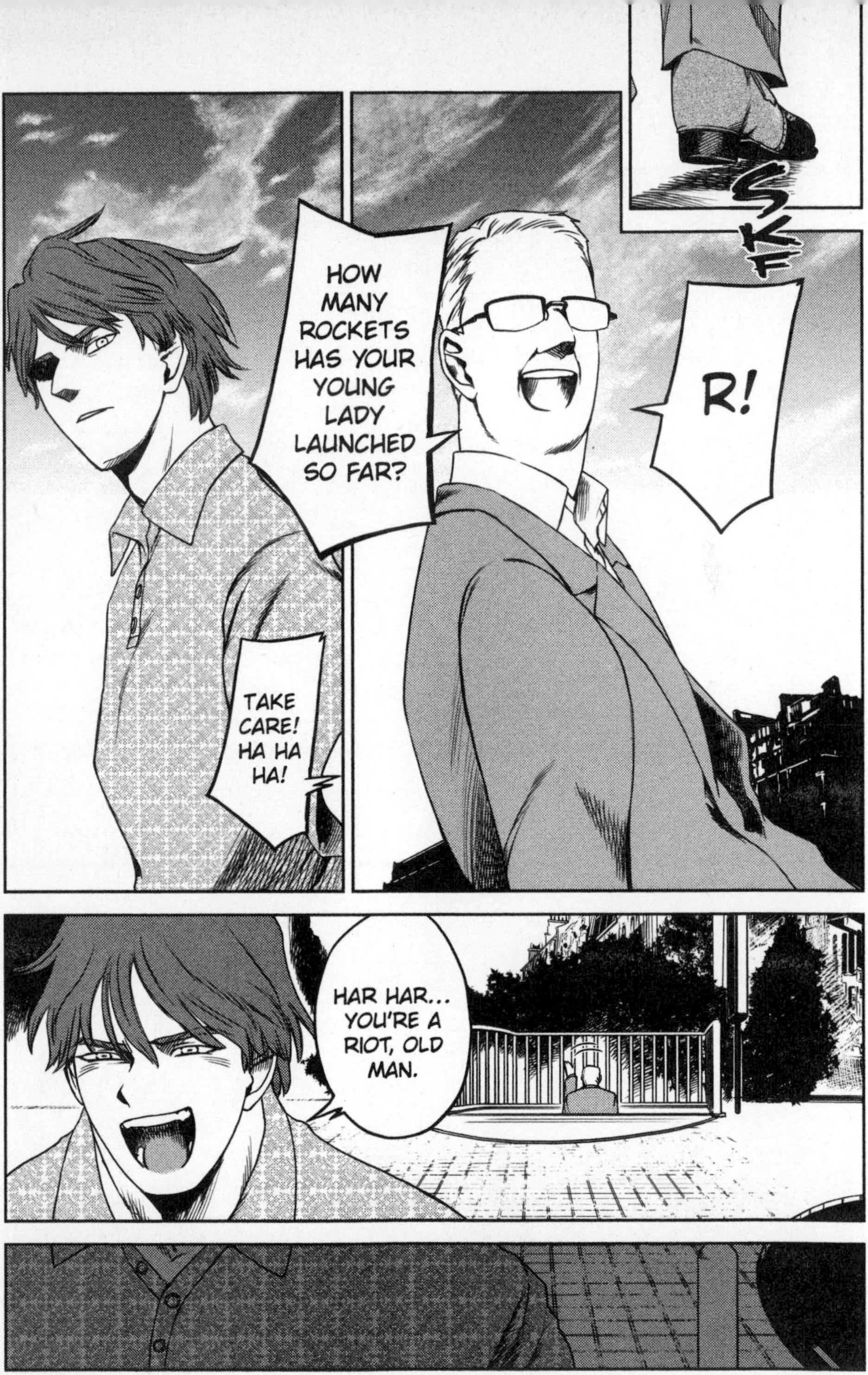
SKF
R!
HOW MANY ROCKETS HAS YOUR YOUNG LADY LAUNCHED SO FAR?
TAKE CARE! HA HA HA!
HAR HAR... YOU'RE A RIOT, OLD MAN.

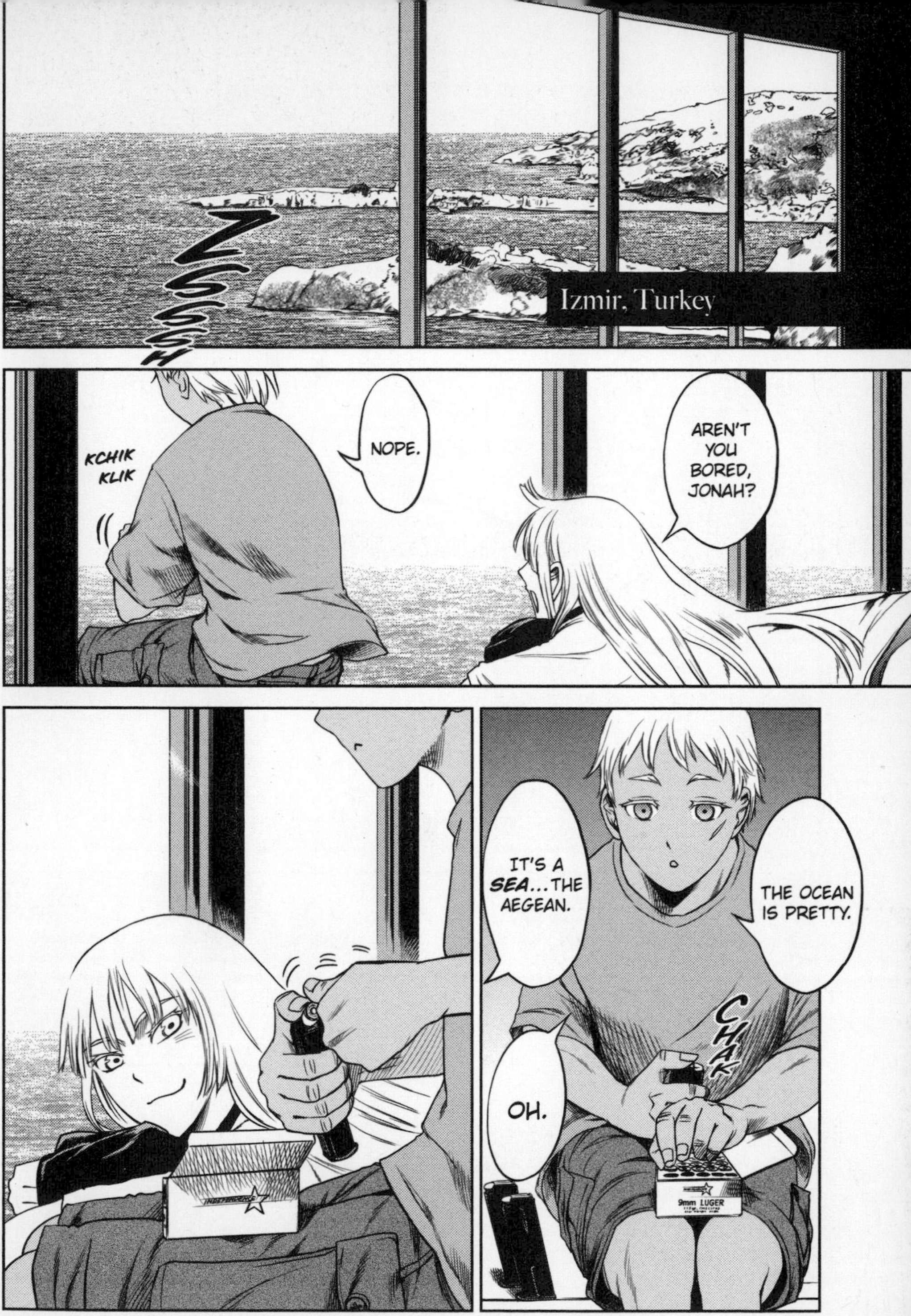
Izmir, Turkey
ZSSSSH
AREN'T YOU BORED, JONAH?
NOPE.
KCHIK KLIK
THE OCEAN IS PRETTY.
IT'S A SEA... THE AEGEAN.
OH.
CHAK
9mm LUGER

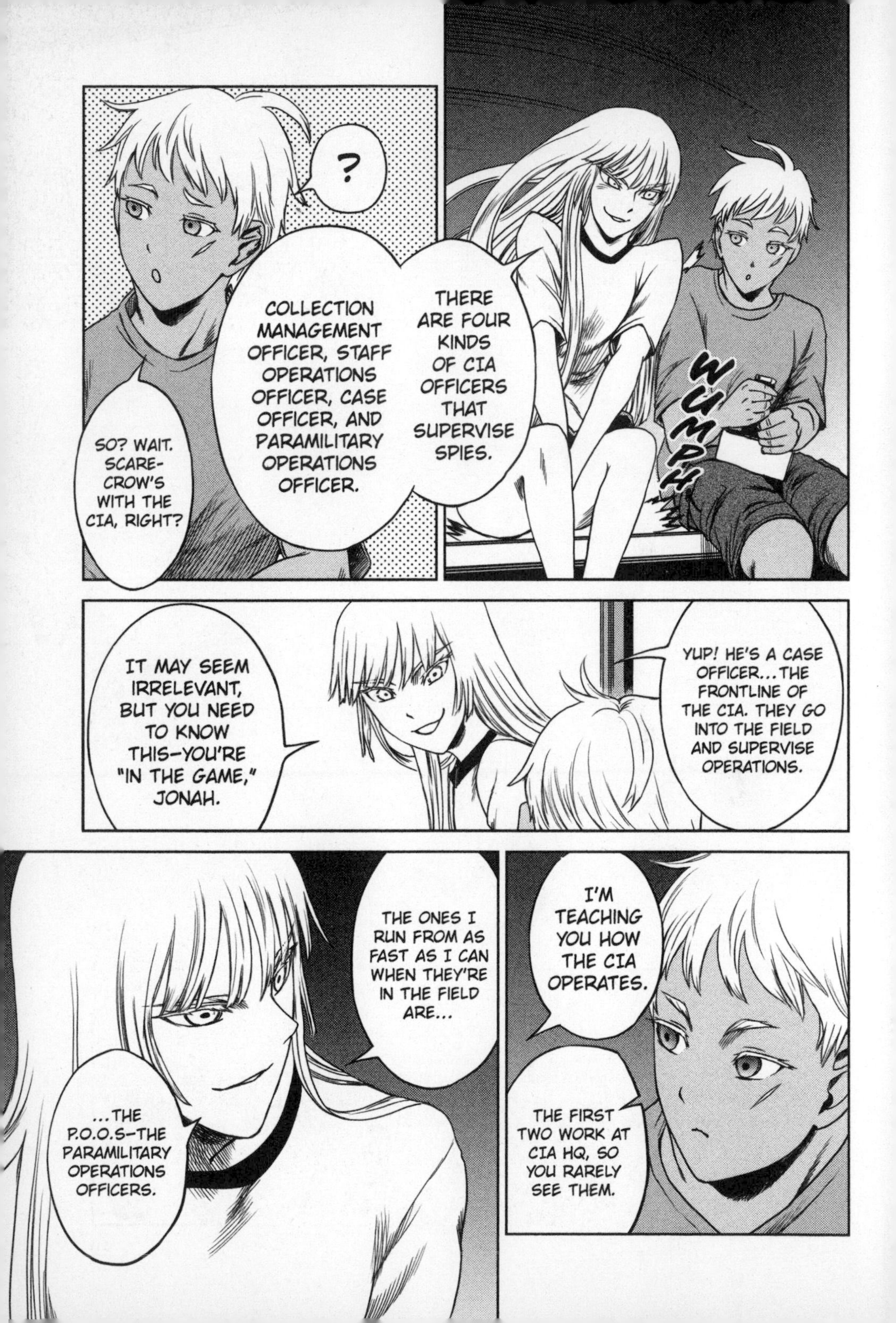
THERE ARE FOUR KINDS OF CIA OFFICERS THAT SUPERVISE SPIES.
WUMPH
COLLECTION MANAGEMENT OFFICER, STAFF OPERATIONS OFFICER, CASE OFFICER, AND PARAMILITARY OPERATIONS OFFICER.
?
SO? WAIT. SCARE-CROW'S WITH THE CIA, RIGHT?
YUP! HE'S A CASE OFFICER...THE FRONTLINE OF THE CIA. THEY GO INTO THE FIELD AND SUPERVISE OPERATIONS.
IT MAY SEEM IRRELEVANT, BUT YOU NEED TO KNOW THIS—YOU'RE "IN THE GAME," JONAH.
I'M TEACHING YOU HOW THE CIA OPERATES.
THE FIRST TWO WORK AT CIA HQ, SO YOU RARELY SEE THEM.
THE ONES I RUN FROM AS FAST AS I CAN WHEN THEY'RE IN THE FIELD ARE...
...THE P.O.O.S—THE PARAMILITARY OPERATIONS OFFICERS.

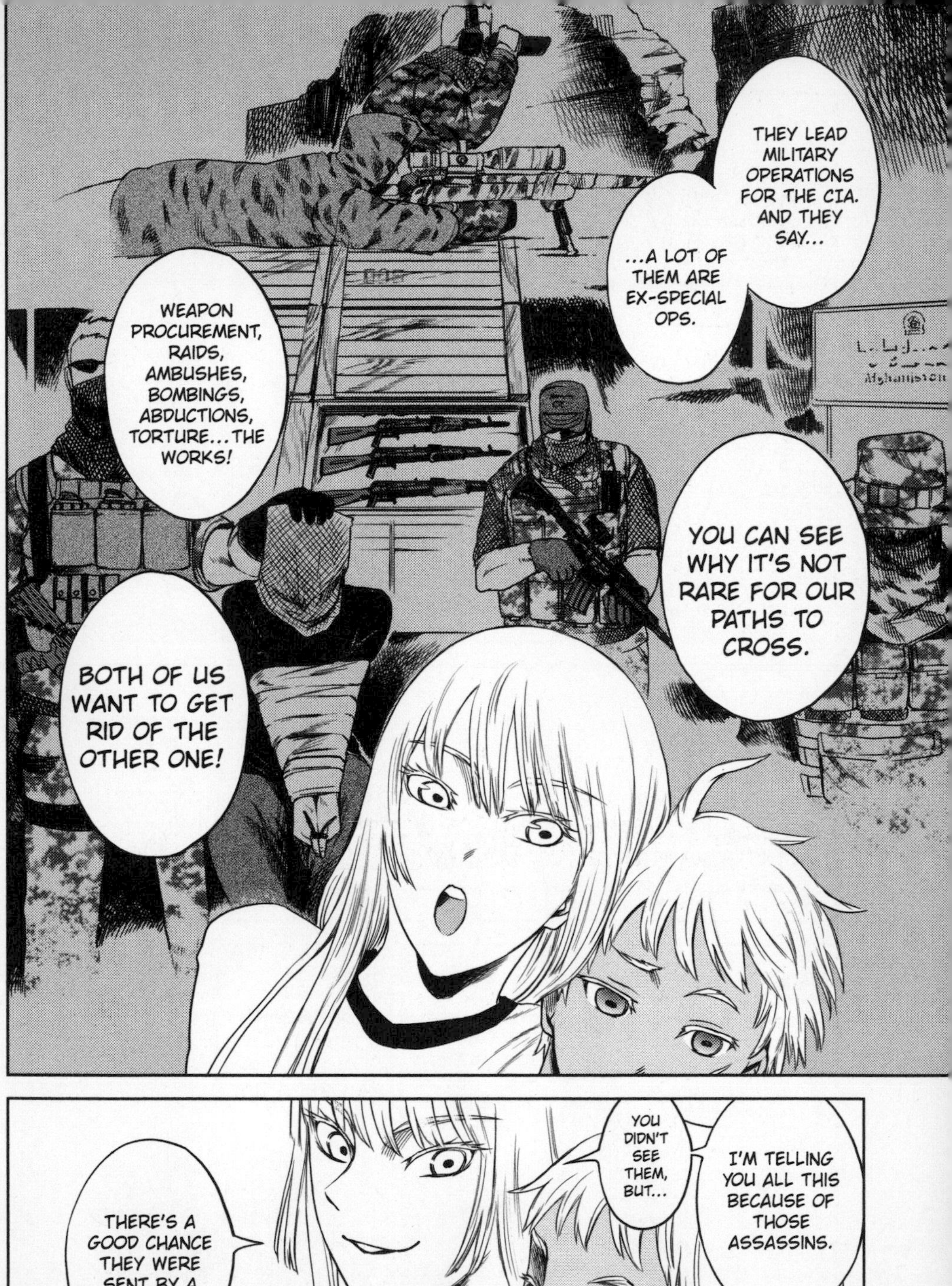
THEY LEAD MILITARY OPERATIONS FOR THE CIA. AND THEY SAY...
...A LOT OF THEM ARE EX-SPECIAL OPS.
WEAPON PROCUREMENT, RAIDS, AMBUSHES, BOMBINGS, ABDUCTIONS, TORTURE...THE WORKS!
YOU CAN SEE WHY IT'S NOT RARE FOR OUR PATHS TO CROSS.
BOTH OF US WANT TO GET RID OF THE OTHER ONE!
I'M TELLING YOU ALL THIS BECAUSE OF THOSE ASSASSINS.
YOU DIDN'T SEE THEM, BUT...
THERE'S A GOOD CHANCE THEY WERE SENT BY A P.O.O.

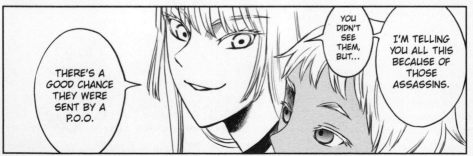

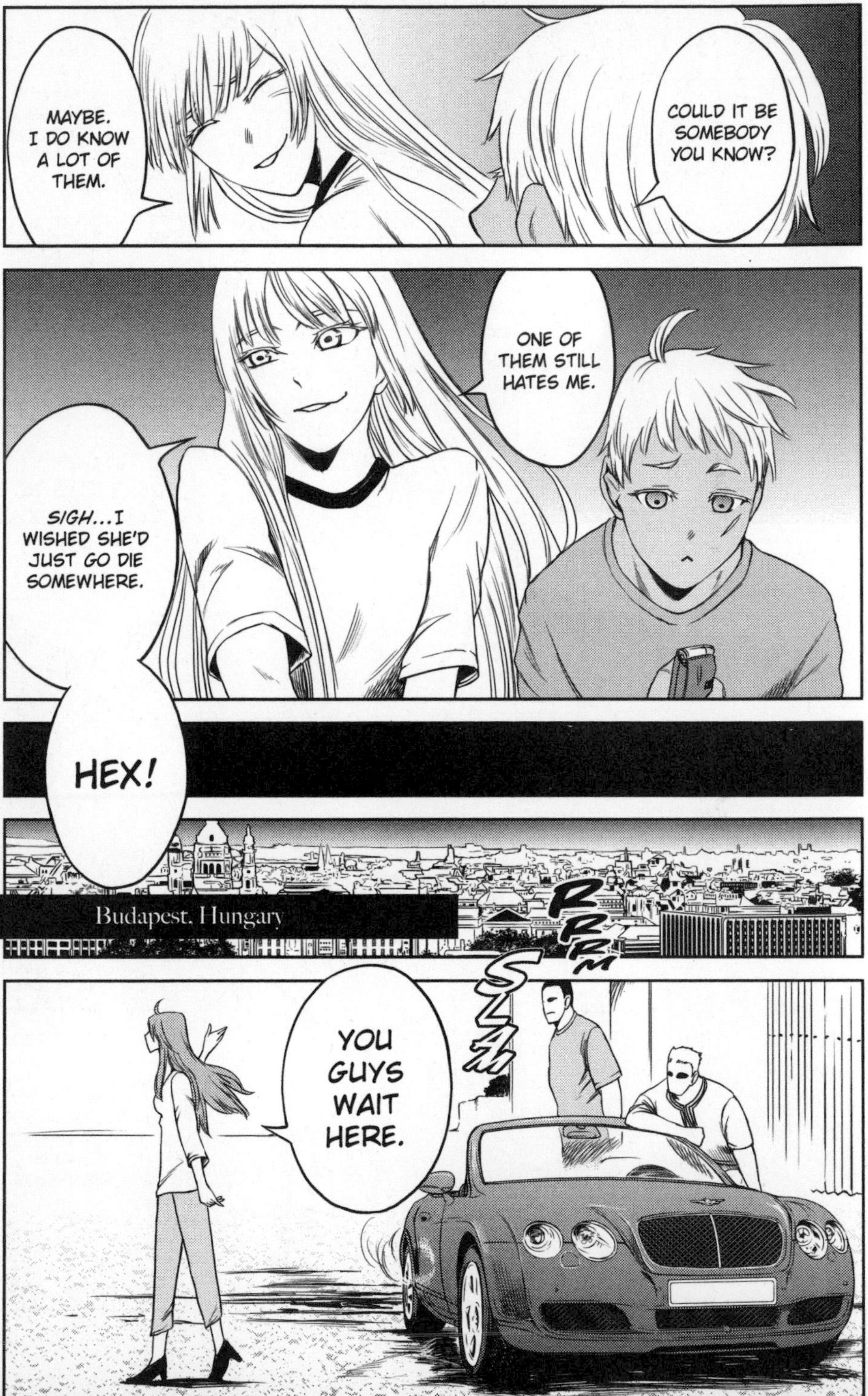
COULD IT BE SOMEBODY YOU KNOW?
MAYBE. I DO KNOW A LOT OF THEM.
ONE OF THEM STILL HATES ME.
SIGH...I WISHED SHE'D JUST GO DIE SOMEWHERE.
HEX!
Budapest, Hungary
RRRM
SLAM
YOU GUYS WAIT HERE.

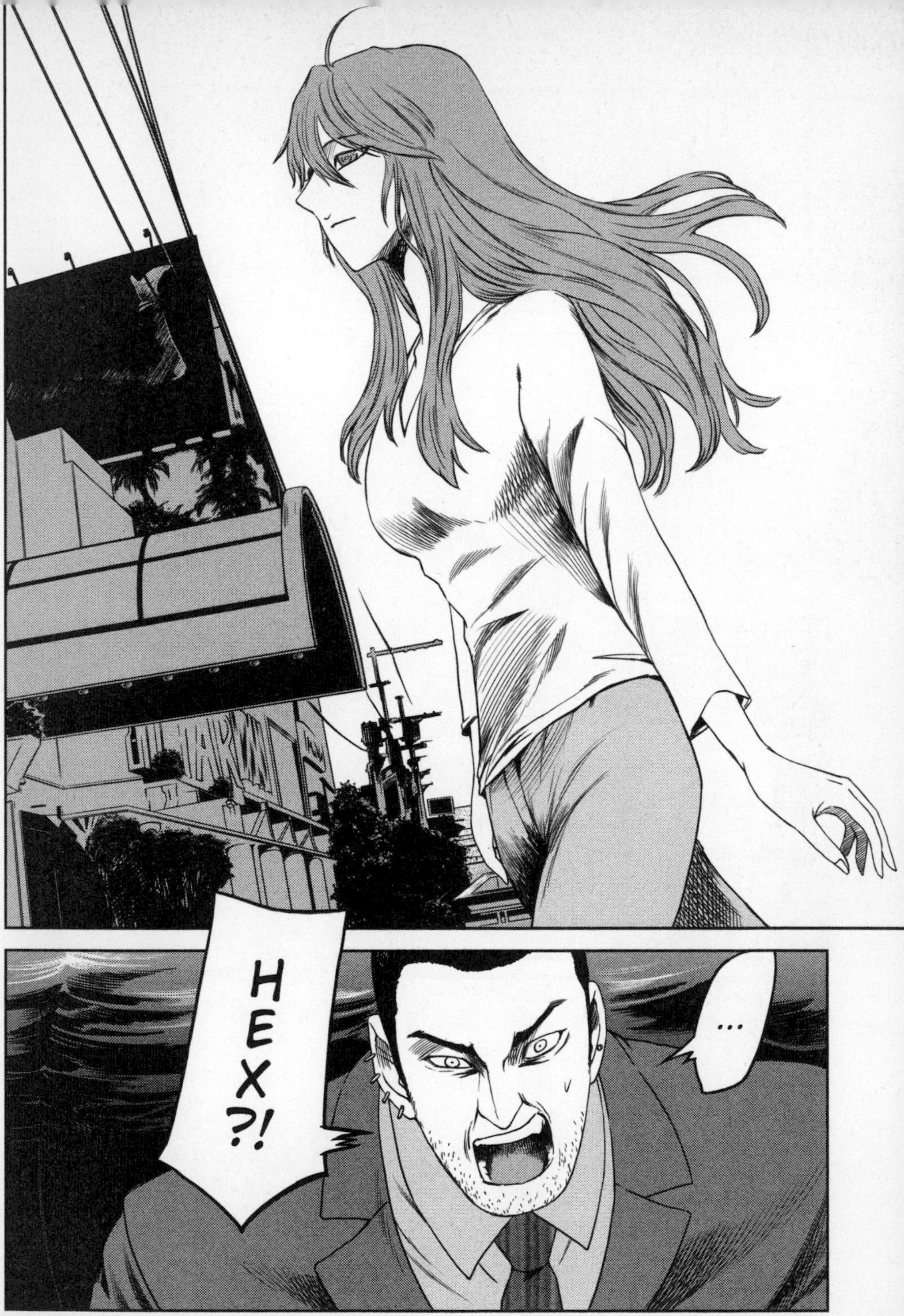
...
HEX?!

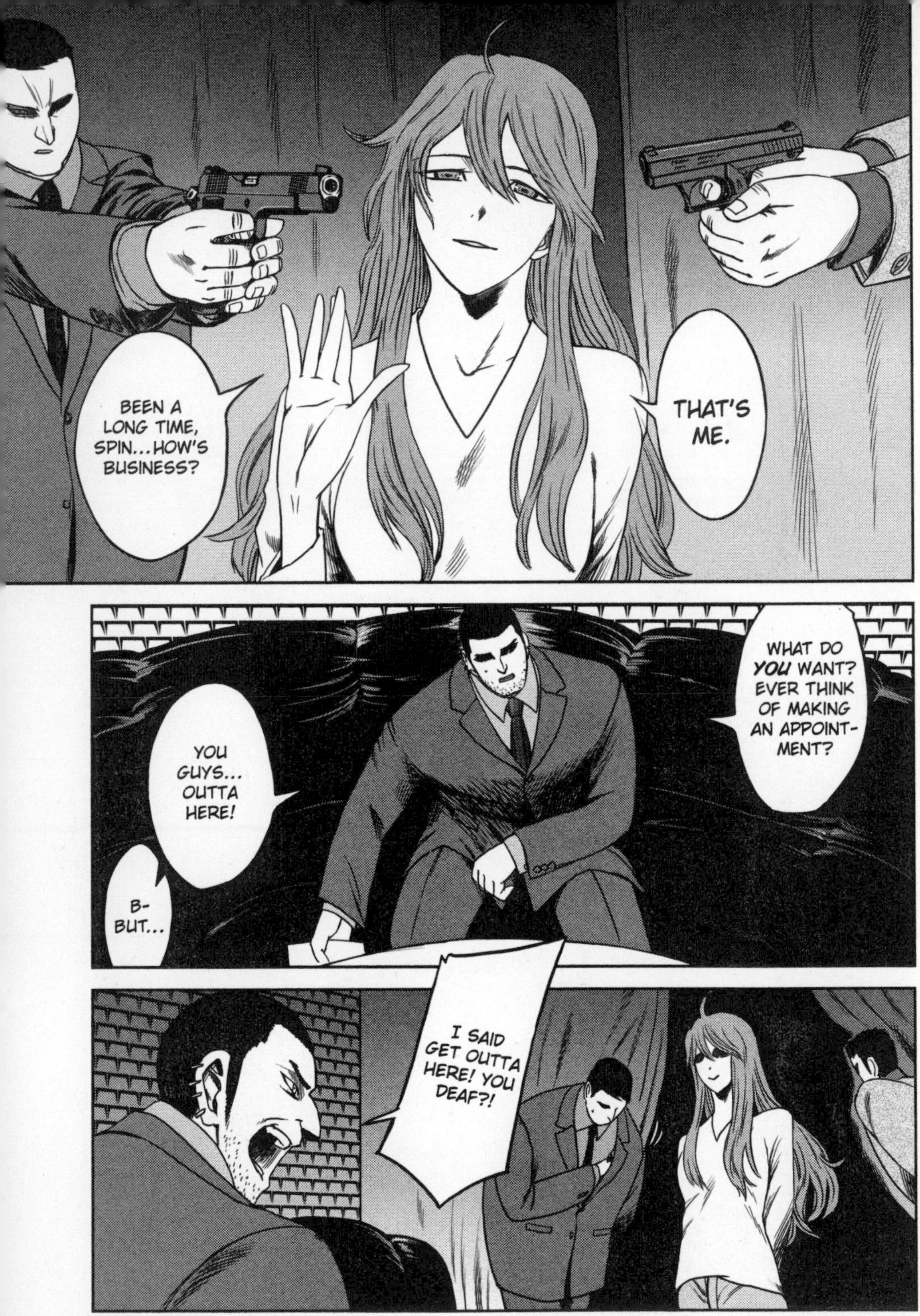
THAT'S ME.
BEEN A LONG TIME, SPIN...HOW'S BUSINESS?
WHAT DO YOU WANT? EVER THINK OF MAKING AN APPOINT-MENT?
YOU GUYS... OUTTA HERE!
B-BUT...
I SAID GET OUTTA HERE! YOU DEAF?!

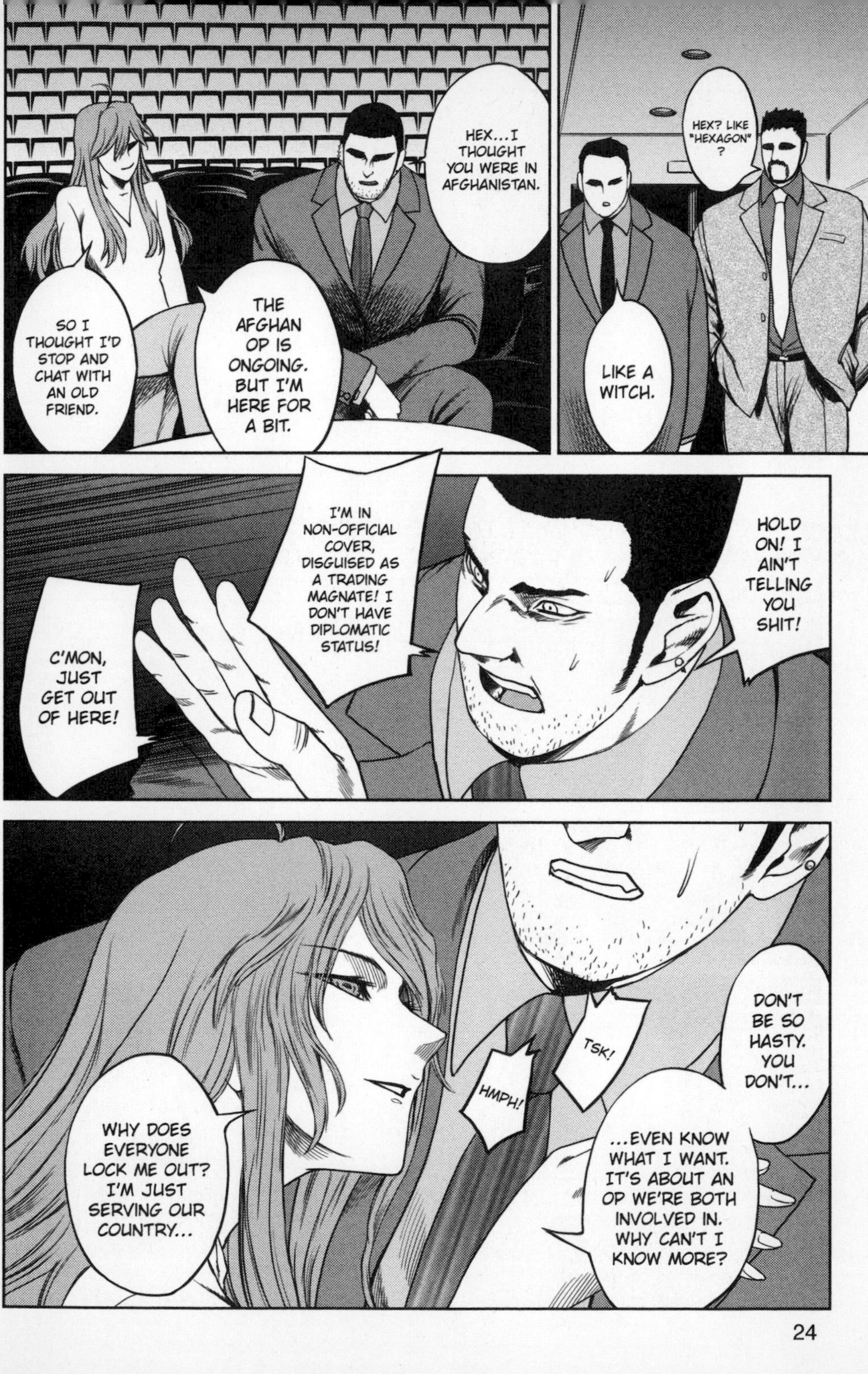
HEX? LIKE "HEXAGON"?
LIKE A WITCH.
HEX...I THOUGHT YOU WERE IN AFGHANISTAN.
THE AFGHAN OP IS ONGOING. BUT I'M HERE FOR A BIT.
SO I THOUGHT I'D STOP AND CHAT WITH AN OLD FRIEND.
HOLD ON! I AIN'T TELLING YOU SHIT!
I'M IN NON-OFFICIAL COVER, DISGUISED AS A TRADING MAGNATE! I DON'T HAVE DIPLOMATIC STATUS!
C'MON, JUST GET OUT OF HERE!
DON'T BE SO HASTY. YOU DON'T...
TSK!
HMPH!
...EVEN KNOW WHAT I WANT. IT'S ABOUT AN OP WE'RE BOTH INVOLVED IN. WHY CAN'T I KNOW MORE?
WHY DOES EVERYONE LOCK ME OUT? I'M JUST SERVING OUR COUNTRY...

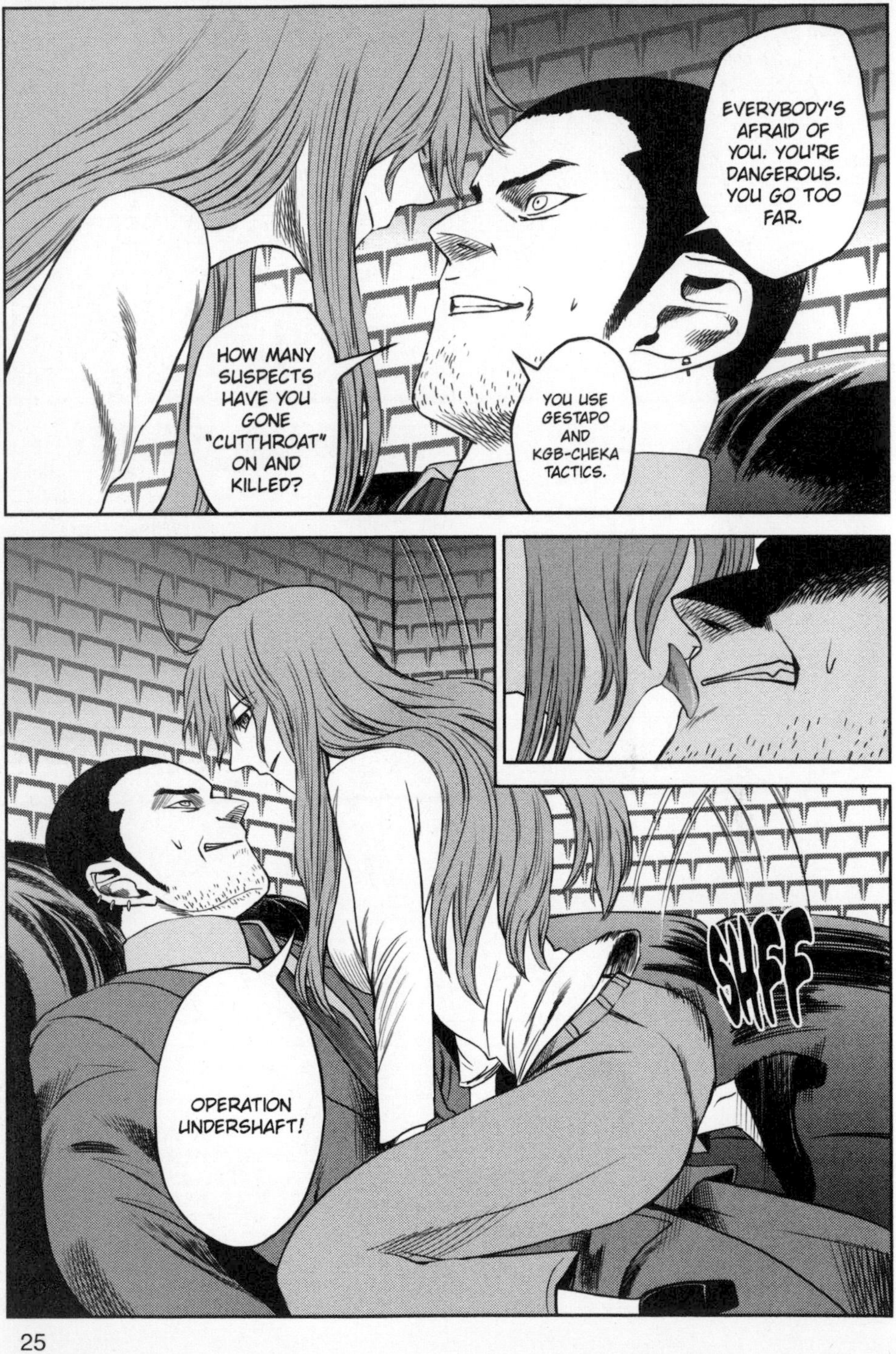
EVERYBODY'S AFRAID OF YOU. YOU'RE DANGEROUS. YOU GO TOO FAR.
YOU USE GESTAPO AND KGB-CHEKA TACTICS.
HOW MANY SUSPECTS HAVE YOU GONE "CUTTHROAT" ON AND KILLED?
SHFF
OPERATION UNDERSHAFT!

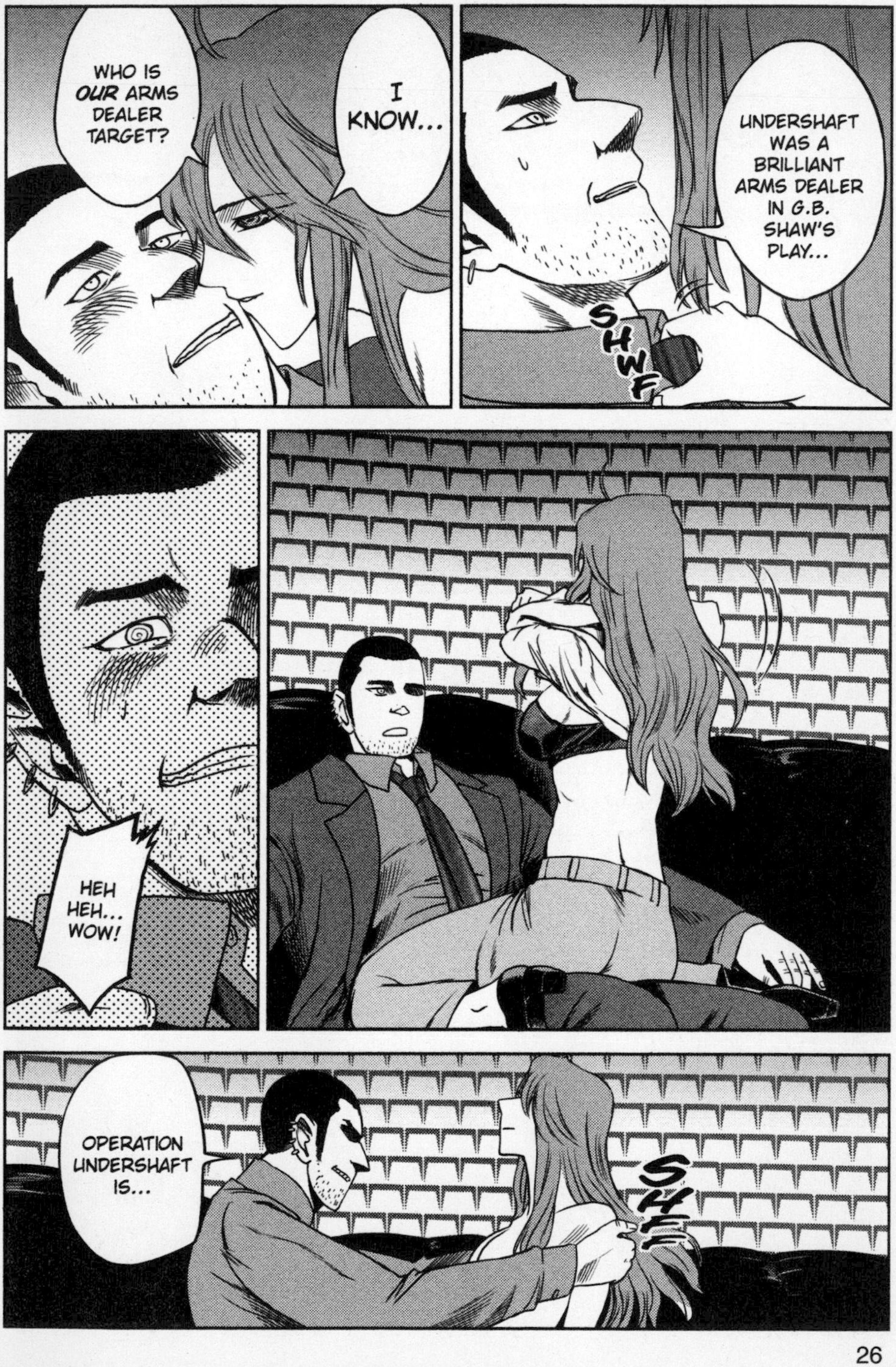
UNDERSHAFT WAS A BRILLIANT ARMS DEALER IN G.B. SHAW'S PLAY...
SHWF
I KNOW...
WHO IS *OUR* ARMS DEALER TARGET?
HEH HEH... WOW!
SHFF
OPERATION UNDERSHAFT IS...

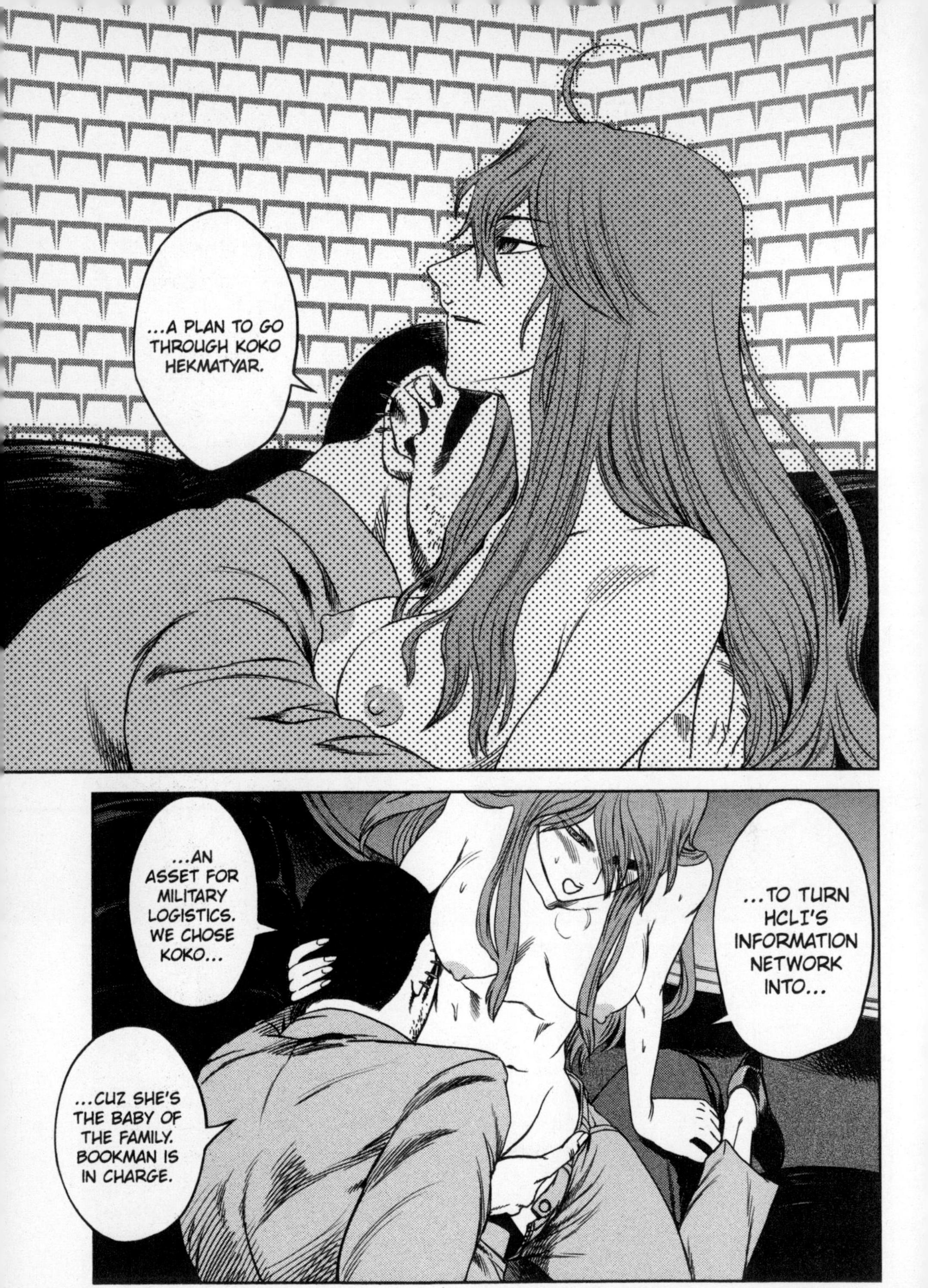
...A PLAN TO GO THROUGH KOKO HEKMATYAR.
...TO TURN HCLI'S INFORMATION NETWORK INTO...
...AN ASSET FOR MILITARY LOGISTICS. WE CHOSE KOKO...
...CUZ SHE'S THE BABY OF THE FAMILY. BOOKMAN IS IN CHARGE.

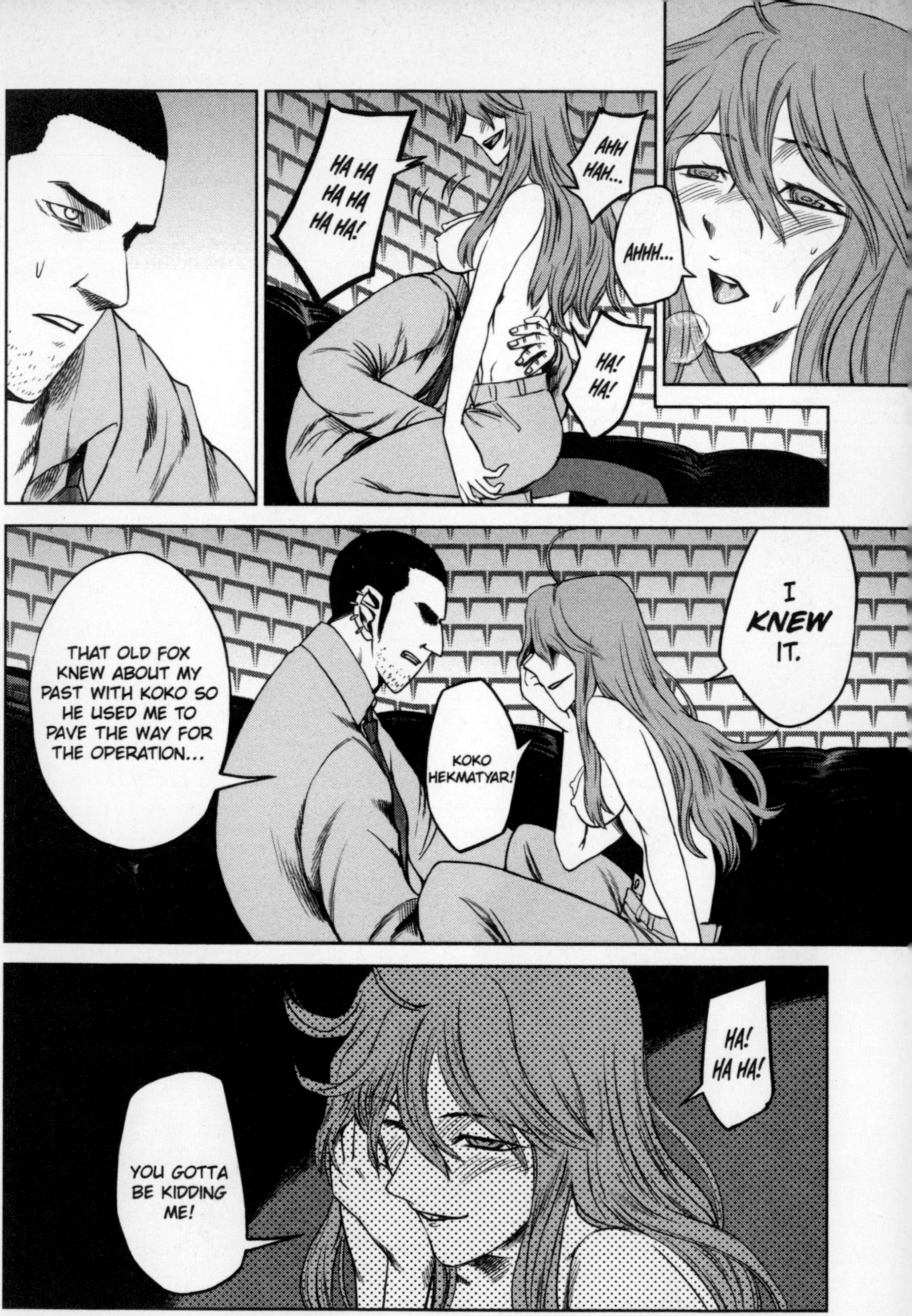
AHHH...
AHH HAH...
HA HA HA HA HA HA!
HA! HA!
I KNEW IT.
KOKO HEKMATYAR!
THAT OLD FOX KNEW ABOUT MY PAST WITH KOKO SO HE USED ME TO PAVE THE WAY FOR THE OPERATION...
HA! HA HA!
YOU GOTTA BE KIDDING ME!

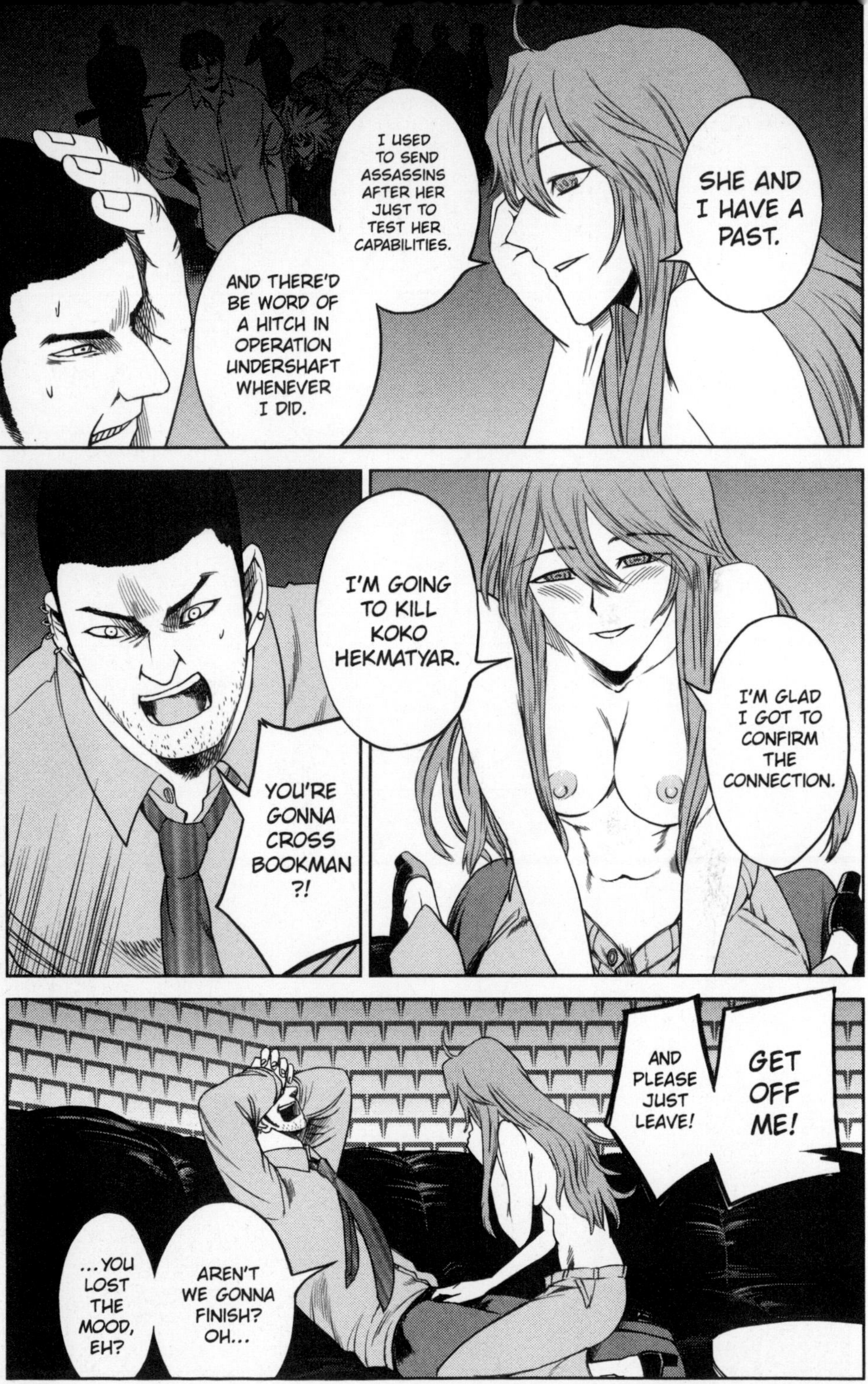
SHE AND I HAVE A PAST.
I USED TO SEND ASSASSINS AFTER HER JUST TO TEST HER CAPABILITIES.
AND THERE'D BE WORD OF A HITCH IN OPERATION UNDERSHAFT WHENEVER I DID.
I'M GOING TO KILL KOKO HEKMATYAR.
I'M GLAD I GOT TO CONFIRM THE CONNECTION.
YOU'RE GONNA CROSS BOOKMAN?!
GET OFF ME!
AND PLEASE JUST LEAVE!
AREN'T WE GONNA FINISH? OH...
...YOU LOST THE MOOD, EH?

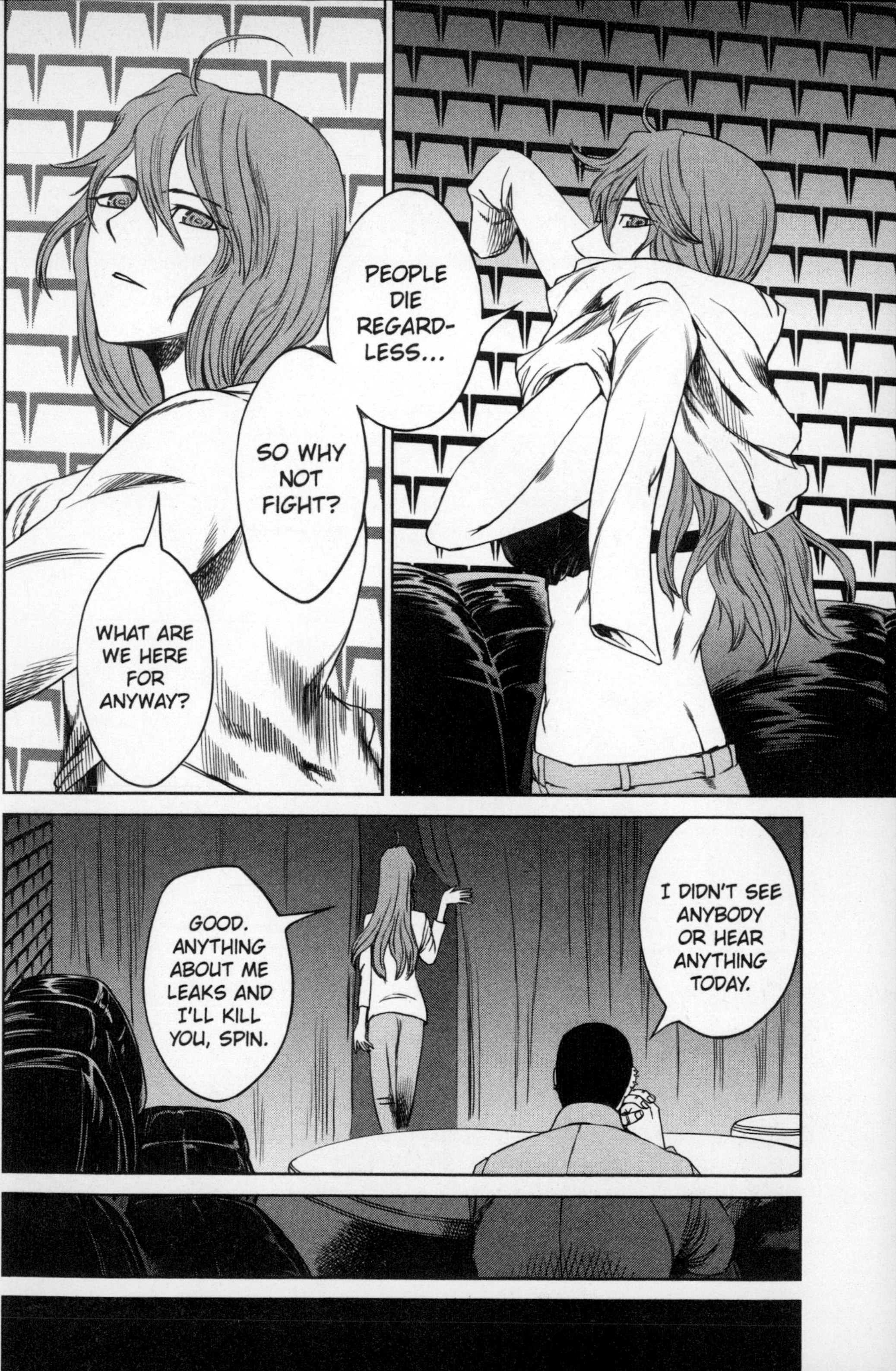
PEOPLE DIE REGARDLESS...
SO WHY NOT FIGHT?
WHAT ARE WE HERE FOR ANYWAY?
I DIDN'T SEE ANYBODY OR HEAR ANYTHING TODAY.
GOOD. ANYTHING ABOUT ME LEAKS AND I'LL KILL YOU, SPIN.

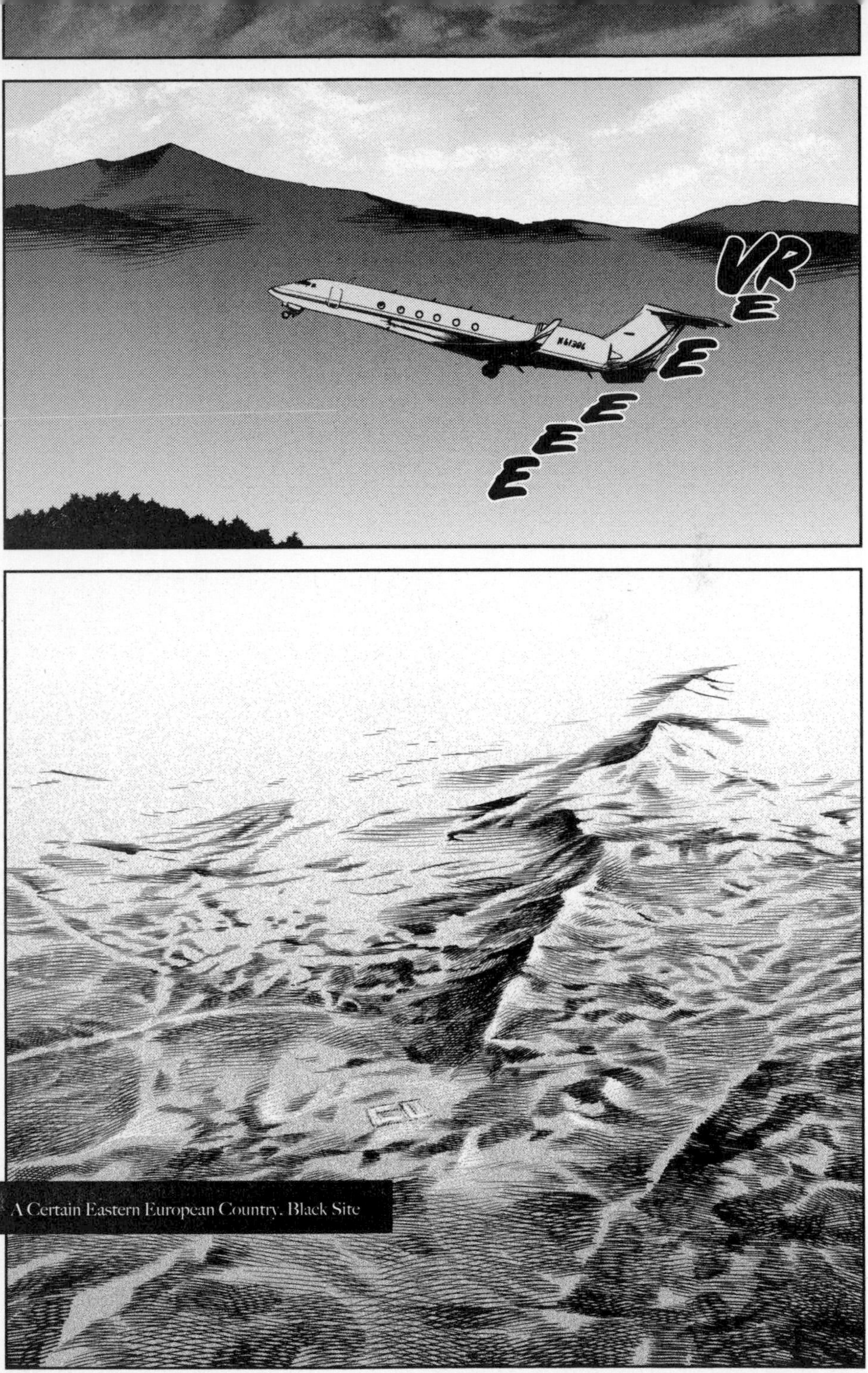
VREEEEE
A Certain Eastern European Country, Black Site

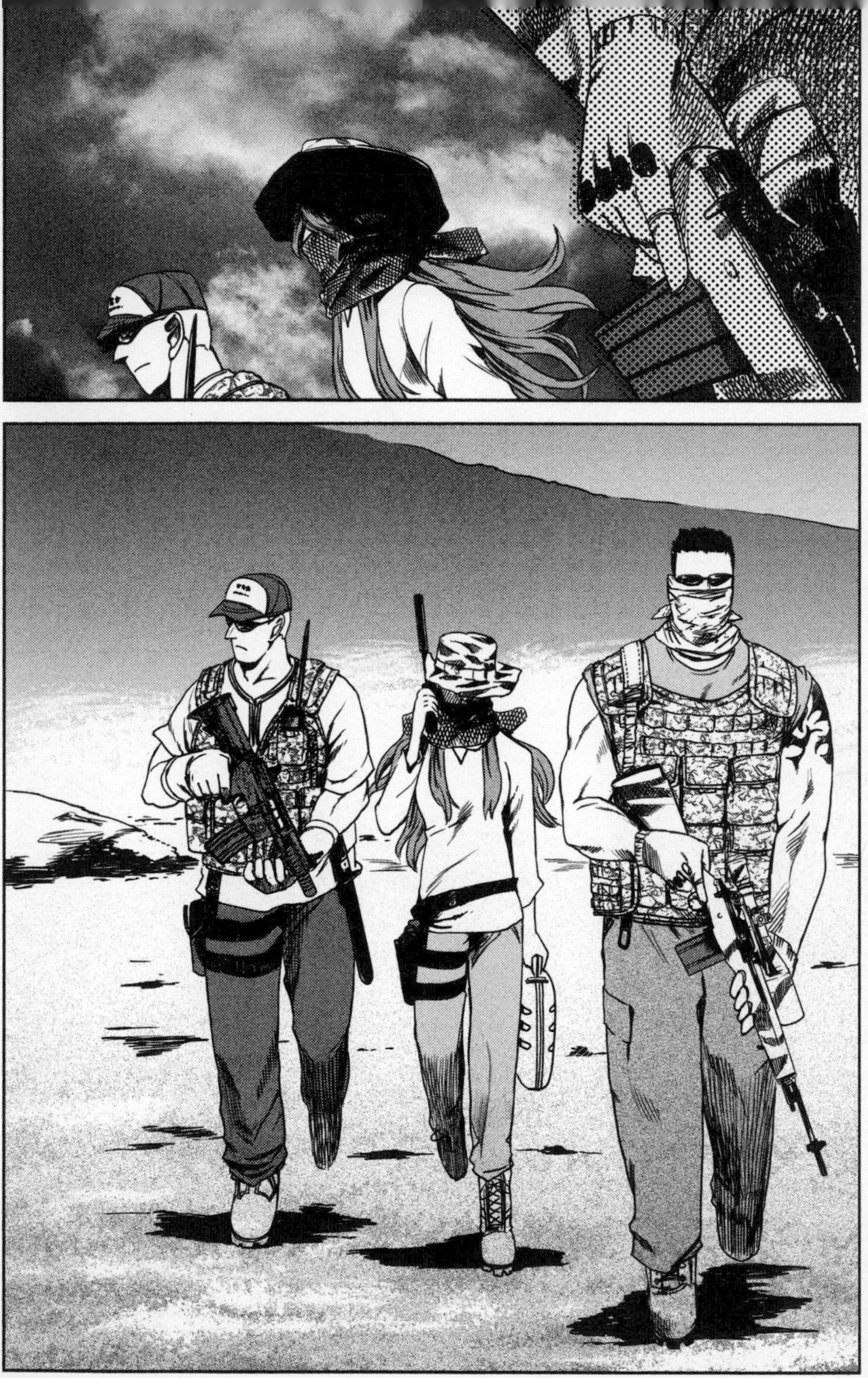

I'M BEAT.

WHEW...

NUMBER 24?

NOT TALKING. WHADDAYA WANNA DO, HEX?

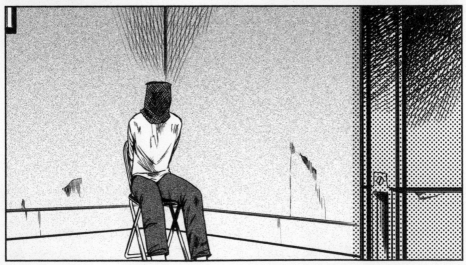

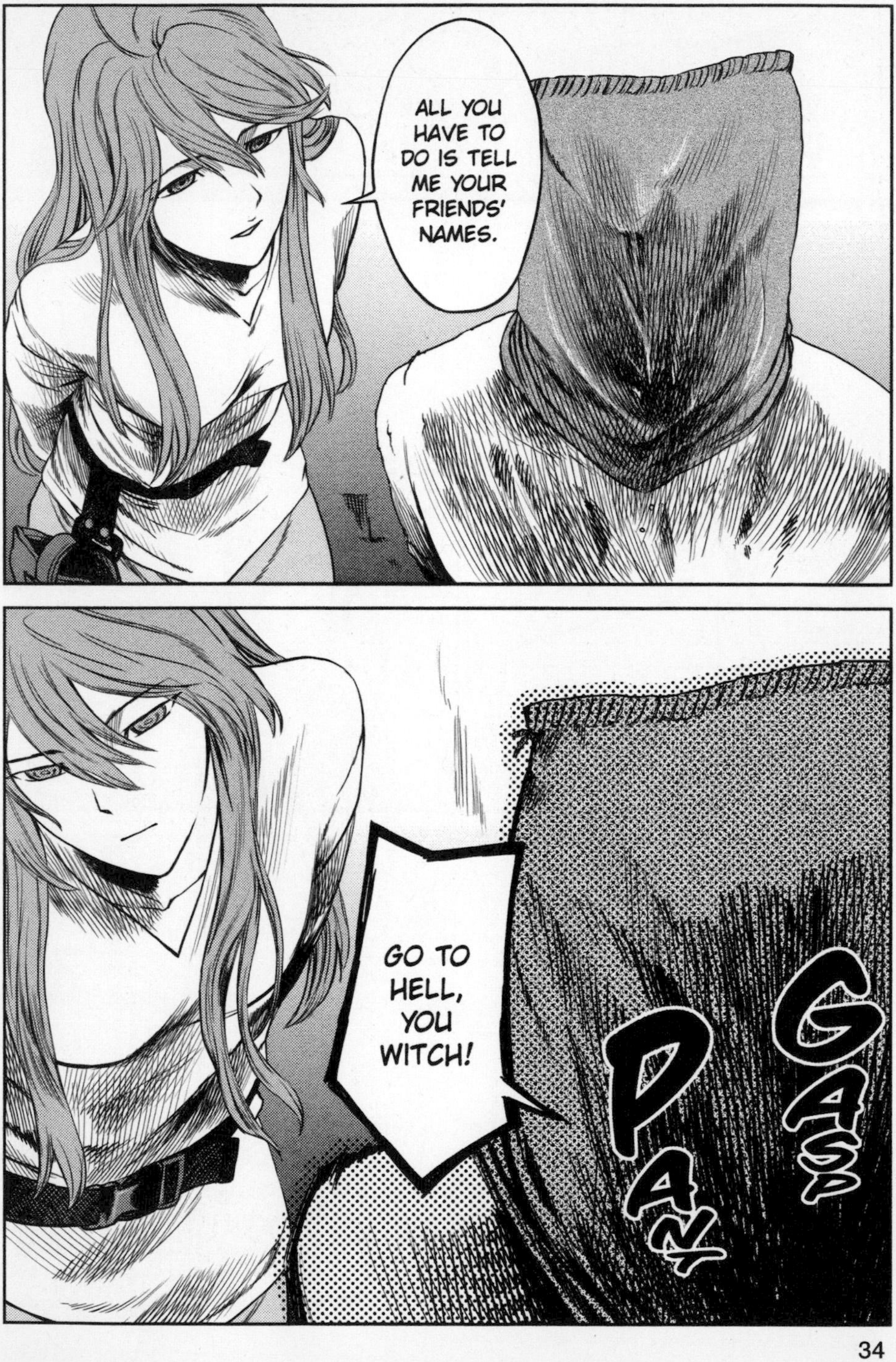
ALL YOU HAVE TO DO IS TELL ME YOUR FRIENDS' NAMES.
GASP
PANT
GO TO HELL, YOU WITCH!

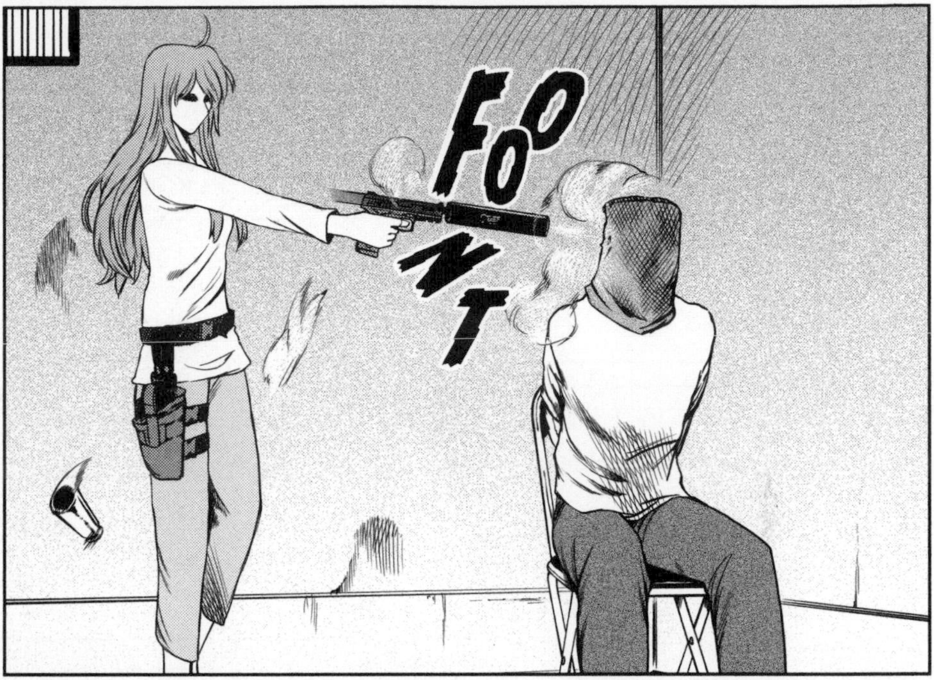
FOONT
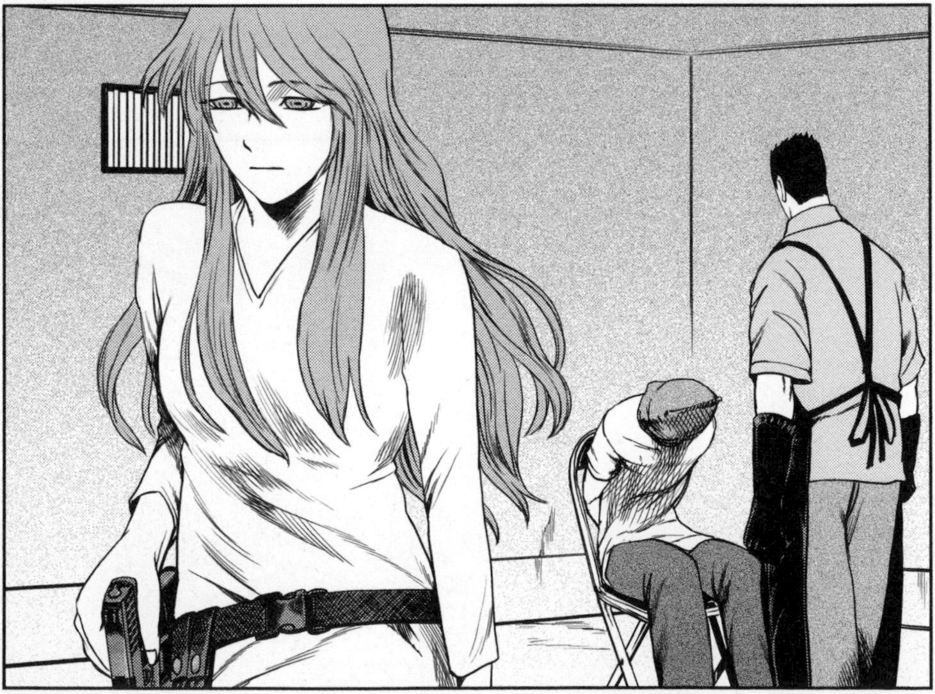

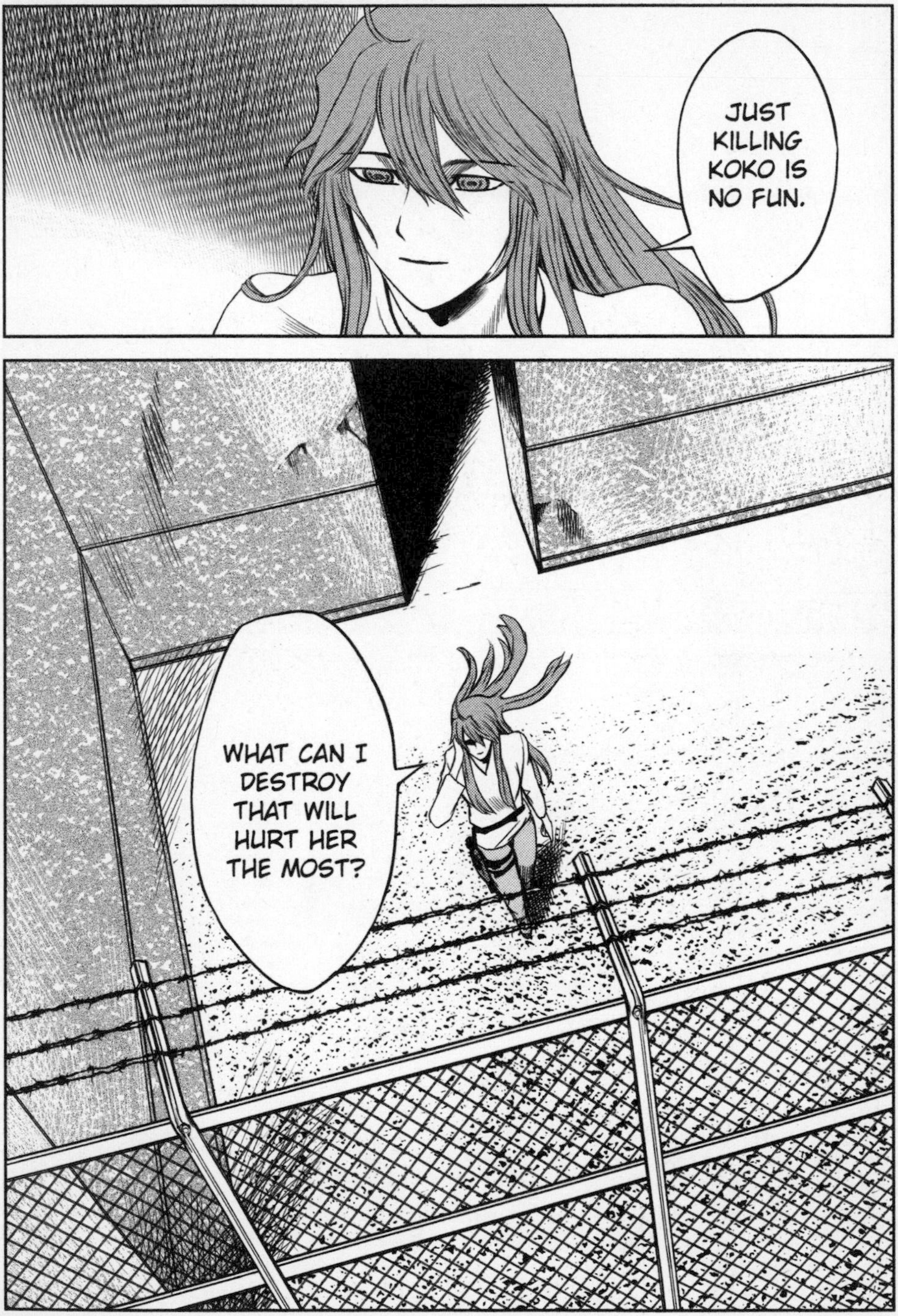
JUST KILLING KOKO IS NO FUN.
WHAT CAN I DESTROY THAT WILL HURT HER THE MOST?

Chapter 38: Dance with Undershaft (phase 2)

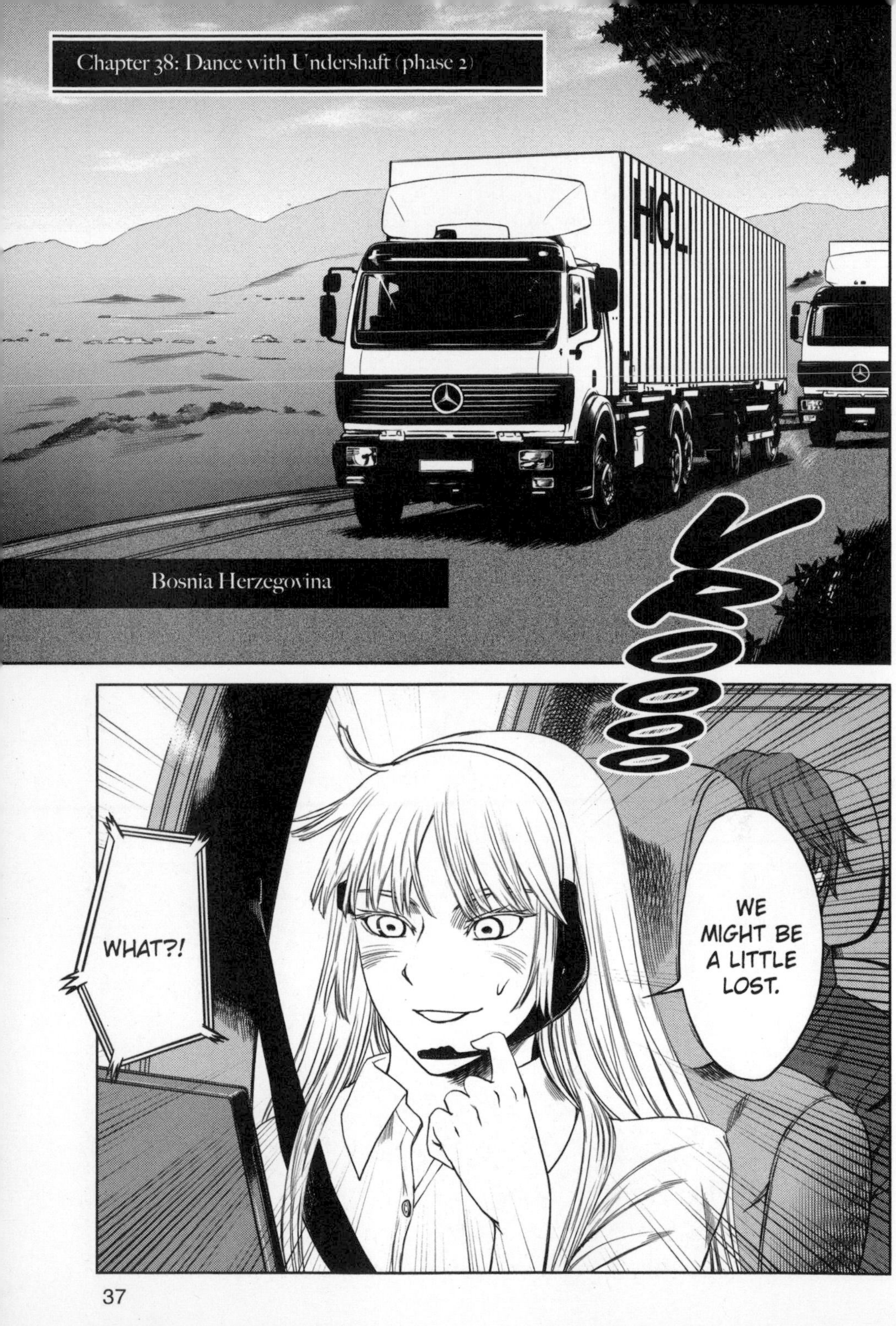
HCLI
Bosnia Herzegovina
VROOOOOO
WE MIGHT BE A LITTLE LOST.
WHAT?!

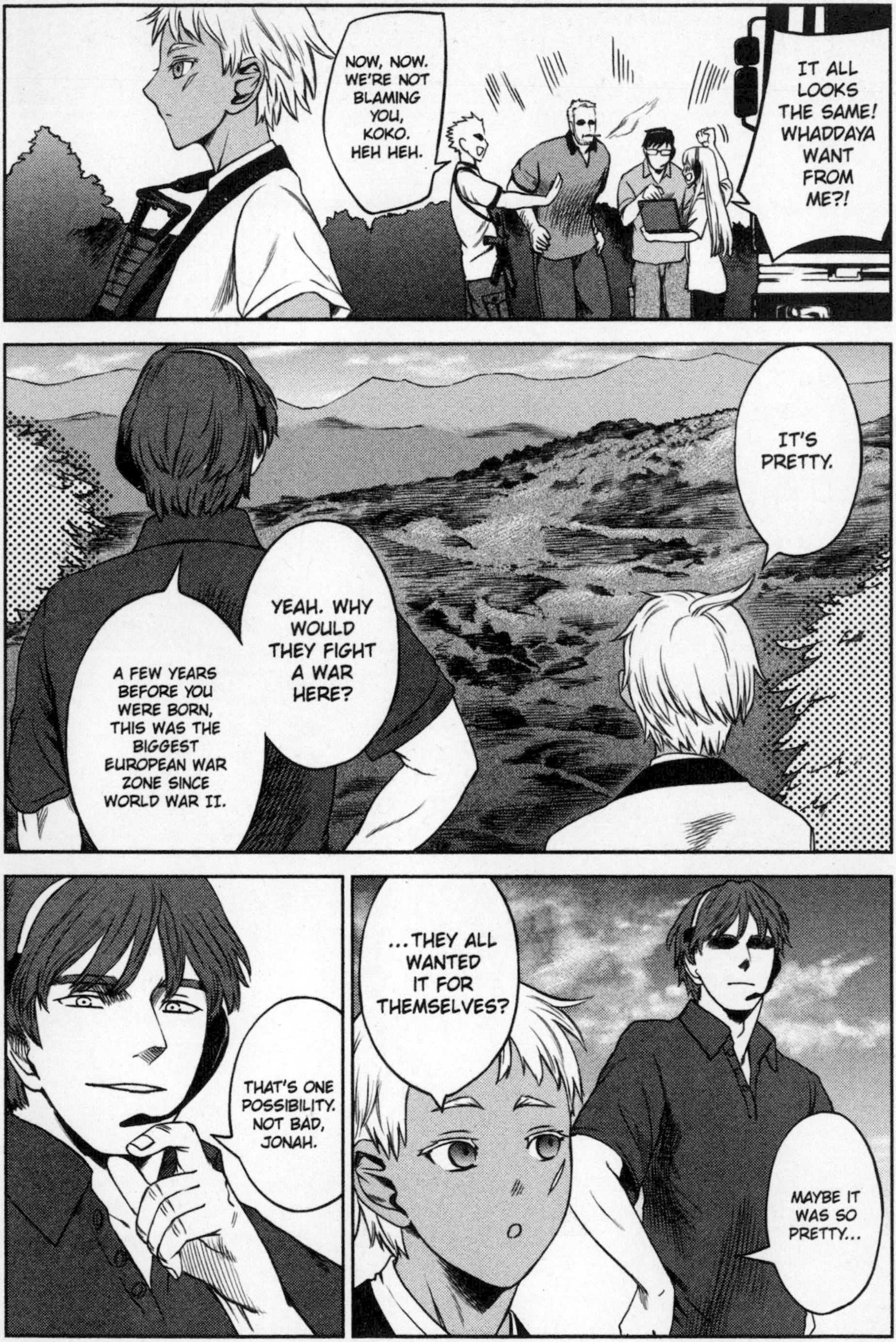
IT ALL LOOKS THE SAME! WHADDAYA WANT FROM ME?!
NOW, NOW. WE'RE NOT BLAMING YOU, KOKO. HEH HEH.
IT'S PRETTY.
YEAH. WHY WOULD THEY FIGHT A WAR HERE?
A FEW YEARS BEFORE YOU WERE BORN, THIS WAS THE BIGGEST EUROPEAN WAR ZONE SINCE WORLD WAR II.
MAYBE IT WAS SO PRETTY...
...THEY ALL WANTED IT FOR THEMSELVES?
THAT'S ONE POSSIBILITY. NOT BAD, JONAH.

Chapter 38: Dance with Undershaft (phase 2)

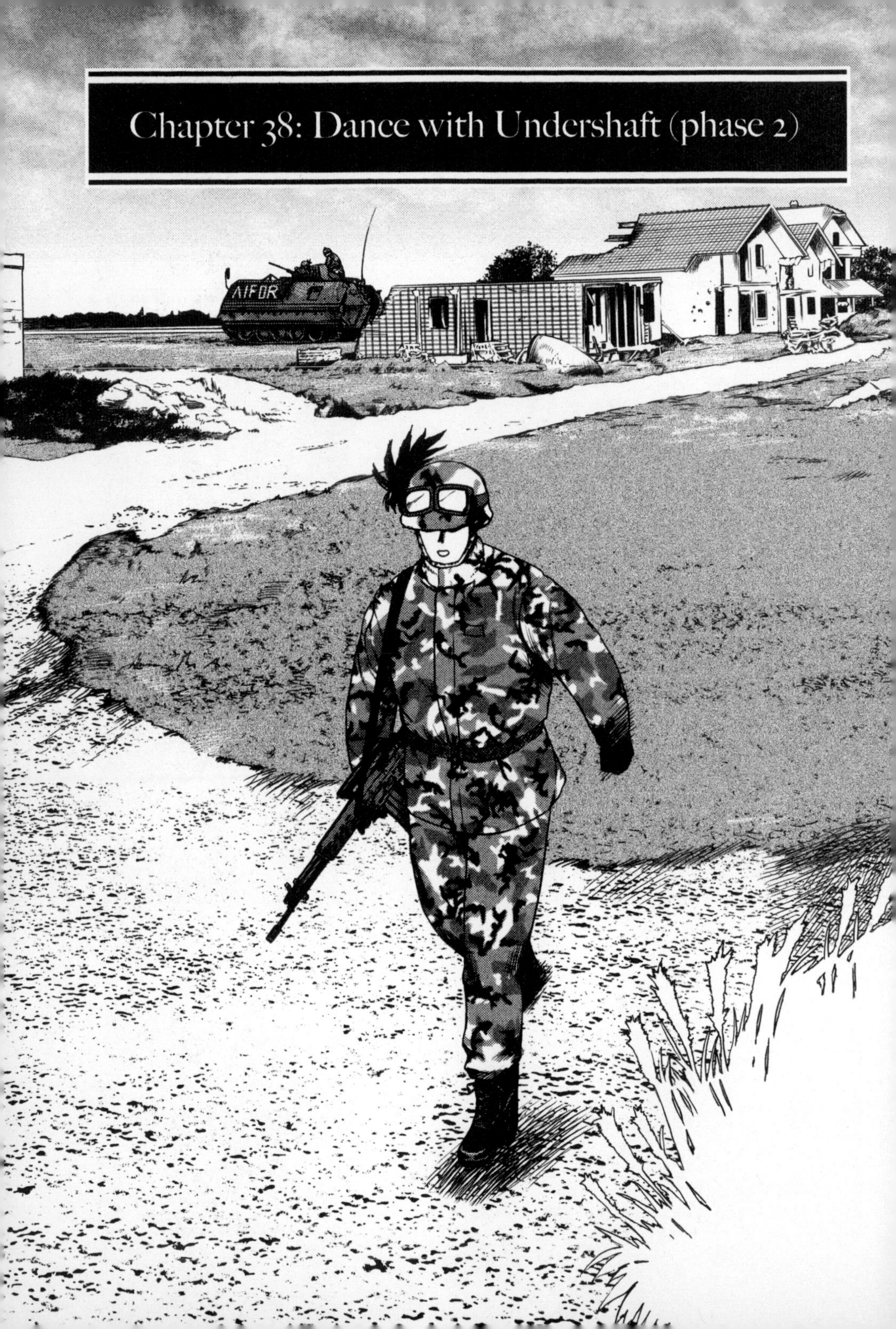
AIFOR

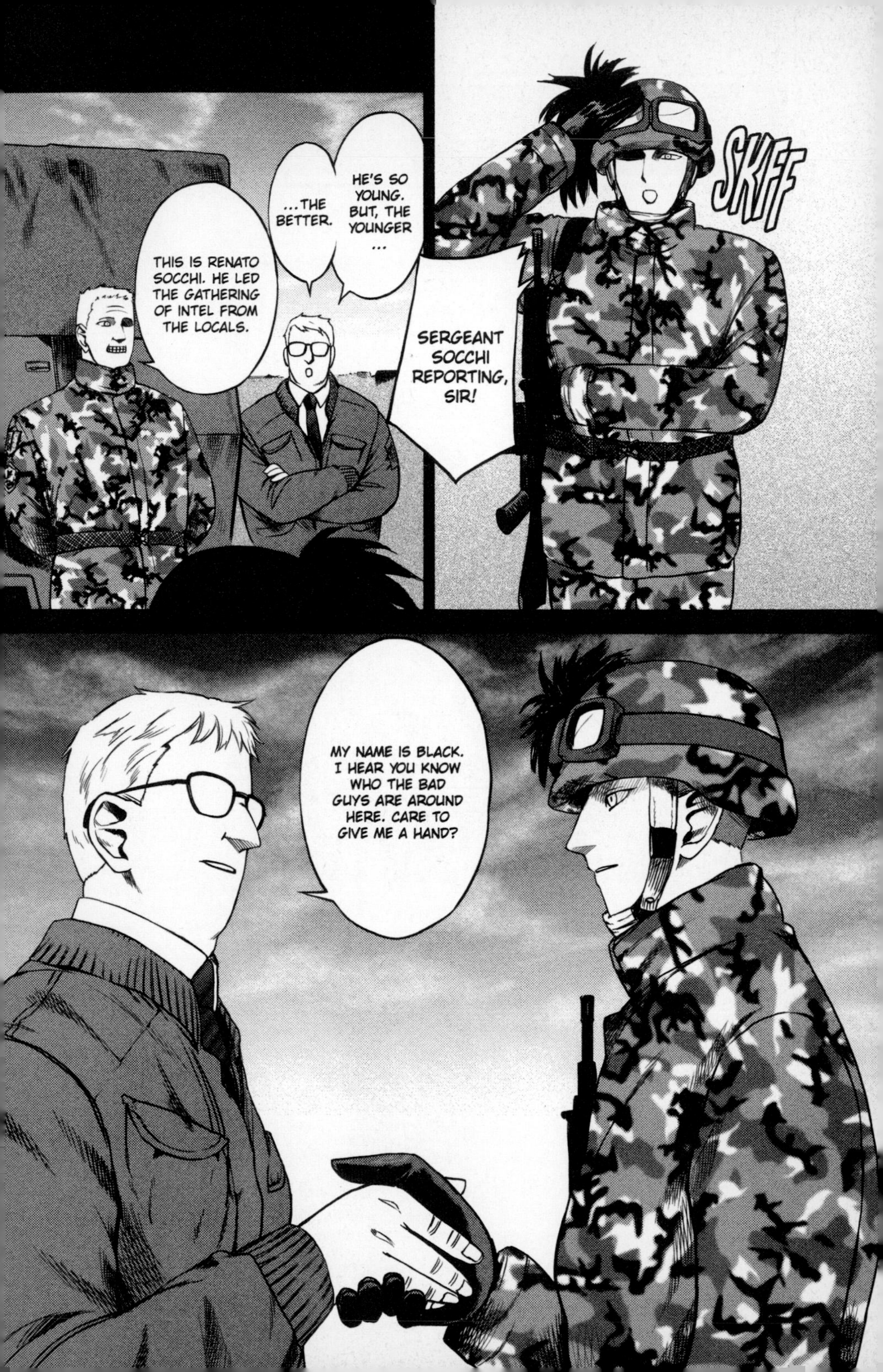
SKFF
SERGEANT SOCCHI REPORTING, SIR!
HE'S SO YOUNG. BUT, THE YOUNGER ...
...THE BETTER.
THIS IS RENATO SOCCHI. HE LED THE GATHERING OF INTEL FROM THE LOCALS.
MY NAME IS BLACK. I HEAR YOU KNOW WHO THE BAD GUYS ARE AROUND HERE. CARE TO GIVE ME A HAND?

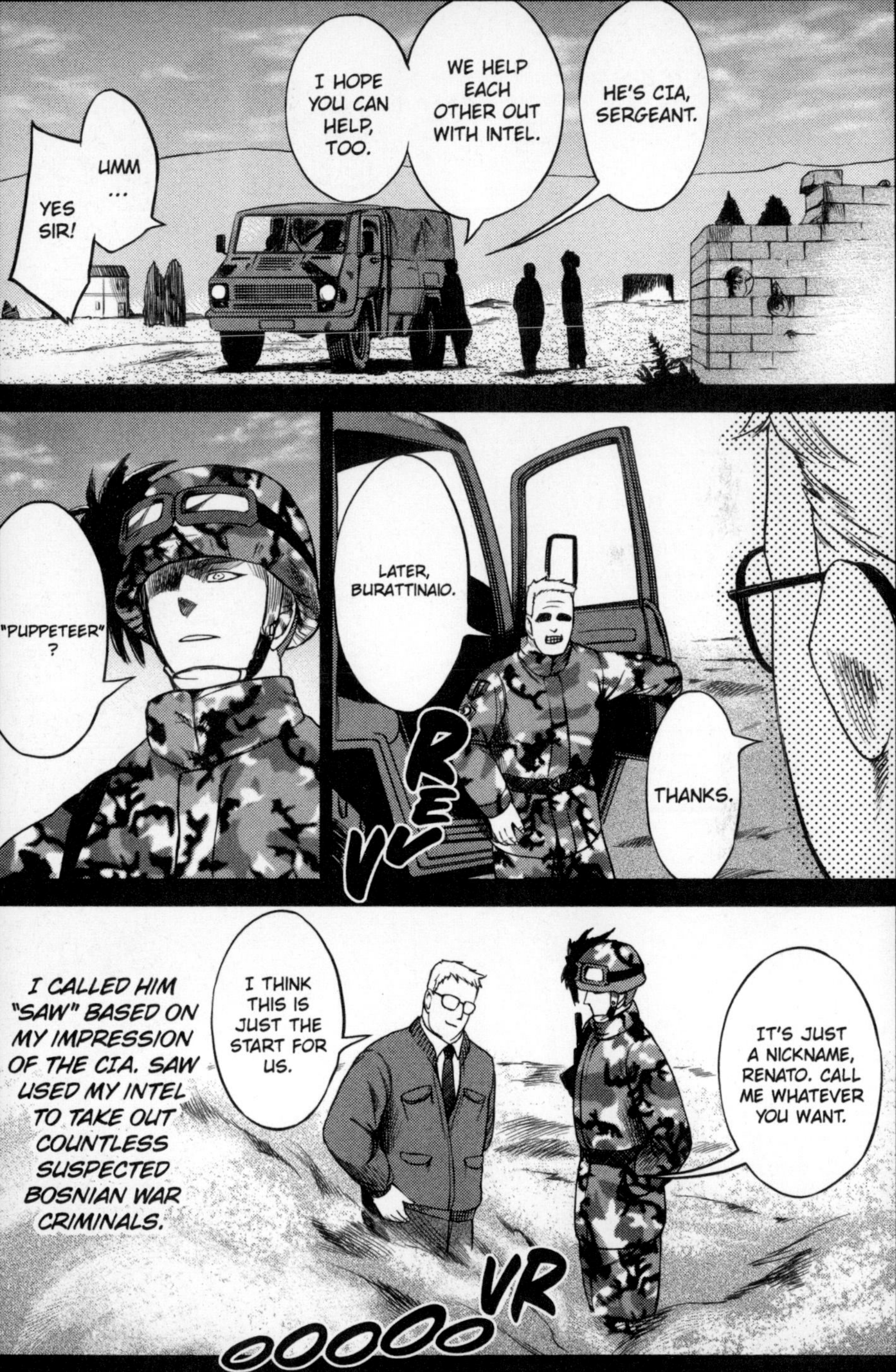
HE'S CIA, SERGEANT.
WE HELP EACH OTHER OUT WITH INTEL.
I HOPE YOU CAN HELP, TOO.
UMM ...
YES SIR!
THANKS.
LATER, BURATTINAIO.
REVV
"PUPPETEER" ?
IT'S JUST A NICKNAME, RENATO. CALL ME WHATEVER YOU WANT.
I THINK THIS IS JUST THE START FOR US.
I CALLED HIM "SAW" BASED ON MY IMPRESSION OF THE CIA. SAW USED MY INTEL TO TAKE OUT COUNTLESS SUSPECTED BOSNIAN WAR CRIMINALS.
VROOOOO

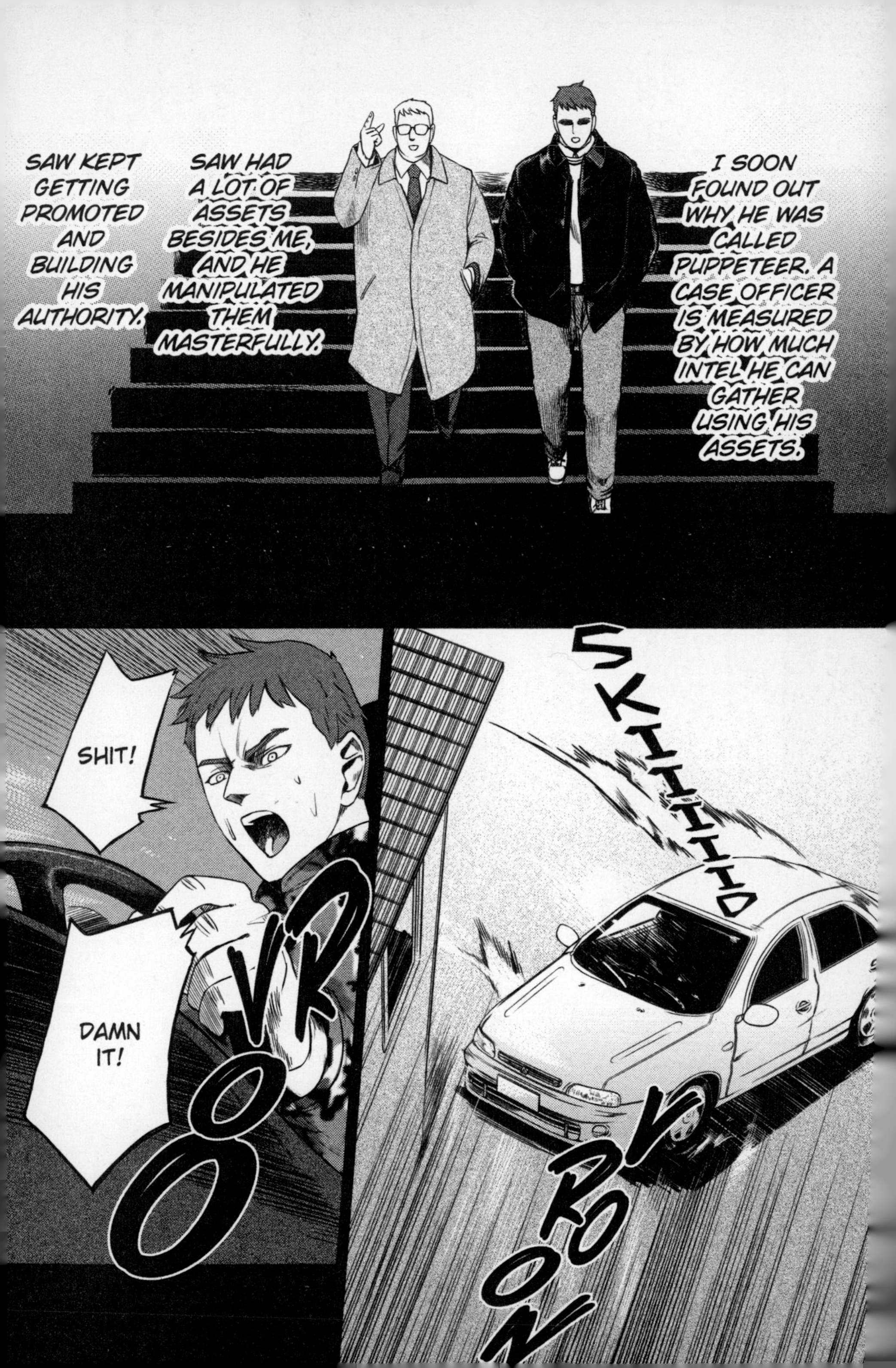
I SOON FOUND OUT WHY HE WAS CALLED PUPPETEER. A CASE OFFICER IS MEASURED BY HOW MUCH INTEL HE CAN GATHER USING HIS ASSETS.
SAW HAD A LOT OF ASSETS BESIDES ME, AND HE MANIPULATED THEM MASTERFULLY.
SAW KEPT GETTING PROMOTED AND BUILDING HIS AUTHORITY.
SKIIIIIID
VROON
SHIT!
DAMN IT!
VROOO

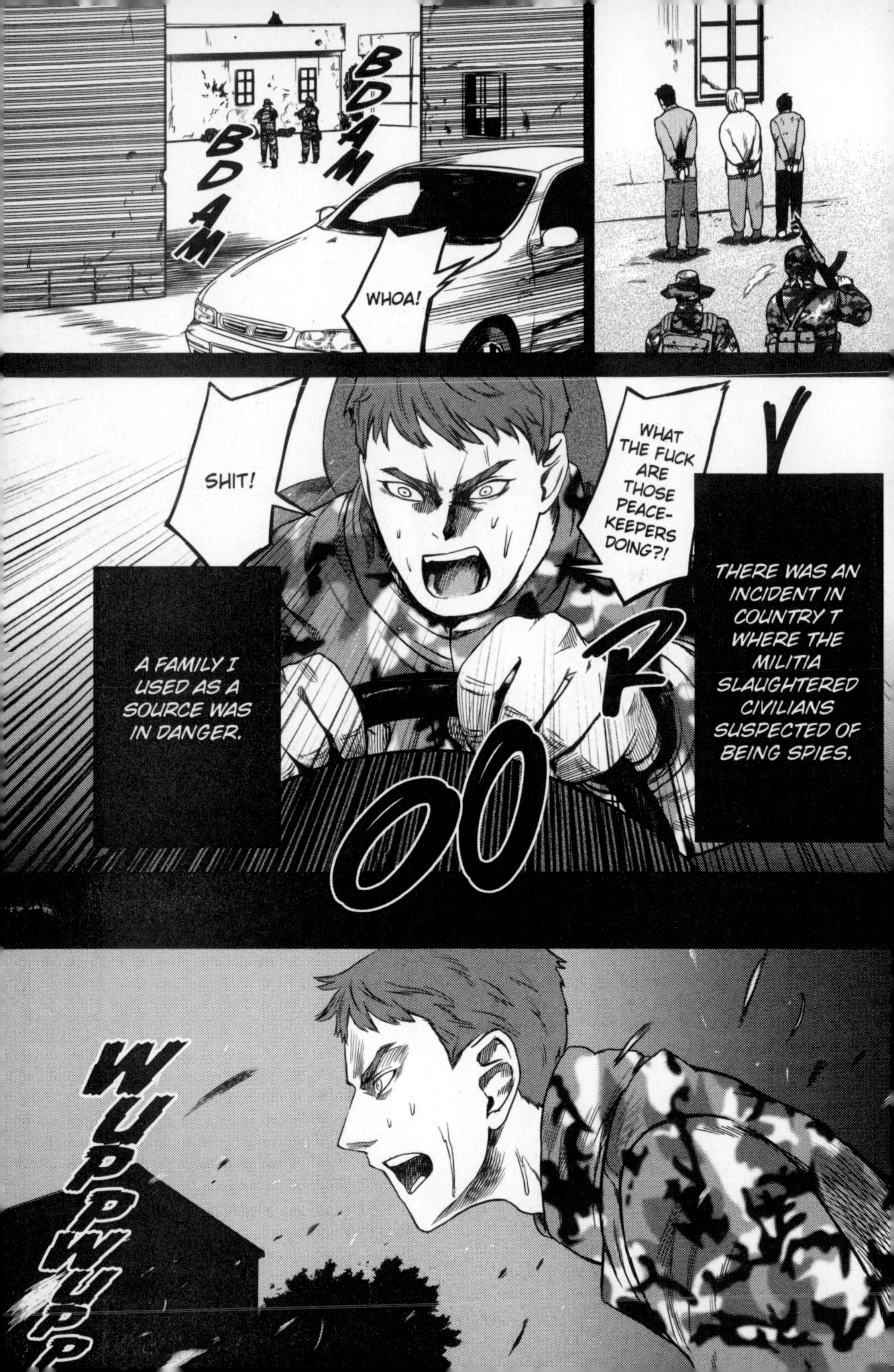
BDAM
BDAM
WHOA!
WHAT THE FUCK ARE THOSE PEACE-KEEPERS DOING?!
THERE WAS AN INCIDENT IN COUNTRY T WHERE THE MILITIA SLAUGHTERED CIVILIANS SUSPECTED OF BEING SPIES.
SHIT!
A FAMILY I USED AS A SOURCE WAS IN DANGER.
VROO
WUPPWUPP

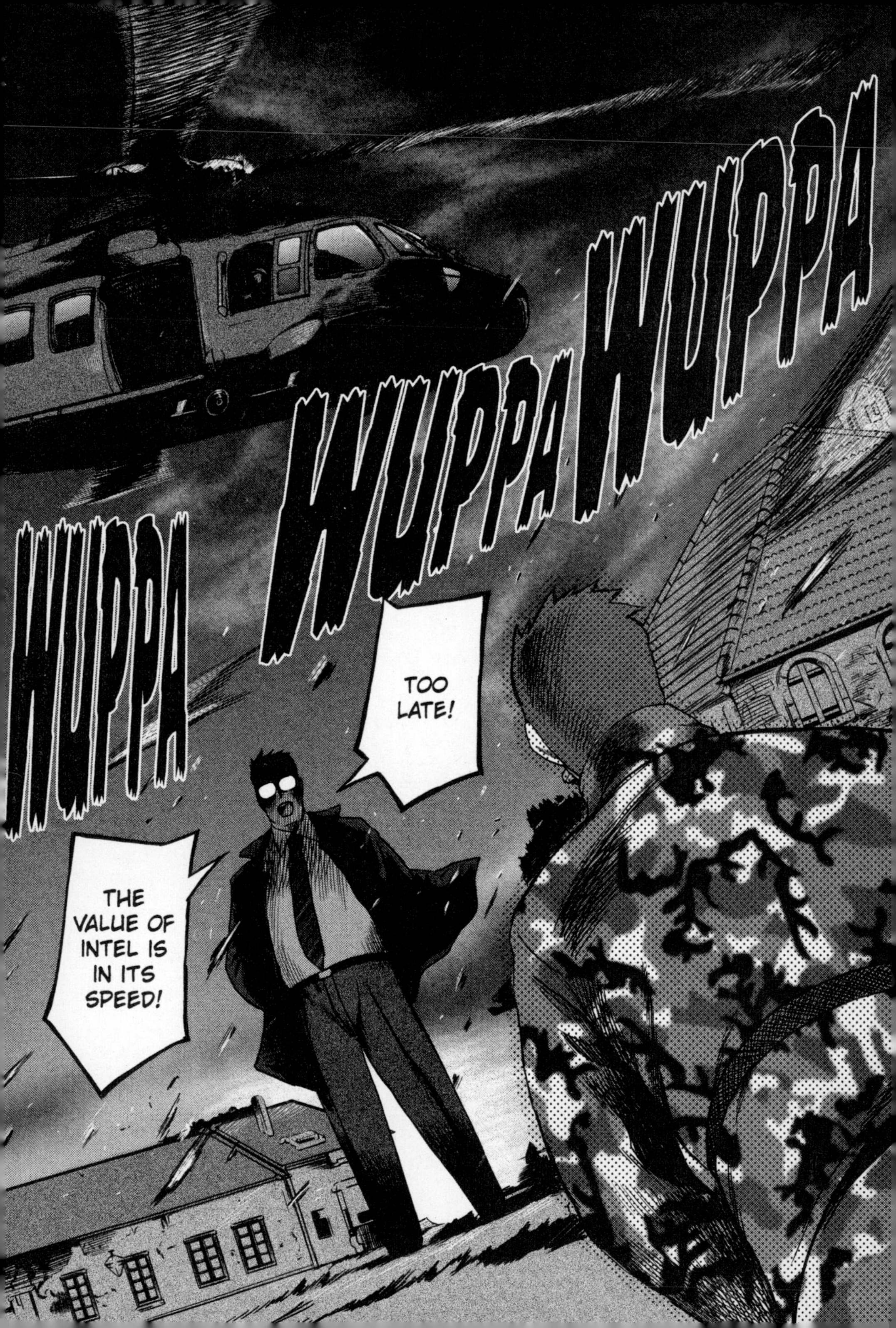
WUPPA WUPPA
WUPPA
TOO LATE!
THE VALUE OF INTEL IS IN ITS SPEED!

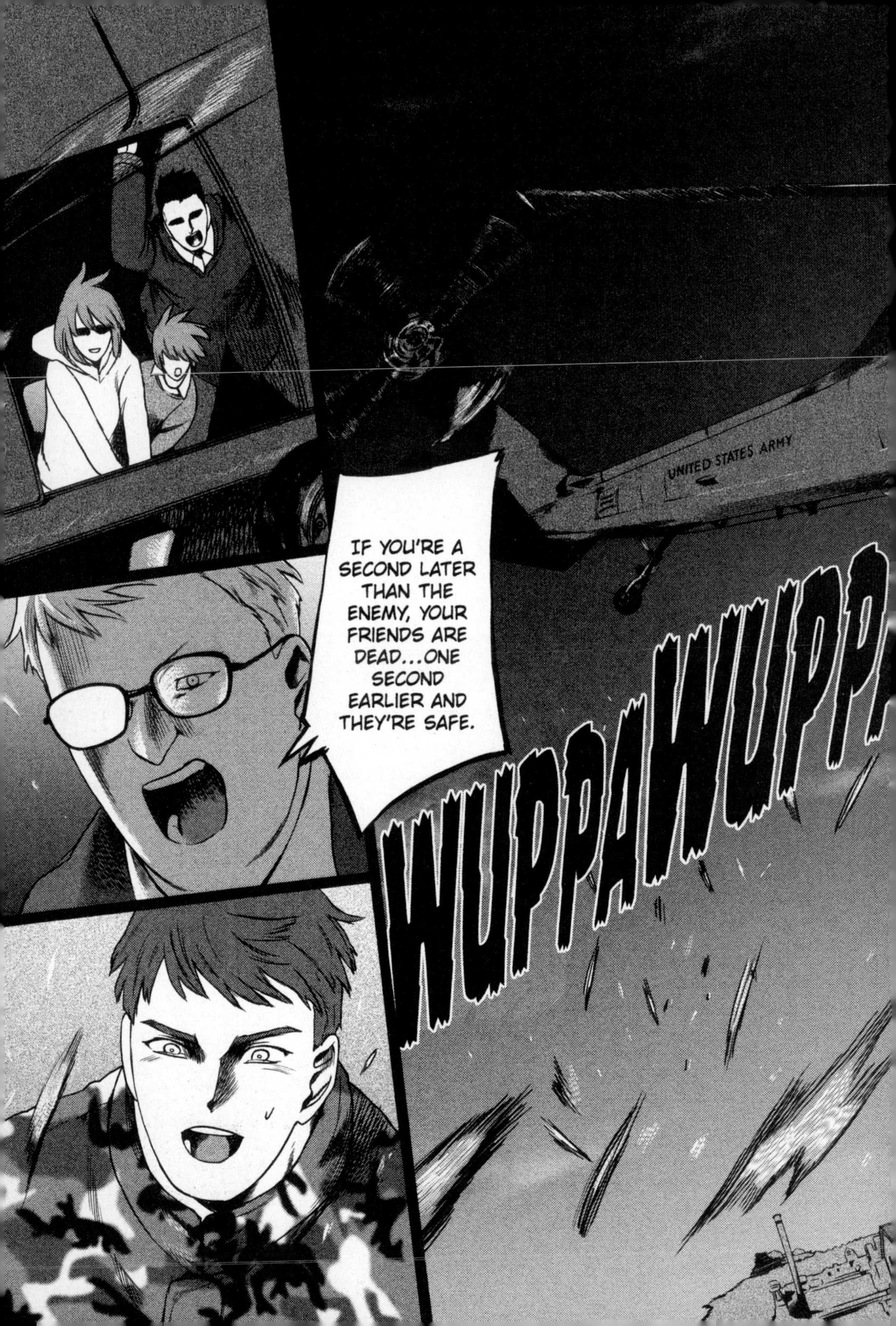
UNITED STATES ARMY
IF YOU'RE A SECOND LATER THAN THE ENEMY, YOUR FRIENDS ARE DEAD...ONE SECOND EARLIER AND THEY'RE SAFE.
WUPPAWUPP

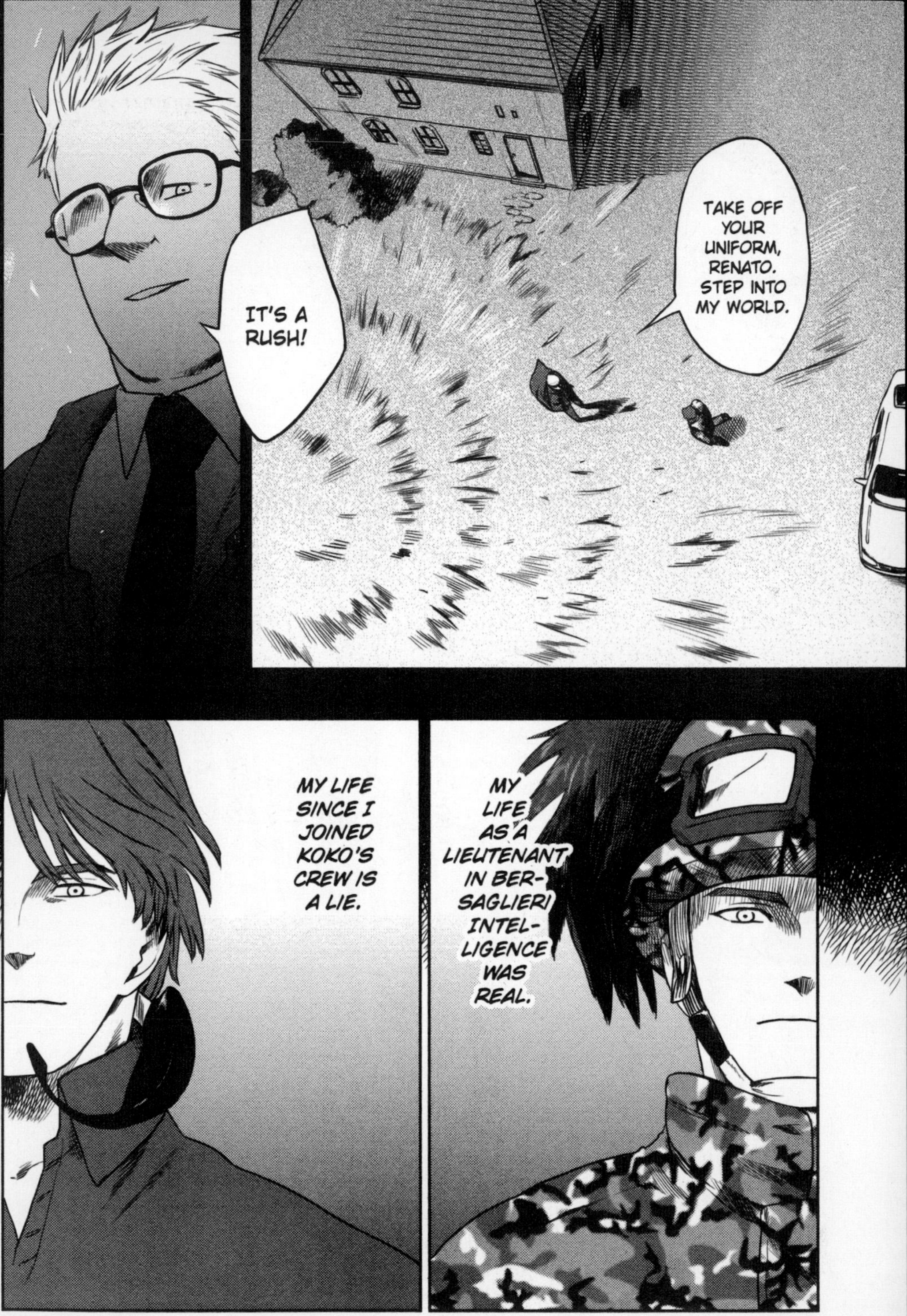
TAKE OFF YOUR UNIFORM, RENATO. STEP INTO MY WORLD.
IT'S A RUSH!
MY LIFE AS A LIEUTENANT IN BERSAGLIERI INTELLIGENCE WAS REAL.
MY LIFE SINCE I JOINED KOKO'S CREW IS A LIE.

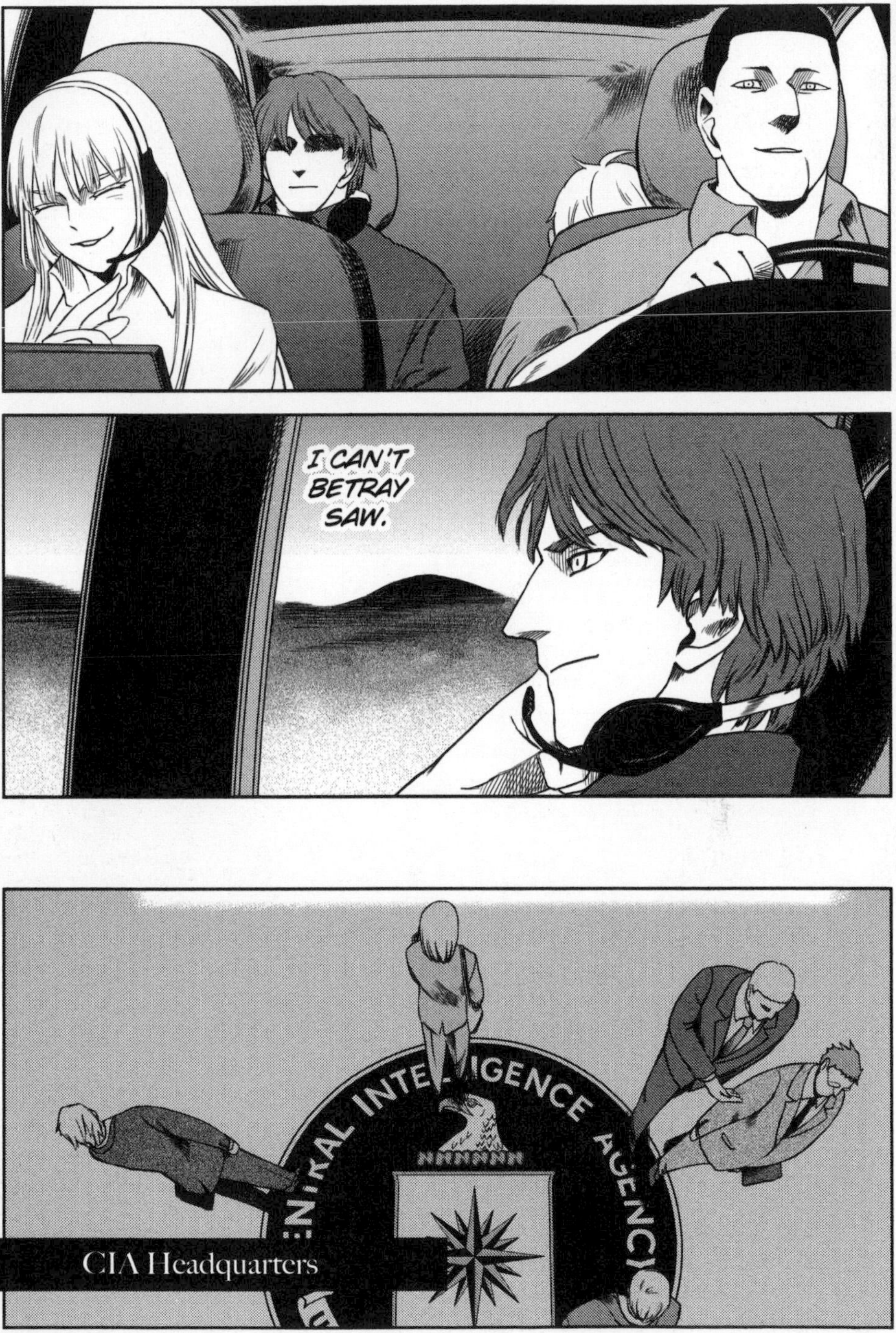
I CAN'T BETRAY SAW.
CENTRAL INTELLIGENCE AGENCY
CIA Headquarters

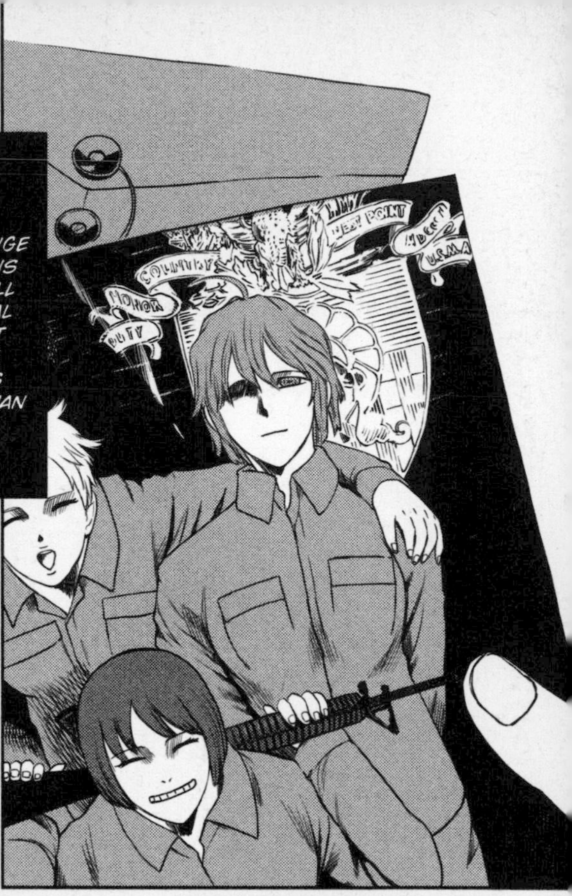

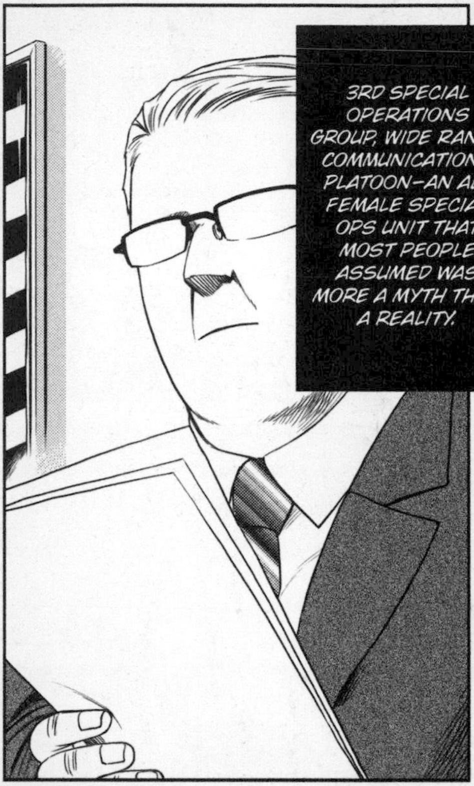
3RD SPECIAL OPERATIONS GROUP, WIDE RANGE COMMUNICATIONS PLATOON—AN ALL FEMALE SPECIAL OPS UNIT THAT MOST PEOPLE ASSUMED WAS MORE A MYTH THAN A REALITY.

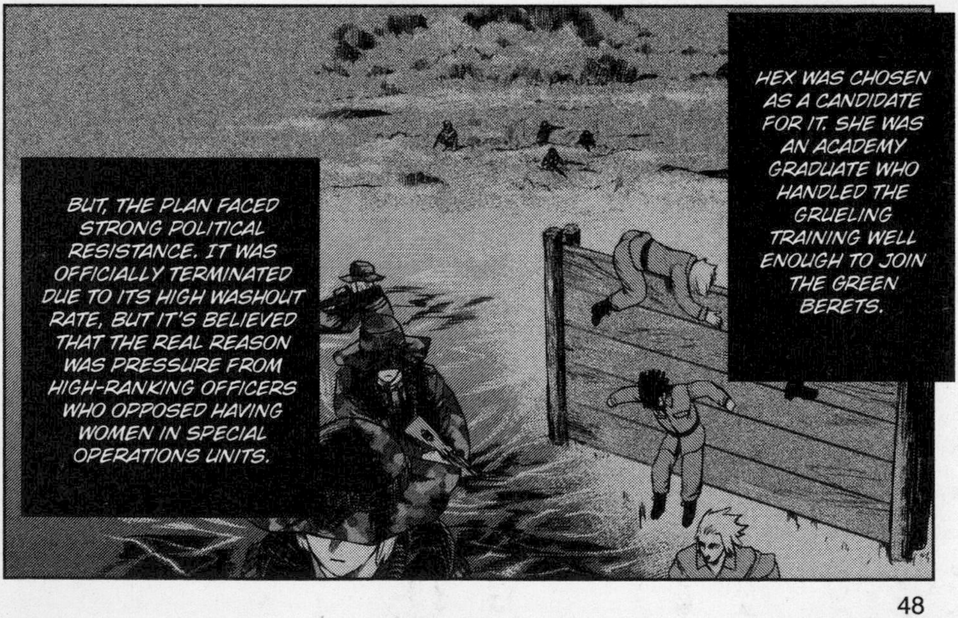
HEX WAS CHOSEN AS A CANDIDATE FOR IT. SHE WAS AN ACADEMY GRADUATE WHO HANDLED THE GRUELING TRAINING WELL ENOUGH TO JOIN THE GREEN BERETS.
BUT, THE PLAN FACED STRONG POLITICAL RESISTANCE. IT WAS OFFICIALLY TERMINATED DUE TO ITS HIGH WASHOUT RATE, BUT IT'S BELIEVED THAT THE REAL REASON WAS PRESSURE FROM HIGH-RANKING OFFICERS WHO OPPOSED HAVING WOMEN IN SPECIAL OPERATIONS UNITS.

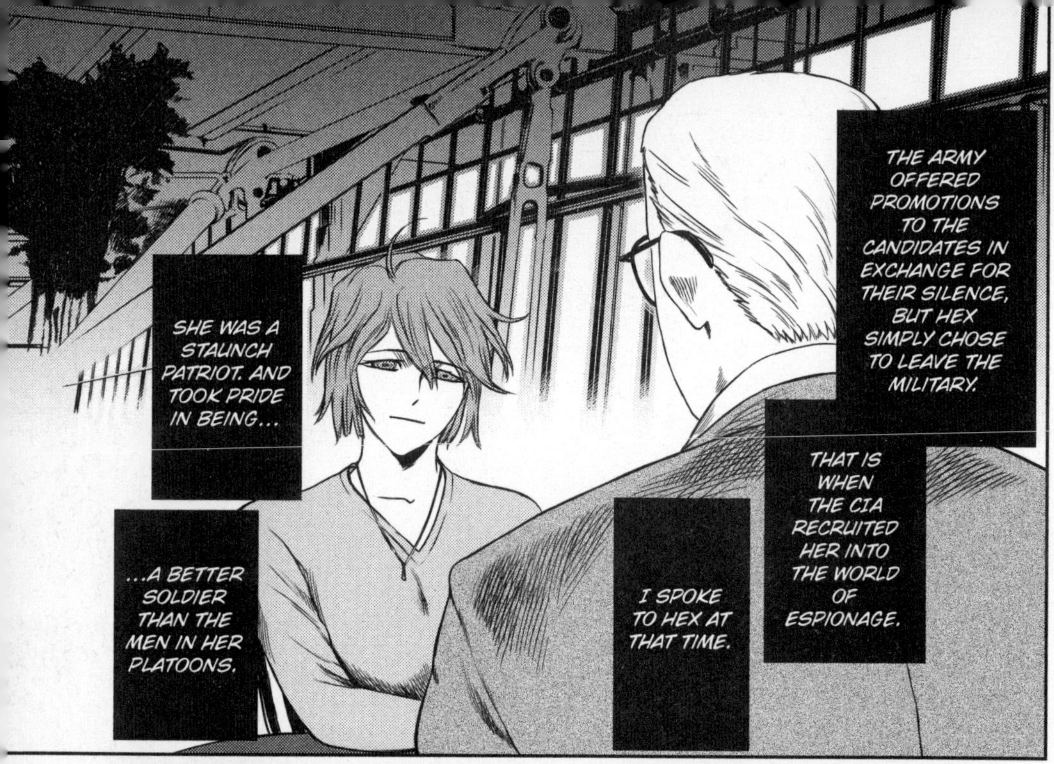
THE ARMY OFFERED PROMOTIONS TO THE CANDIDATES IN EXCHANGE FOR THEIR SILENCE, BUT HEX SIMPLY CHOSE TO LEAVE THE MILITARY.
THAT IS WHEN THE CIA RECRUITED HER INTO THE WORLD OF ESPIONAGE.
I SPOKE TO HEX AT THAT TIME.
SHE WAS A STAUNCH PATRIOT. AND TOOK PRIDE IN BEING...
...A BETTER SOLDIER THAN THE MEN IN HER PLATOONS.

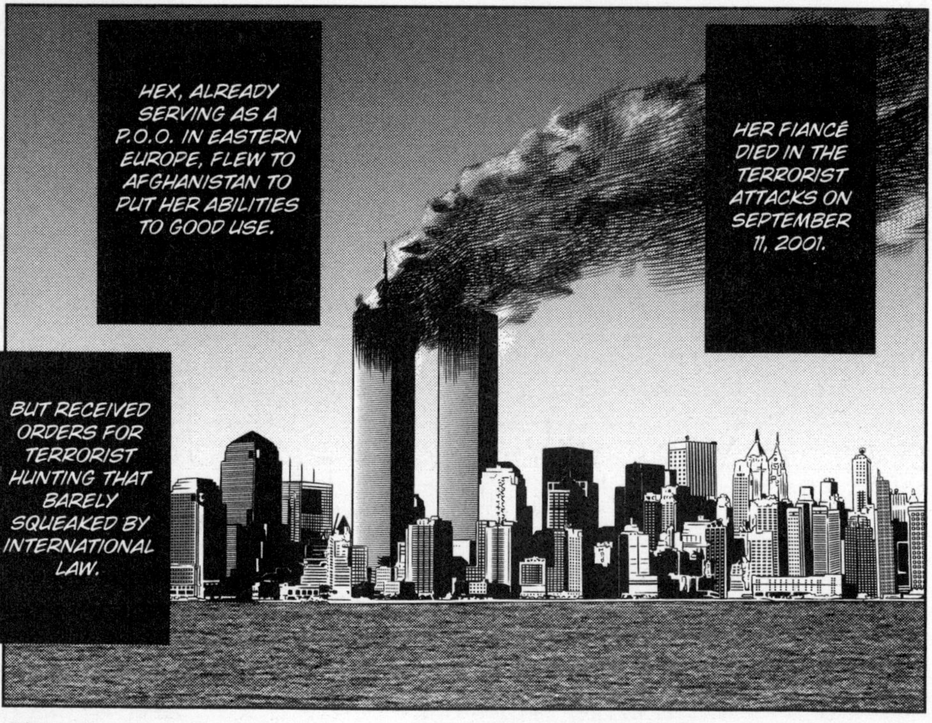
HER FIANCÉ DIED IN THE TERRORIST ATTACKS ON SEPTEMBER 11, 2001.
HEX, ALREADY SERVING AS A P.O.O. IN EASTERN EUROPE, FLEW TO AFGHANISTAN TO PUT HER ABILITIES TO GOOD USE.
BUT RECEIVED ORDERS FOR TERRORIST HUNTING THAT BARELY SQUEAKED BY INTERNATIONAL LAW.

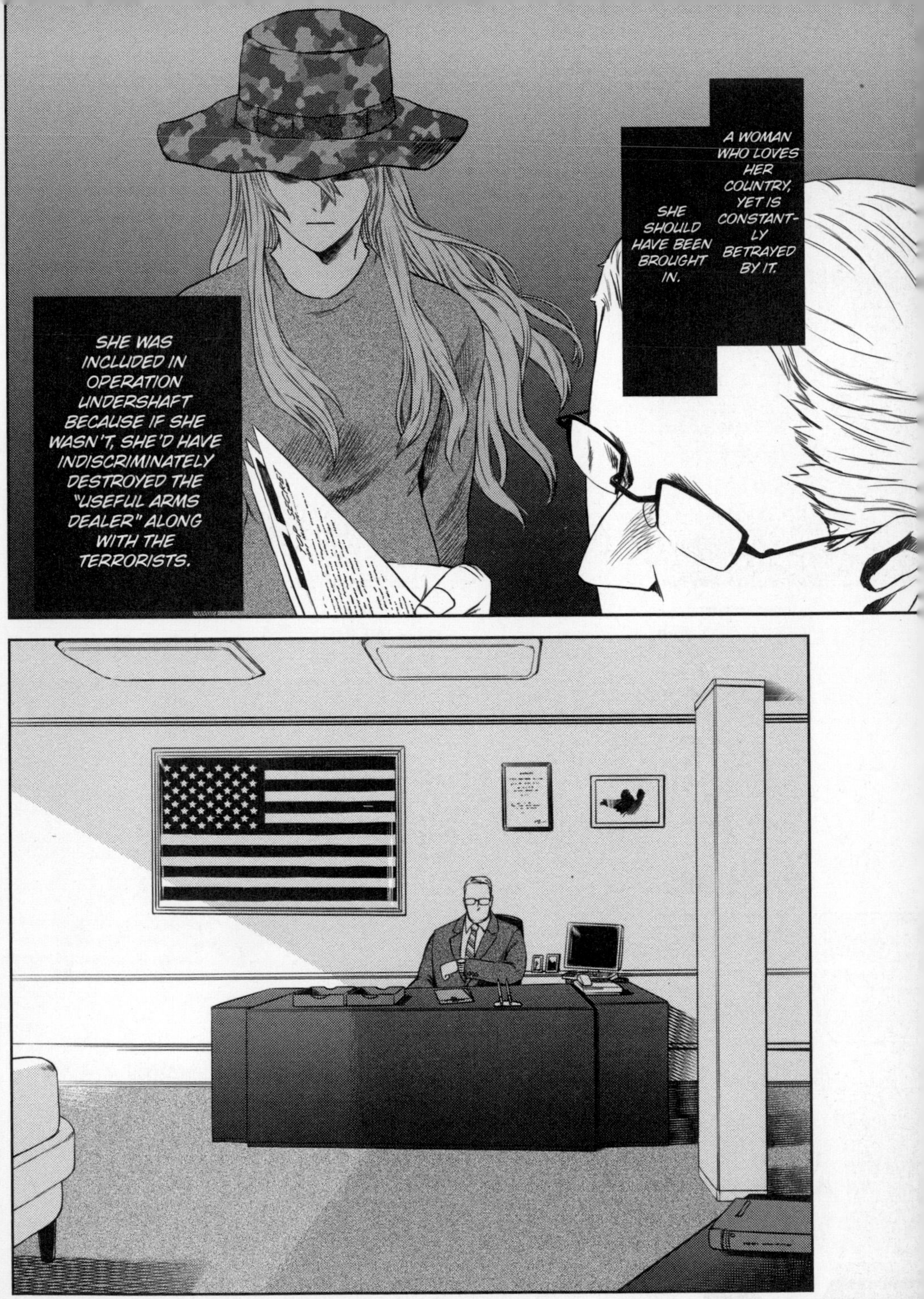
A WOMAN WHO LOVES HER COUNTRY, YET IS CONSTANT-LY BETRAYED BY IT.
SHE SHOULD HAVE BEEN BROUGHT IN.
SHE WAS INCLUDED IN OPERATION UNDERSHAFT BECAUSE IF SHE WASN'T, SHE'D HAVE INDISCRIMINATELY DESTROYED THE "USEFUL ARMS DEALER" ALONG WITH THE TERRORISTS.

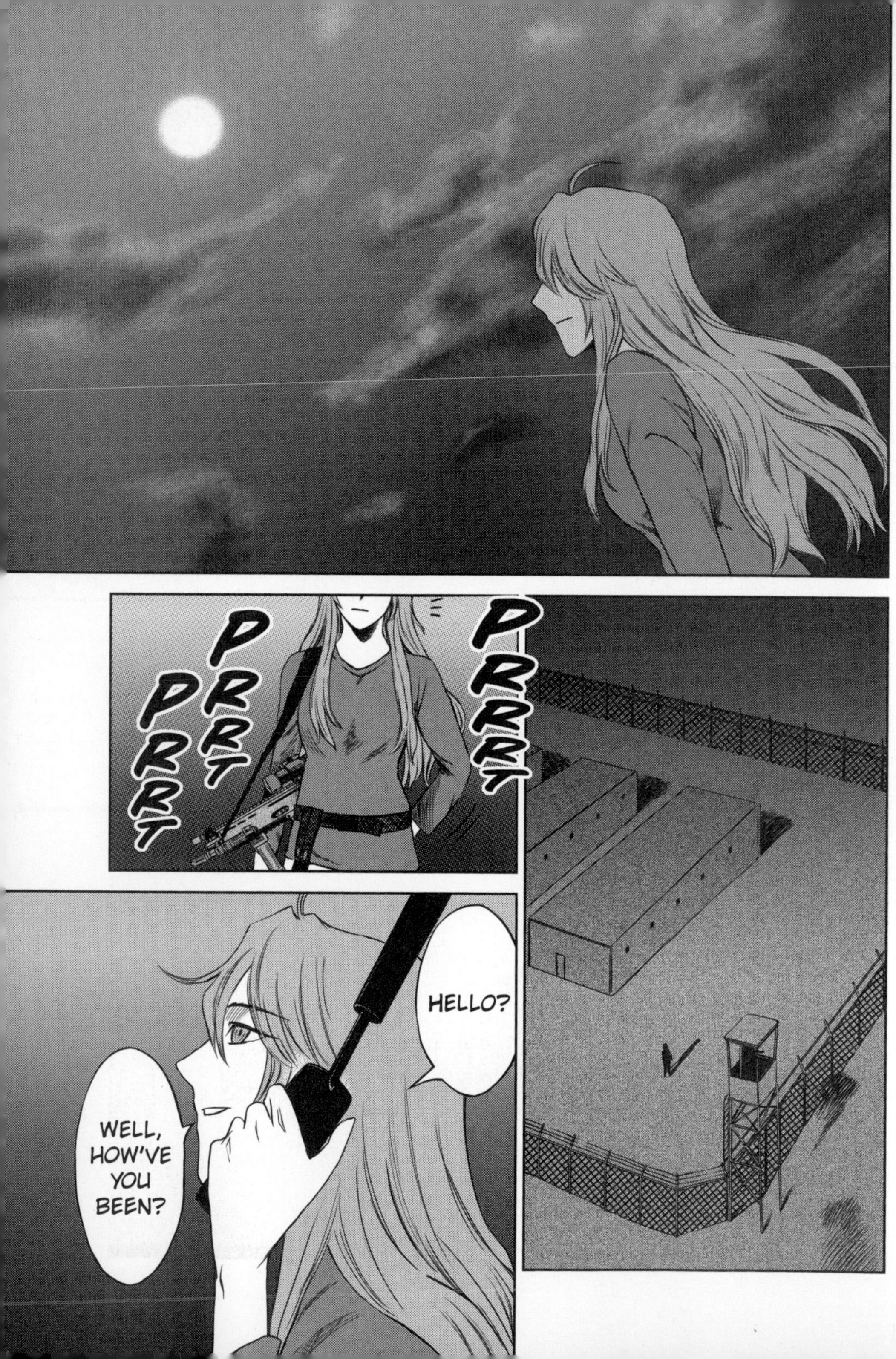
PRRRRT
PRRT
PRRRT
HELLO?
WELL, HOW'VE YOU BEEN?

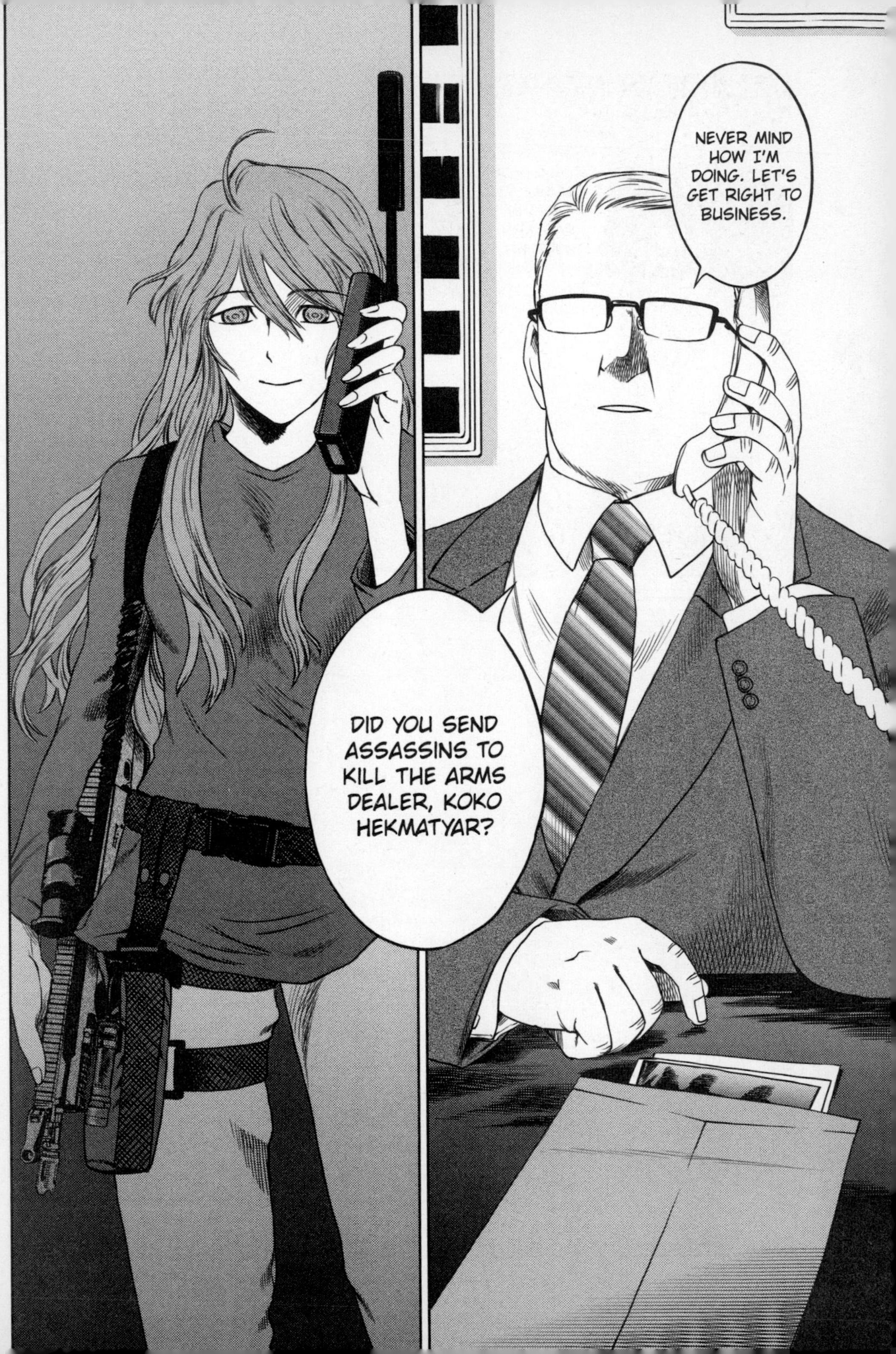
NEVER MIND HOW I'M DOING. LET'S GET RIGHT TO BUSINESS.
DID YOU SEND ASSASSINS TO KILL THE ARMS DEALER, KOKO HEKMATYAR?

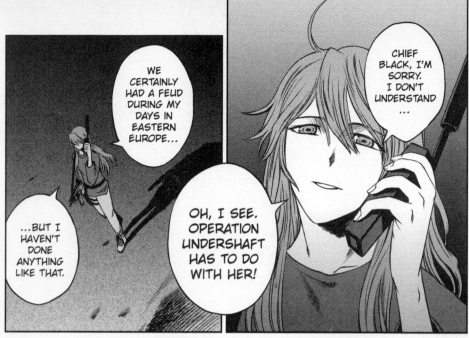

CHIEF BLACK, I'M SORRY. I DON'T UNDERSTAND ...
OH, I SEE. OPERATION UNDERSHAFT HAS TO DO WITH HER!
WE CERTAINLY HAD A FEUD DURING MY DAYS IN EASTERN EUROPE...
...BUT I HAVEN'T DONE ANYTHING LIKE THAT.
GLAD TO HEAR IT. I WANT YOU TO KEEP IT THAT WAY.
TAP
TAP
TAP
THAT'S AN ORDER.

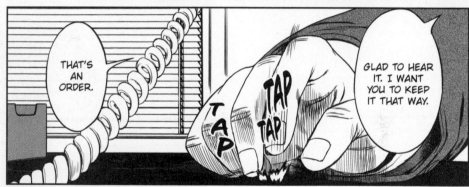

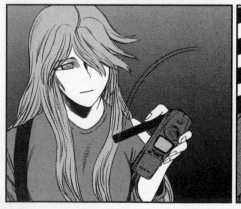

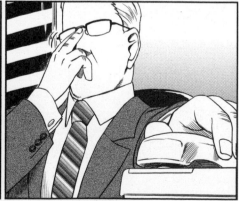

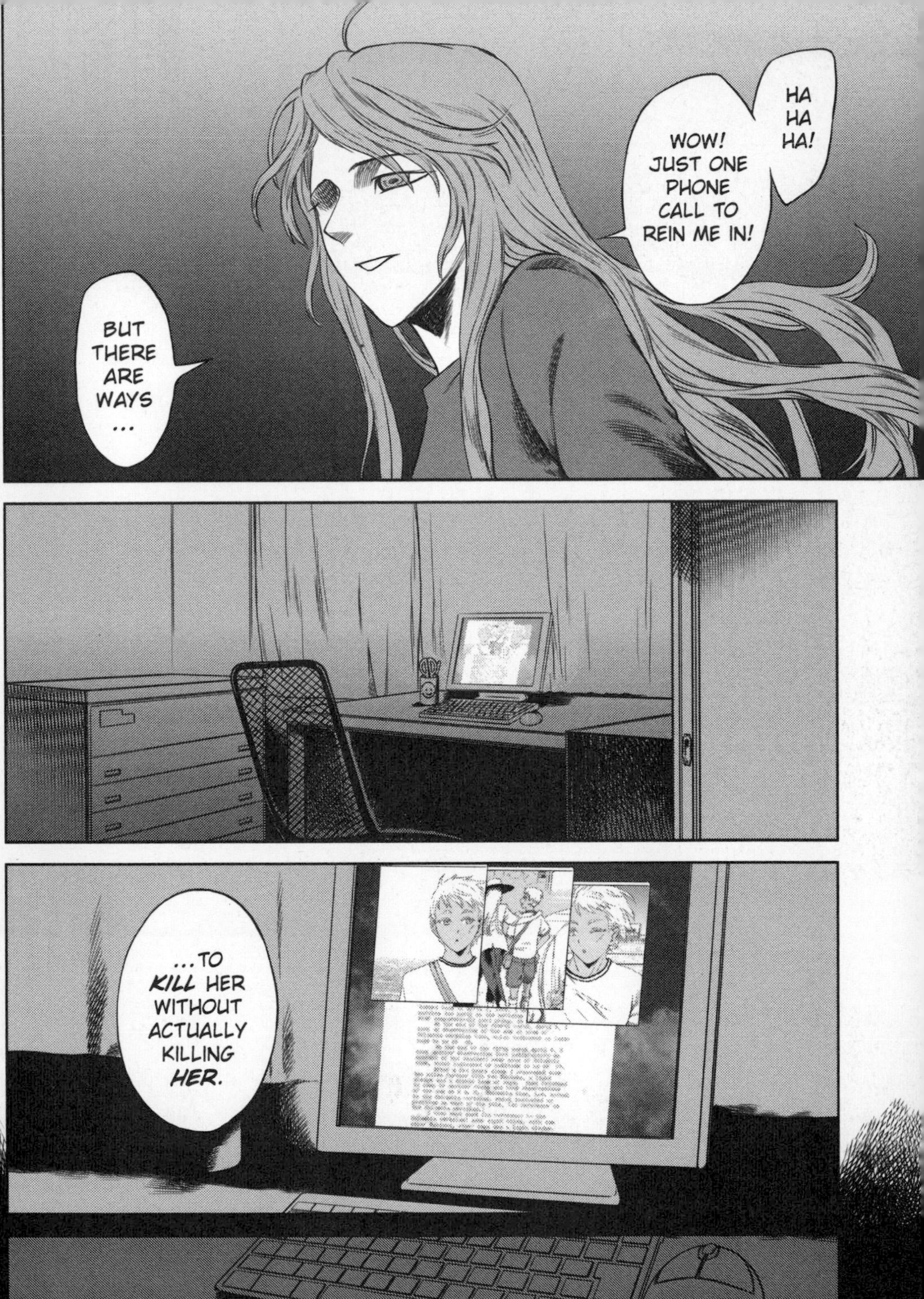
HA HA HA!
WOW! JUST ONE PHONE CALL TO REIN ME IN!
BUT THERE ARE WAYS ...
...TO KILL HER WITHOUT ACTUALLY KILLING HER.

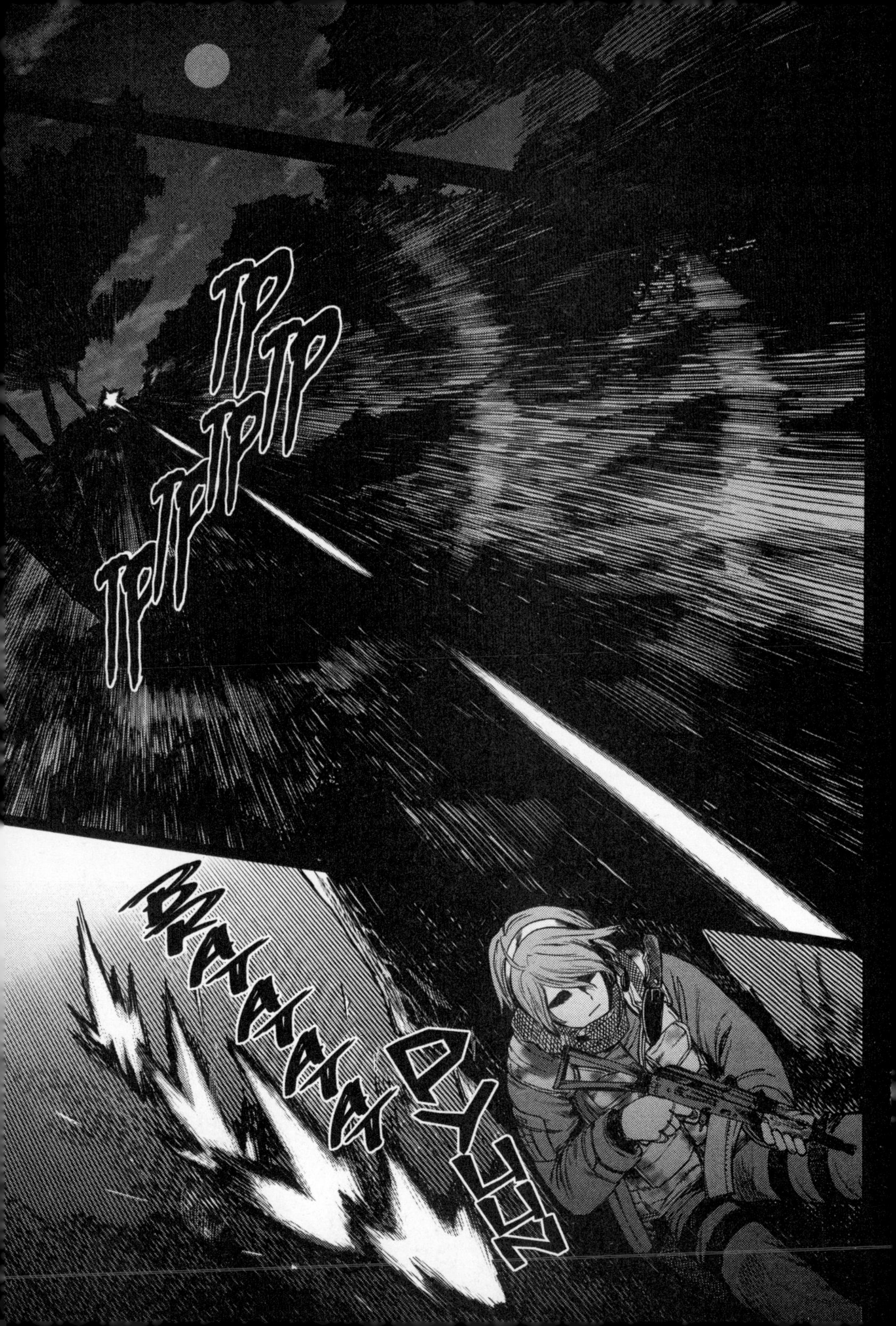
TPTPTPTPTP
BATATATAT
DYUUN

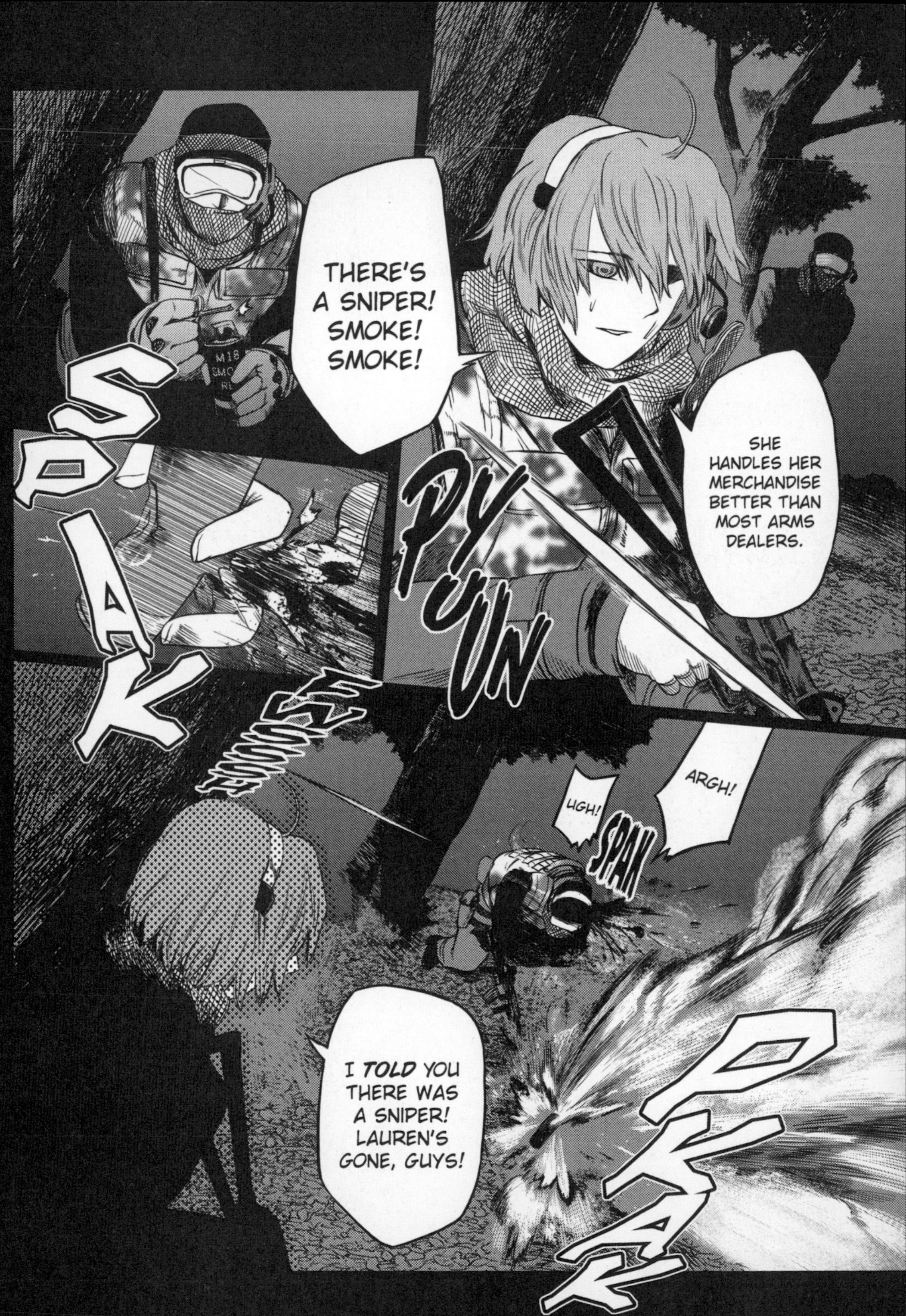
SHE HANDLES HER MERCHANDISE BETTER THAN MOST ARMS DEALERS.
PYUUN
THERE'S A SNIPER! SMOKE! SMOKE!
M18 SMOKE
SPAK
ARGH!
UGH!
SPAK
PAKAK
I *TOLD* YOU THERE WAS A SNIPER! LAUREN'S GONE, GUYS!

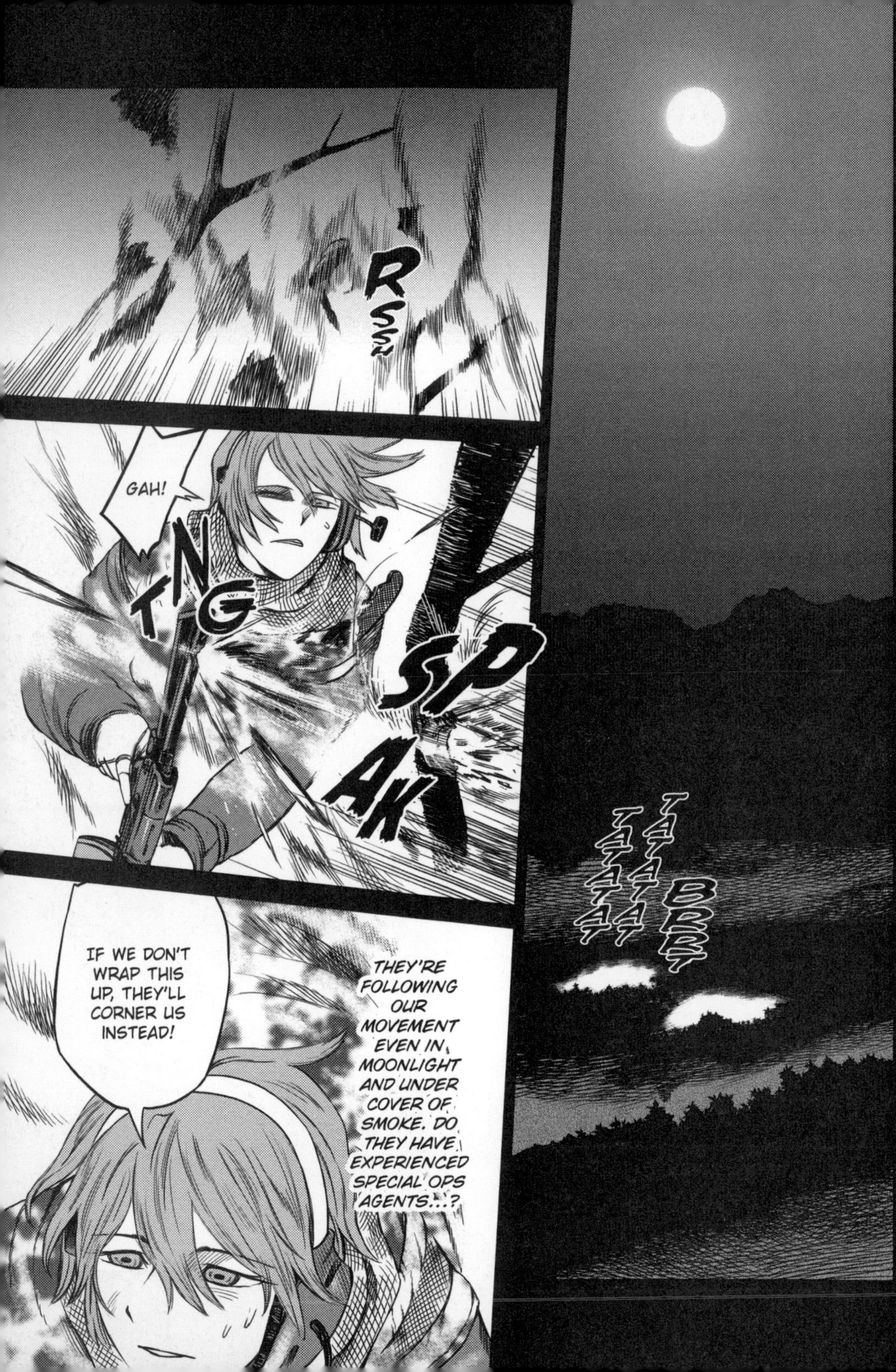
BRRT
TATATAT
TATATAT
RSSH
GAH!
TNG
SPAK
THEY'RE FOLLOWING OUR MOVEMENT EVEN IN MOONLIGHT AND UNDER COVER OF SMOKE. DO THEY HAVE EXPERIENCED SPECIAL OPS AGENTS...?
IF WE DON'T WRAP THIS UP, THEY'LL CORNER US INSTEAD!

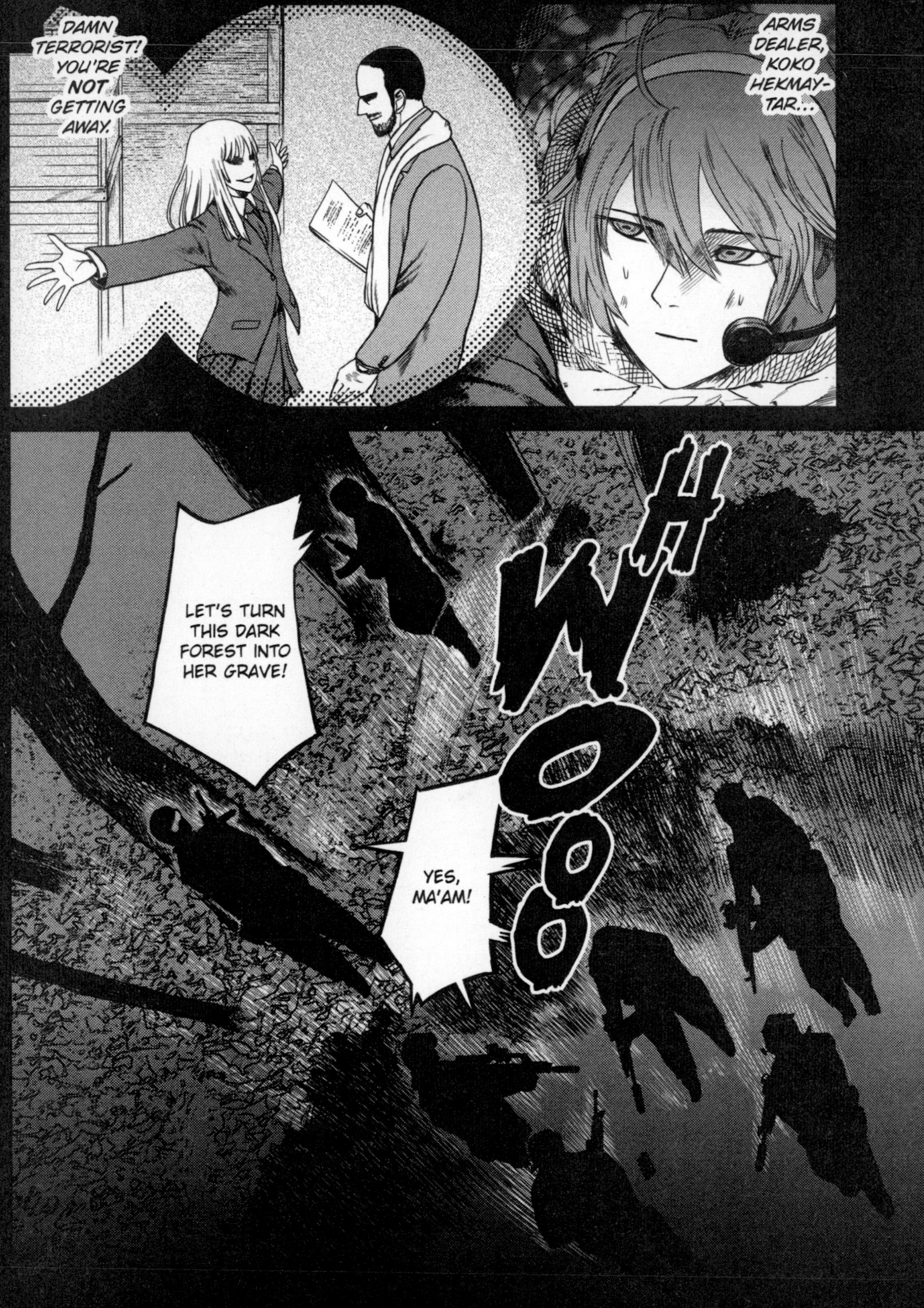
ARMS DEALER, KOKO HEKMAY-TAR...
DAMN TERRORIST! YOU'RE NOT GETTING AWAY.
HWOOO
LET'S TURN THIS DARK FOREST INTO HER GRAVE!
YES, MA'AM!

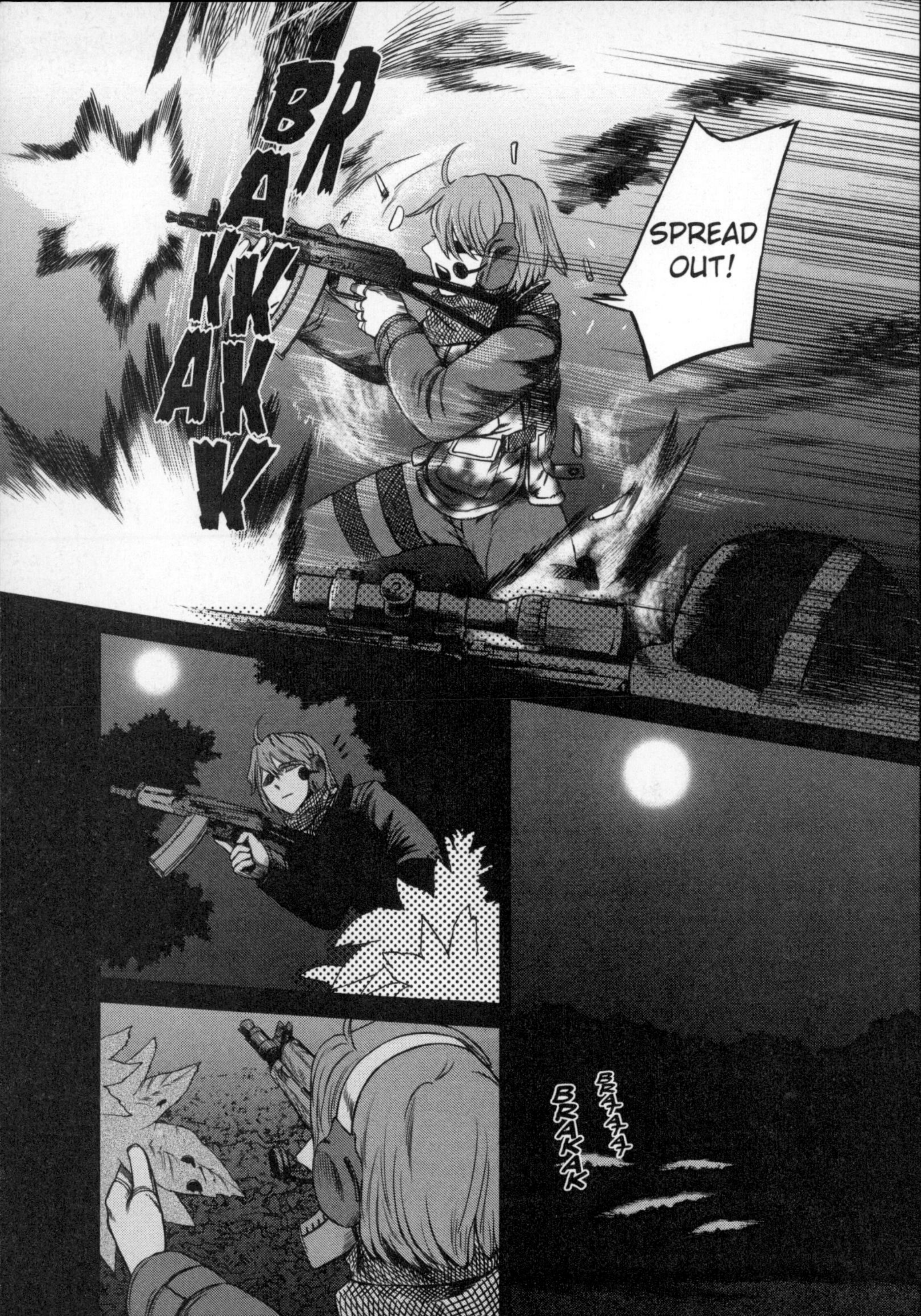
SPREAD OUT!
BRAKKAKAKK
BRATATA
BRAKAK

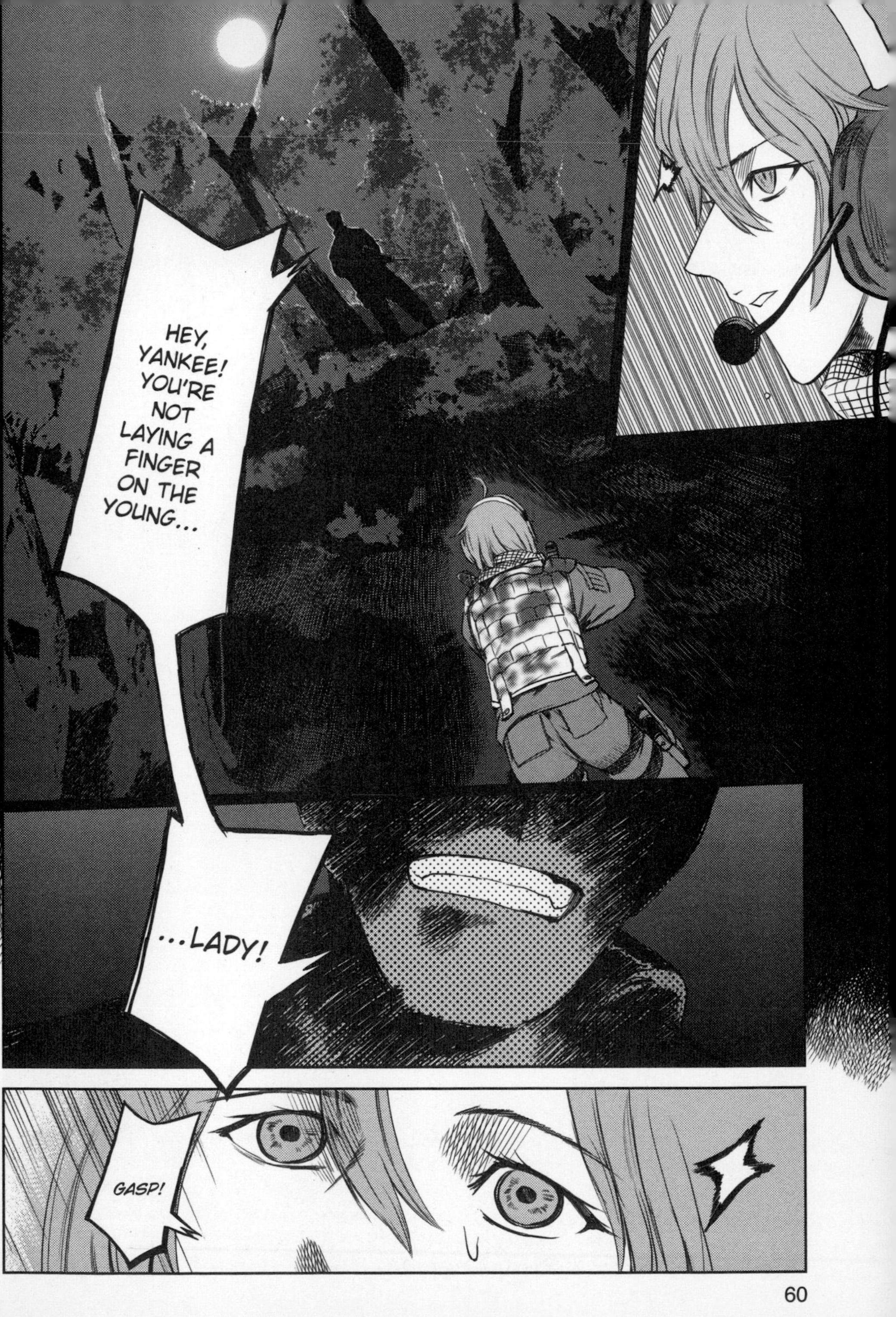
HEY, YANKEE! YOU'RE NOT LAYING A FINGER ON THE YOUNG...
...LADY!
GASP!

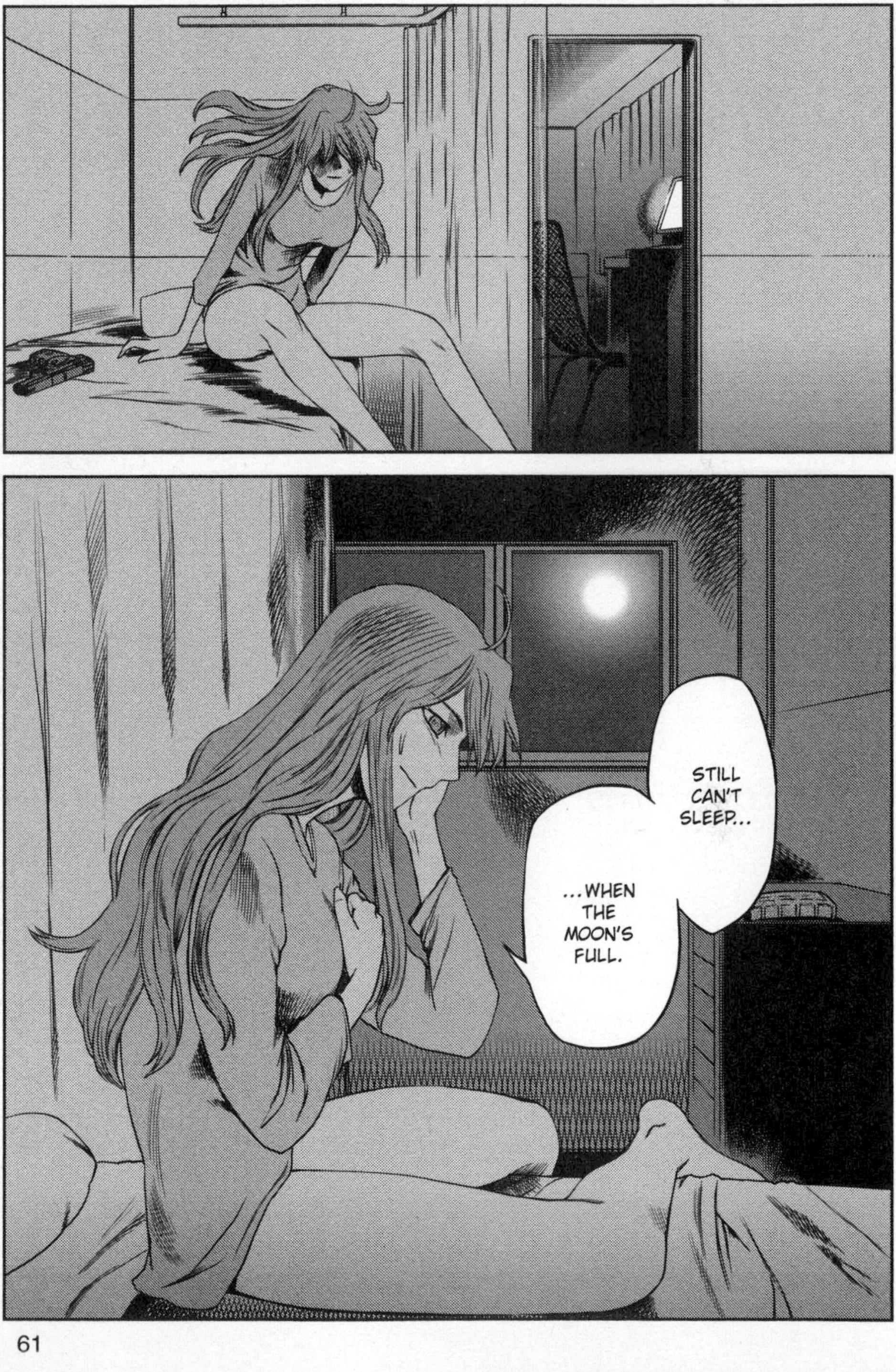
STILL CAN'T SLEEP...
...WHEN THE MOON'S FULL.

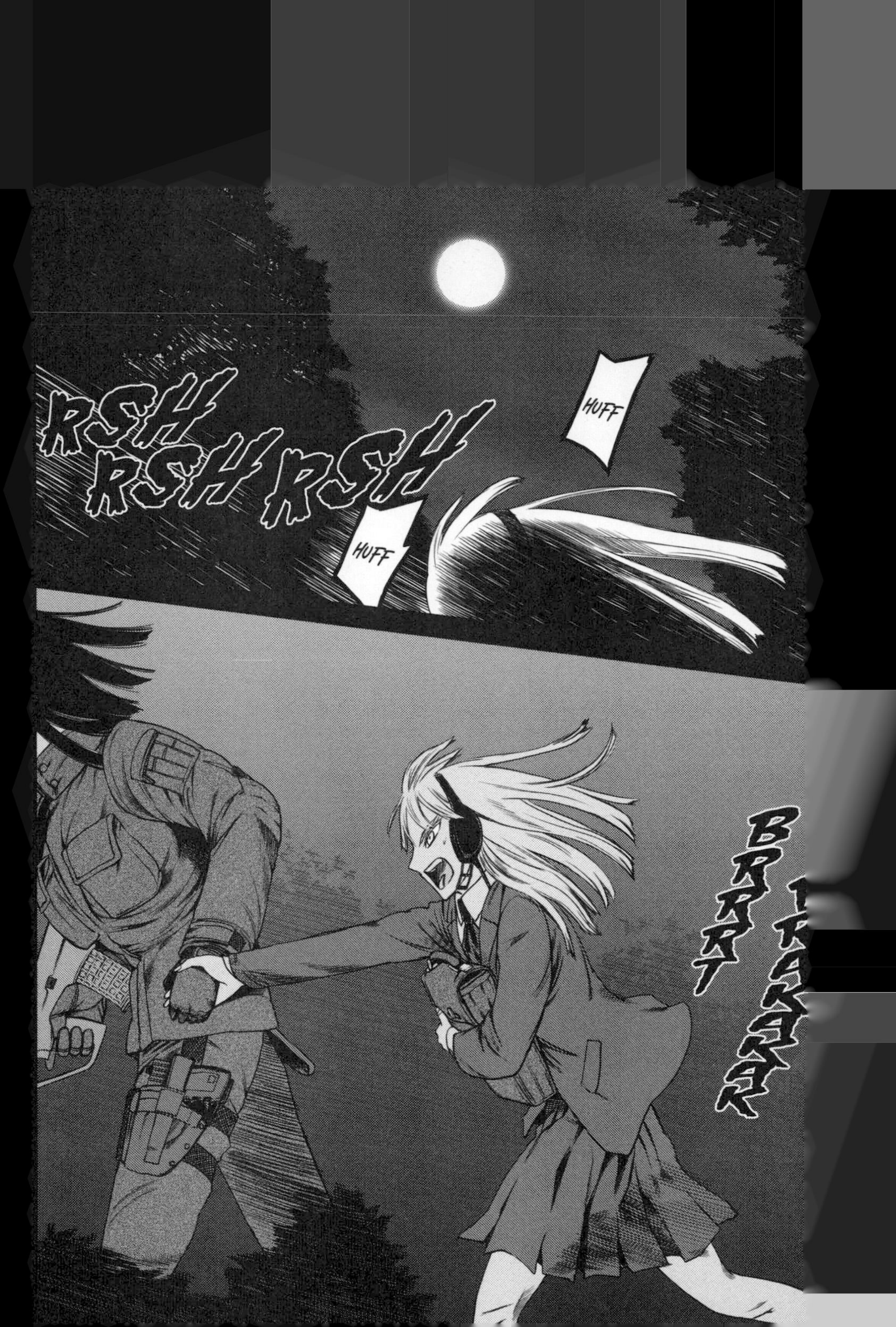
HUFF
RSH
RSH
RSH
RSH
HUFF
BRRRT

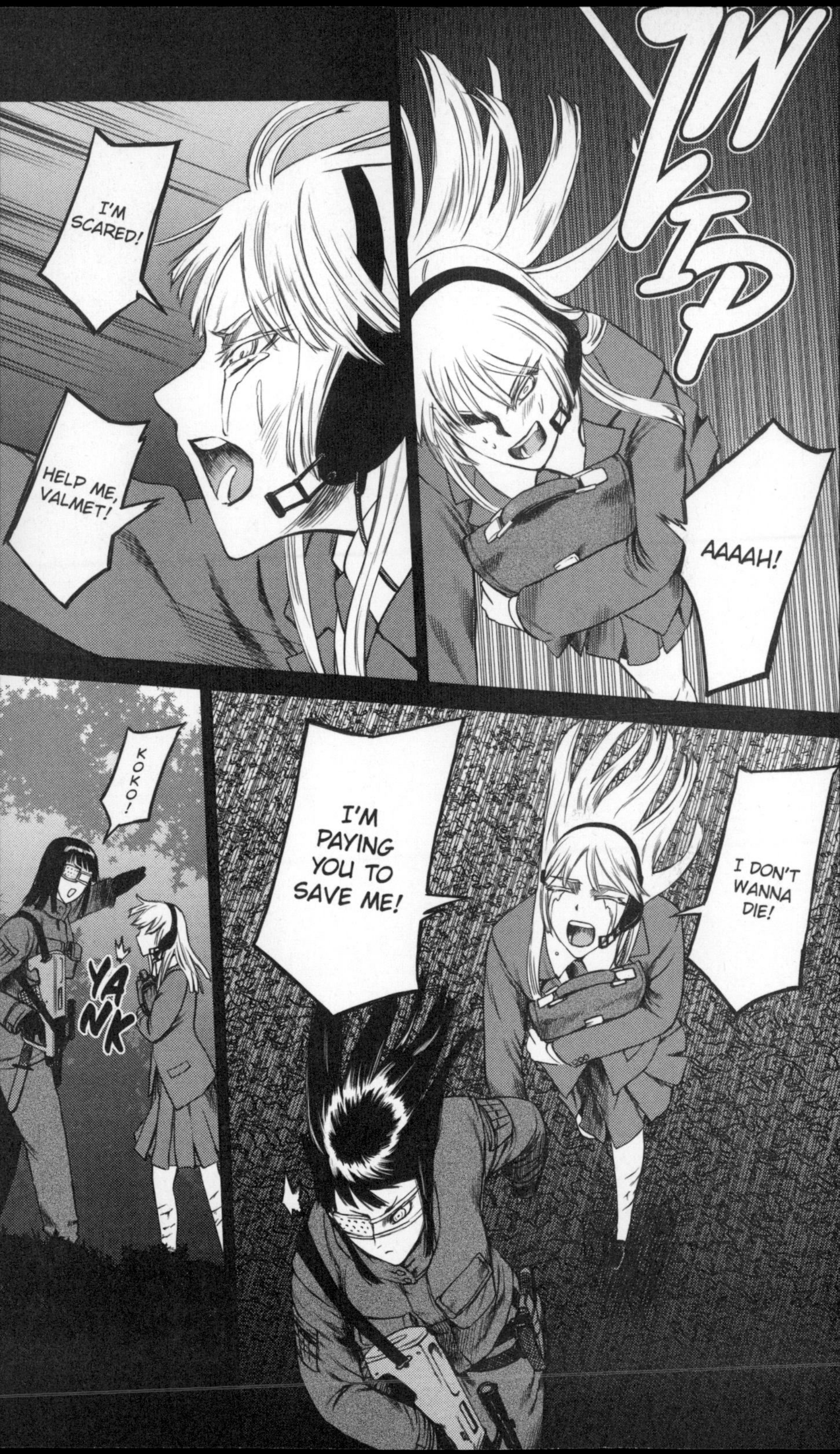
WHIP
AAAAH!
I'M SCARED!
HELP ME, VALMET!
I DON'T WANNA DIE!
I'M PAYING YOU TO SAVE ME!
KOKO!
YANK

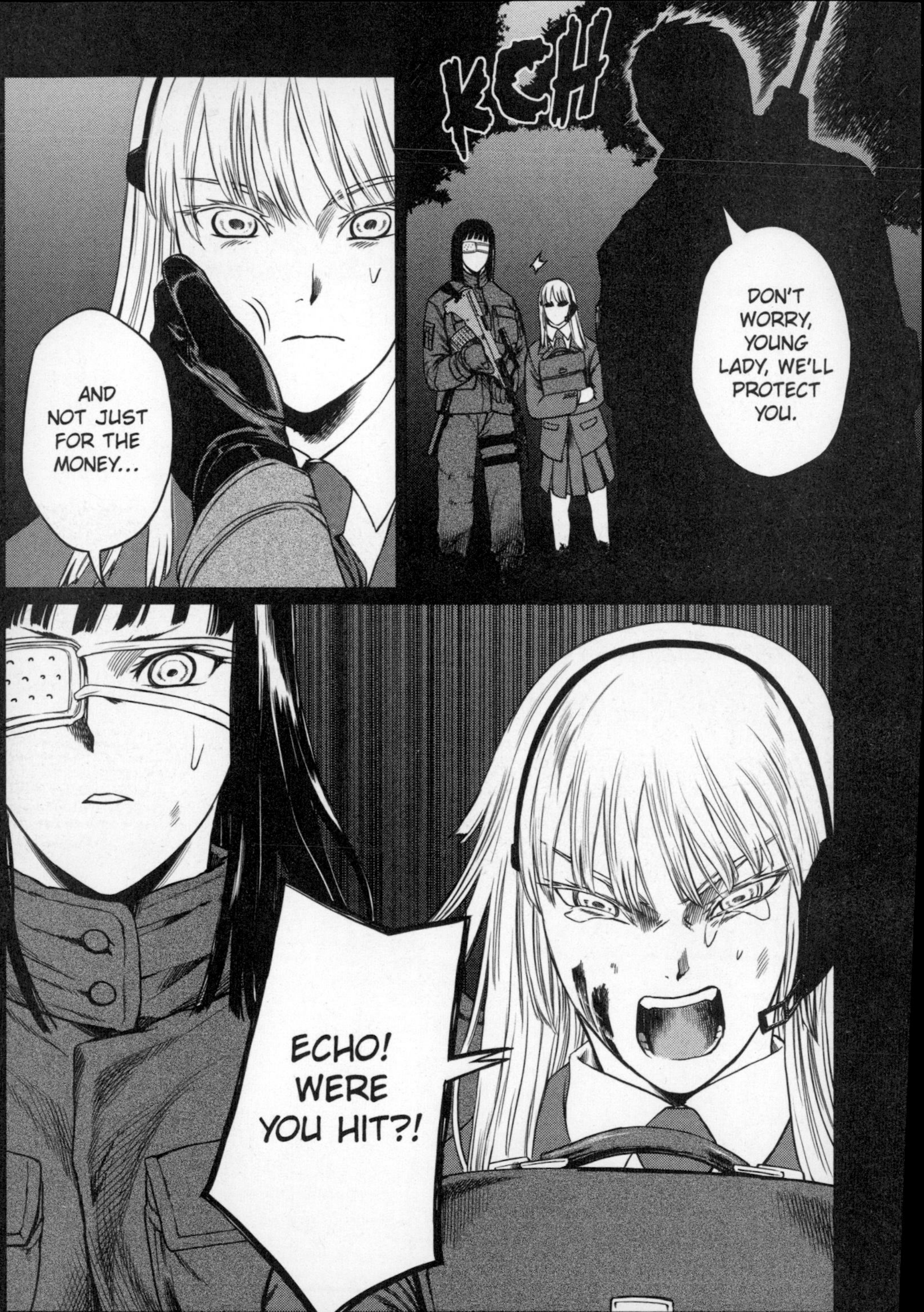
KCH
DON'T WORRY, YOUNG LADY, WE'LL PROTECT YOU.
AND NOT JUST FOR THE MONEY...
ECHO! WERE YOU HIT?!

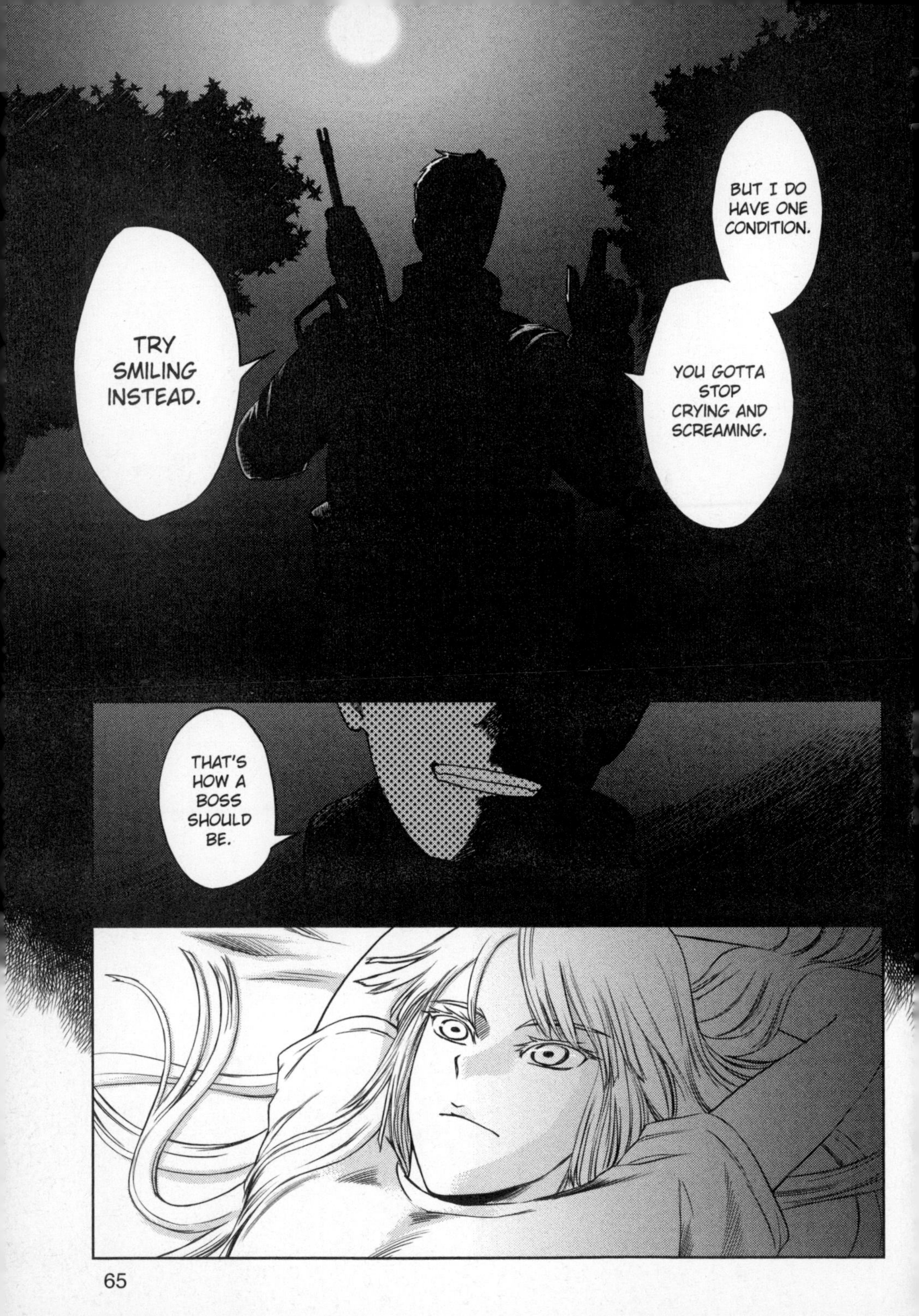
BUT I DO HAVE ONE CONDITION.
YOU GOTTA STOP CRYING AND SCREAMING.
TRY SMILING INSTEAD.
THAT'S HOW A BOSS SHOULD BE.

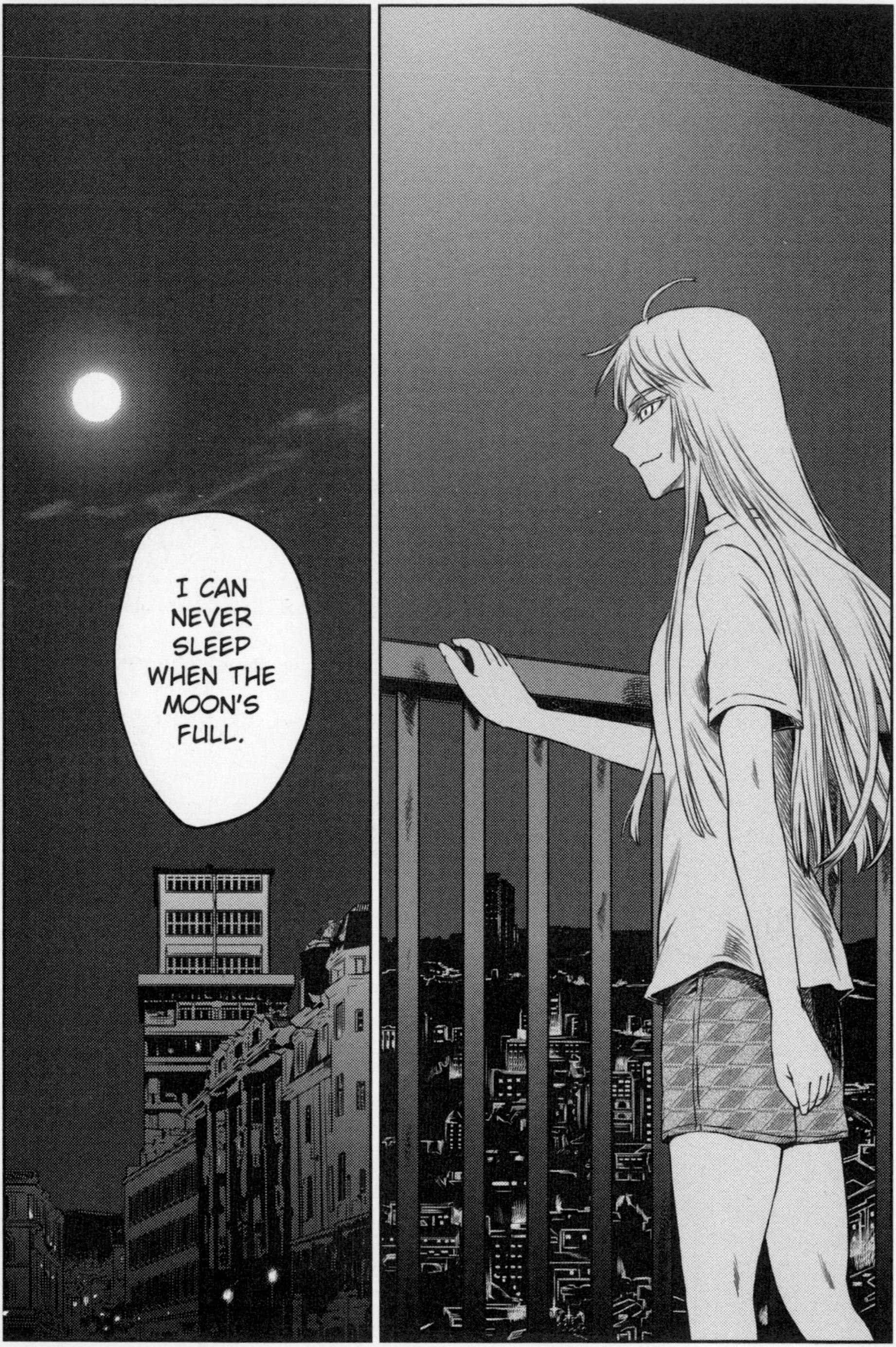
I CAN NEVER SLEEP WHEN THE MOON'S FULL.

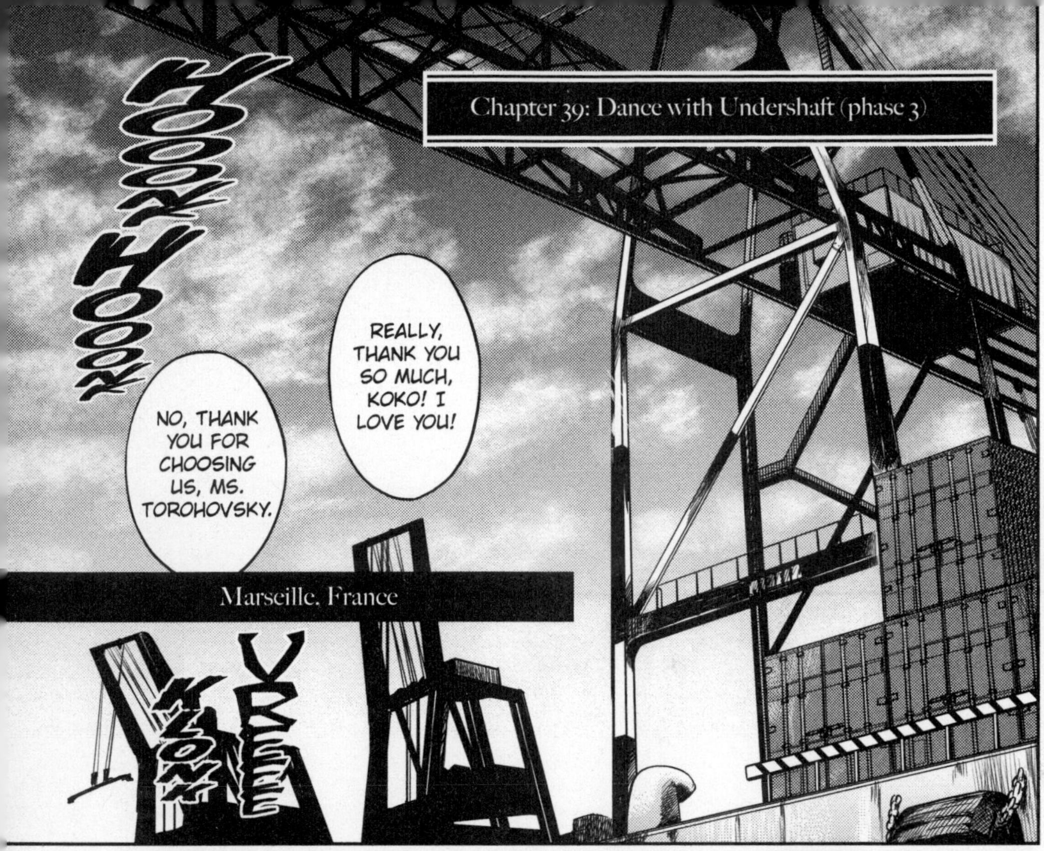
Chapter 39: Dance with Undershaft (phase 3)
REALLY, THANK YOU SO MUCH, KOKO! I LOVE YOU!
NO, THANK YOU FOR CHOOSING US, MS. TOROHOVSKY.
Marseille, France

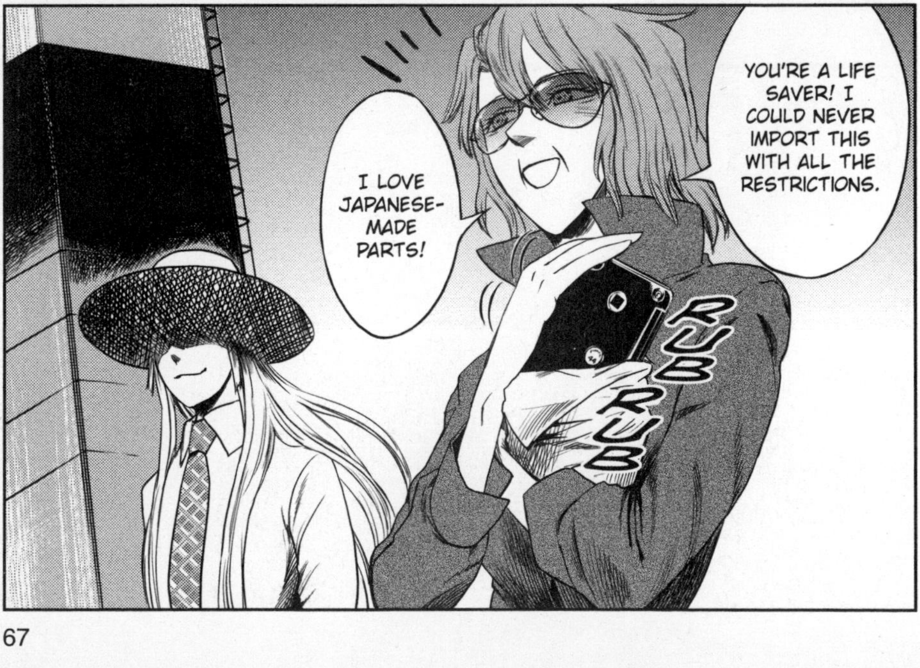
YOU'RE A LIFE SAVER! I COULD NEVER IMPORT THIS WITH ALL THE RESTRICTIONS.
I LOVE JAPANESE-MADE PARTS!
RUB RUB

Chapter 39: Dance with Undershaft (phase 3)

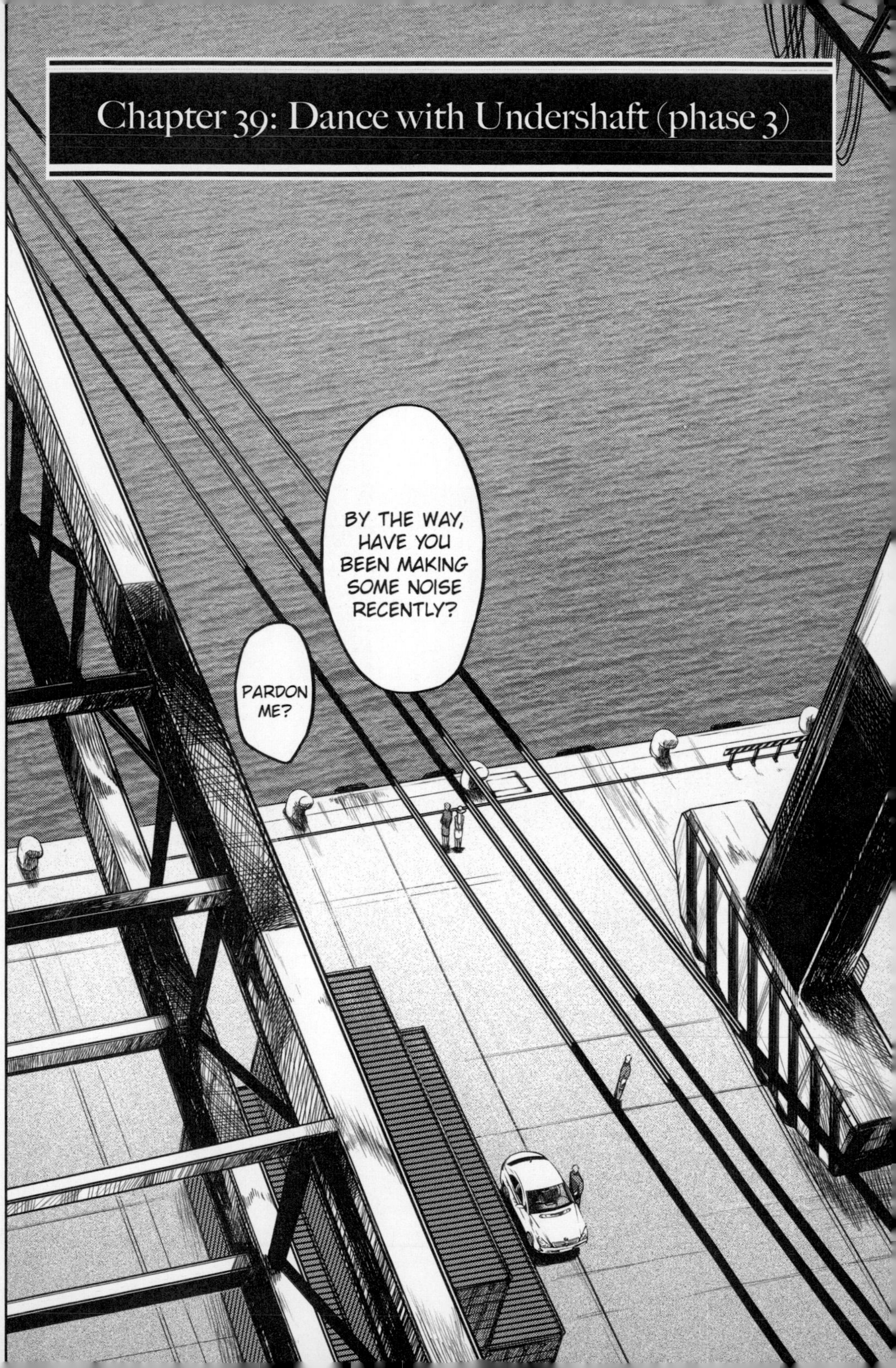
BY THE WAY, HAVE YOU BEEN MAKING SOME NOISE RECENTLY?
PARDON ME?

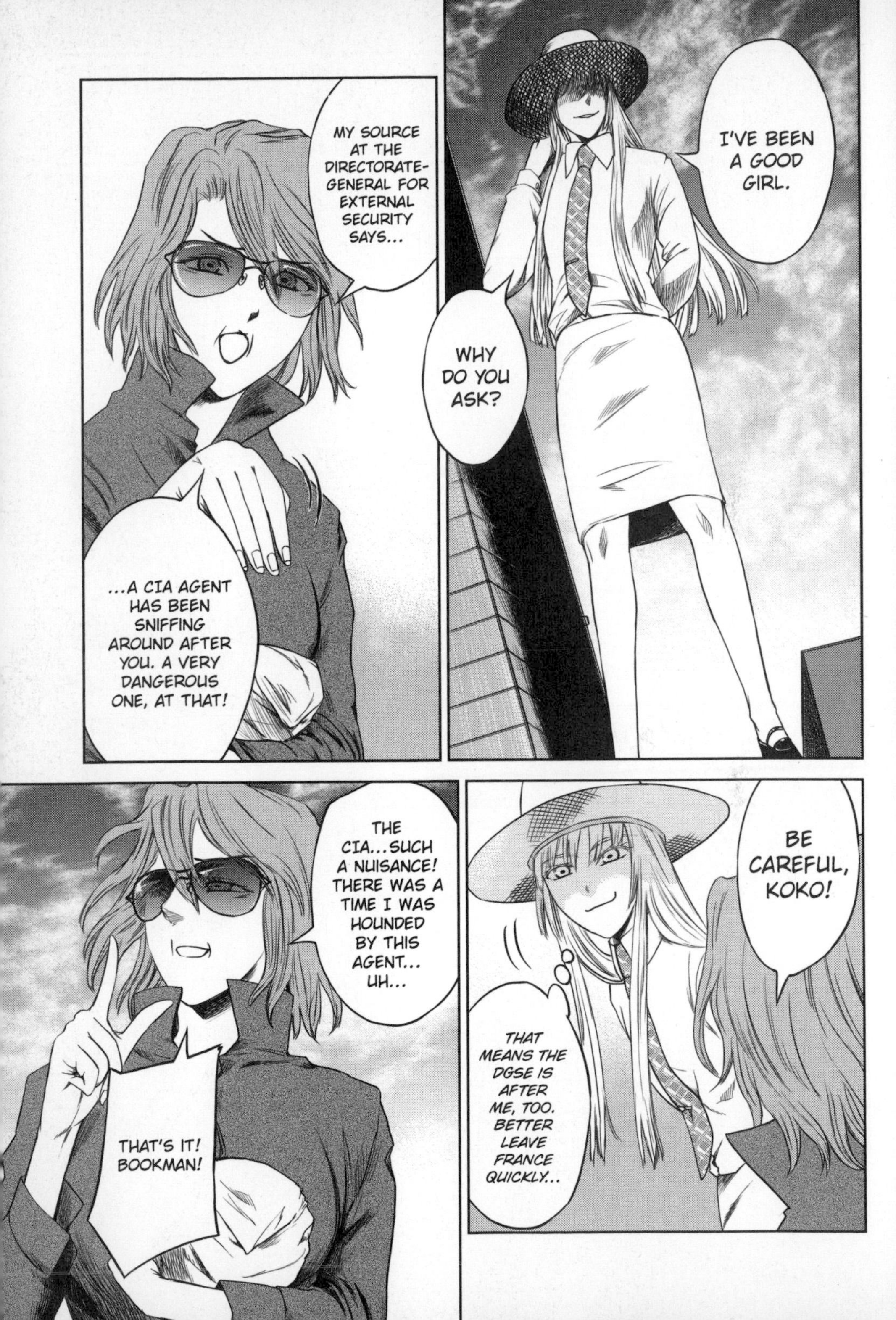
I'VE BEEN A GOOD GIRL.
WHY DO YOU ASK?
MY SOURCE AT THE DIRECTORATE-GENERAL FOR EXTERNAL SECURITY SAYS...
...A CIA AGENT HAS BEEN SNIFFING AROUND AFTER YOU. A VERY DANGEROUS ONE, AT THAT!
BE CAREFUL, KOKO!
THAT MEANS THE DGSE IS AFTER ME, TOO. BETTER LEAVE FRANCE QUICKLY...
THE CIA...SUCH A NUISANCE! THERE WAS A TIME I WAS HOUNDED BY THIS AGENT... UH...
THAT'S IT! BOOKMAN!

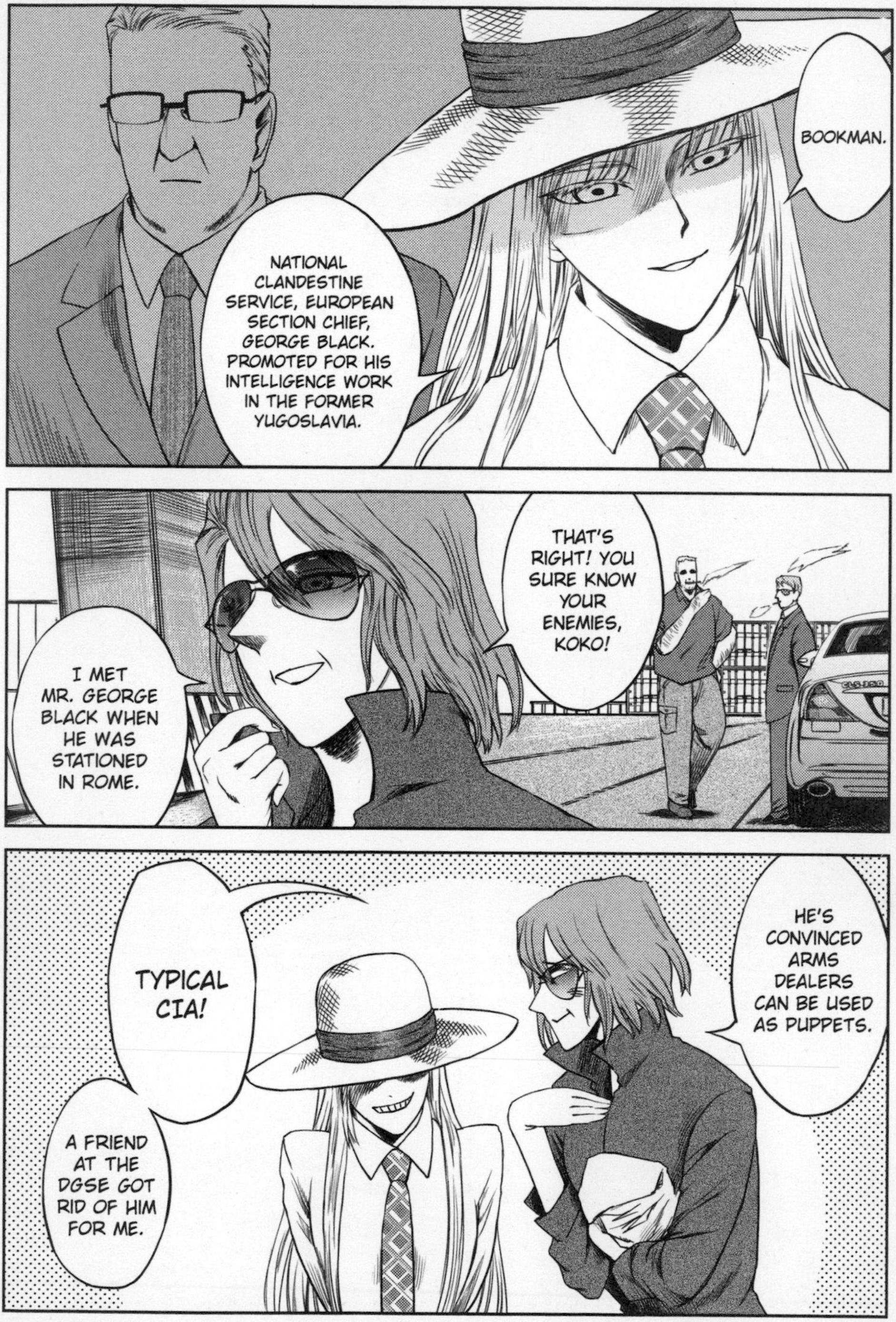
BOOKMAN.
NATIONAL CLANDESTINE SERVICE, EUROPEAN SECTION CHIEF, GEORGE BLACK. PROMOTED FOR HIS INTELLIGENCE WORK IN THE FORMER YUGOSLAVIA.
THAT'S RIGHT! YOU SURE KNOW YOUR ENEMIES, KOKO!
I MET MR. GEORGE BLACK WHEN HE WAS STATIONED IN ROME.
HE'S CONVINCED ARMS DEALERS CAN BE USED AS PUPPETS.
TYPICAL CIA!
A FRIEND AT THE DGSE GOT RID OF HIM FOR ME.

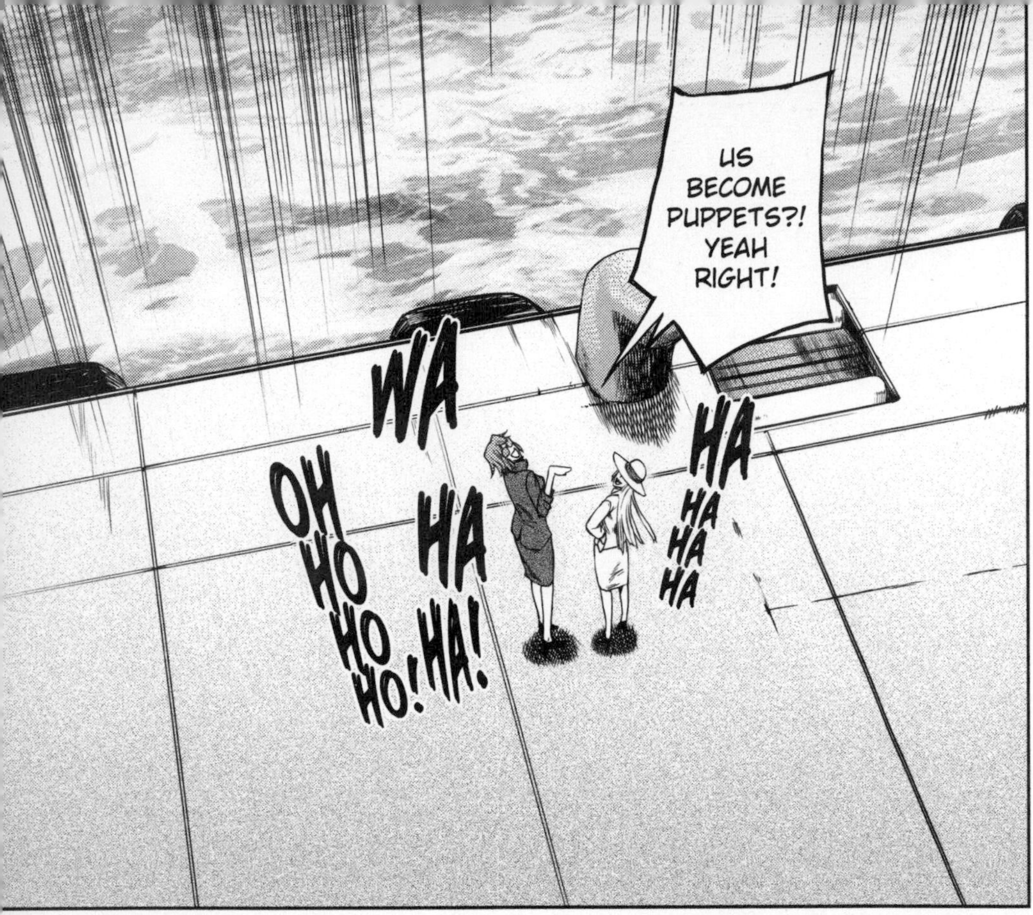
US BECOME PUPPETS?! YEAH RIGHT!
HA HA HA HA HA
WA HA HA HA!
OH HO HO HO HO!

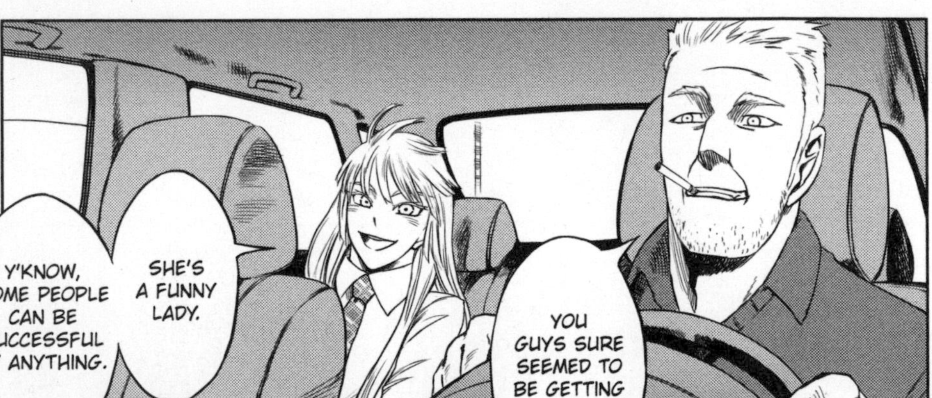
YOU GUYS SURE SEEMED TO BE GETTING ALONG.
SHE'S A FUNNY LADY.
Y'KNOW, SOME PEOPLE CAN BE SUCCESSFUL AT ANYTHING.

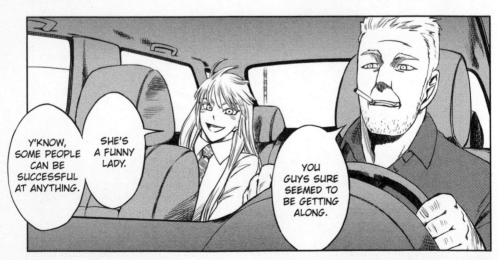

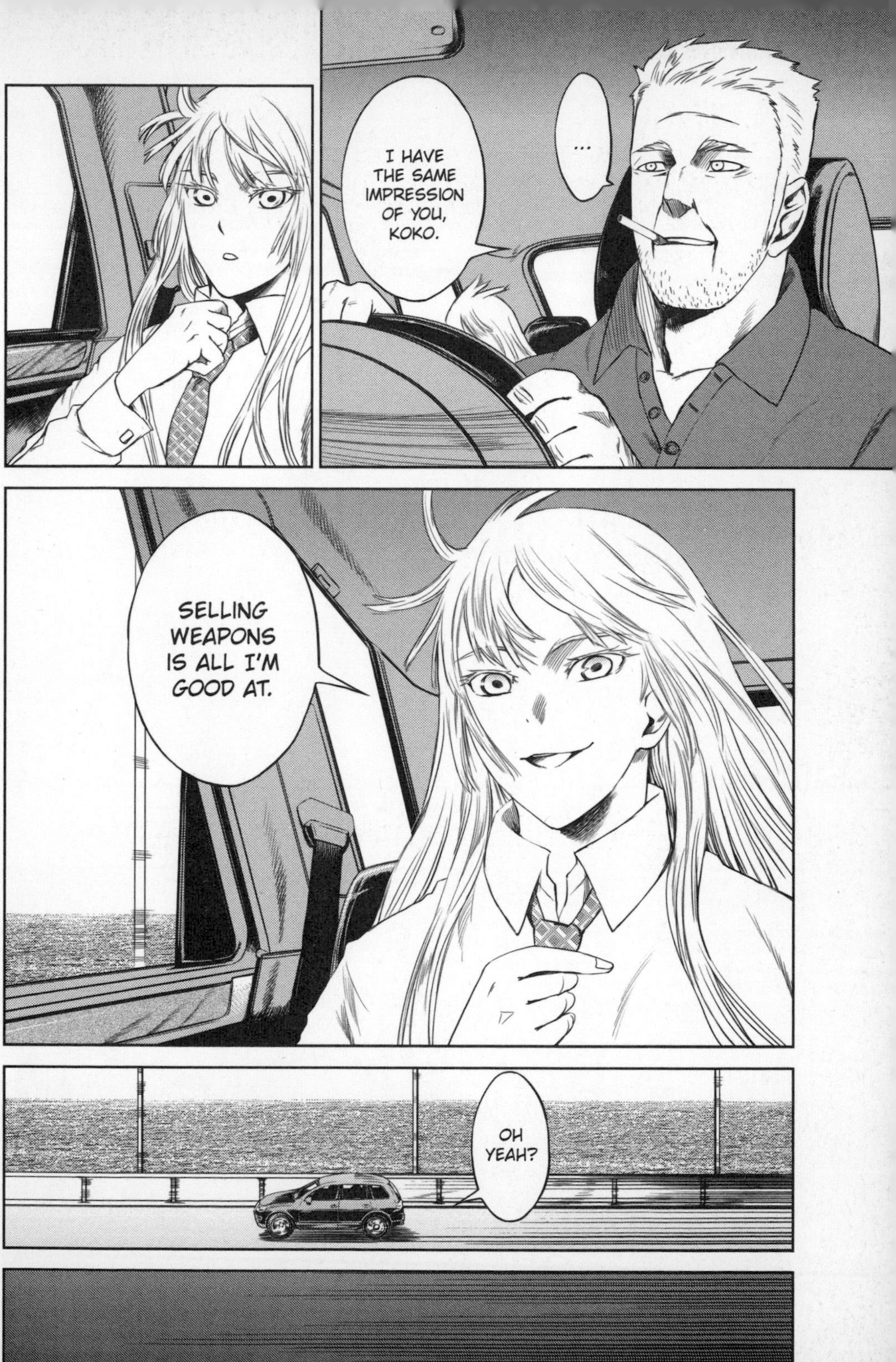
...
I HAVE THE SAME IMPRESSION OF YOU, KOKO.
SELLING WEAPONS IS ALL I'M GOOD AT.
OH YEAH?

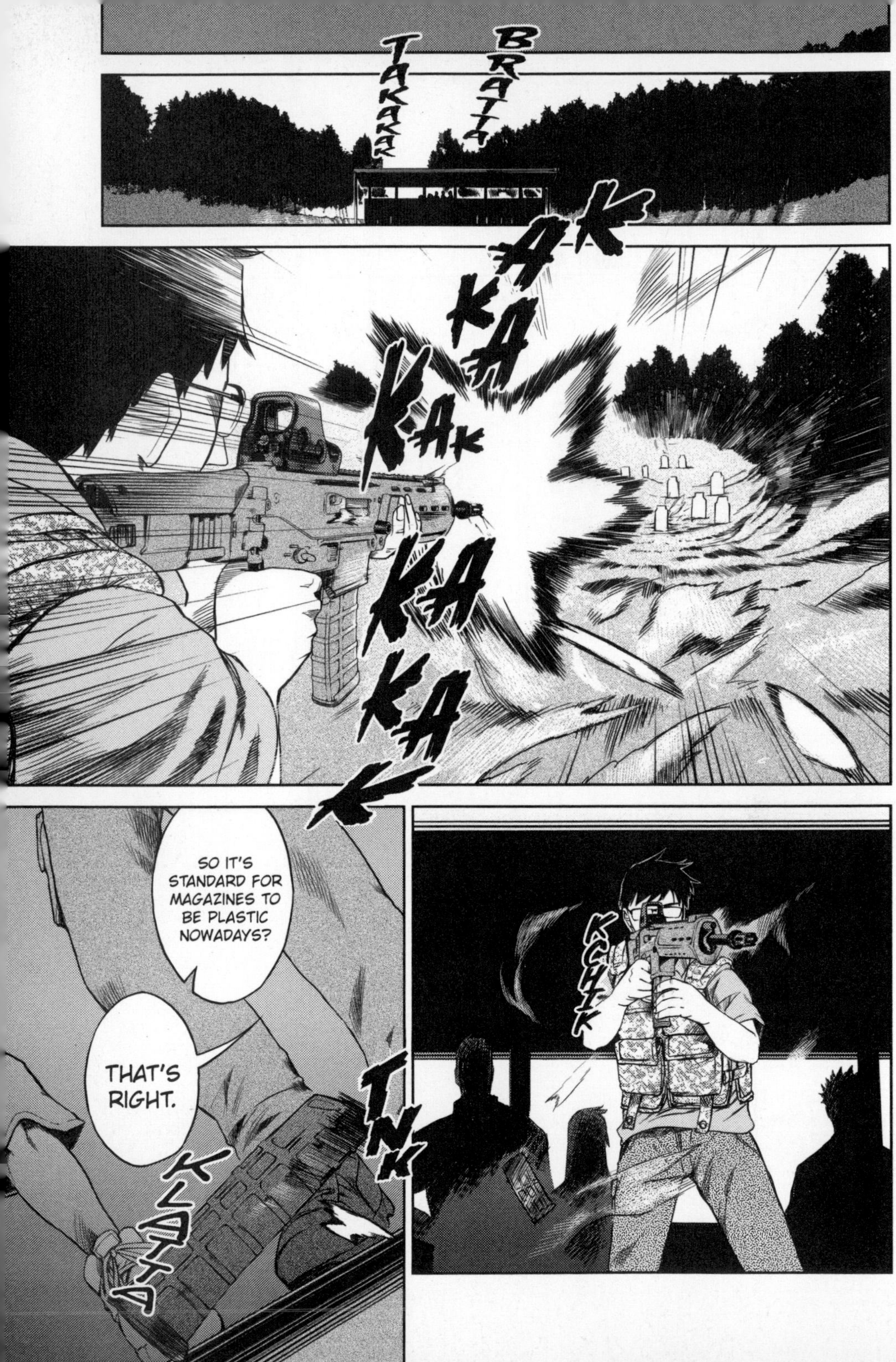
BRATTA
TAKAKAK
AKKAKAKAKKAKAK
KCHIK
TNK
SO IT'S STANDARD FOR MAGAZINES TO BE PLASTIC NOWADAYS?
THAT'S RIGHT.
KLATTA

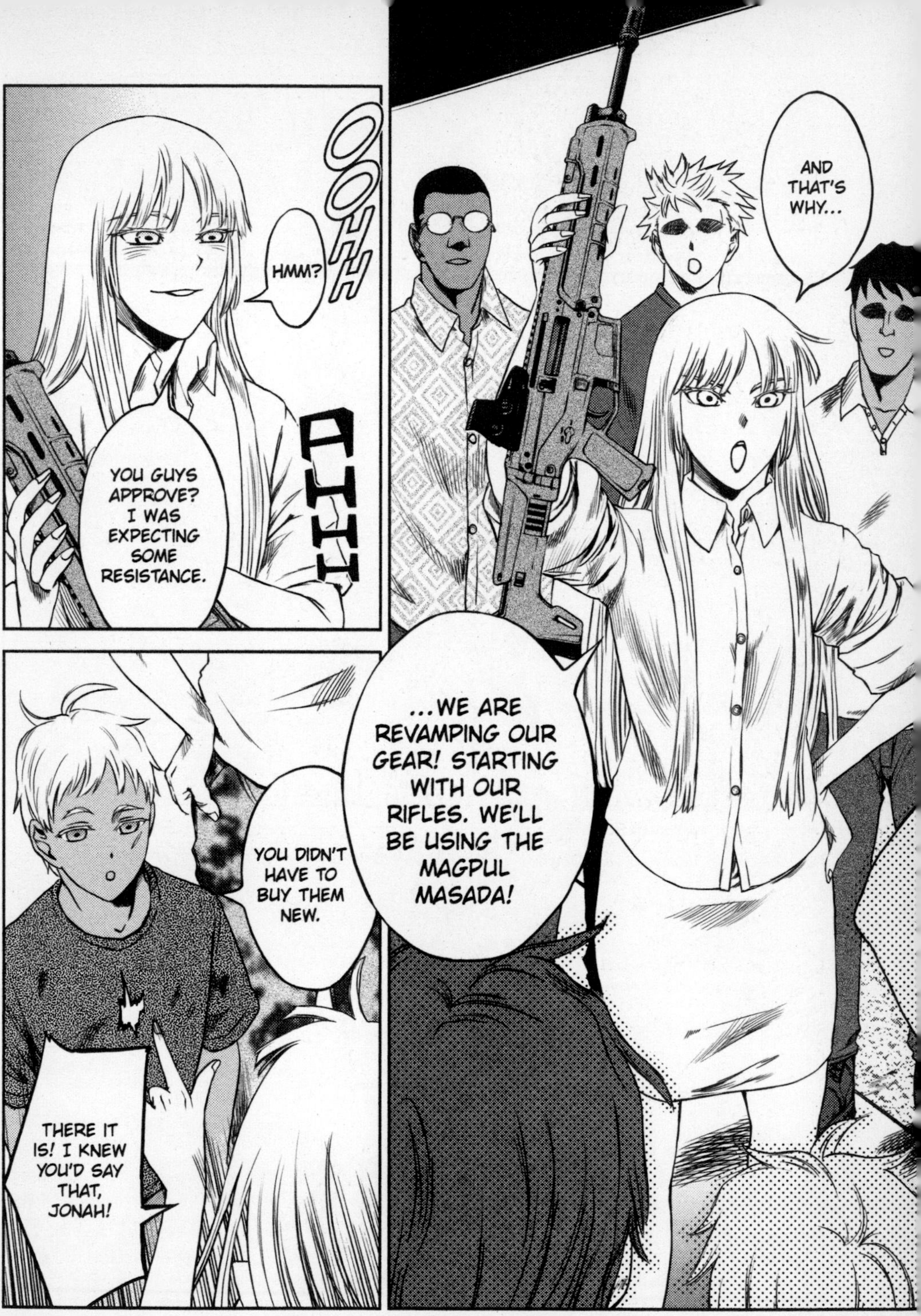
AND THAT'S WHY...
...WE ARE REVAMPING OUR GEAR! STARTING WITH OUR RIFLES. WE'LL BE USING THE MAGPUL MASADA!
OOOHHH
AHHH
HMM?
YOU GUYS APPROVE? I WAS EXPECTING SOME RESISTANCE.
YOU DIDN'T HAVE TO BUY THEM NEW.
THERE IT IS! I KNEW YOU'D SAY THAT, JONAH!

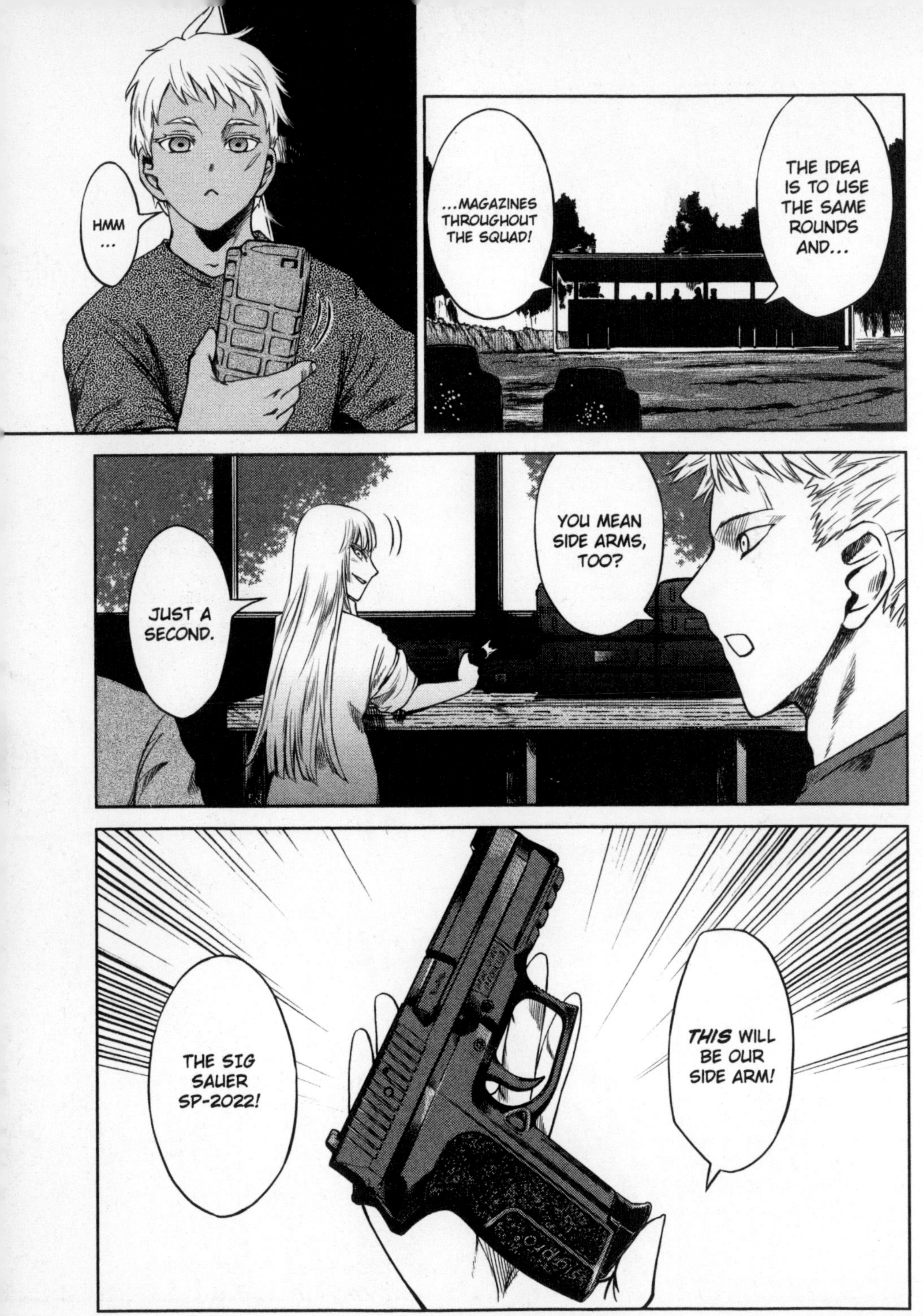
THE IDEA IS TO USE THE SAME ROUNDS AND...
...MAGAZINES THROUGHOUT THE SQUAD!
HMM ...
YOU MEAN SIDE ARMS, TOO?
JUST A SECOND.
THIS WILL BE OUR SIDE ARM!
THE SIG SAUER SP-2022!

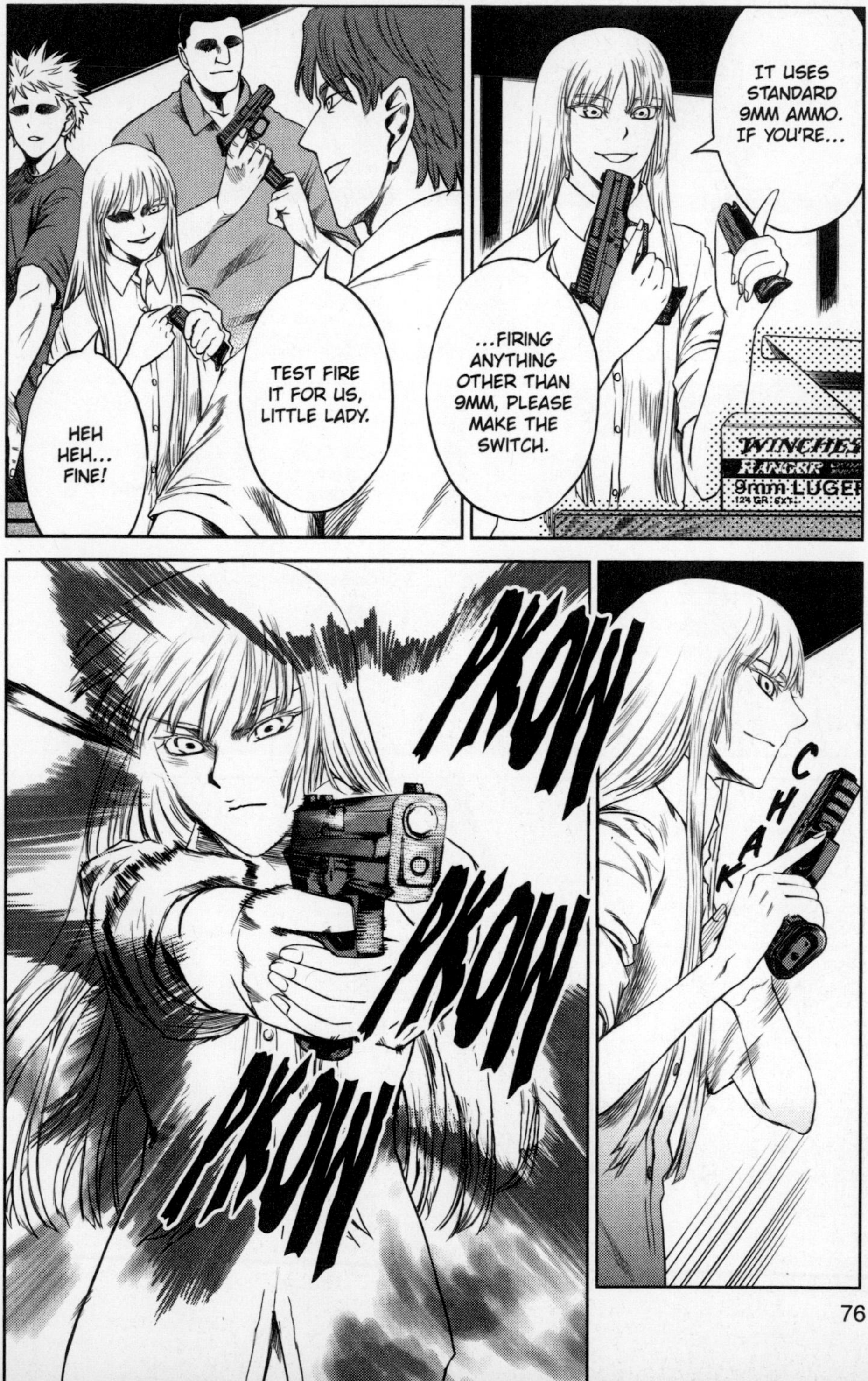
IT USES STANDARD 9MM AMMO. IF YOU'RE...
...FIRING ANYTHING OTHER THAN 9MM, PLEASE MAKE THE SWITCH.
TEST FIRE IT FOR US, LITTLE LADY.
HEH HEH... FINE!
CHAK
PKOW
PKOW
PKOW

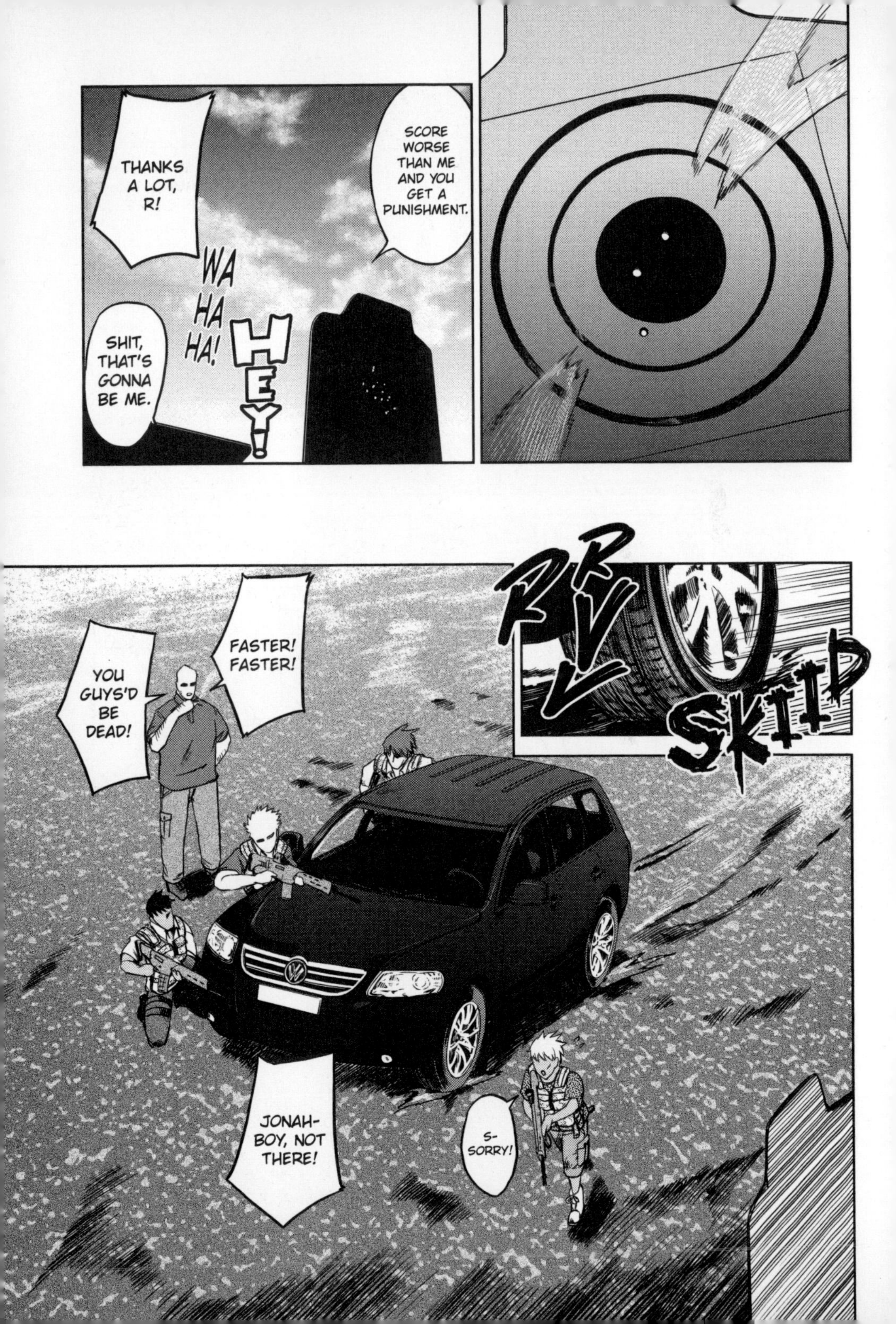
SCORE WORSE THAN ME AND YOU GET A PUNISHMENT.
THANKS A LOT, R!
HEY!
WA HA HA!
SHIT, THAT'S GONNA BE ME.
RRV
SKID
FASTER! FASTER!
YOU GUYS'D BE DEAD!
JONAH-BOY, NOT THERE!
S-SORRY!

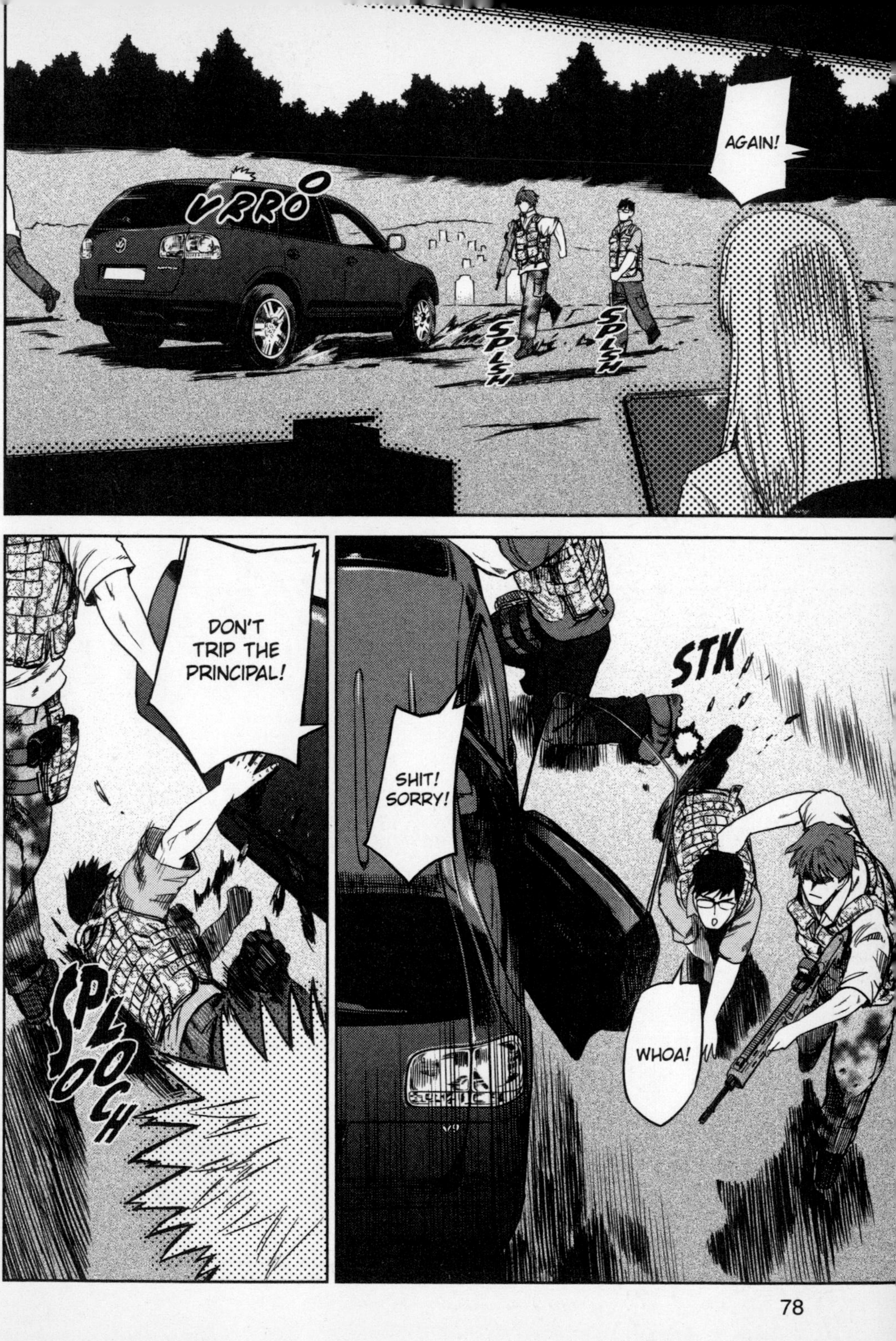
AGAIN!
SPLSH
SPLSH
VRROO
STK
SHIT! SORRY!
WHOA!
DON'T TRIP THE PRINCIPAL!
SPLOOCH

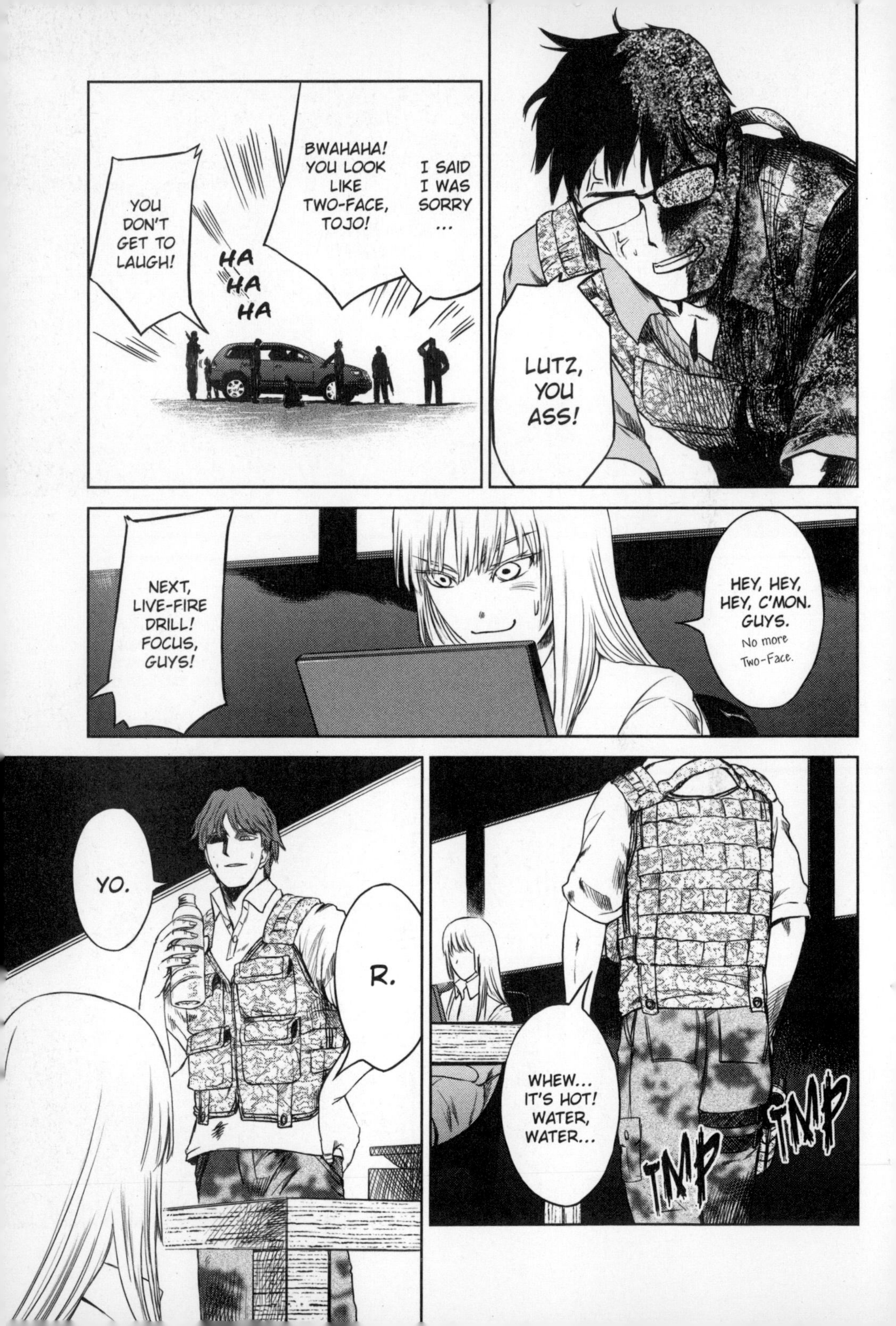
LUTZ, YOU ASS!
I SAID I WAS SORRY...
BWAHAHA! YOU LOOK LIKE TWO-FACE, TOJO!
HA HA HA
YOU DON'T GET TO LAUGH!
HEY, HEY, HEY, C'MON. GUYS. No more Two-Face.
NEXT, LIVE-FIRE DRILL! FOCUS, GUYS!
WHEW... IT'S HOT! WATER, WATER...
TMP TMP
R.
YO.

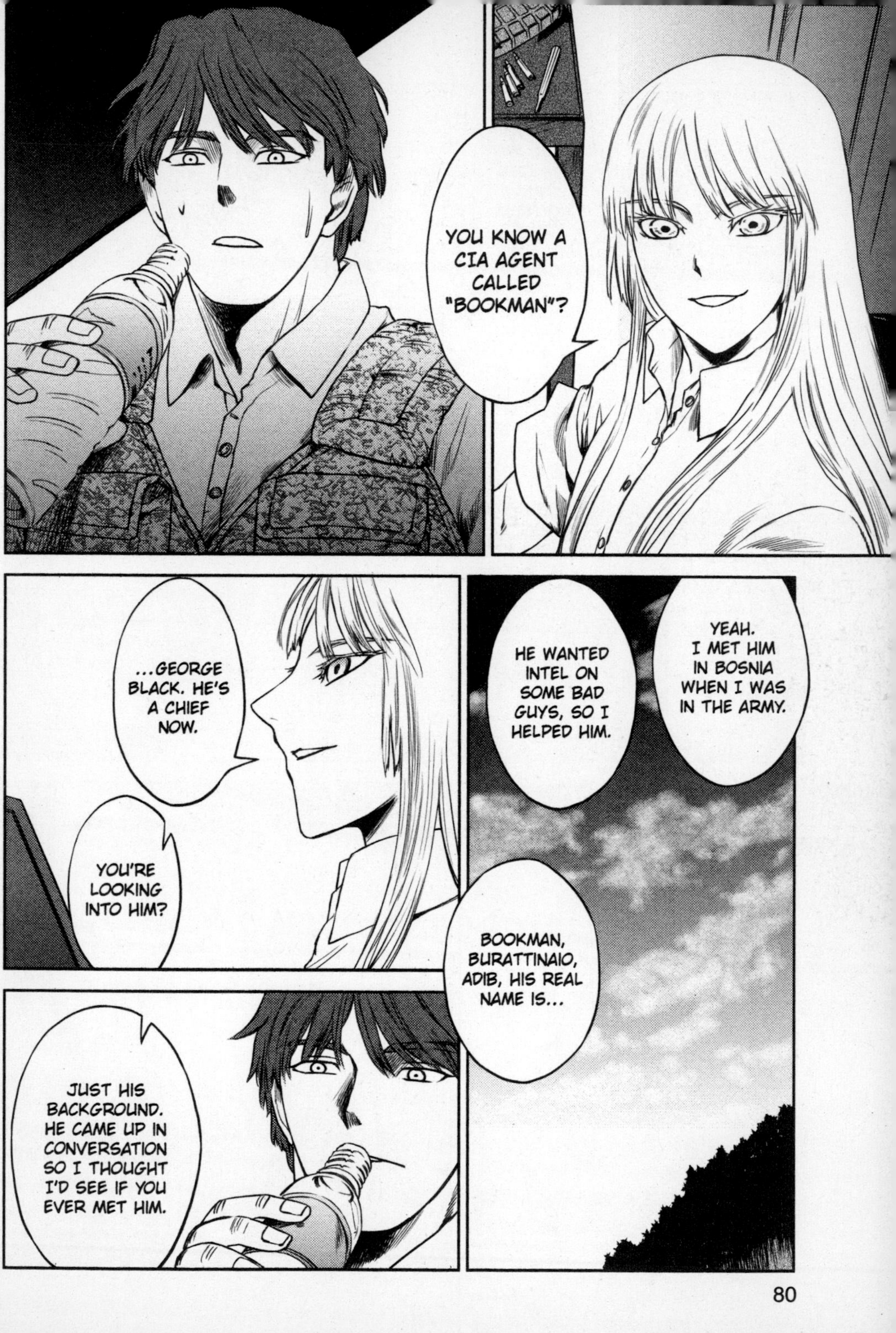
YOU KNOW A CIA AGENT CALLED "BOOKMAN"?
YEAH. I MET HIM IN BOSNIA WHEN I WAS IN THE ARMY.
HE WANTED INTEL ON SOME BAD GUYS, SO I HELPED HIM.
BOOKMAN, BURATTINAIO, ADIB, HIS REAL NAME IS...
...GEORGE BLACK. HE'S A CHIEF NOW.
YOU'RE LOOKING INTO HIM?
JUST HIS BACKGROUND. HE CAME UP IN CONVERSATION SO I THOUGHT I'D SEE IF YOU EVER MET HIM.

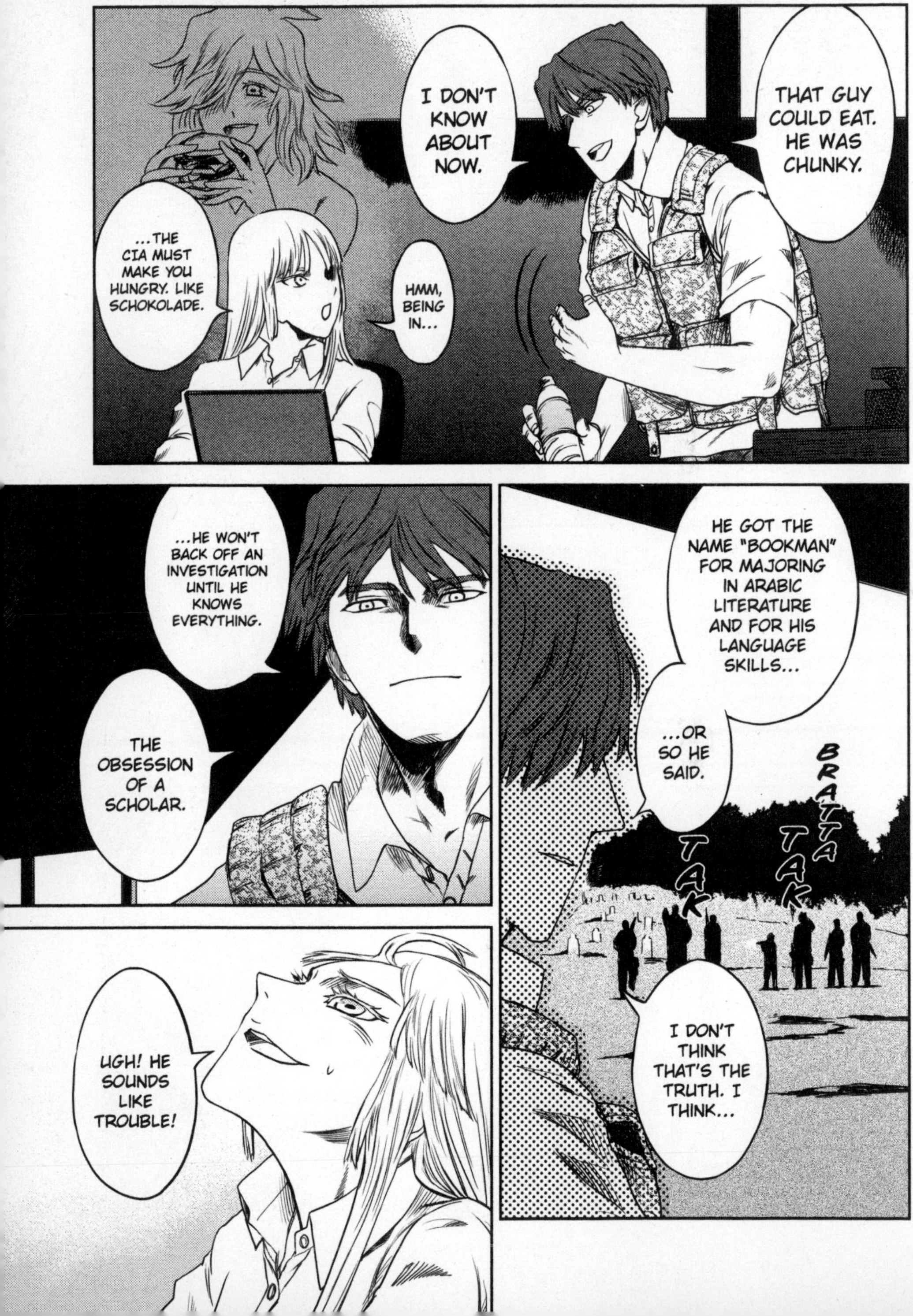
THAT GUY COULD EAT. HE WAS CHUNKY.
I DON'T KNOW ABOUT NOW.
HMM, BEING IN...
...THE CIA MUST MAKE YOU HUNGRY. LIKE SCHOKOLADE.
HE GOT THE NAME "BOOKMAN" FOR MAJORING IN ARABIC LITERATURE AND FOR HIS LANGUAGE SKILLS...
...OR SO HE SAID.
BRATTA
TAK
TAK
I DON'T THINK THAT'S THE TRUTH. I THINK...
...HE WON'T BACK OFF AN INVESTIGATION UNTIL HE KNOWS EVERYTHING.
THE OBSESSION OF A SCHOLAR.
UGH! HE SOUNDS LIKE TROUBLE!

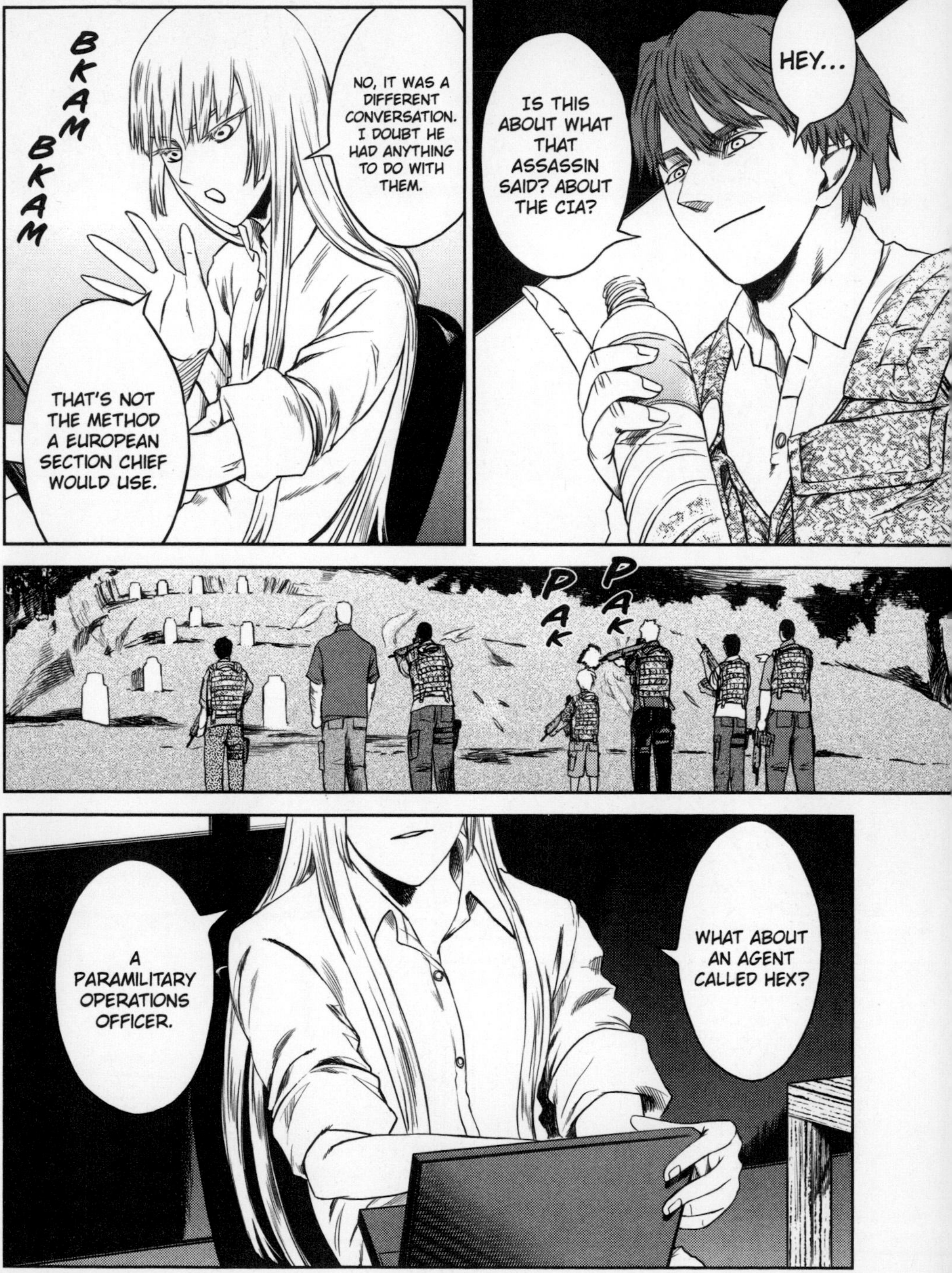
HEY...
IS THIS ABOUT WHAT THAT ASSASSIN SAID? ABOUT THE CIA?
NO, IT WAS A DIFFERENT CONVERSATION. I DOUBT HE HAD ANYTHING TO DO WITH THEM.
BKAM BKAM
THAT'S NOT THE METHOD A EUROPEAN SECTION CHIEF WOULD USE.
PAK PAK
WHAT ABOUT AN AGENT CALLED HEX?
A PARAMILITARY OPERATIONS OFFICER.

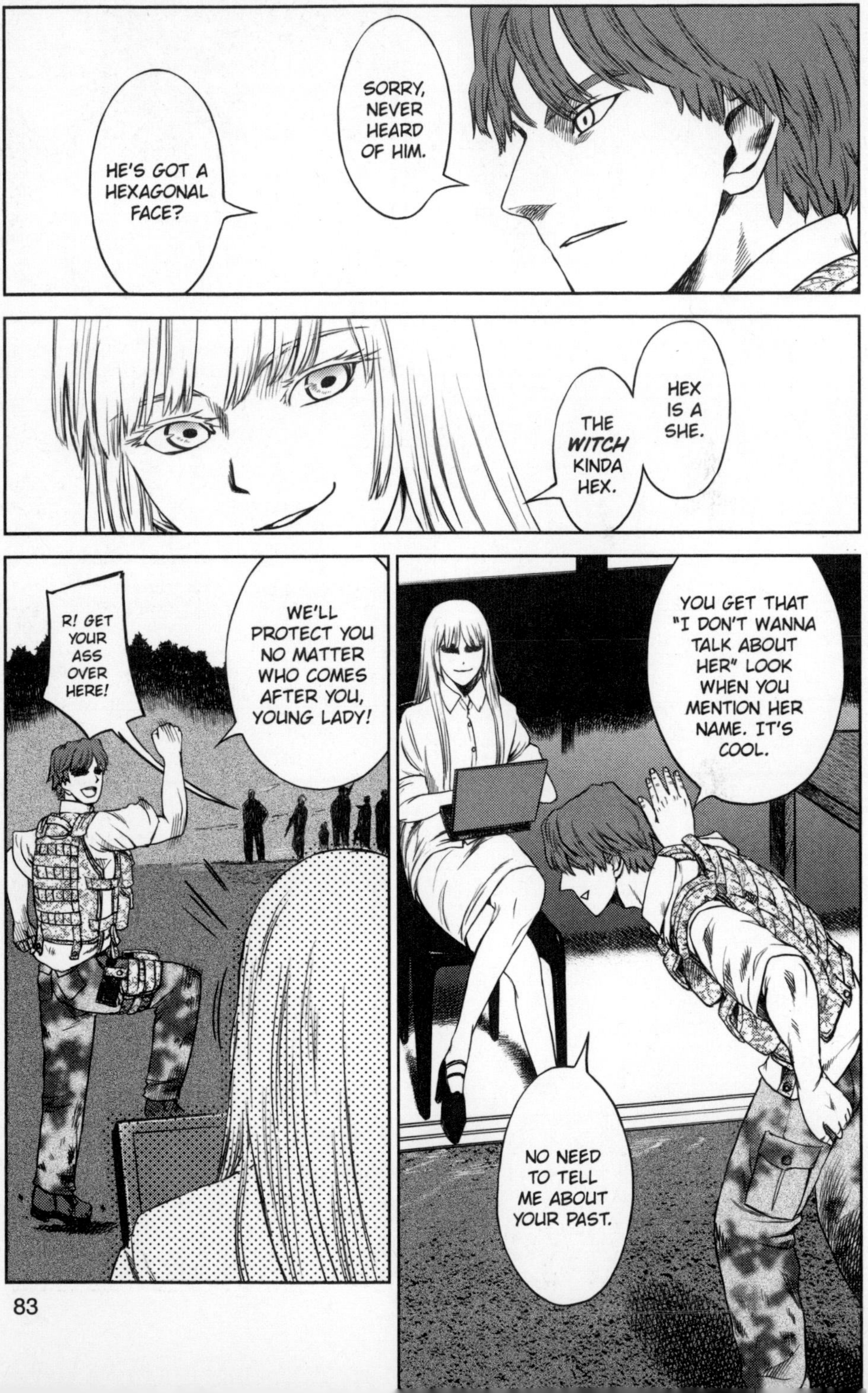
SORRY, NEVER HEARD OF HIM.
HE'S GOT A HEXAGONAL FACE?
HEX IS A SHE.
THE *WITCH* KINDA HEX.
YOU GET THAT "I DON'T WANNA TALK ABOUT HER" LOOK WHEN YOU MENTION HER NAME. IT'S COOL.
NO NEED TO TELL ME ABOUT YOUR PAST.
WE'LL PROTECT YOU NO MATTER WHO COMES AFTER YOU, YOUNG LADY!
R! GET YOUR ASS OVER HERE!

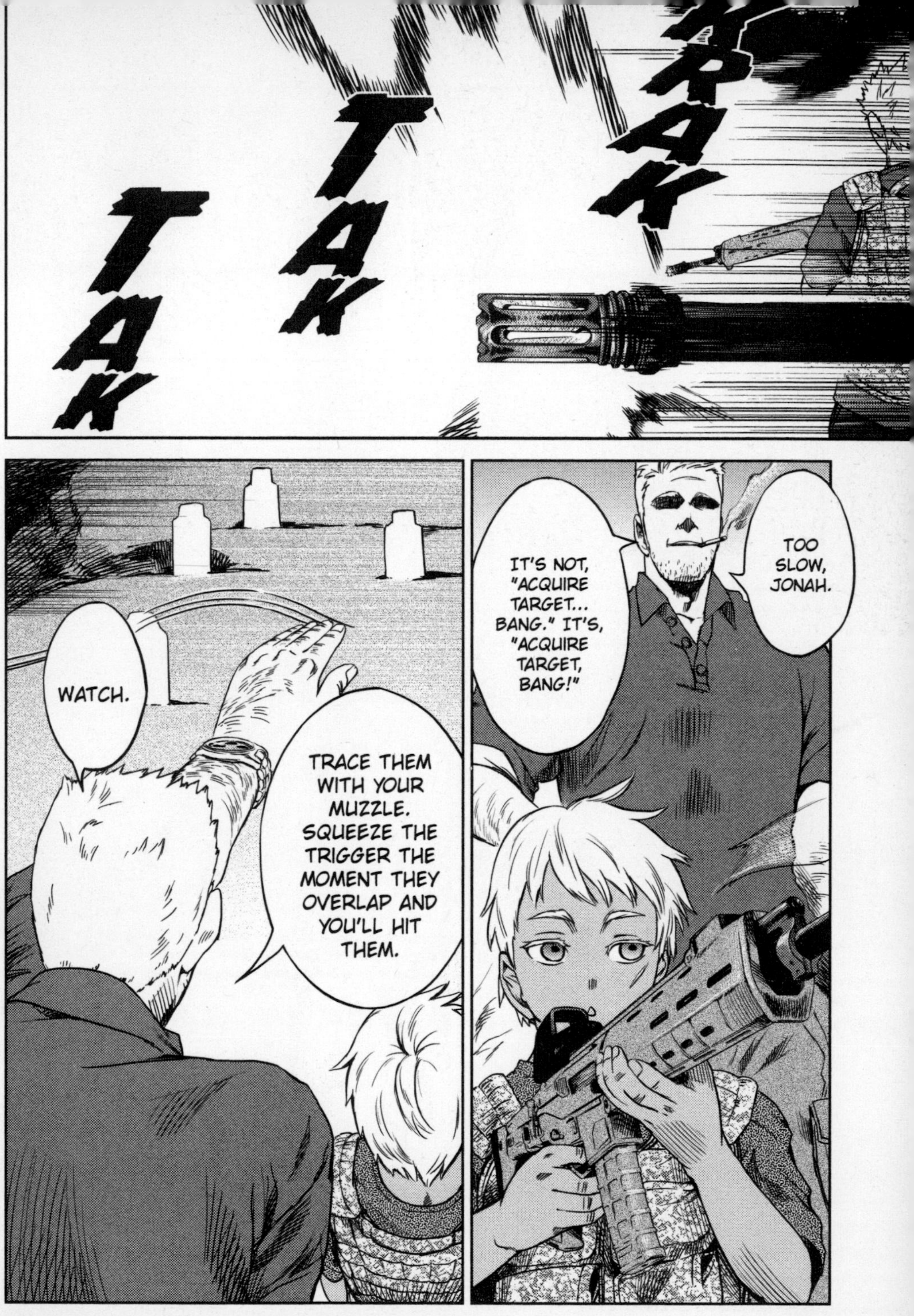
RAK
TAK
TAK
TOO SLOW, JONAH.
IT'S NOT, "ACQUIRE TARGET... BANG." IT'S, "ACQUIRE TARGET, BANG!"
WATCH.
TRACE THEM WITH YOUR MUZZLE. SQUEEZE THE TRIGGER THE MOMENT THEY OVERLAP AND YOU'LL HIT THEM.

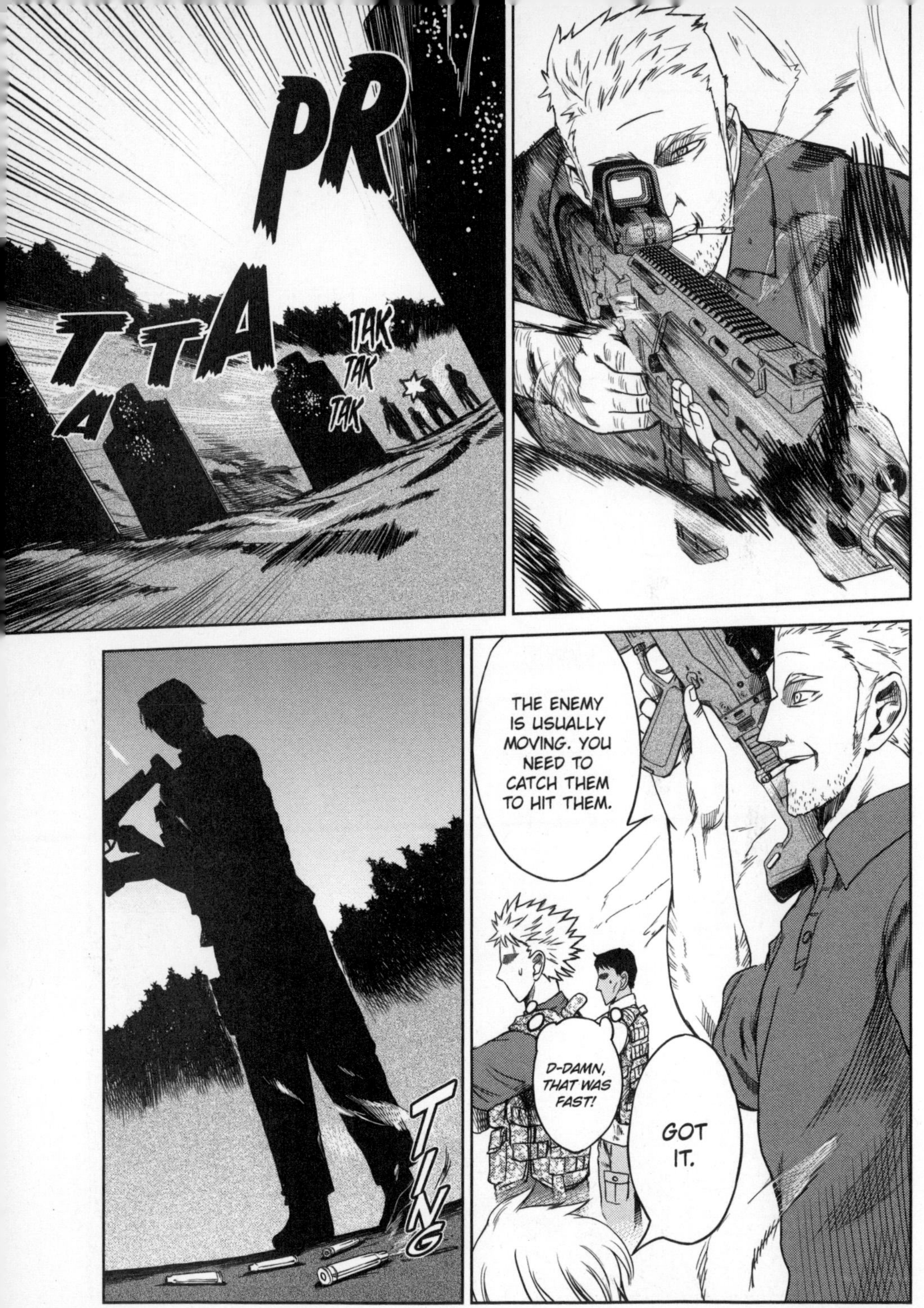
PRTTAA
TAK TAK TAK
THE ENEMY IS USUALLY MOVING. YOU NEED TO CATCH THEM TO HIT THEM.
D-DAMN, THAT WAS FAST!
GOT IT.
TING

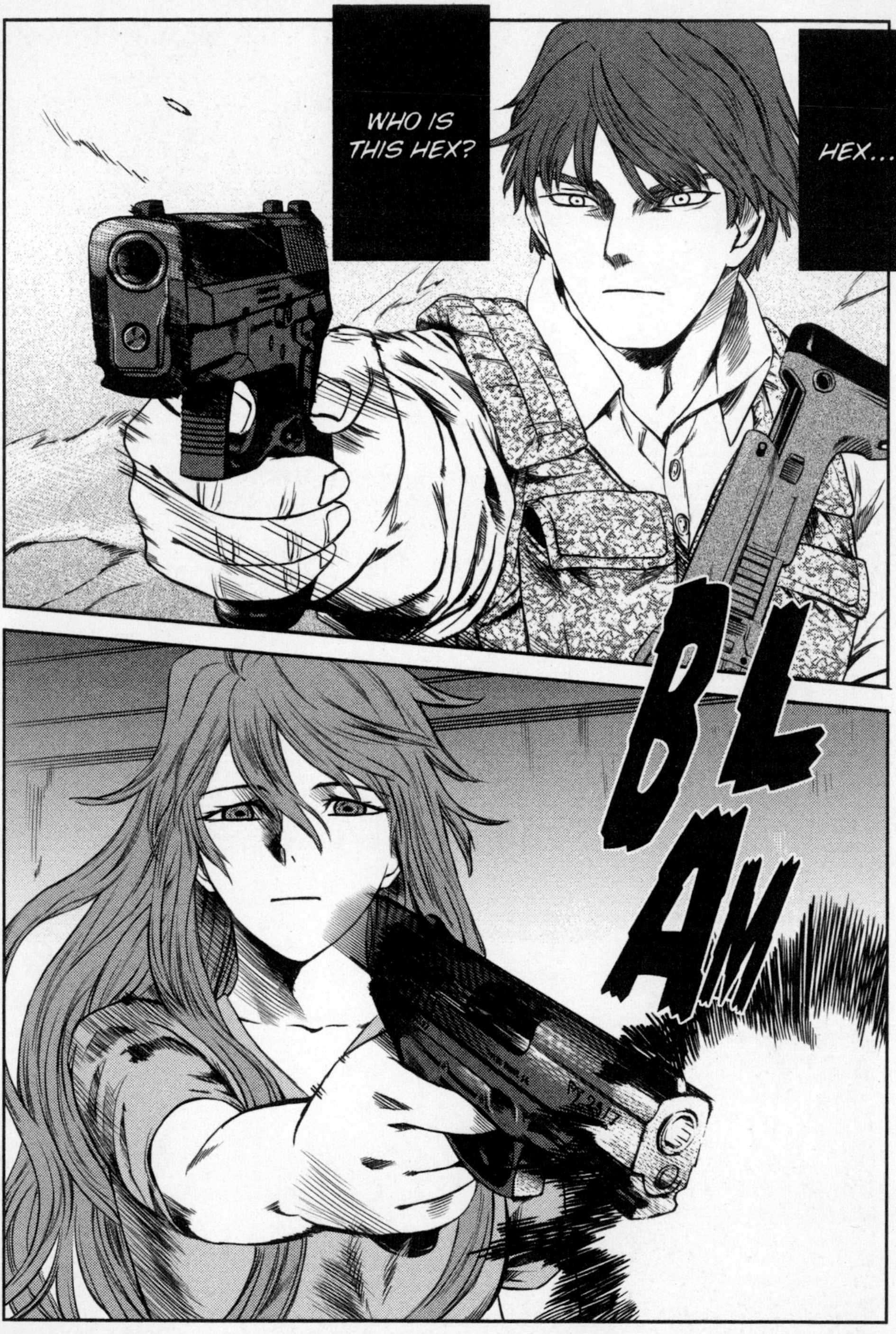
HEX...
WHO IS THIS HEX?
BLAM

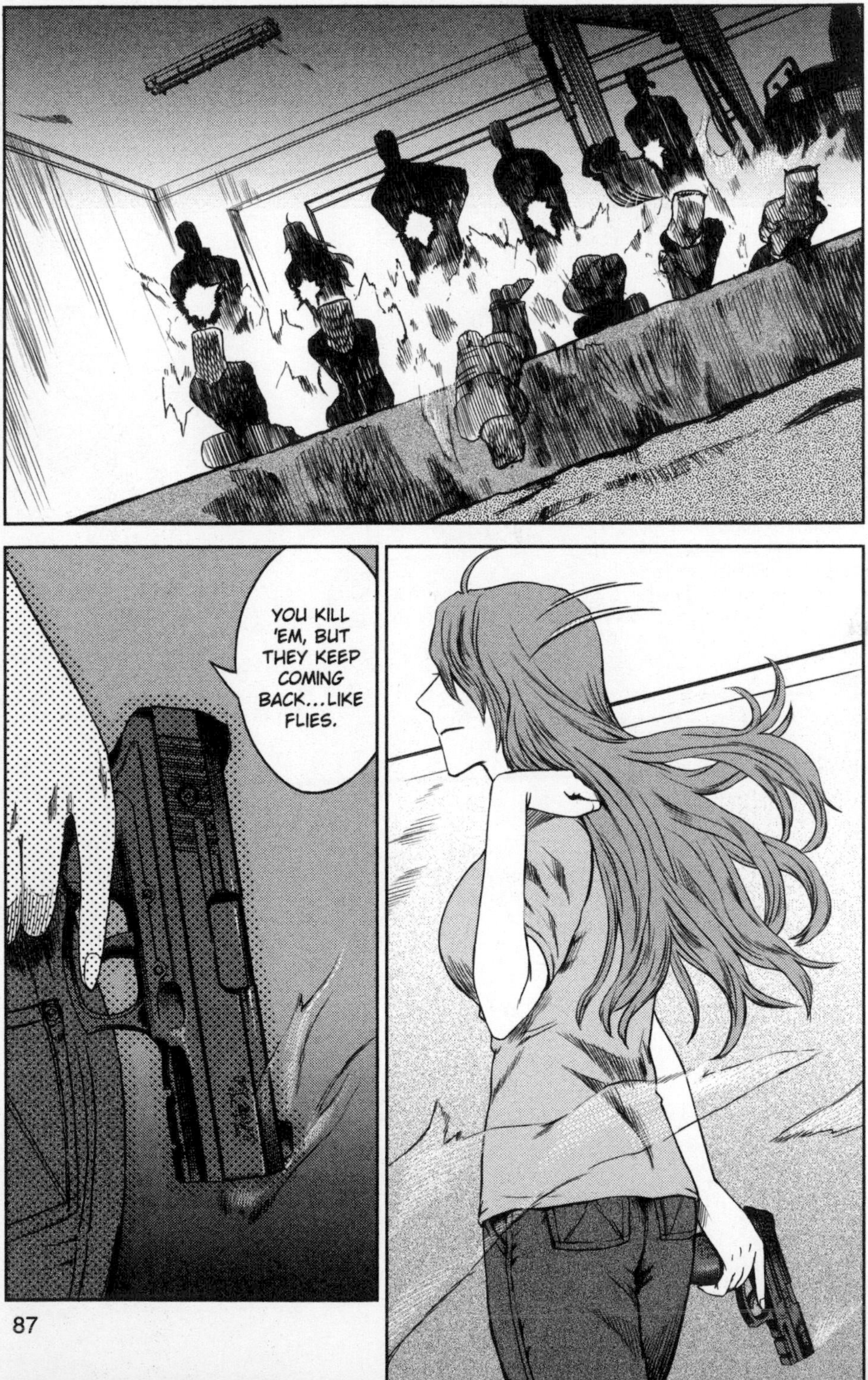
YOU KILL 'EM, BUT THEY KEEP COMING BACK...LIKE FLIES.

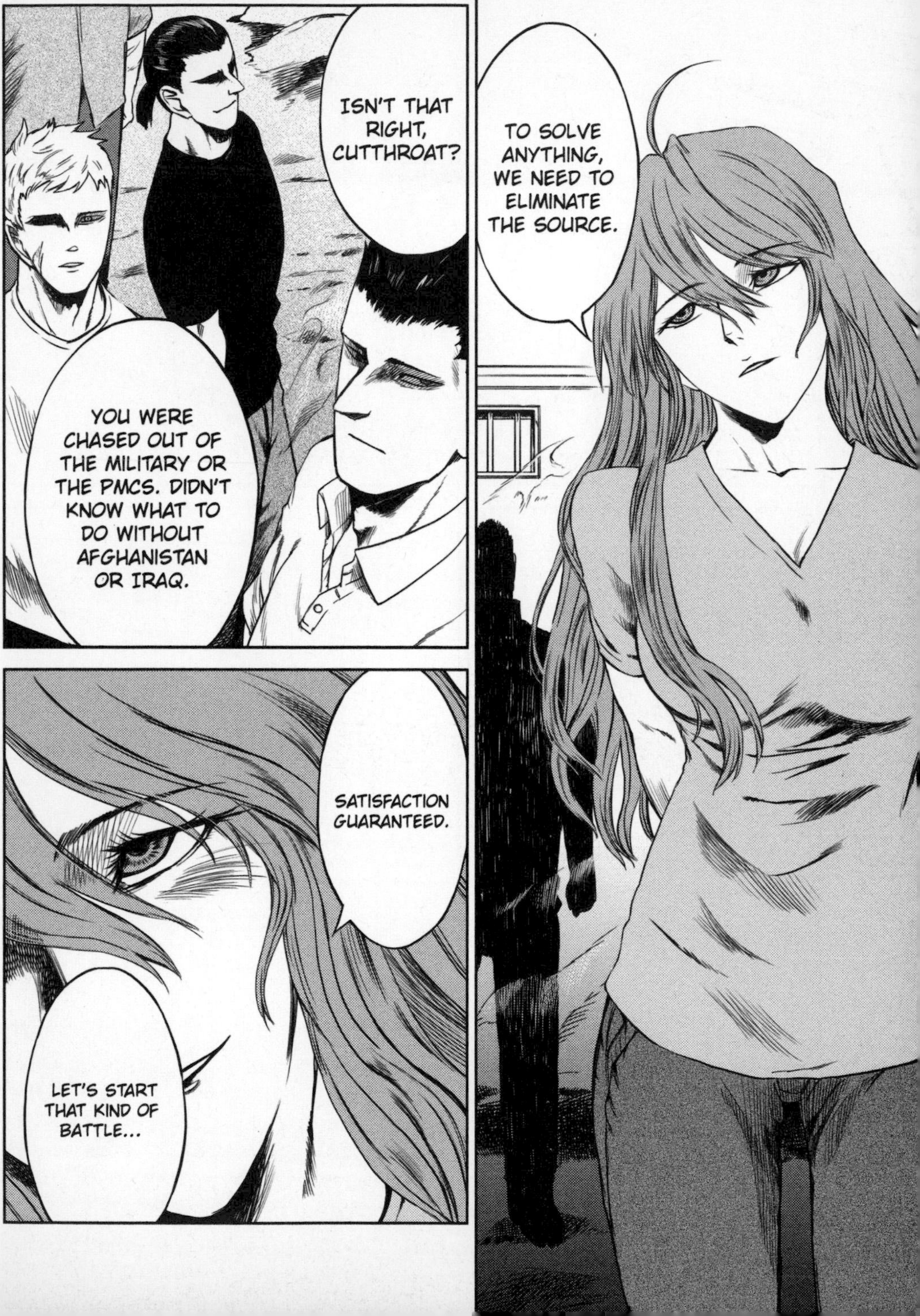
TO SOLVE ANYTHING, WE NEED TO ELIMINATE THE SOURCE.
ISN'T THAT RIGHT, CUTTHROAT?
YOU WERE CHASED OUT OF THE MILITARY OR THE PMCS. DIDN'T KNOW WHAT TO DO WITHOUT AFGHANISTAN OR IRAQ.
SATISFACTION GUARANTEED.
LET'S START THAT KIND OF BATTLE...

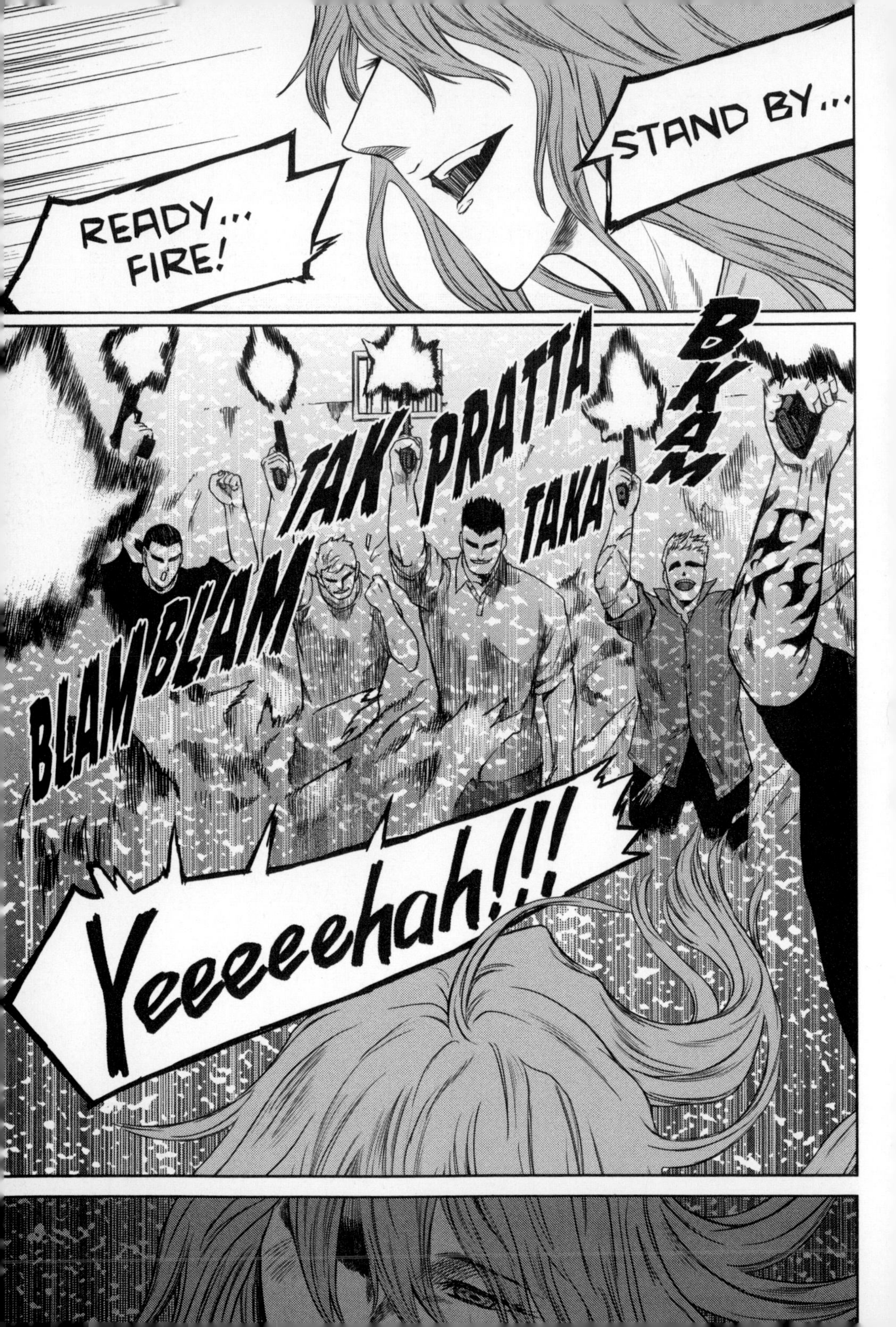
STAND BY...
READY... FIRE!
BKAM
TAKA
PRATTA
TAK
BLAMBLAM
Yeeeeehah!!!

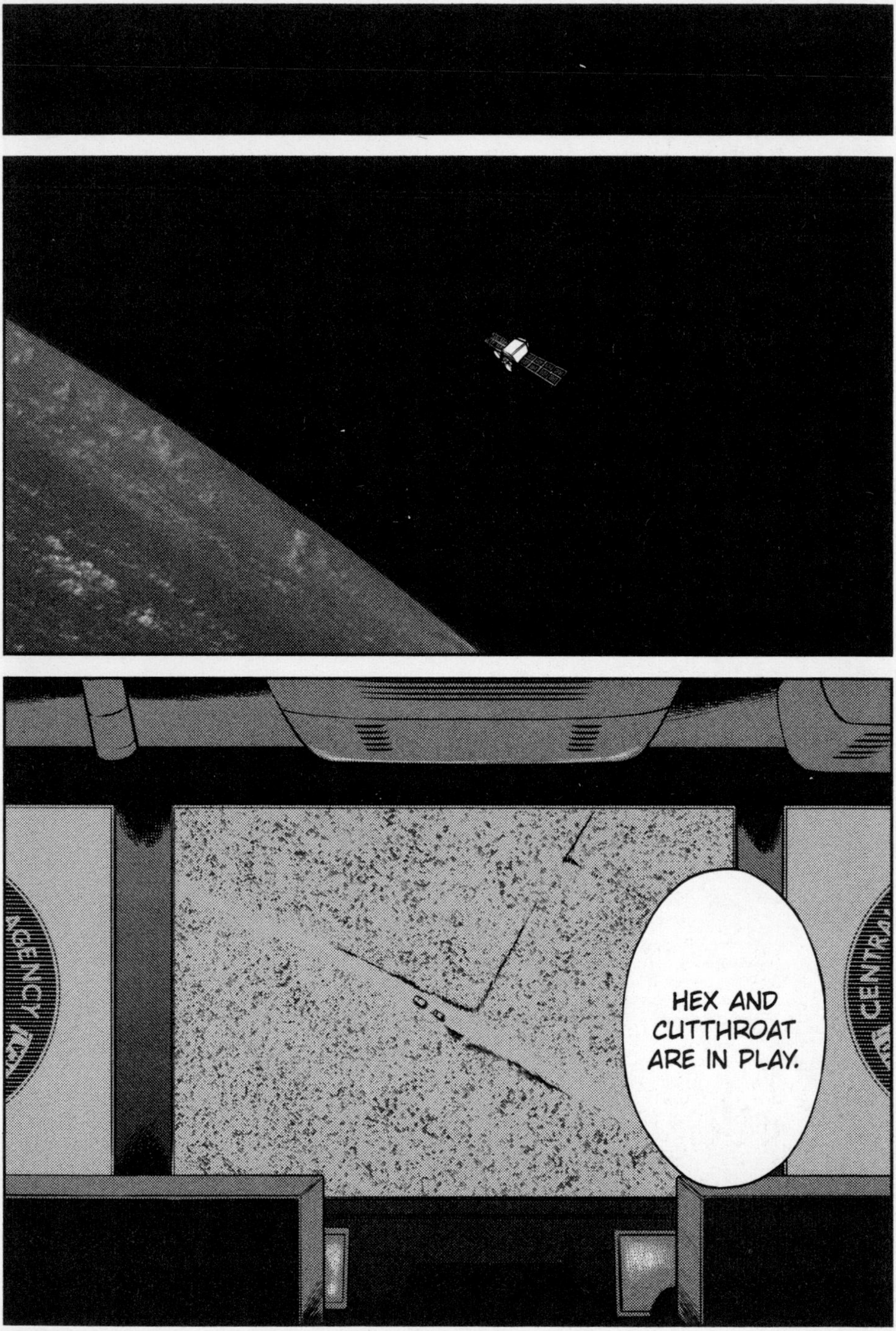
HEX AND CUTTHROAT ARE IN PLAY.
AGENCY

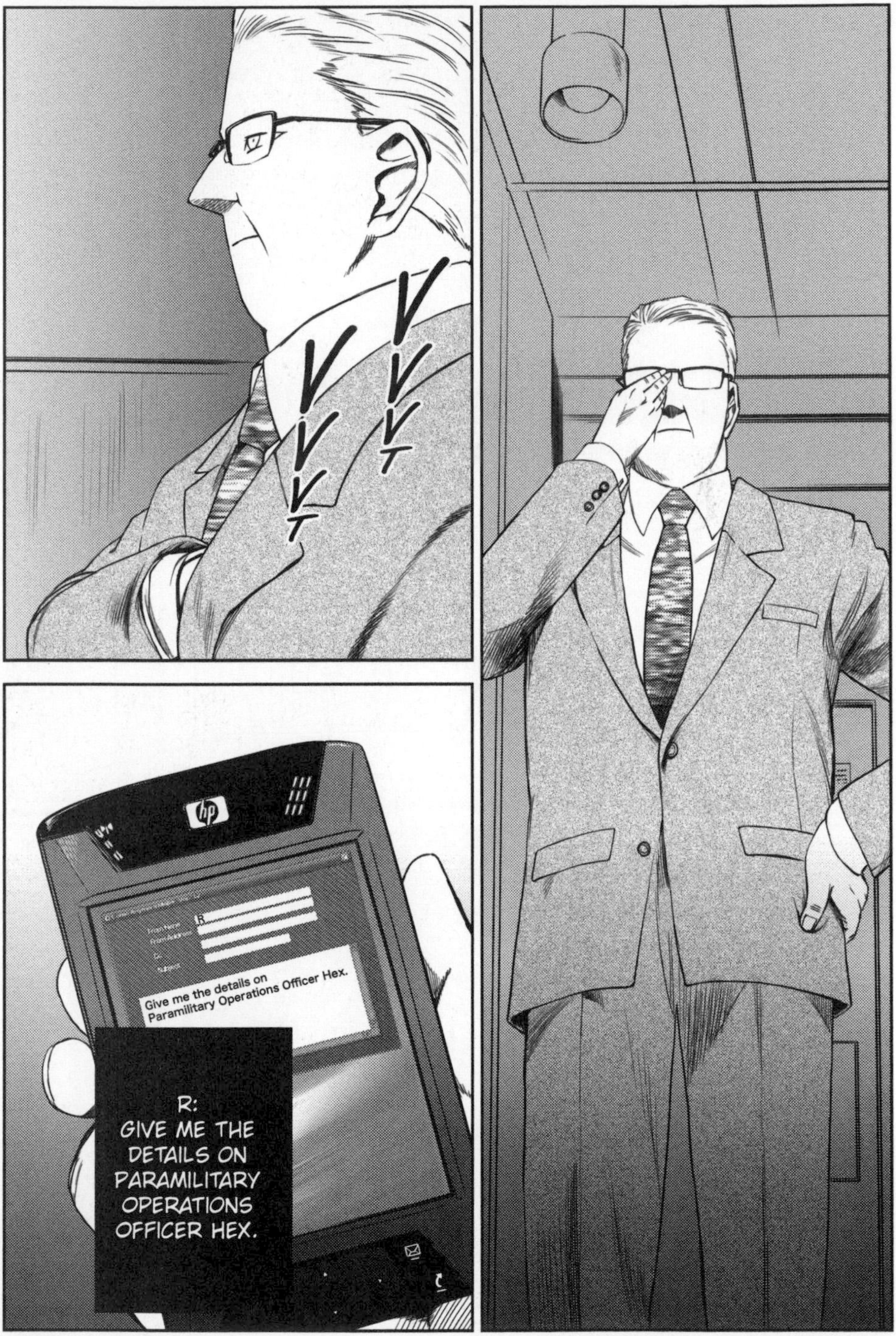
Give me the details on Paramilitary Operations Officer Hex.
R:
GIVE ME THE DETAILS ON PARAMILITARY OPERATIONS OFFICER HEX.

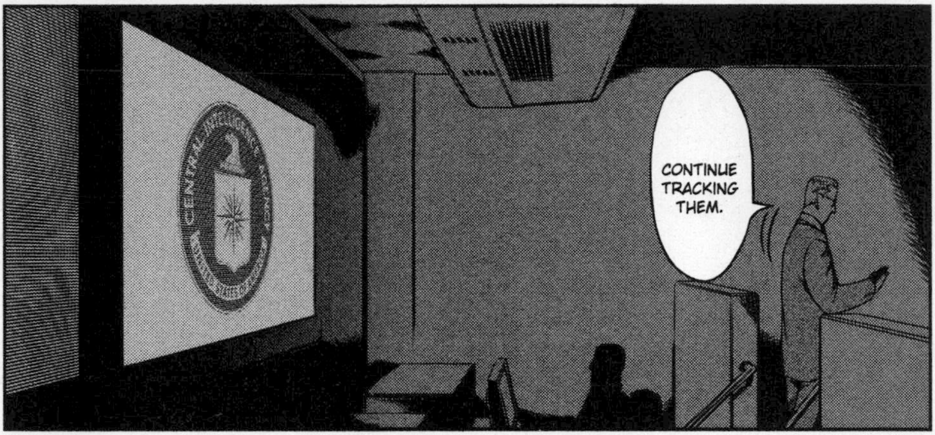
CONTINUE TRACKING THEM.

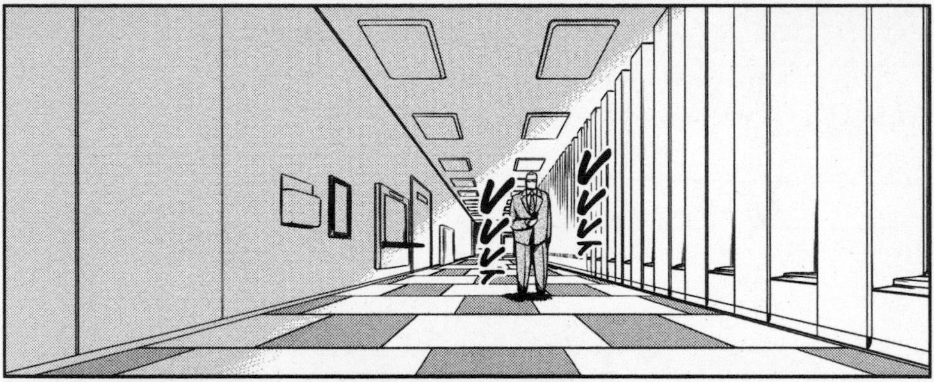

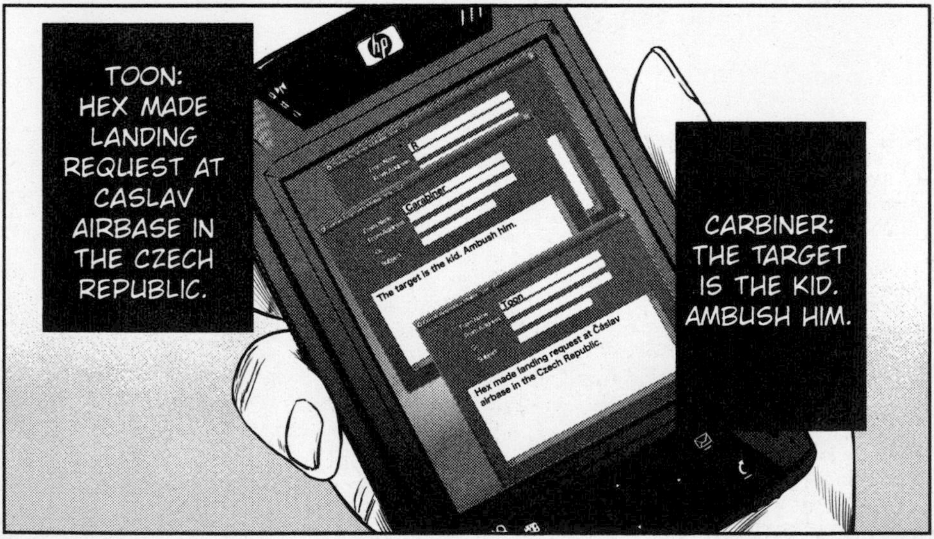
CARBINER: THE TARGET IS THE KID. AMBUSH HIM.
TOON: HEX MADE LANDING REQUEST AT CASLAV AIRBASE IN THE CZECH REPUBLIC.
Carabiner
The target is the kid. Ambush him.
Toon
Hex made landing request at Čáslav airbase in the Czech Republic.

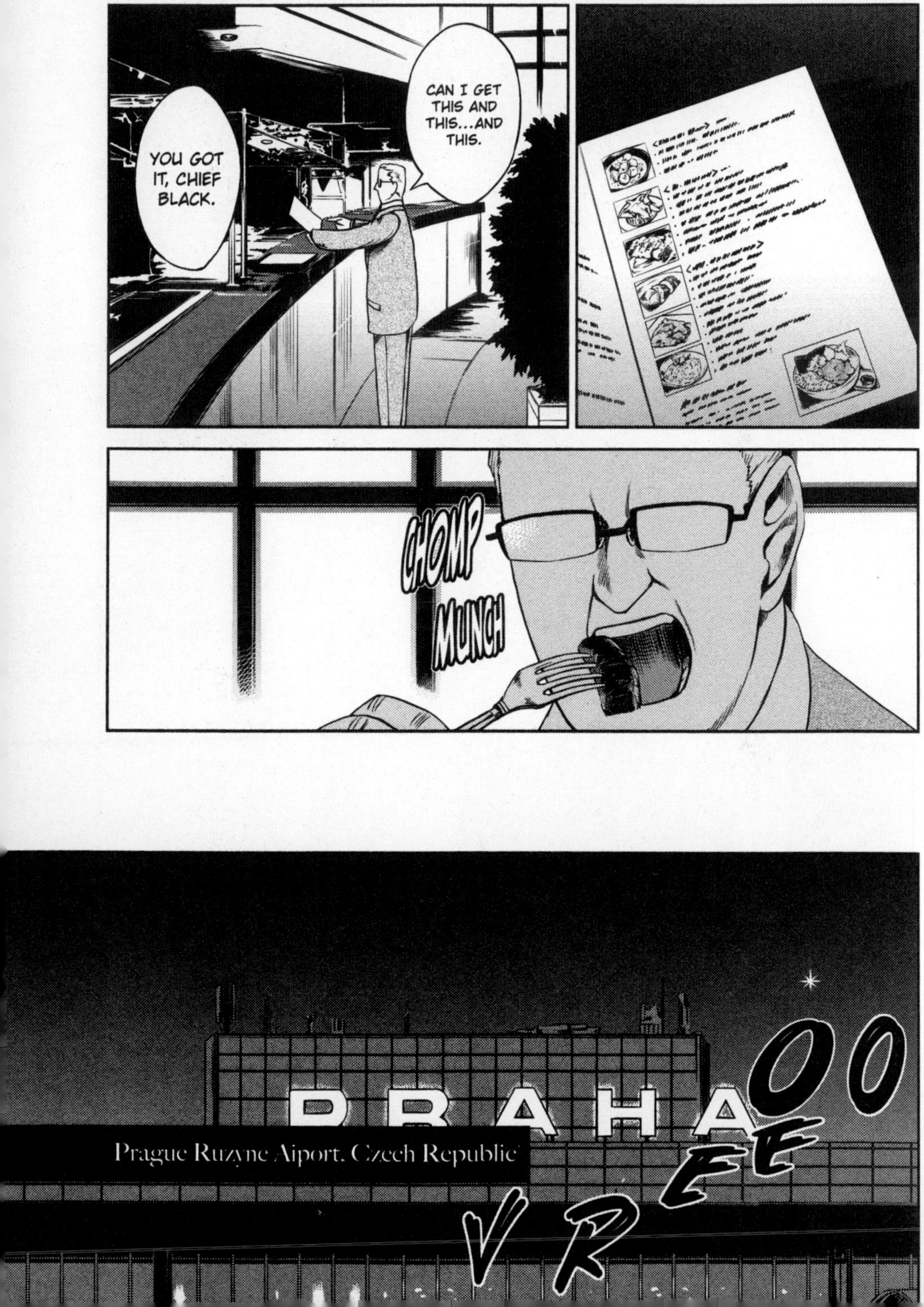
CAN I GET THIS AND THIS...AND THIS.
YOU GOT IT, CHIEF BLACK.
CHOMP
MUNCH
Prague Ruzyne Aiport, Czech Republic
PRAHA
VREEOO

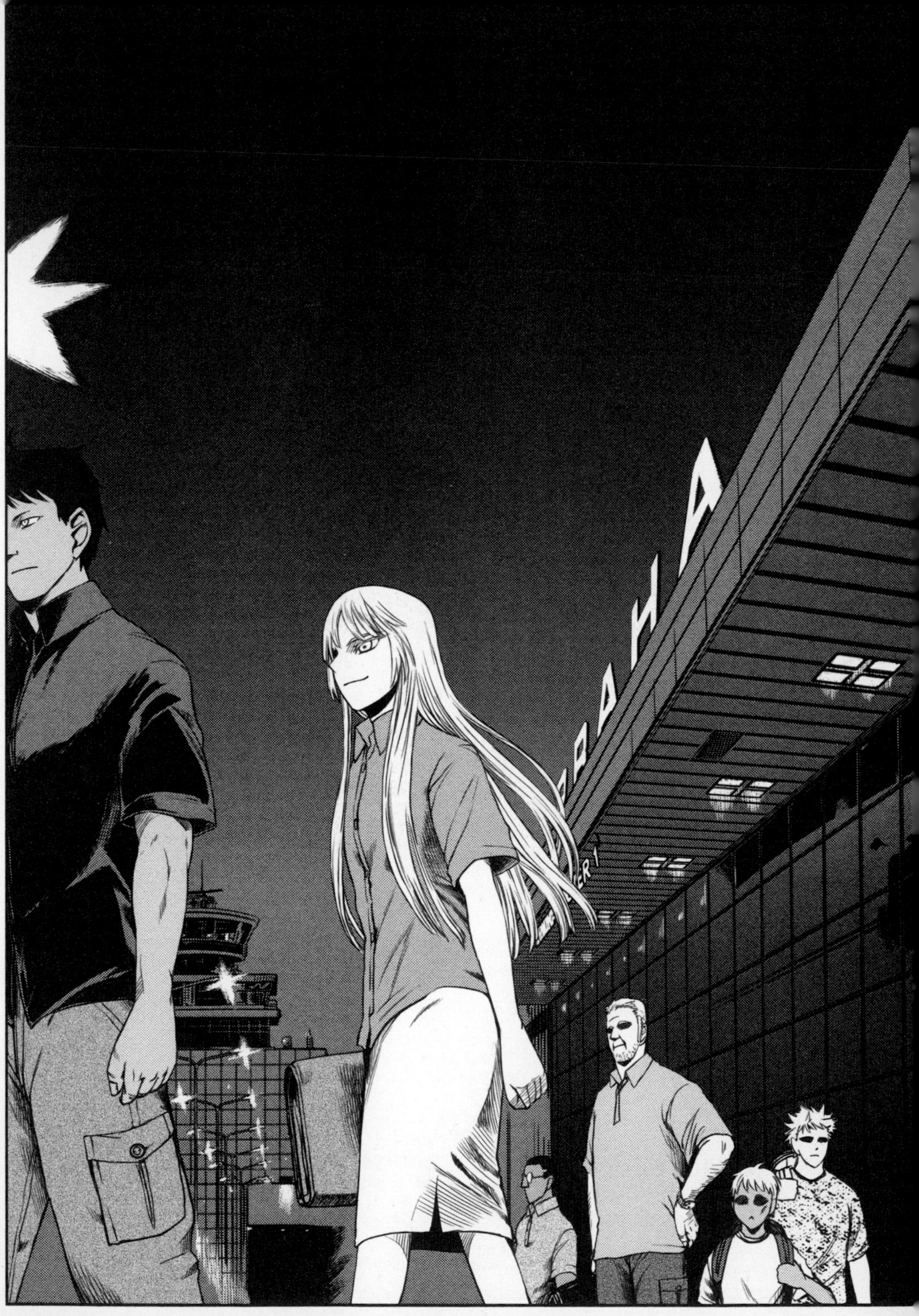
PRAHA

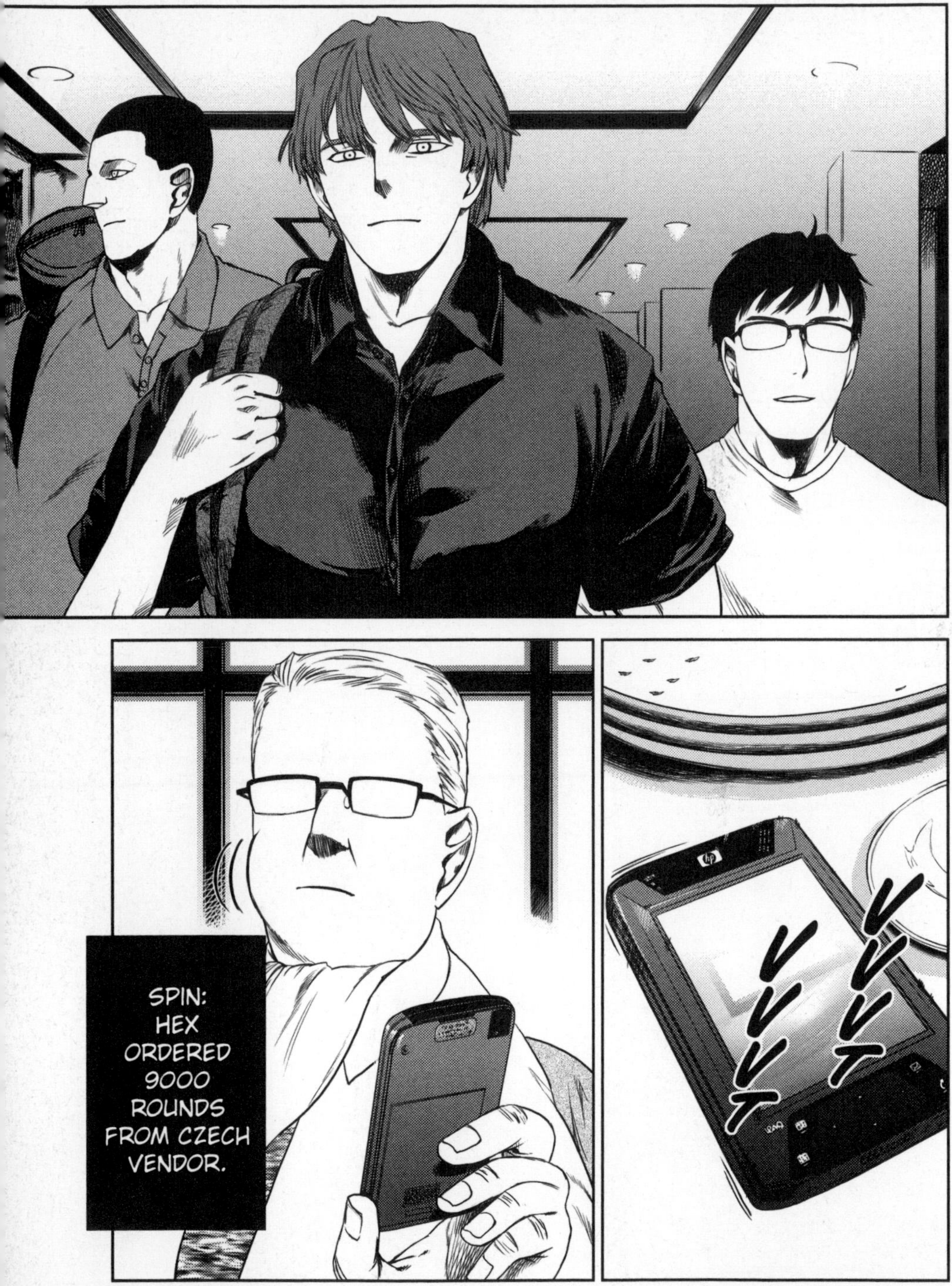
SPIN:
HEX
ORDERED
9000
ROUNDS
FROM CZECH
VENDOR.

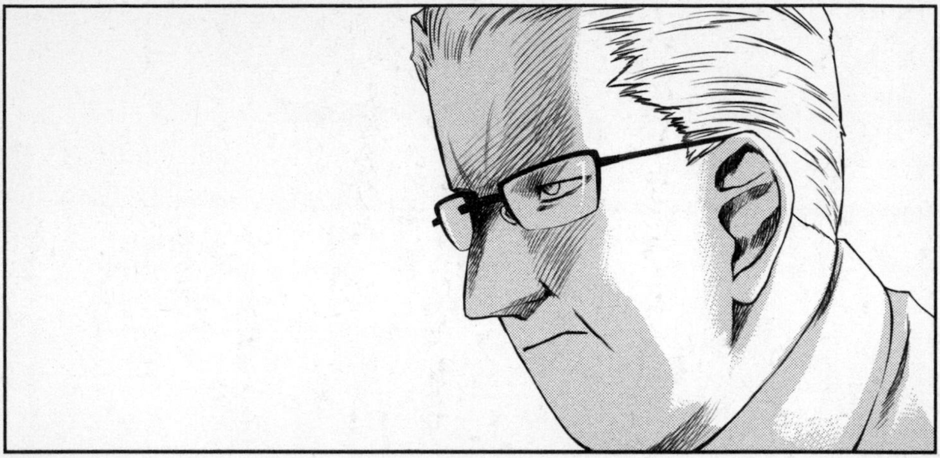

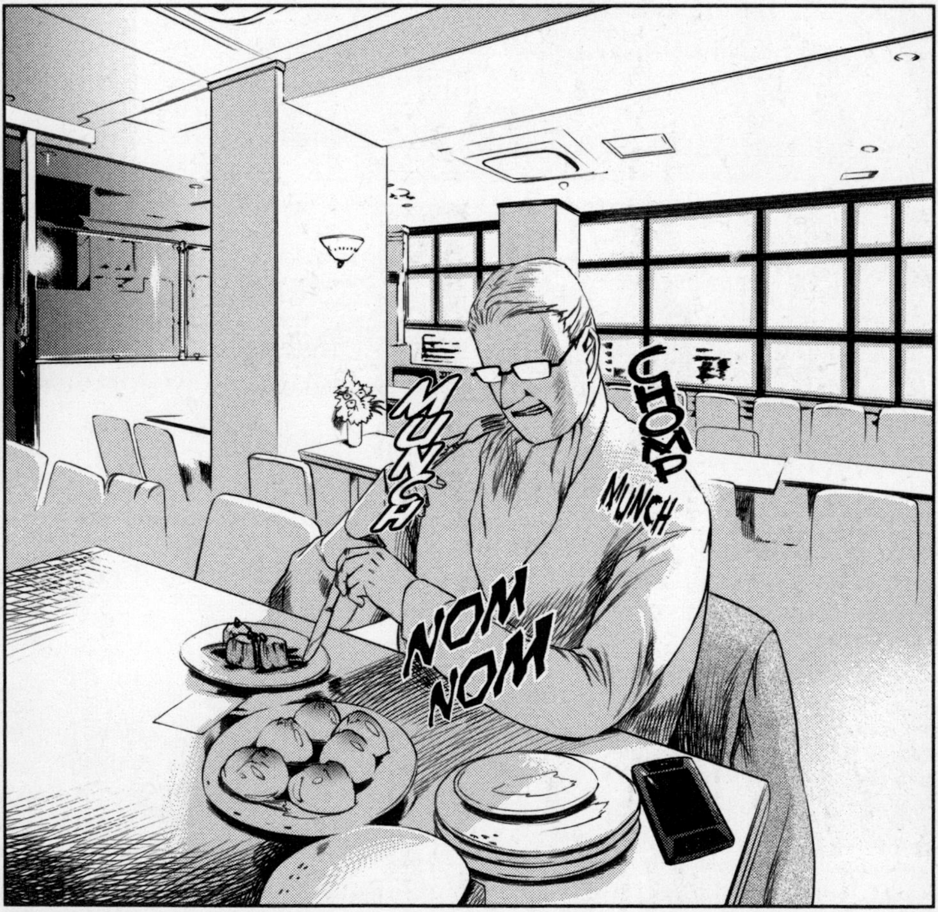
CHOMP
MUNCH
MUNCH
NOM NOM

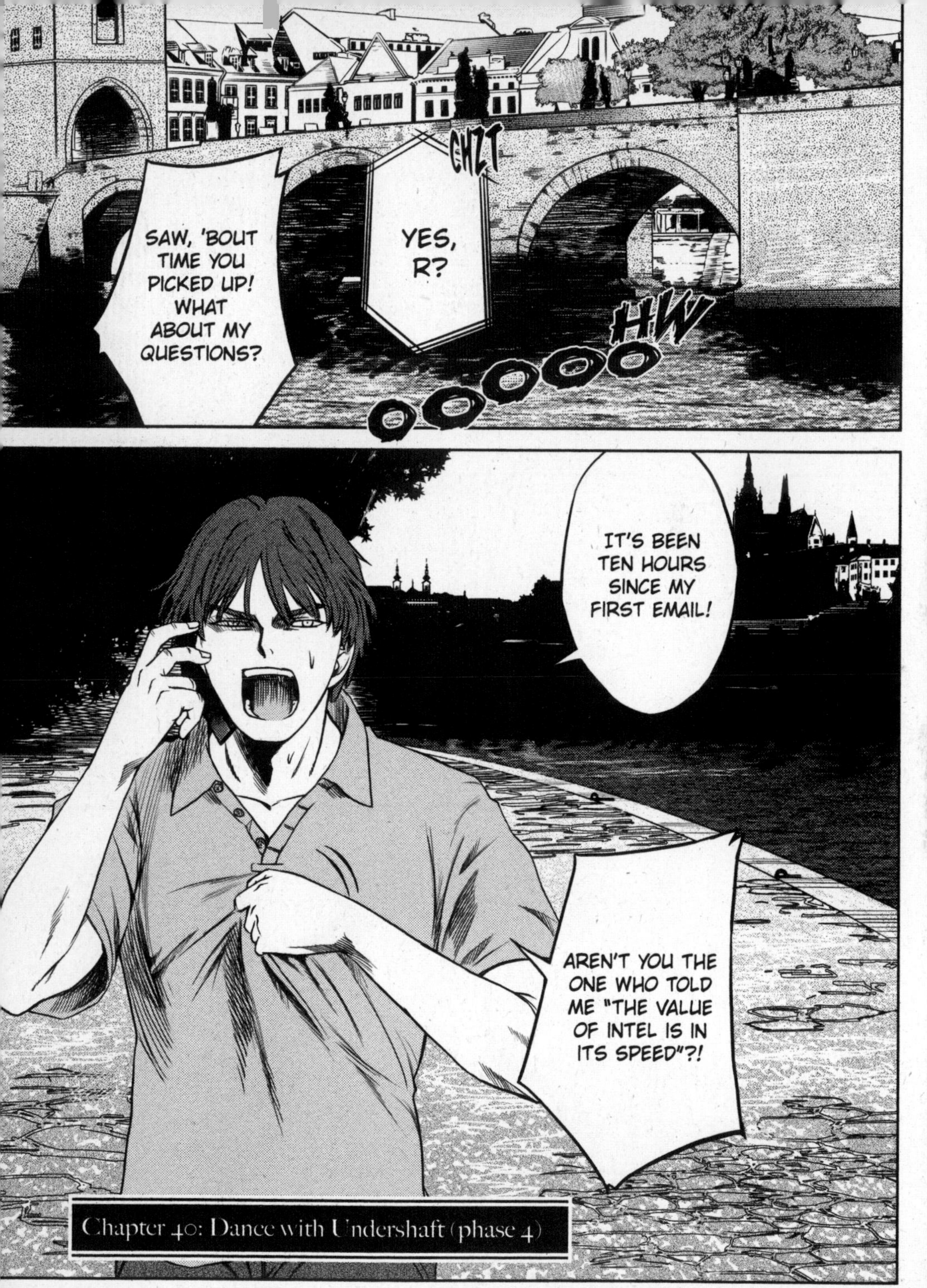
CHZT
YES, R?
SAW, 'BOUT TIME YOU PICKED UP! WHAT ABOUT MY QUESTIONS?
HWOOOOOO
IT'S BEEN TEN HOURS SINCE MY FIRST EMAIL!
AREN'T YOU THE ONE WHO TOLD ME "THE VALUE OF INTEL IS IN ITS SPEED"?!

Chapter 40: Dance with Undershaft (phase 4)

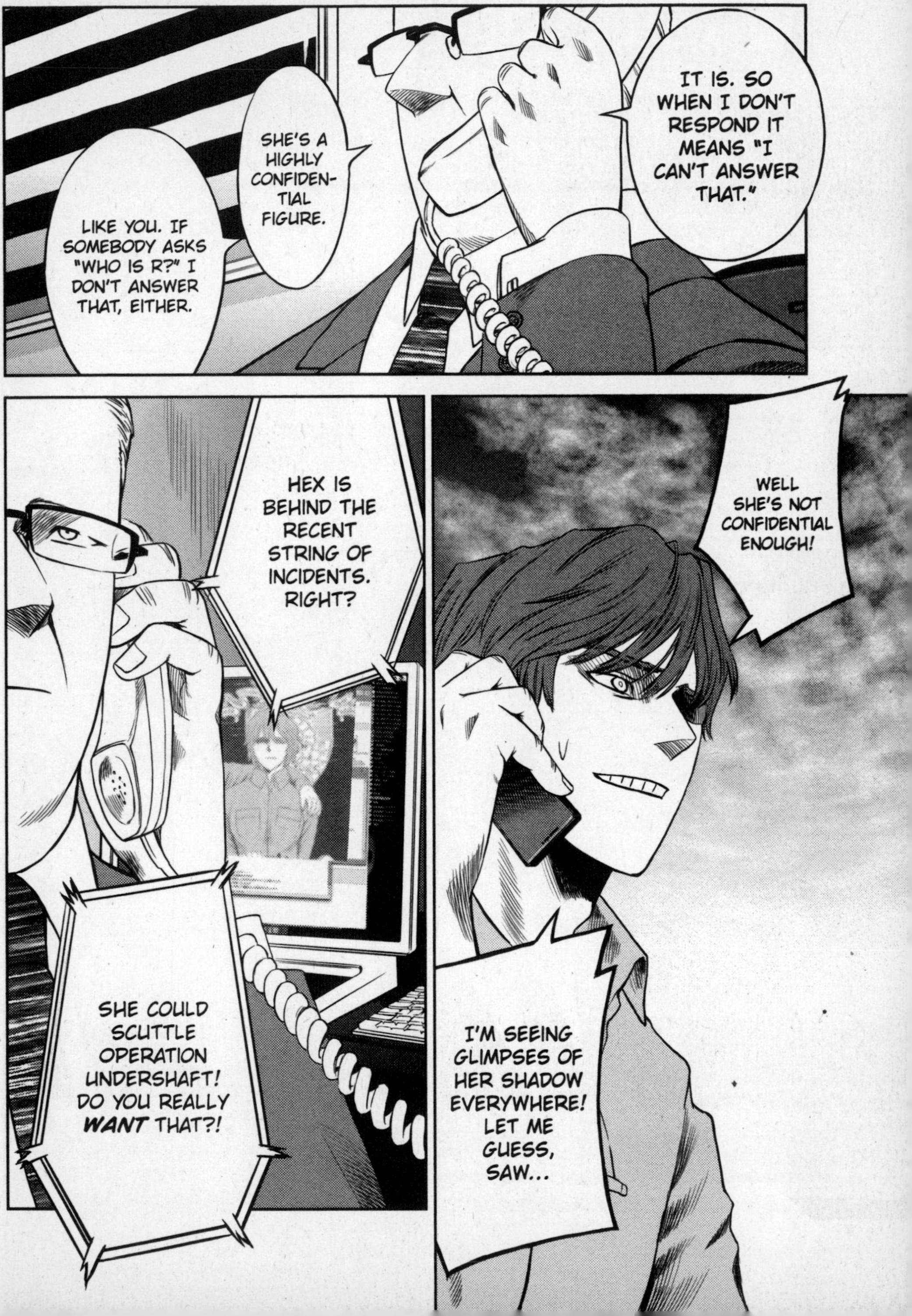
IT IS. SO WHEN I DON'T RESPOND IT MEANS "I CAN'T ANSWER THAT."
SHE'S A HIGHLY CONFIDEN-TIAL FIGURE.
LIKE YOU. IF SOMEBODY ASKS "WHO IS R?" I DON'T ANSWER THAT, EITHER.
WELL SHE'S NOT CONFIDENTIAL ENOUGH!
I'M SEEING GLIMPSES OF HER SHADOW EVERYWHERE! LET ME GUESS, SAW...
HEX IS BEHIND THE RECENT STRING OF INCIDENTS. RIGHT?
SHE COULD SCUTTLE OPERATION UNDERSHAFT! DO YOU REALLY ***WANT*** THAT?!

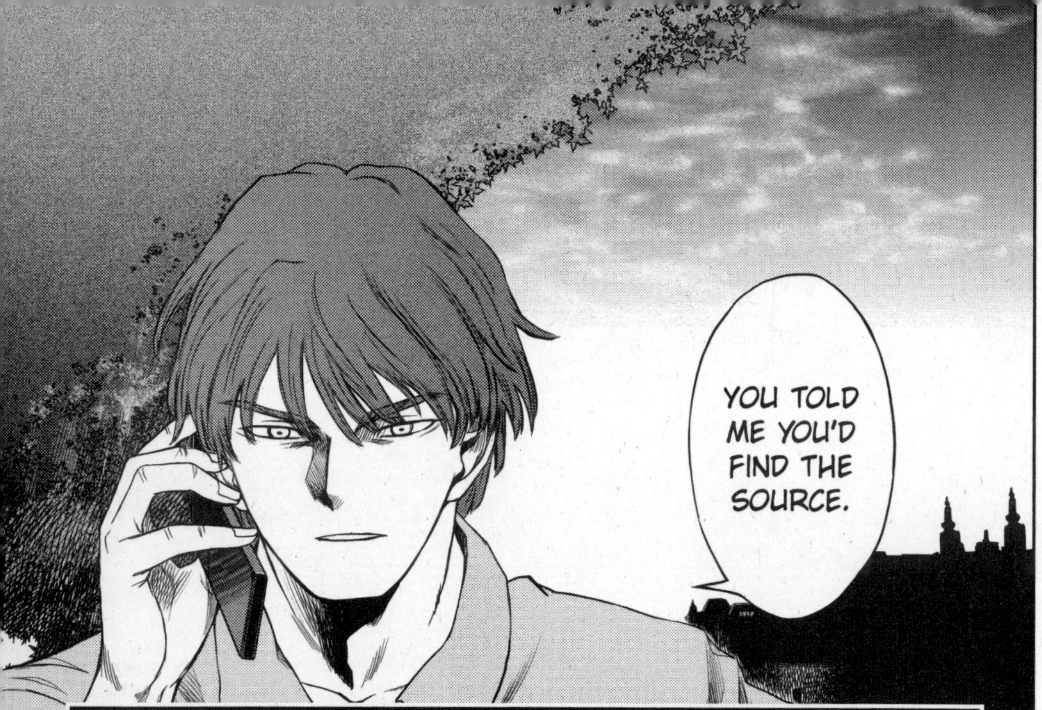
YOU TOLD ME YOU'D FIND THE SOURCE.

Chapter 40: Dance with Undershaft (phase 4)

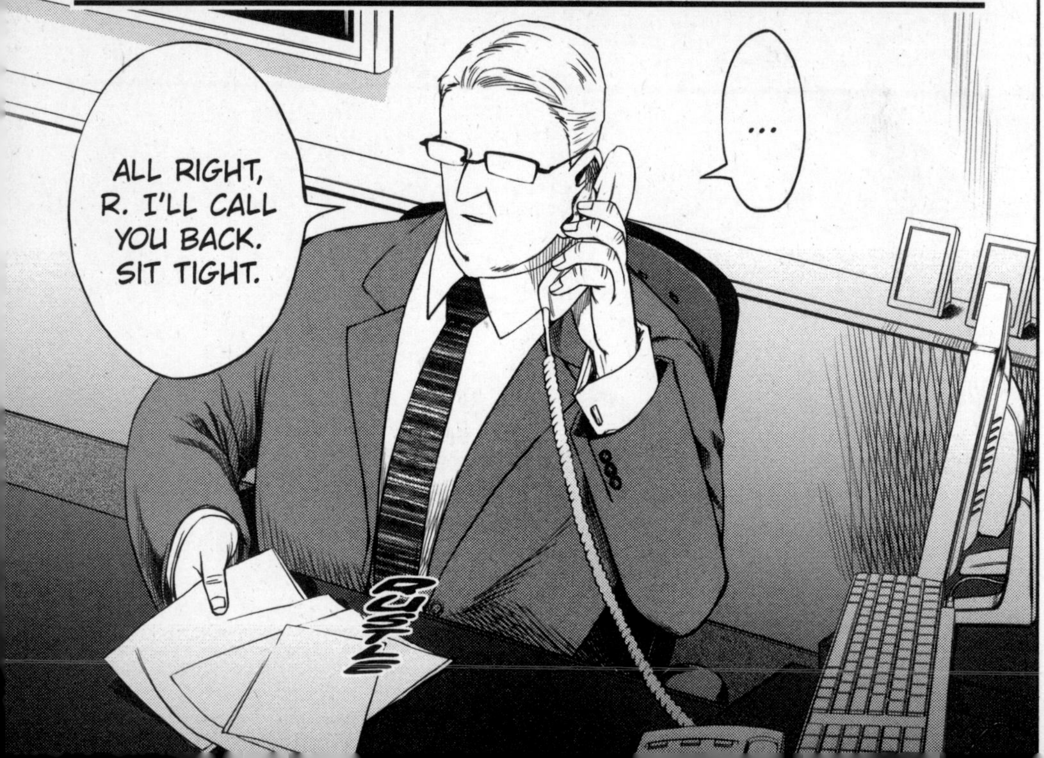
...
ALL RIGHT, R. I'LL CALL YOU BACK. SIT TIGHT.

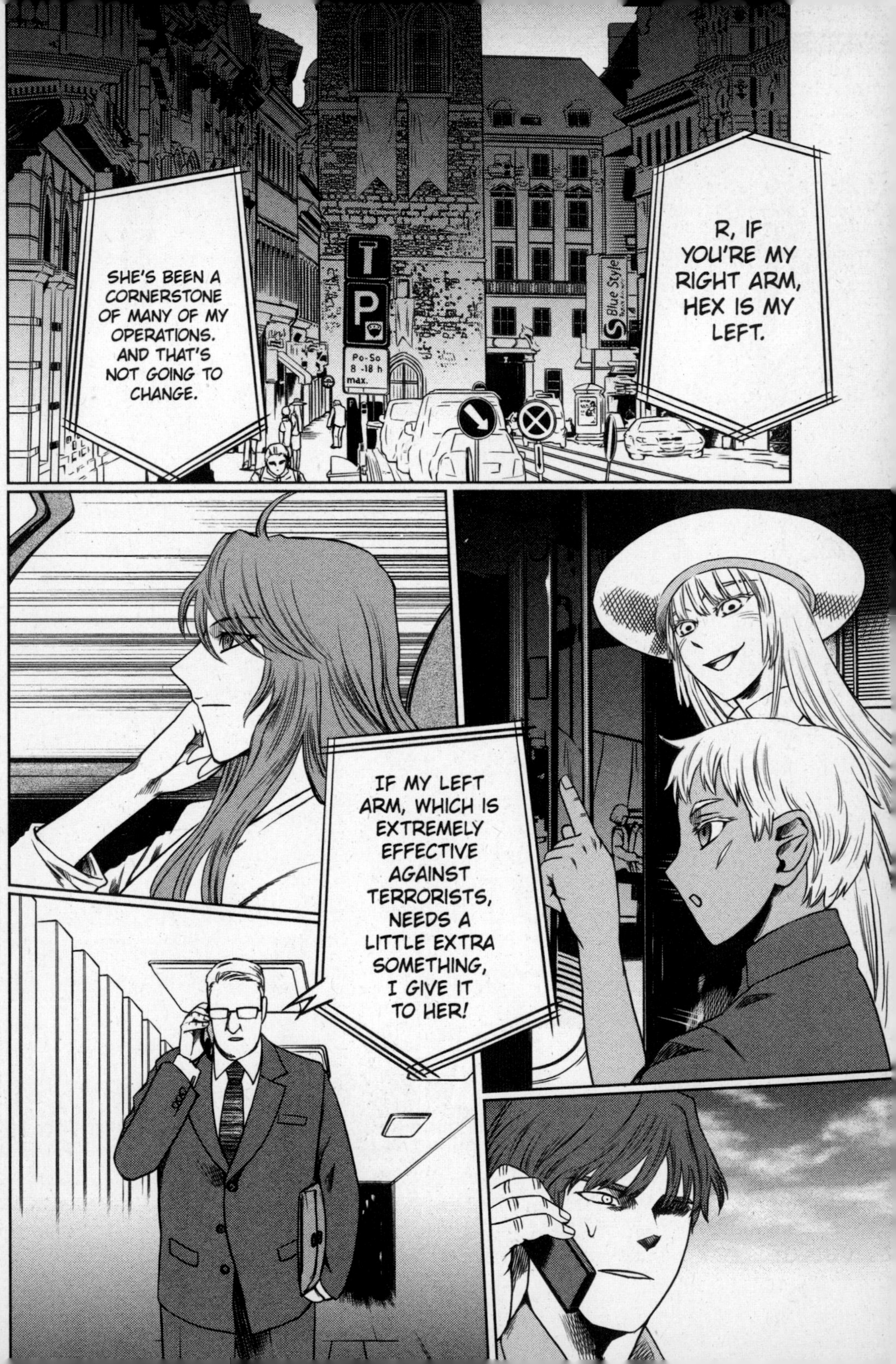
R, IF YOU'RE MY RIGHT ARM, HEX IS MY LEFT.
SHE'S BEEN A CORNERSTONE OF MANY OF MY OPERATIONS. AND THAT'S NOT GOING TO CHANGE.
Blue Style
T
P
Po-So 8 -18 h max.
IF MY LEFT ARM, WHICH IS EXTREMELY EFFECTIVE AGAINST TERRORISTS, NEEDS A LITTLE EXTRA SOMETHING, I GIVE IT TO HER!

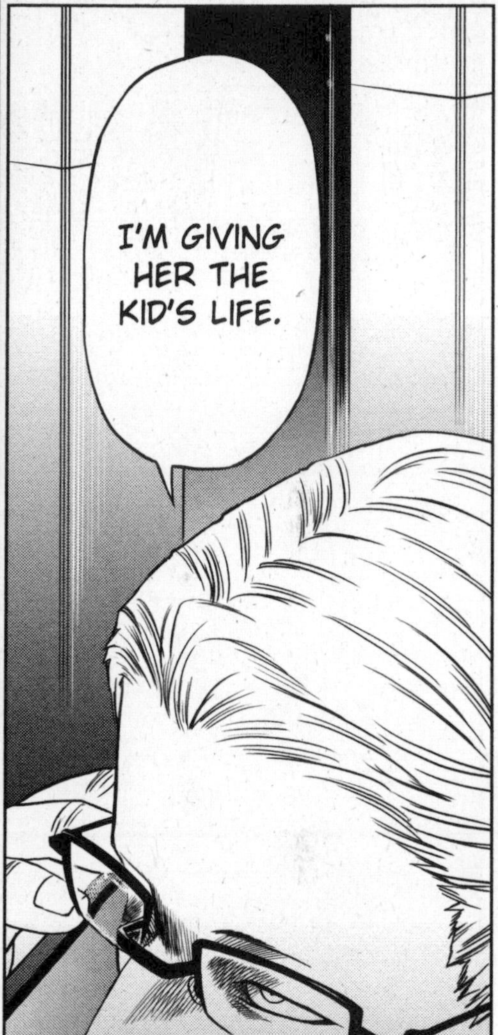
I'M GIVING HER THE KID'S LIFE.

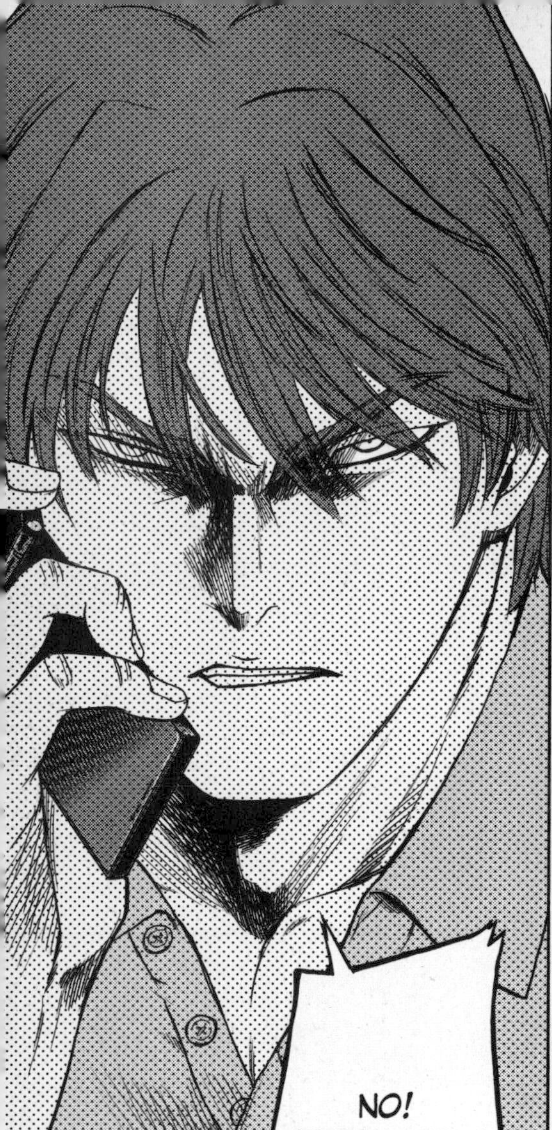
NO! ABSOLUTELY NOT!

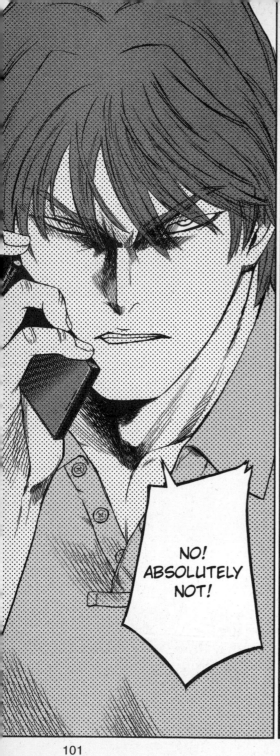

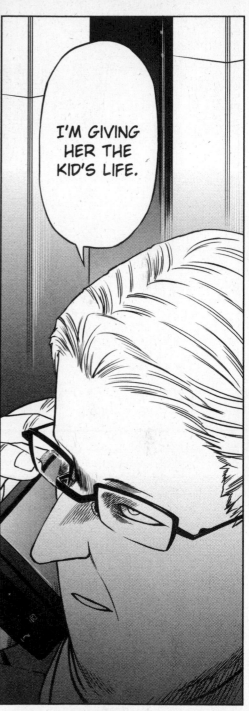

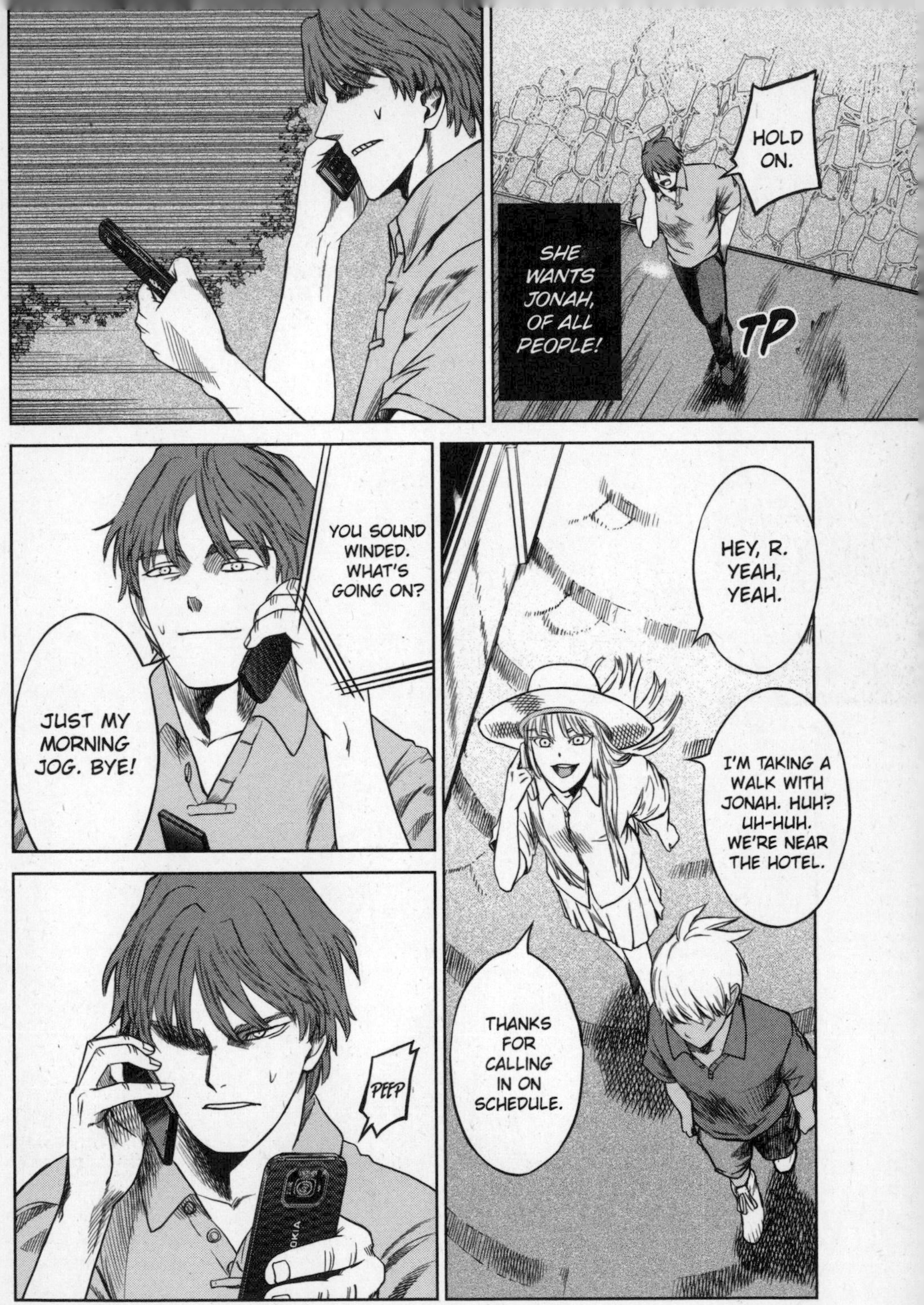
HOLD ON.
SHE WANTS JONAH, OF ALL PEOPLE!
TP
HEY, R. YEAH, YEAH.
I'M TAKING A WALK WITH JONAH. HUH? UH-HUH. WE'RE NEAR THE HOTEL.
THANKS FOR CALLING IN ON SCHEDULE.
YOU SOUND WINDED. WHAT'S GOING ON?
JUST MY MORNING JOG. BYE!
PEEP

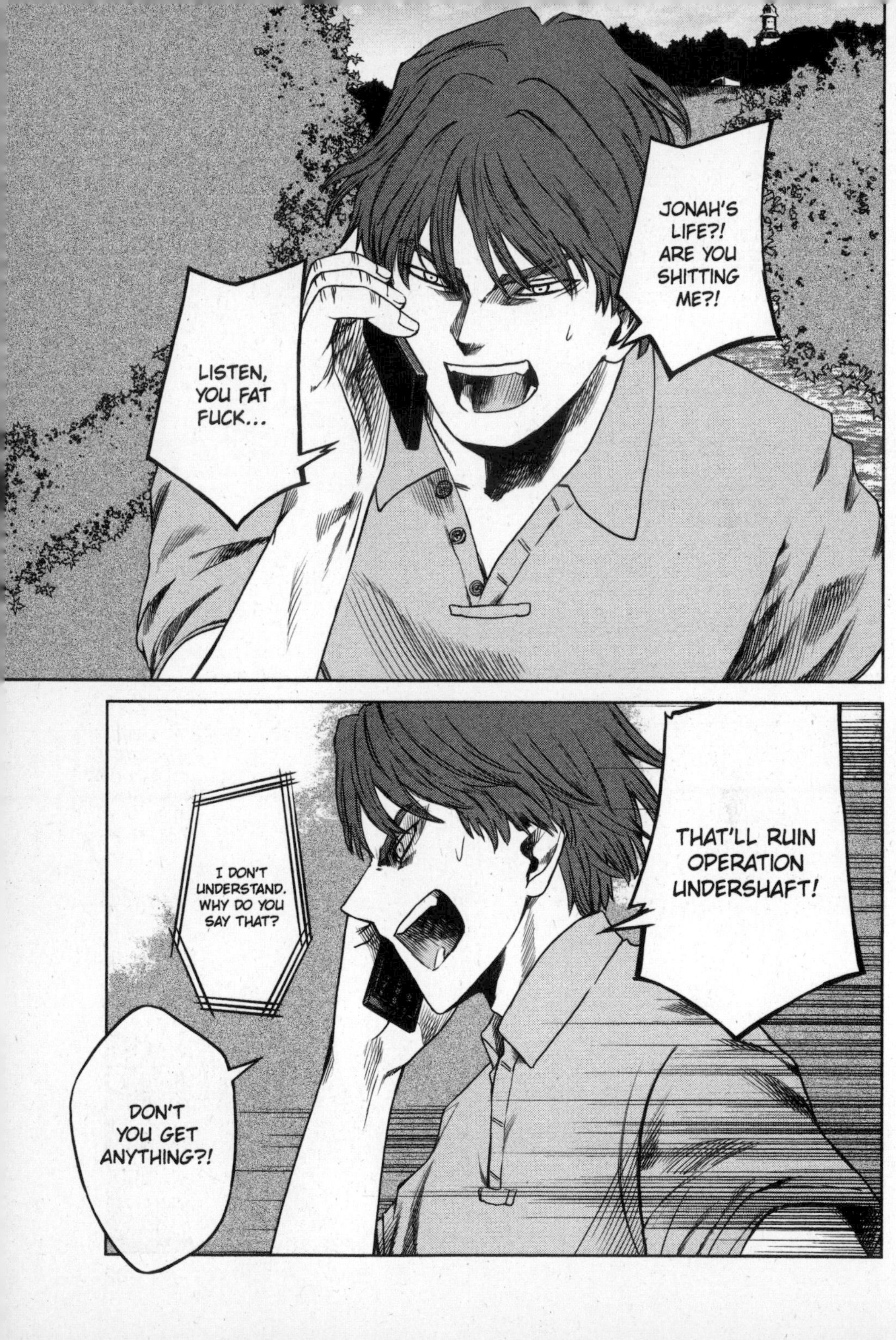
JONAH'S LIFE?! ARE YOU SHITTING ME?!
LISTEN, YOU FAT FUCK...
THAT'LL RUIN OPERATION UNDERSHAFT!
I DON'T UNDERSTAND. WHY DO YOU SAY THAT?
DON'T YOU GET ANYTHING?!

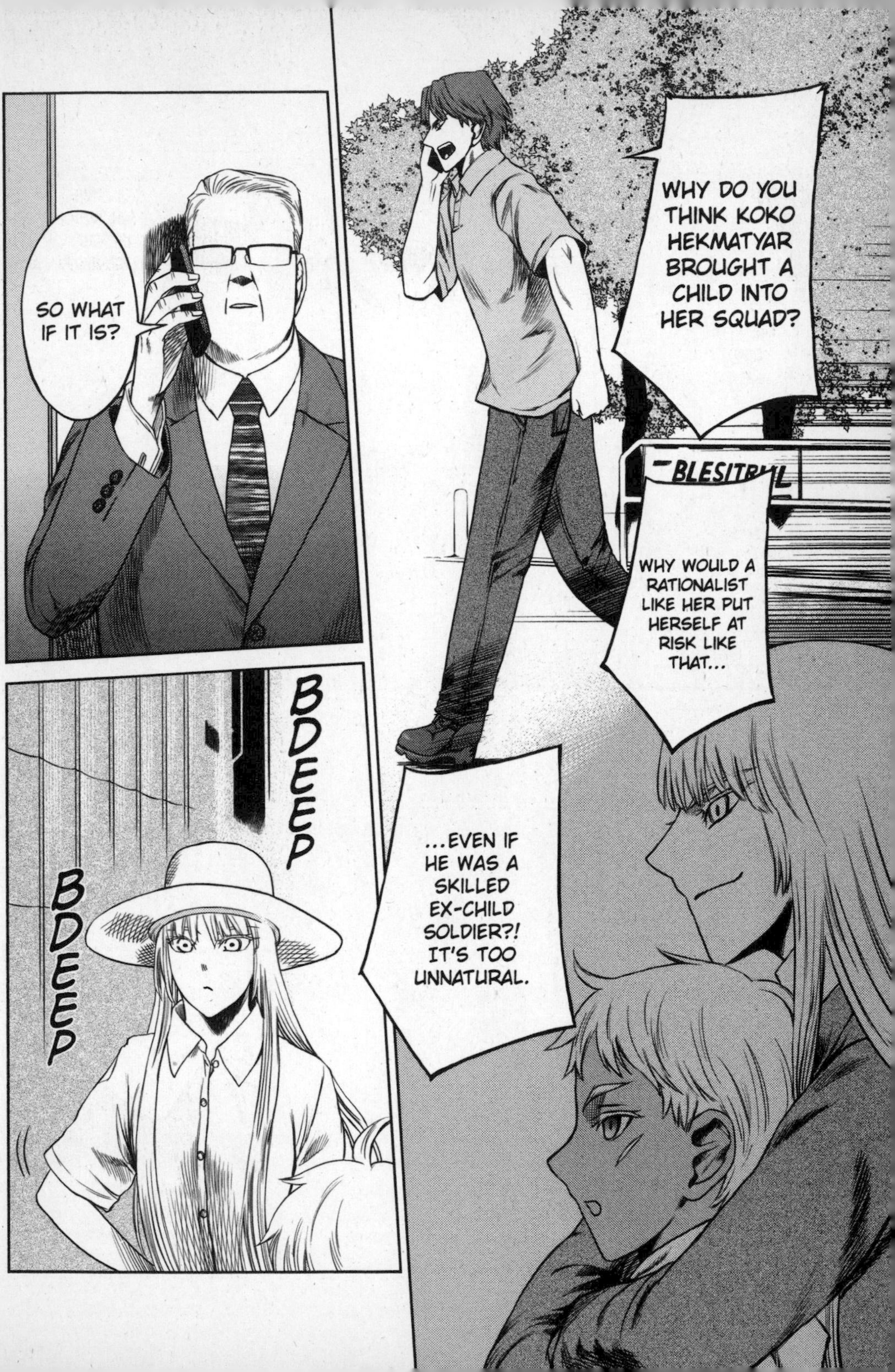
WHY DO YOU THINK KOKO HEKMATYAR BROUGHT A CHILD INTO HER SQUAD?
WHY WOULD A RATIONALIST LIKE HER PUT HERSELF AT RISK LIKE THAT...
...EVEN IF HE WAS A SKILLED EX-CHILD SOLDIER?! IT'S TOO UNNATURAL.
SO WHAT IF IT IS?
BDEEP
BDEEP

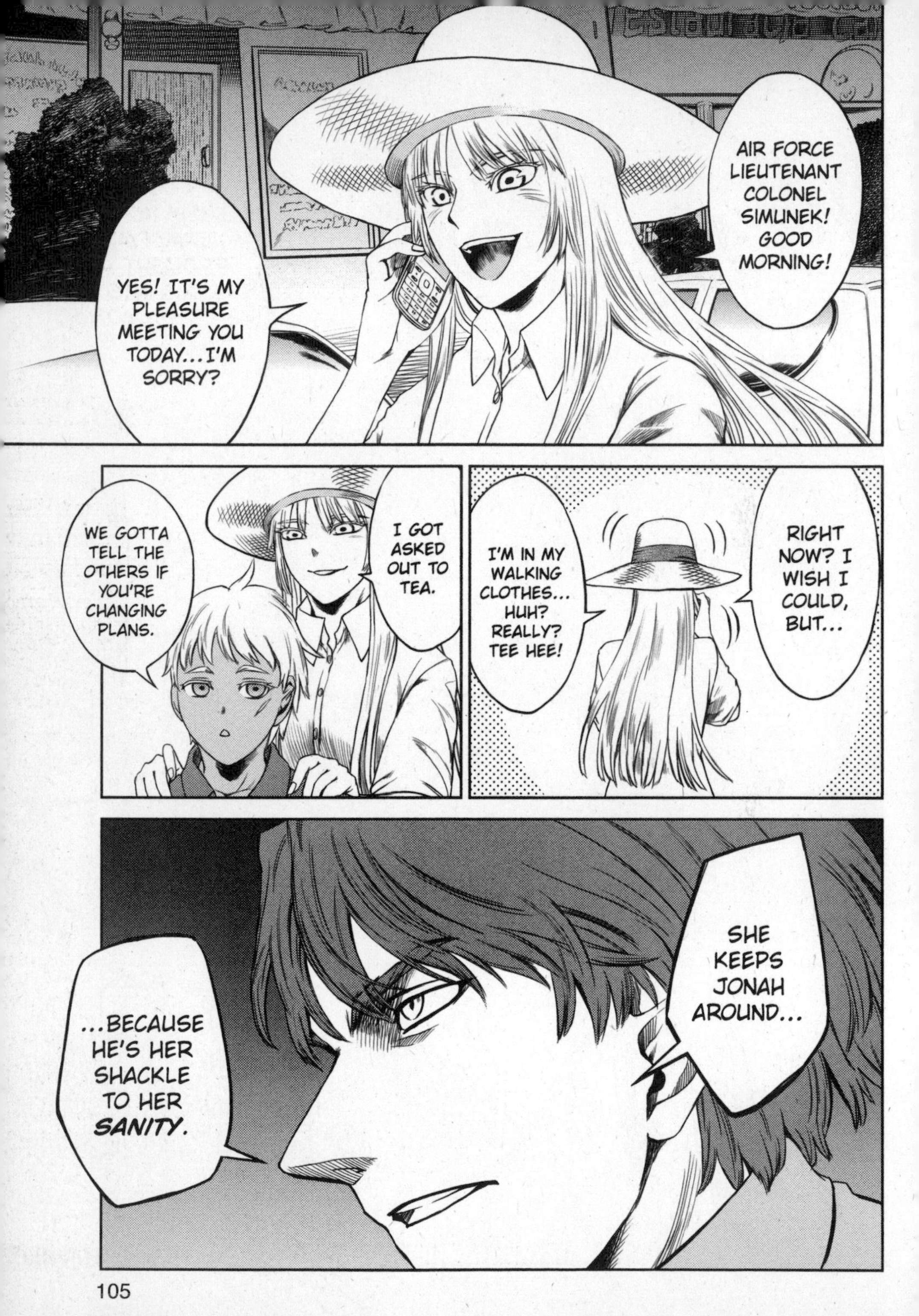
AIR FORCE LIEUTENANT COLONEL SIMUNEK! GOOD MORNING!
YES! IT'S MY PLEASURE MEETING YOU TODAY...I'M SORRY?
RIGHT NOW? I WISH I COULD, BUT...
I'M IN MY WALKING CLOTHES... HUH? REALLY? TEE HEE!
I GOT ASKED OUT TO TEA.
WE GOTTA TELL THE OTHERS IF YOU'RE CHANGING PLANS.
SHE KEEPS JONAH AROUND...
...BECAUSE HE'S HER SHACKLE TO HER ***SANITY***.

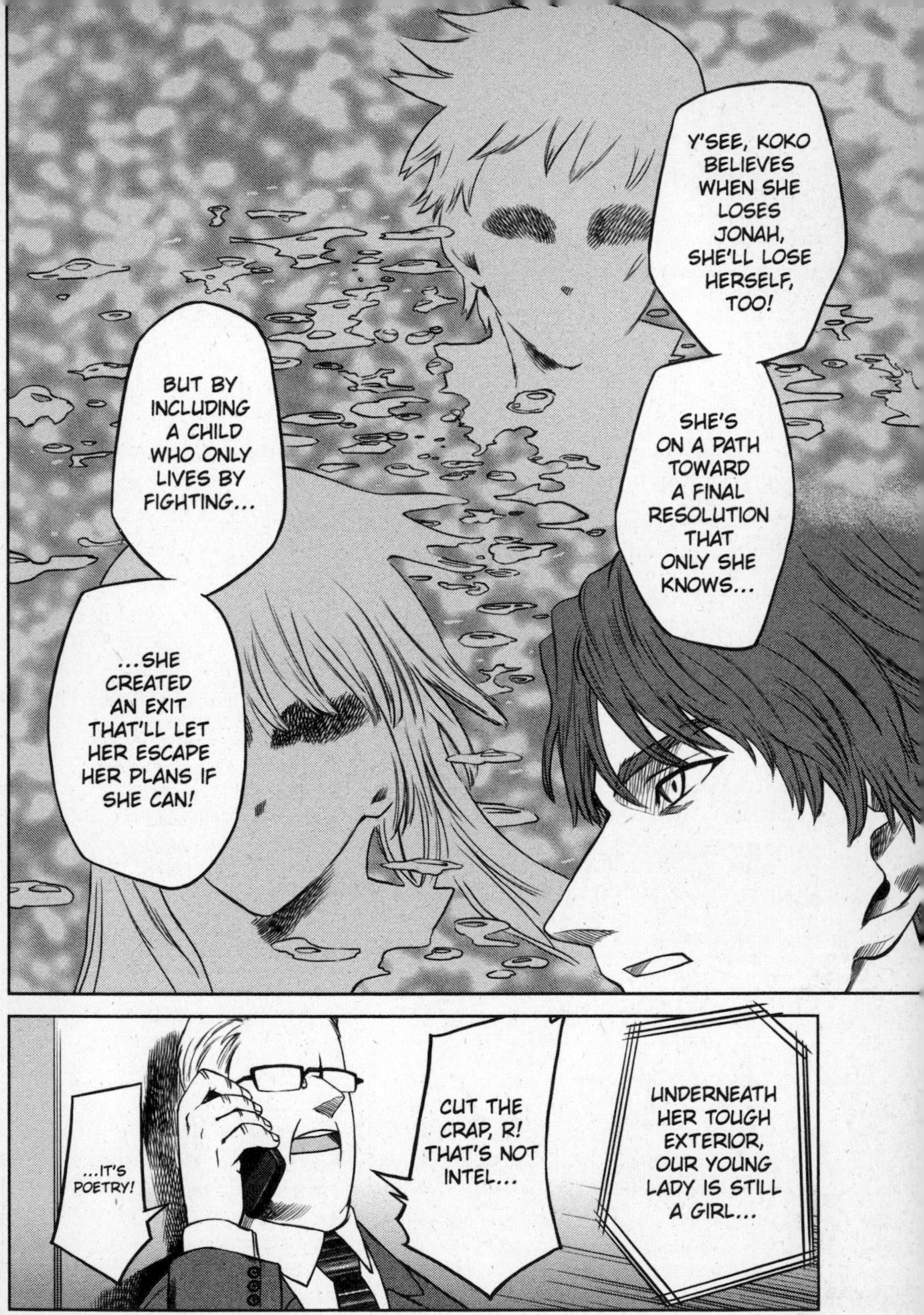
Y'SEE, KOKO BELIEVES WHEN SHE LOSES JONAH, SHE'LL LOSE HERSELF, TOO!
SHE'S ON A PATH TOWARD A FINAL RESOLUTION THAT ONLY SHE KNOWS...
BUT BY INCLUDING A CHILD WHO ONLY LIVES BY FIGHTING...
...SHE CREATED AN EXIT THAT'LL LET HER ESCAPE HER PLANS IF SHE CAN!
UNDERNEATH HER TOUGH EXTERIOR, OUR YOUNG LADY IS STILL A GIRL...
CUT THE CRAP, R! THAT'S NOT INTEL...
...IT'S POETRY!

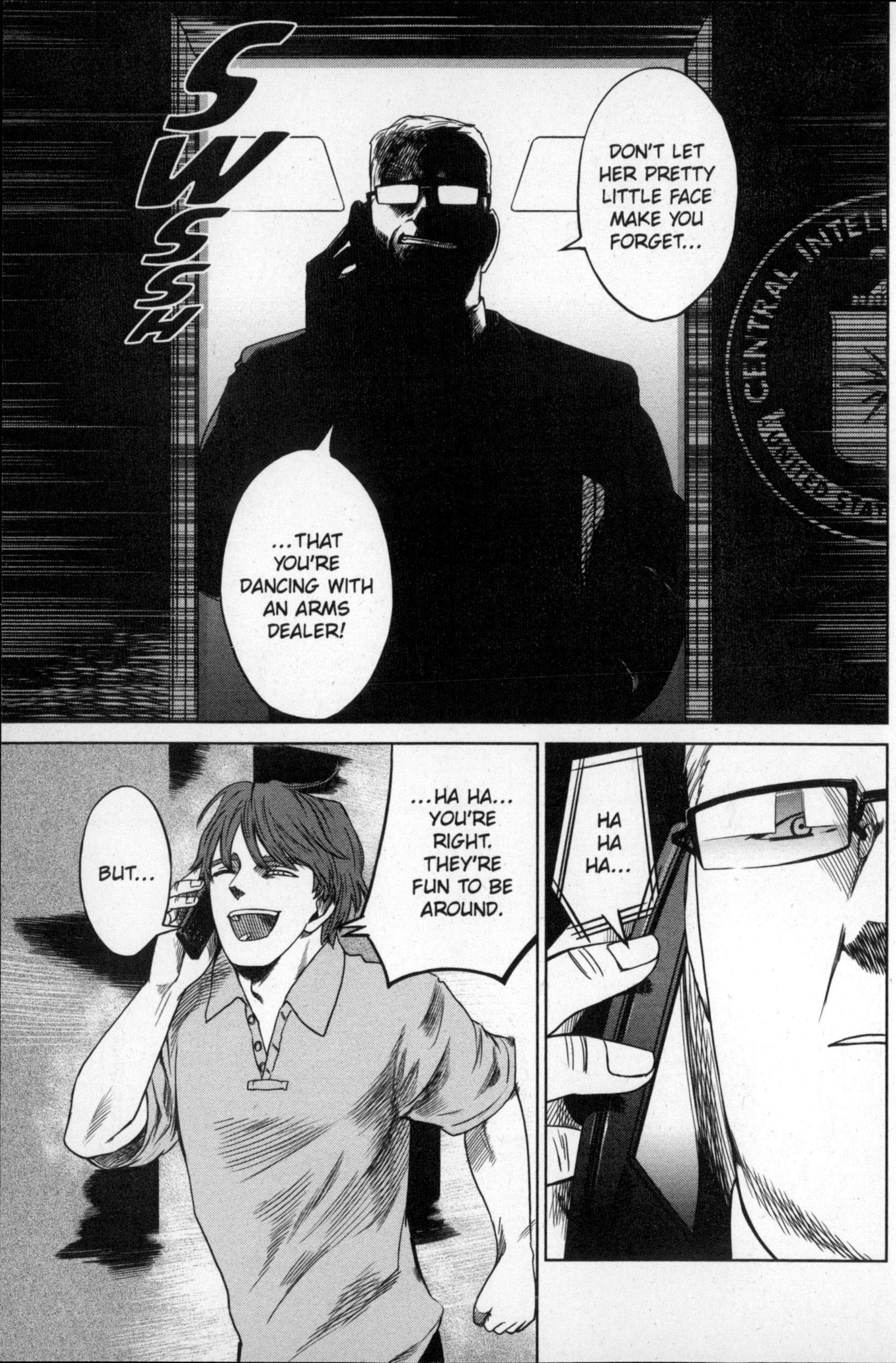
DON'T LET HER PRETTY LITTLE FACE MAKE YOU FORGET...
SWSSH
...THAT YOU'RE DANCING WITH AN ARMS DEALER!
HA HA HA...
...HA HA... YOU'RE RIGHT. THEY'RE FUN TO BE AROUND.
BUT...

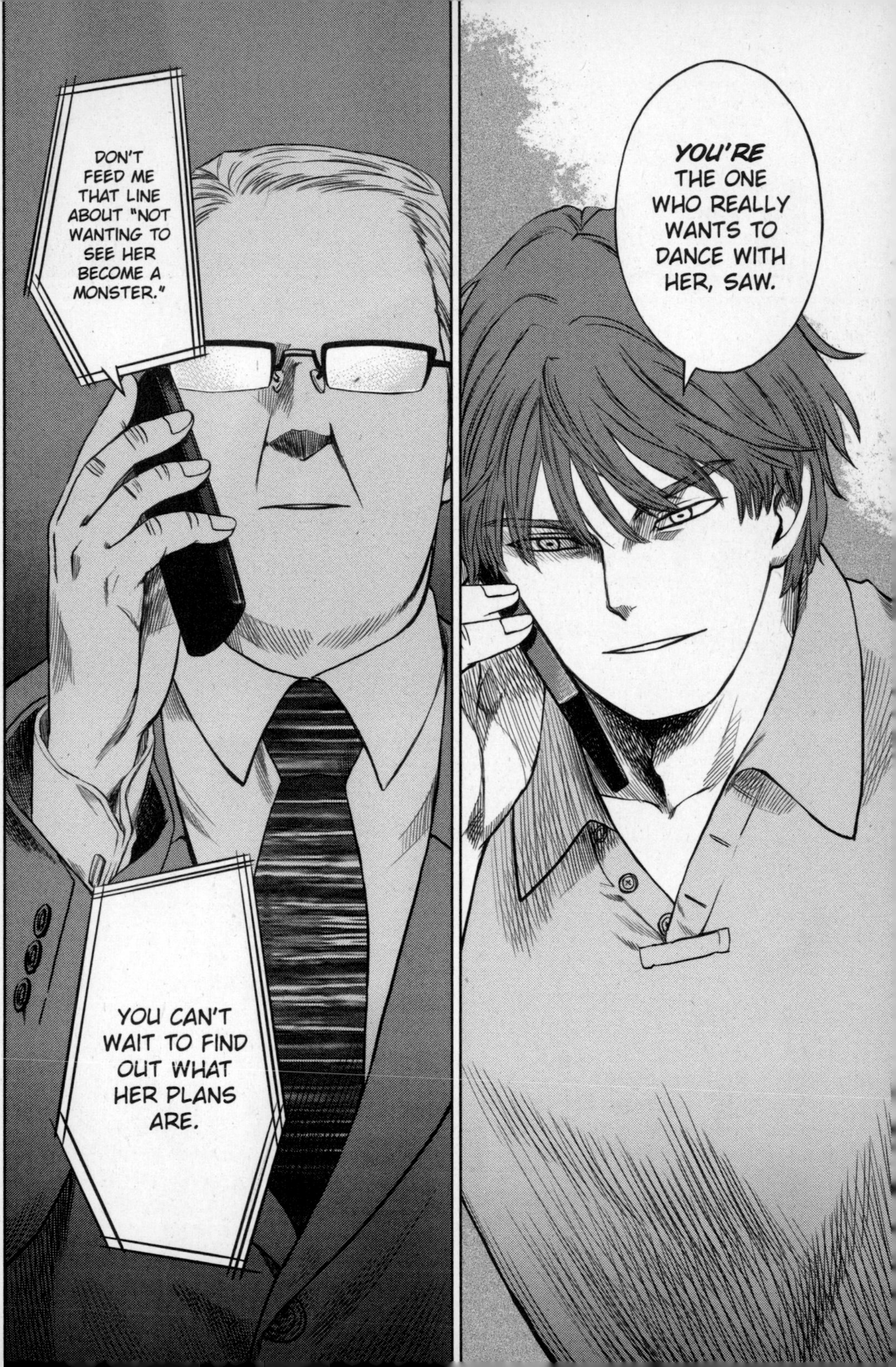
YOU'RE THE ONE WHO REALLY WANTS TO DANCE WITH HER, SAW.
DON'T FEED ME THAT LINE ABOUT "NOT WANTING TO SEE HER BECOME A MONSTER."
YOU CAN'T WAIT TO FIND OUT WHAT HER PLANS ARE.

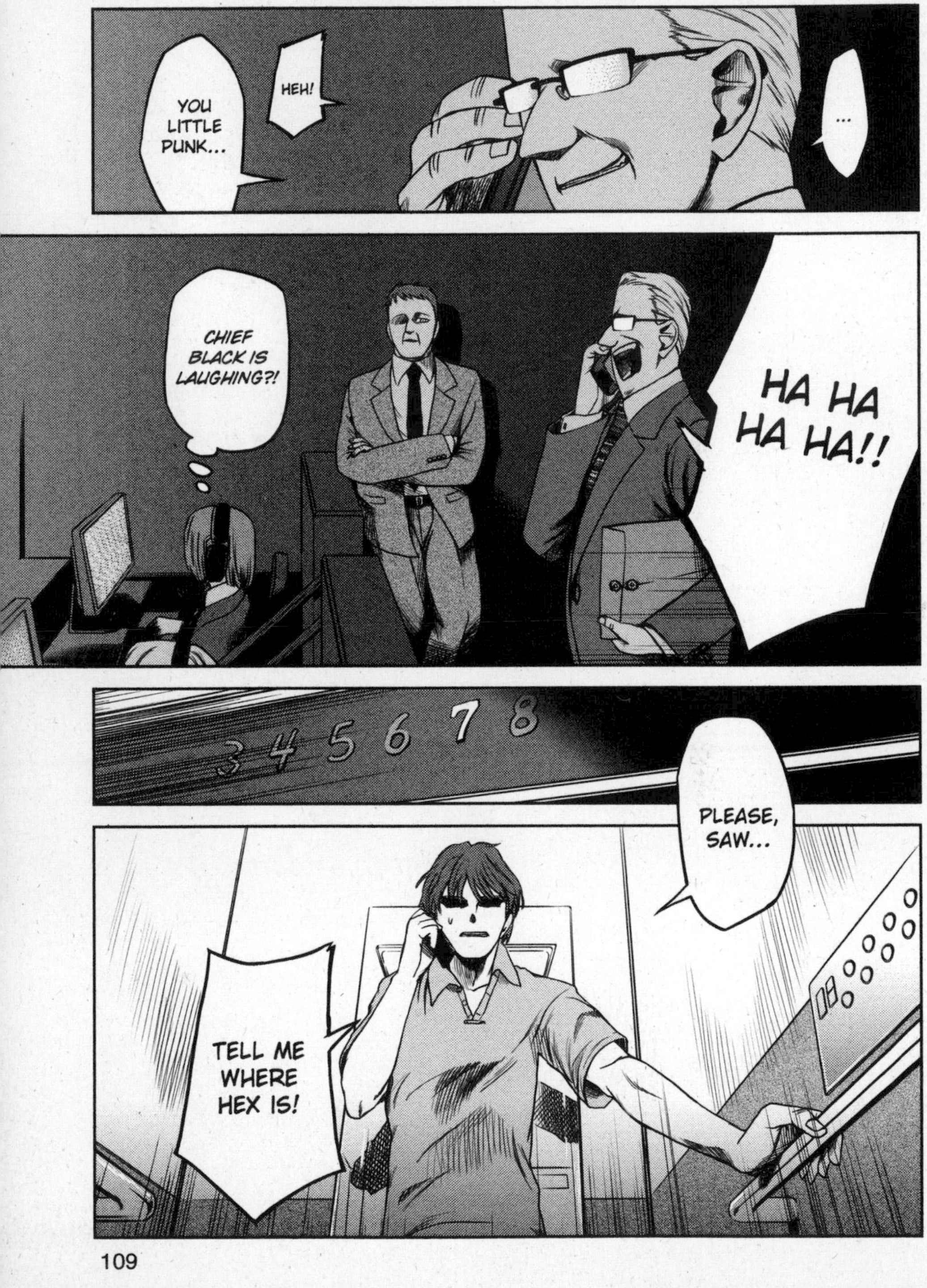
...
HEH!
YOU LITTLE PUNK...
HA HA HA HA!!
CHIEF BLACK IS LAUGHING?!
3 4 5 6 7 8
PLEASE, SAW...
TELL ME WHERE HEX IS!

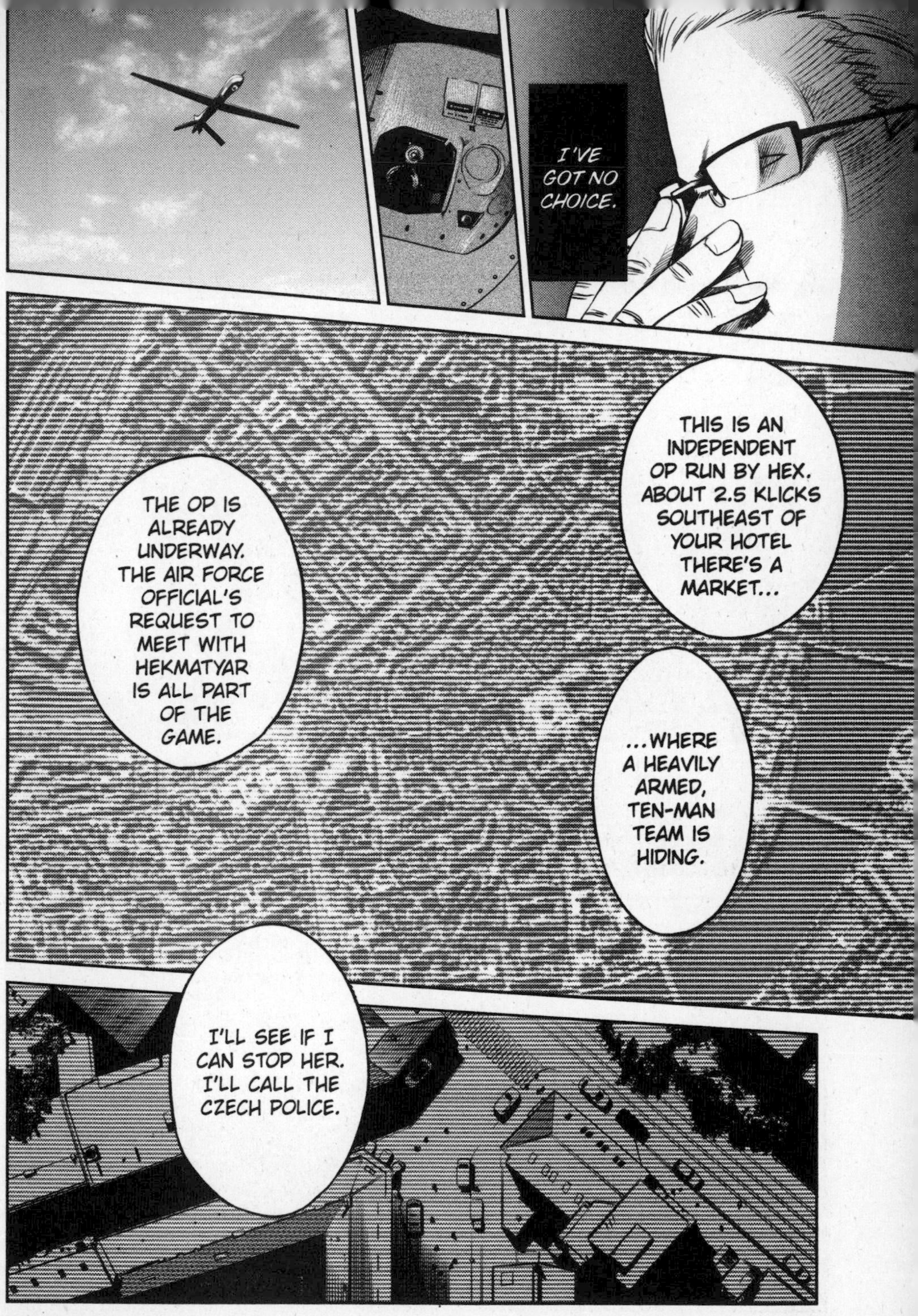
I'VE GOT NO CHOICE.
THIS IS AN INDEPENDENT OP RUN BY HEX. ABOUT 2.5 KLICKS SOUTHEAST OF YOUR HOTEL THERE'S A MARKET...
...WHERE A HEAVILY ARMED, TEN-MAN TEAM IS HIDING.
THE OP IS ALREADY UNDERWAY. THE AIR FORCE OFFICIAL'S REQUEST TO MEET WITH HEKMATYAR IS ALL PART OF THE GAME.
I'LL SEE IF I CAN STOP HER. I'LL CALL THE CZECH POLICE.

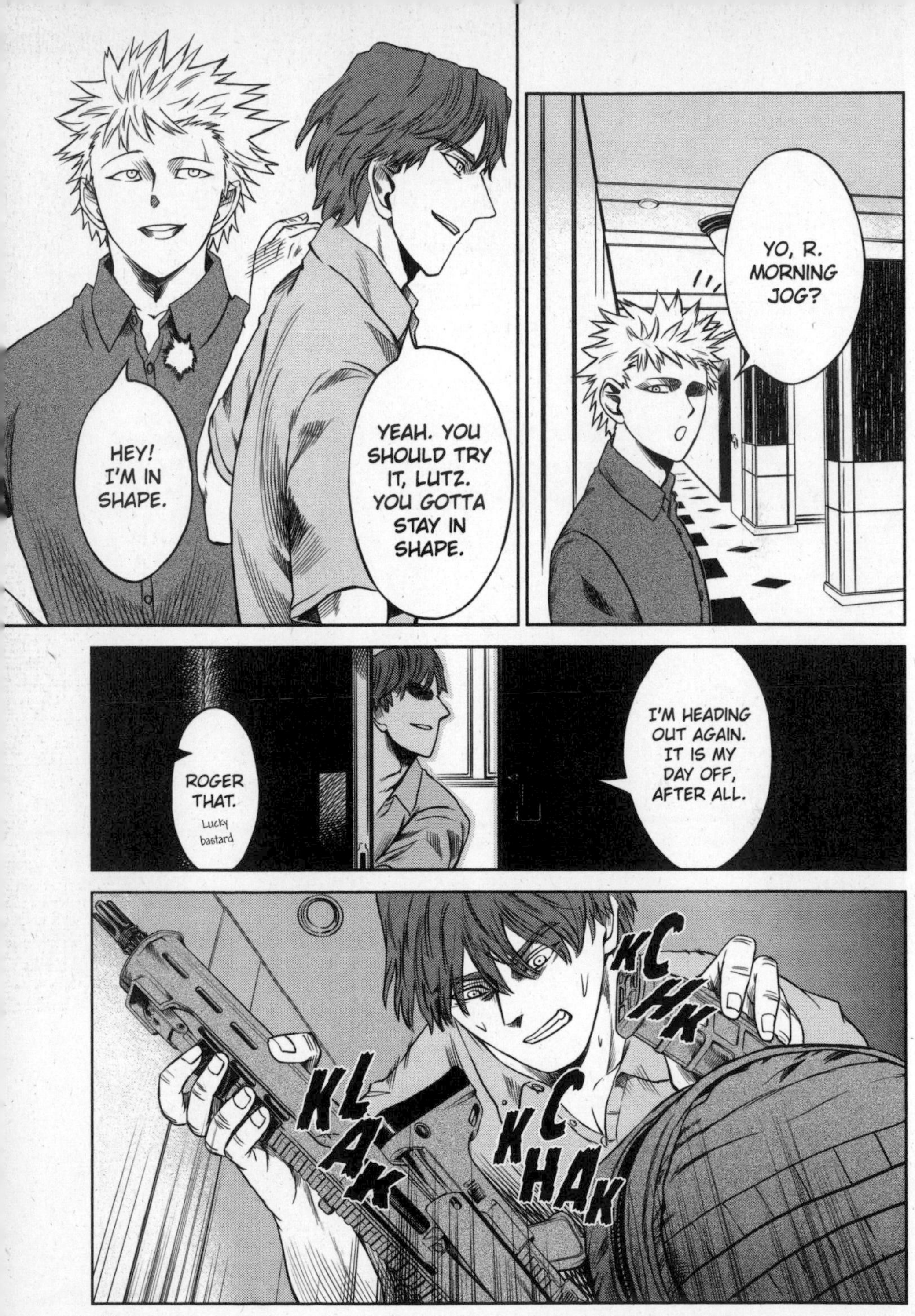
YO, R. MORNING JOG?
YEAH. YOU SHOULD TRY IT, LUTZ. YOU GOTTA STAY IN SHAPE.
HEY! I'M IN SHAPE.
I'M HEADING OUT AGAIN. IT IS MY DAY OFF, AFTER ALL.
ROGER THAT.
Lucky bastard
KCHK
KCHAK
KLAK

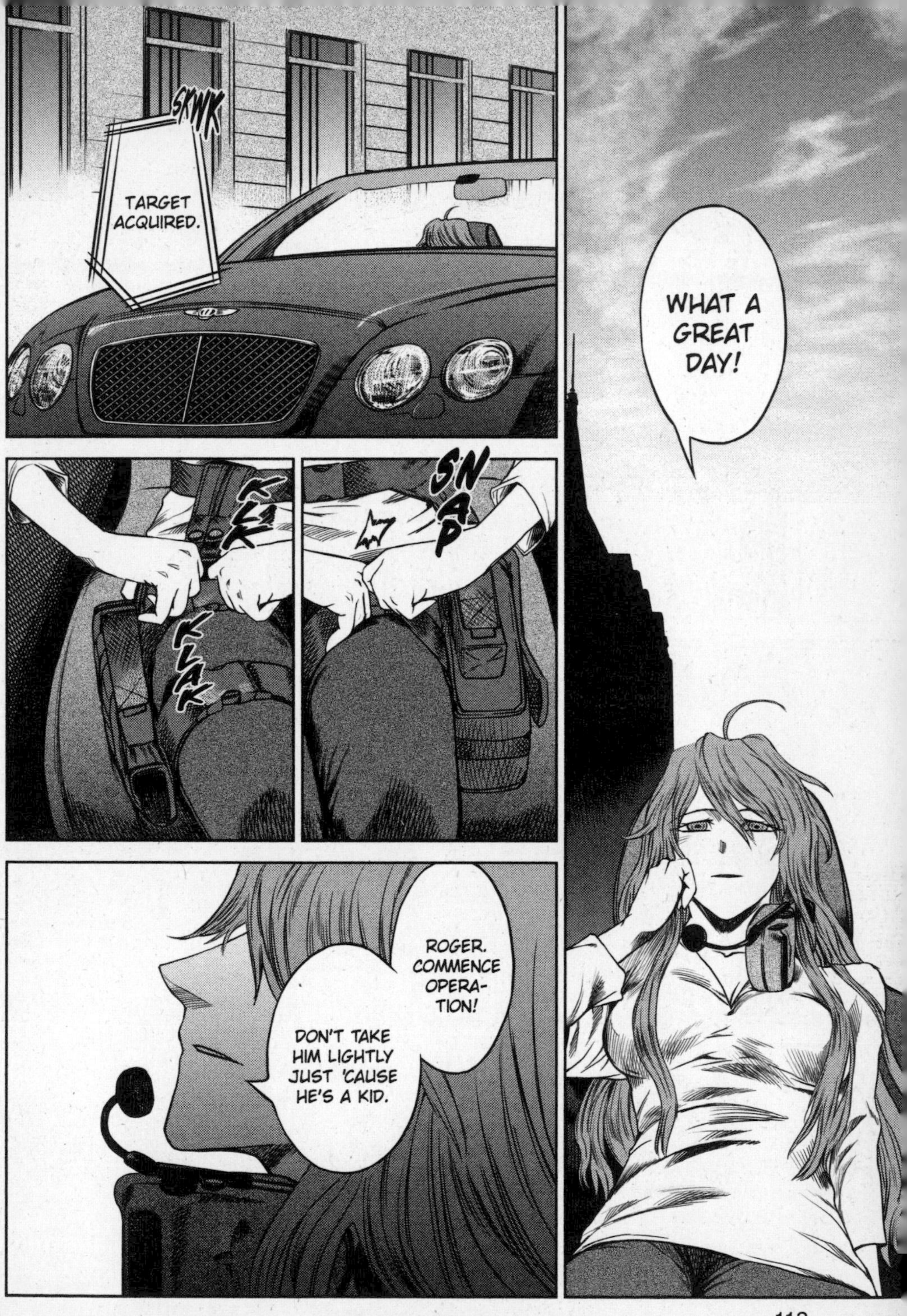
WHAT A GREAT DAY!
SKWK
TARGET ACQUIRED.
SNAP
KLAK
ROGER. COMMENCE OPERA-TION!
DON'T TAKE HIM LIGHTLY JUST 'CAUSE HE'S A KID.

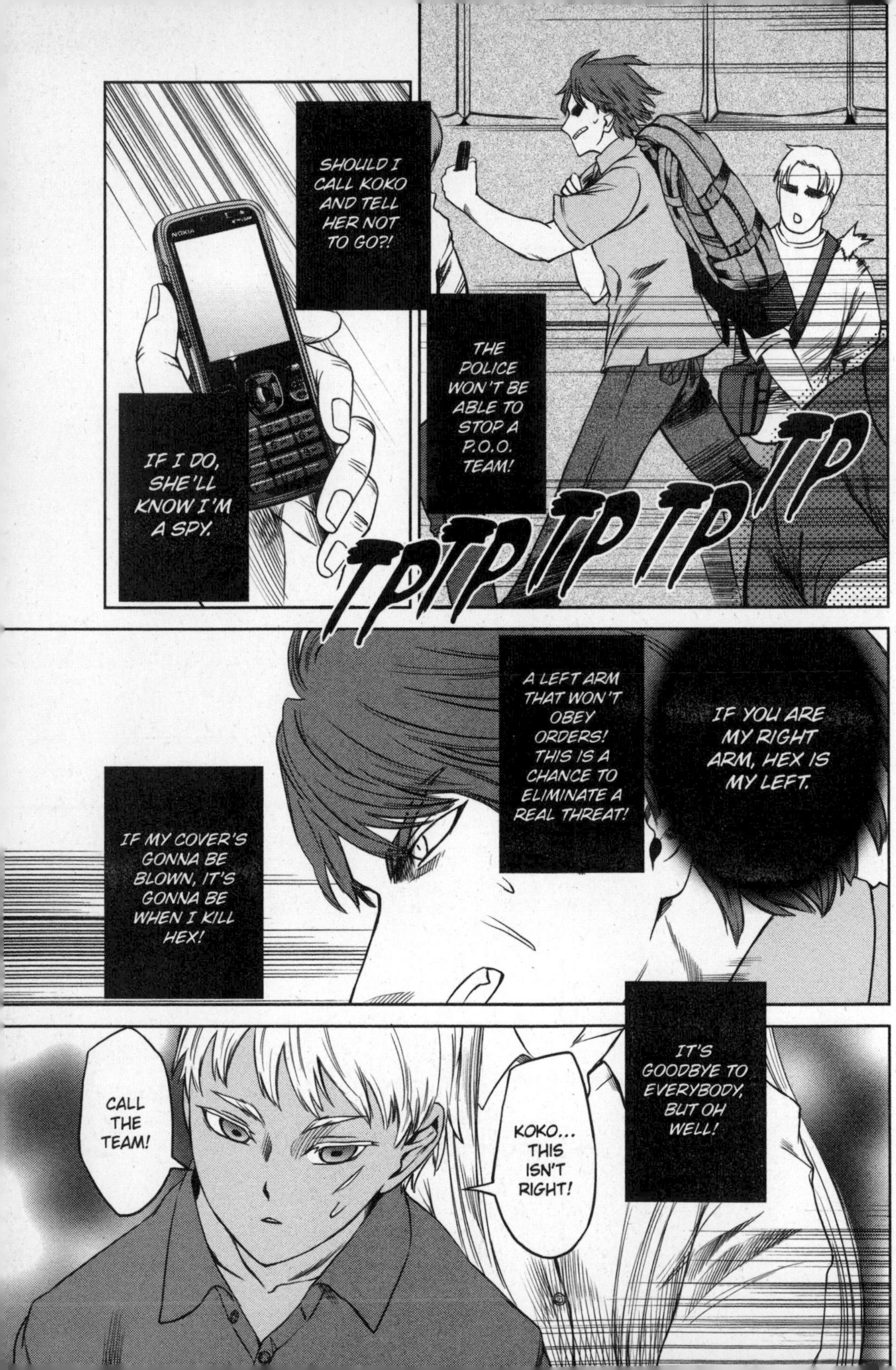
SHOULD I CALL KOKO AND TELL HER NOT TO GO?!
THE POLICE WON'T BE ABLE TO STOP A P.O.O. TEAM!
TP TP TP TP TP TP
IF I DO, SHE'LL KNOW I'M A SPY.
IF YOU ARE MY RIGHT ARM, HEX IS MY LEFT.
A LEFT ARM THAT WON'T OBEY ORDERS! THIS IS A CHANCE TO ELIMINATE A REAL THREAT!
IF MY COVER'S GONNA BE BLOWN, IT'S GONNA BE WHEN I KILL HEX!
IT'S GOODBYE TO EVERYBODY, BUT OH WELL!
KOKO... THIS ISN'T RIGHT!
CALL THE TEAM!

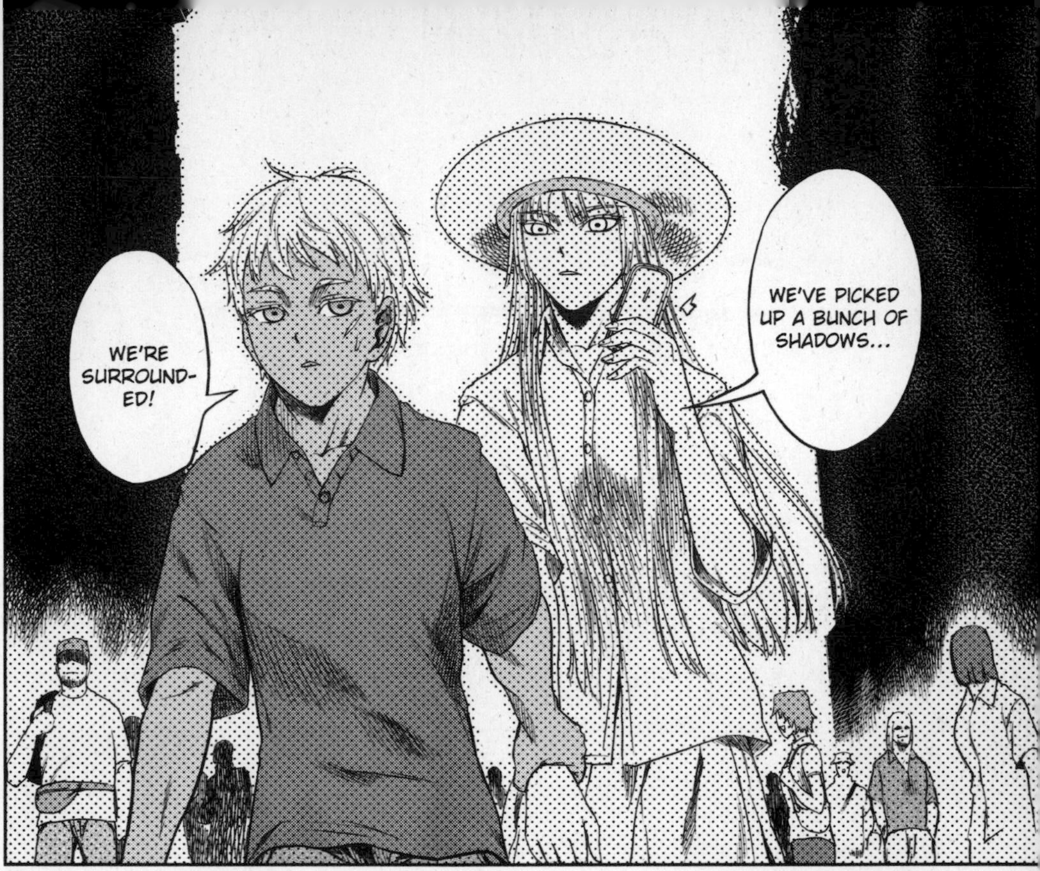
WE'VE PICKED UP A BUNCH OF SHADOWS...
WE'RE SURROUNDED!
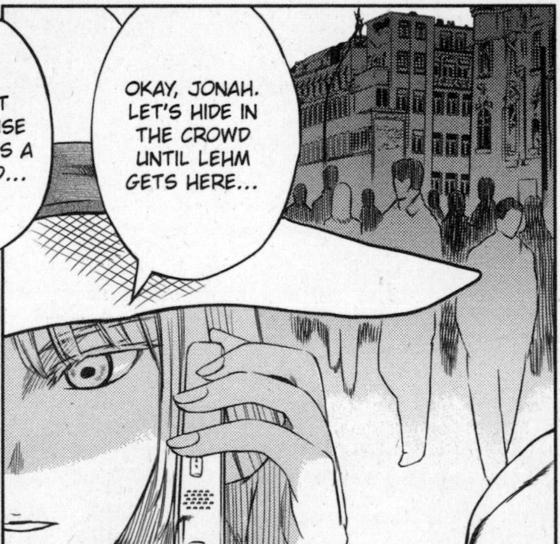
OKAY, JONAH. LET'S HIDE IN THE CROWD UNTIL LEHM GETS HERE...
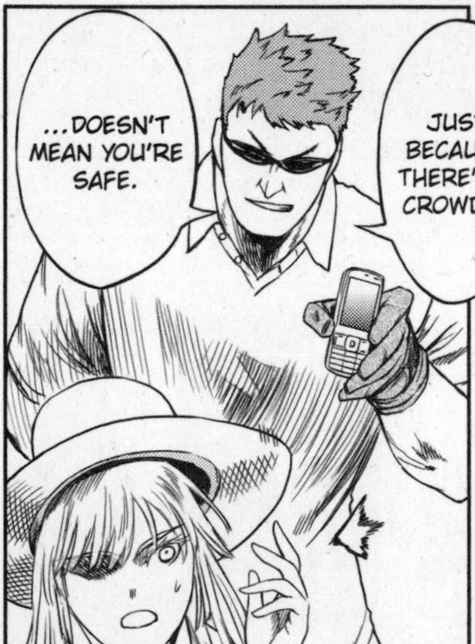
JUST BECAUSE THERE'S A CROWD...
...DOESN'T MEAN YOU'RE SAFE.

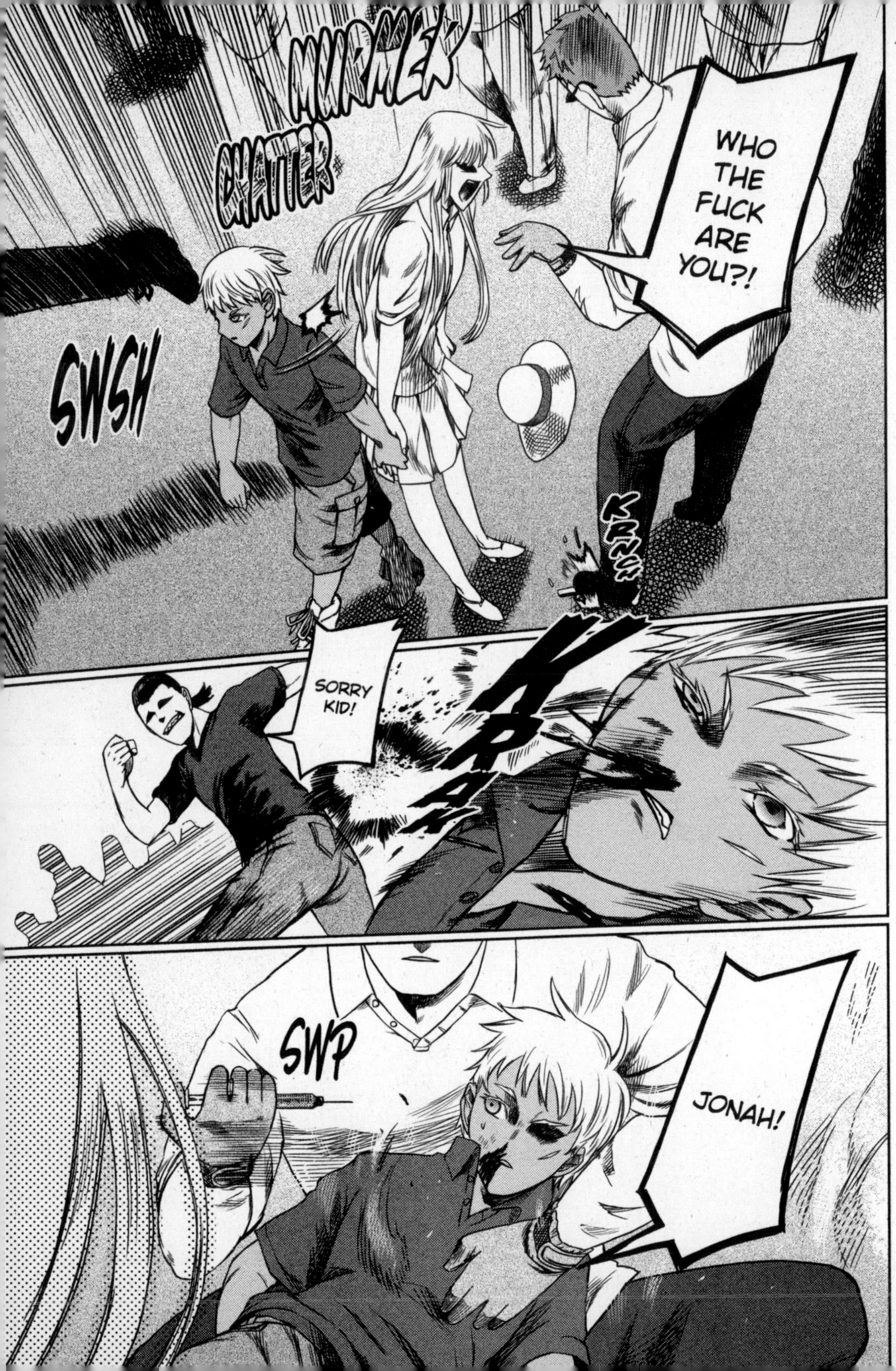
WHO THE FUCK ARE YOU?!
CHATTER
SWSH
KRNCH
KRAK
SORRY KID!
JONAH!
SWP

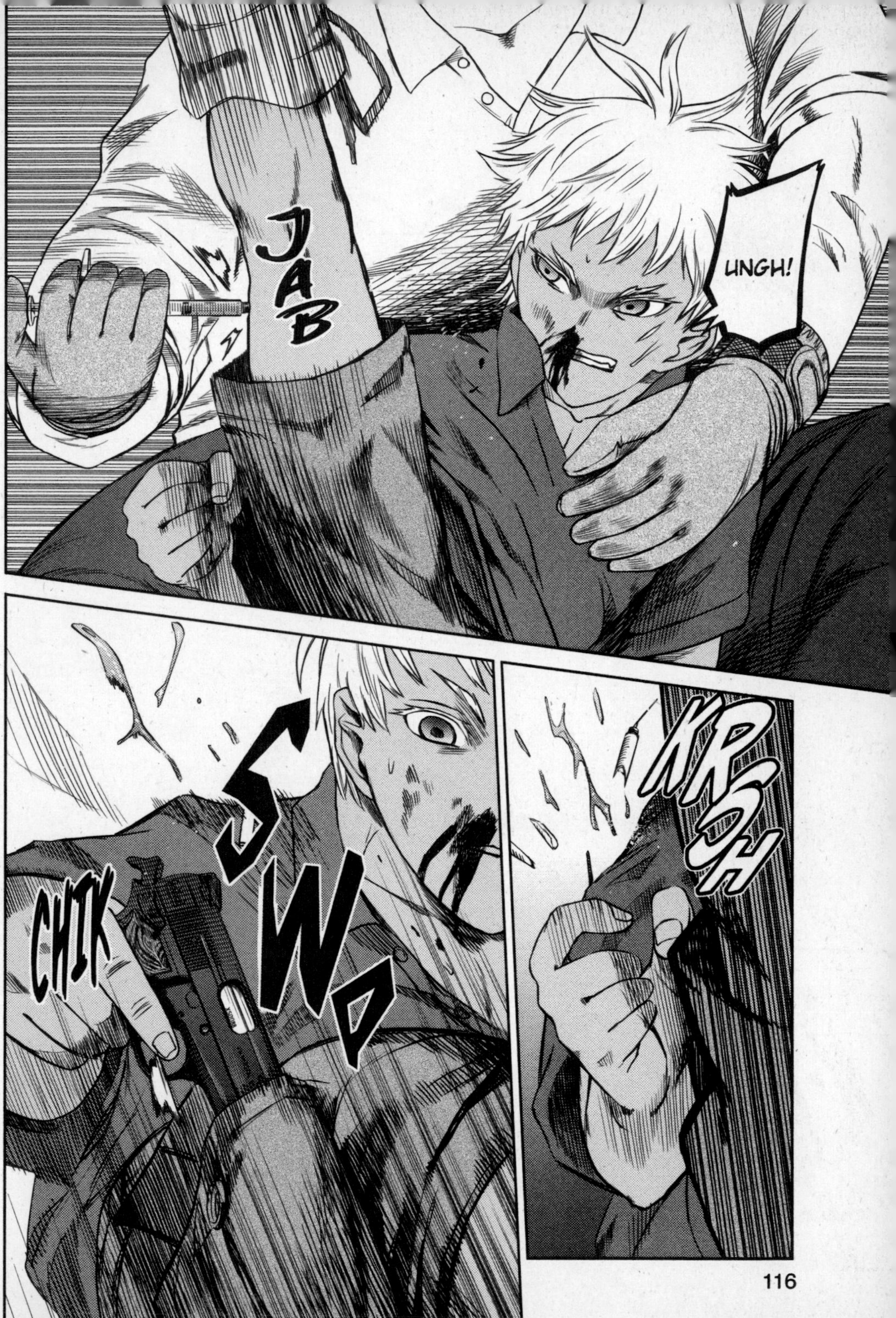
JAB
UNGH!
KRSH
SWD
CHIK

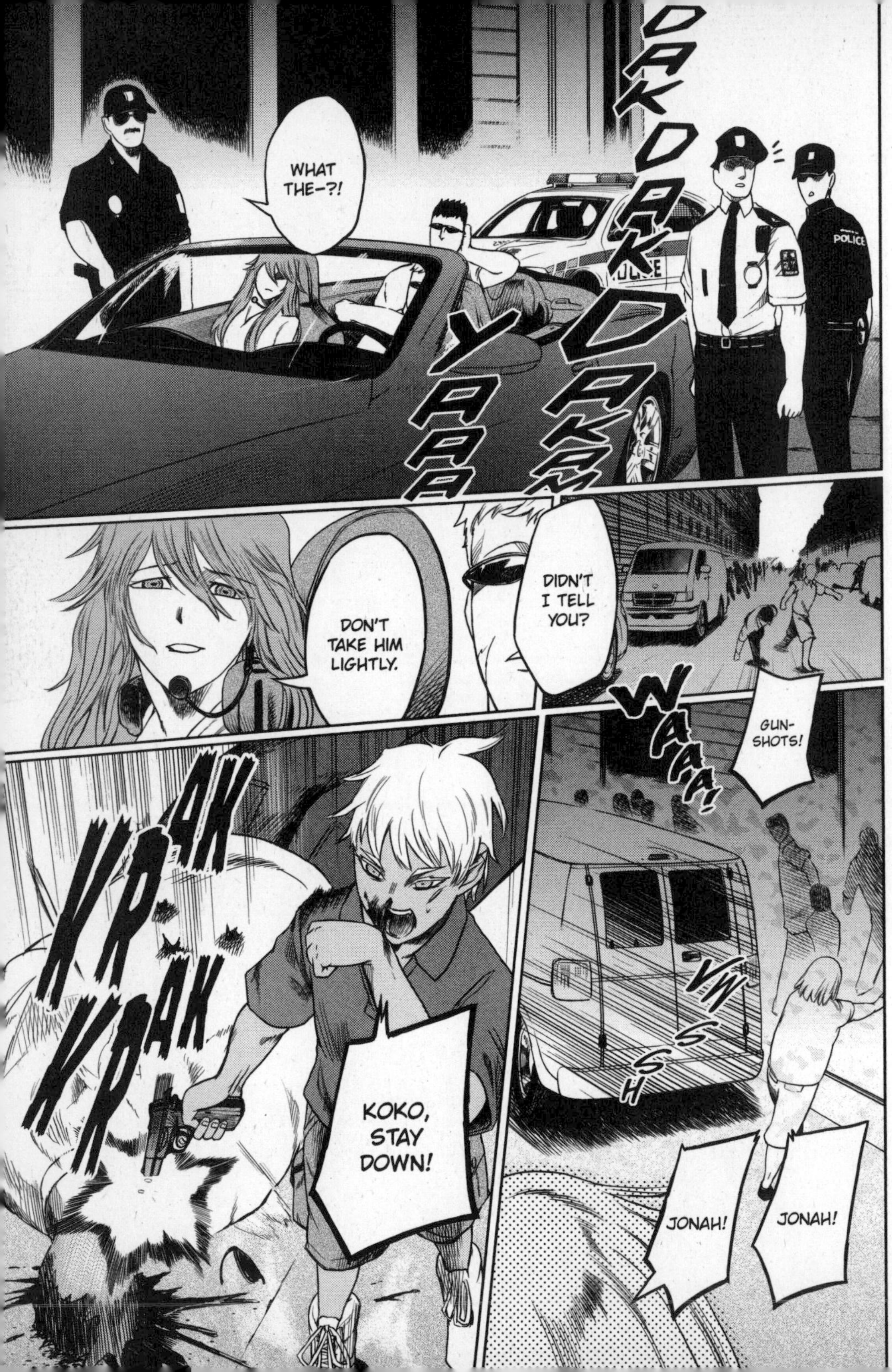
DAKDAKDAKM
YAAAA
WHAT THE–?!
GUN-SHOTS!
WAAAA!
DIDN'T I TELL YOU?
DON'T TAKE HIM LIGHTLY.
VWSSH
JONAH!
JONAH!
KRAK KRAK KRAK
KOKO, STAY DOWN!

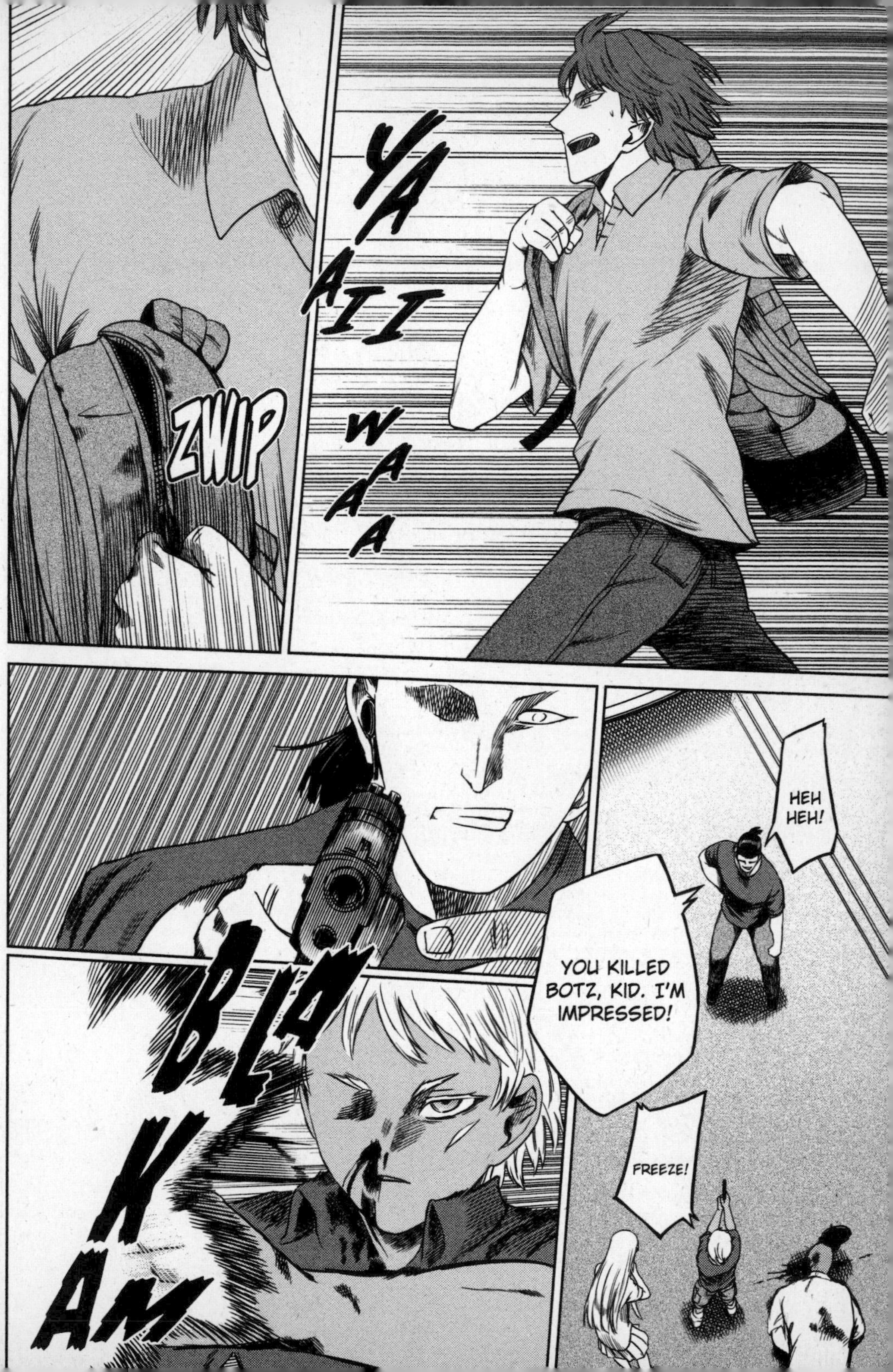

YAAII
WAAAA
ZWIP
HEH HEH!
YOU KILLED BOTZ, KID. I'M IMPRESSED!
FREEZE!
BLAKAM

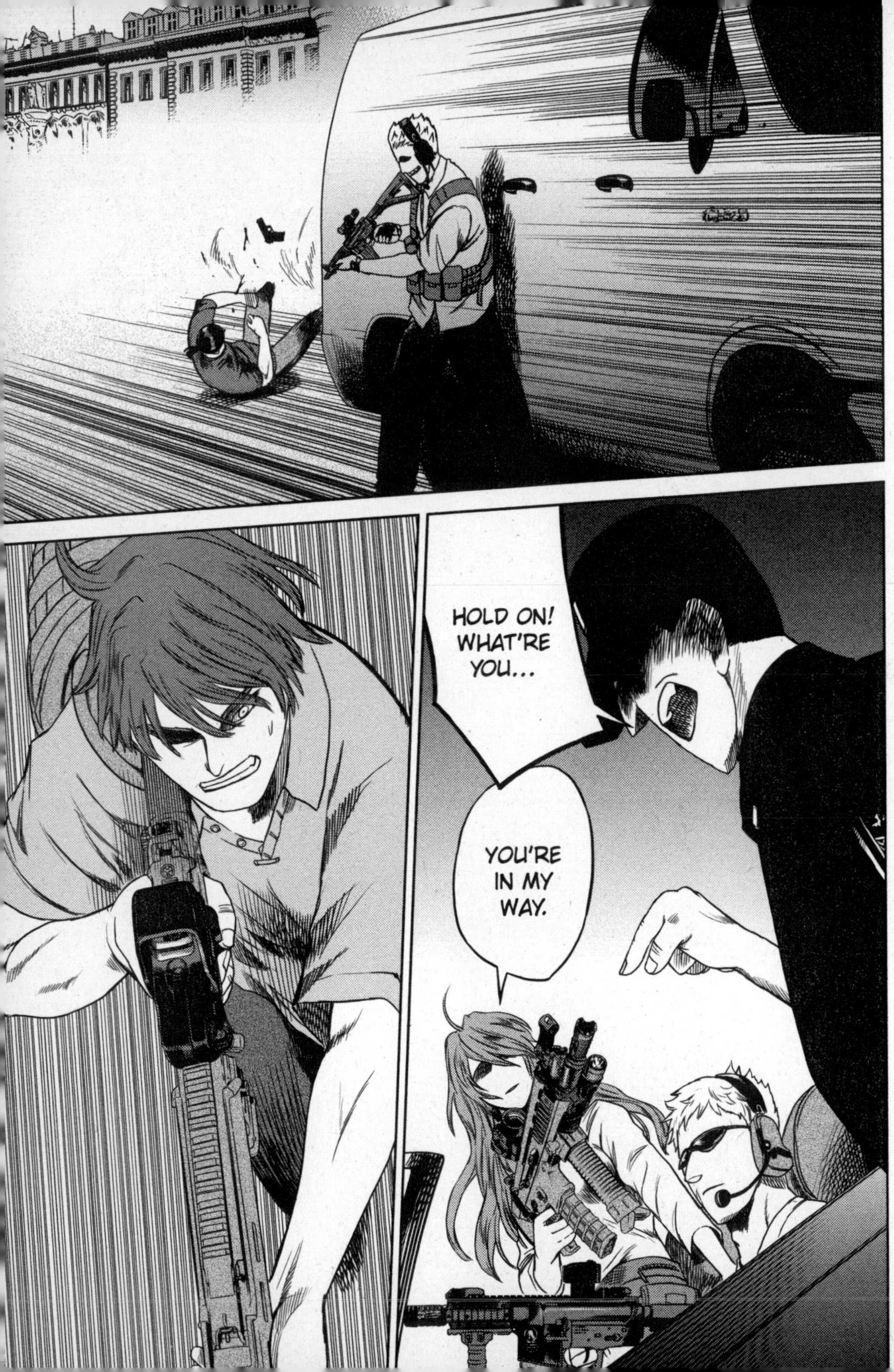
HOLD ON! WHAT'RE YOU...
YOU'RE IN MY WAY.

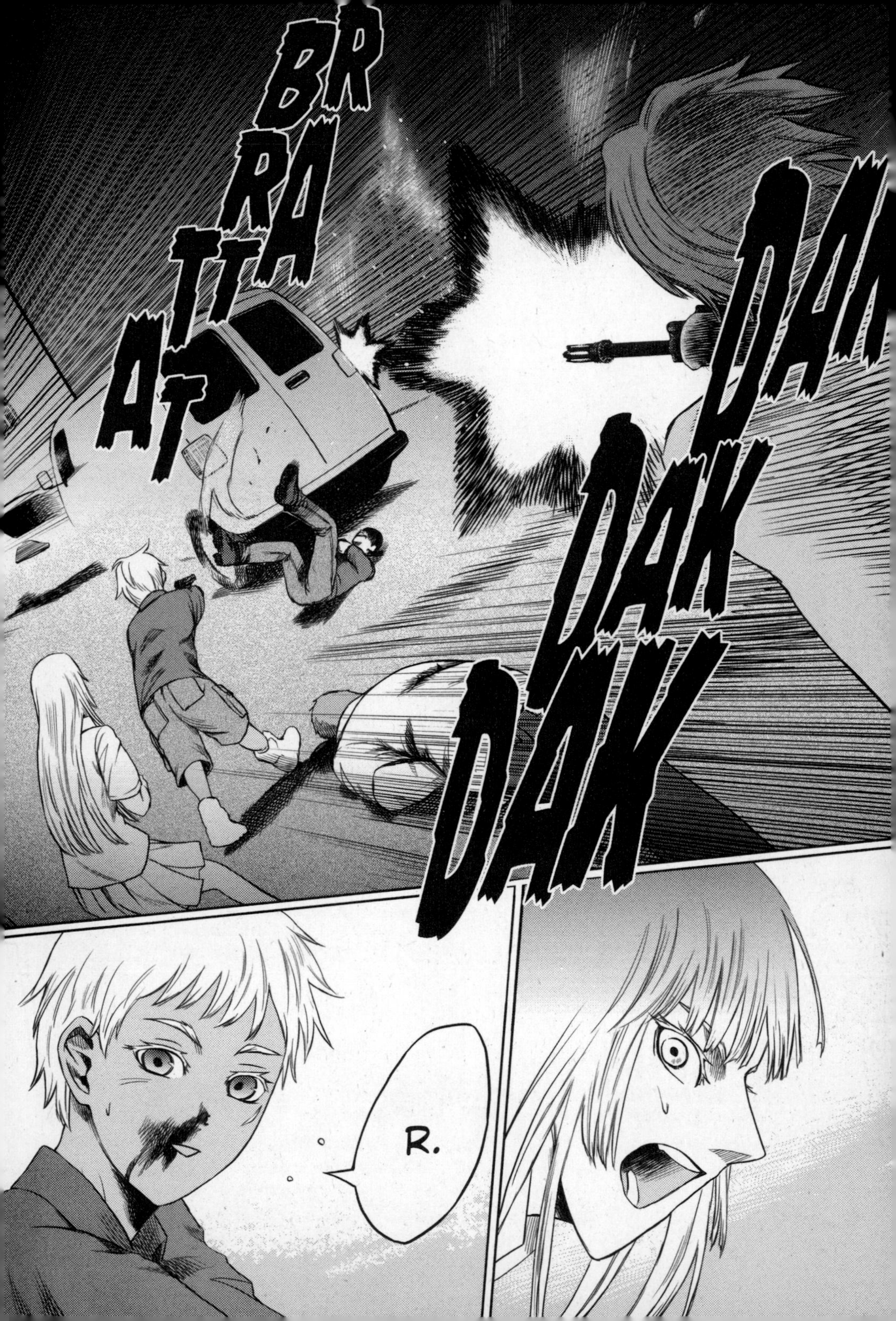
DAK
DAK
DAK
BRRATTATT
R.

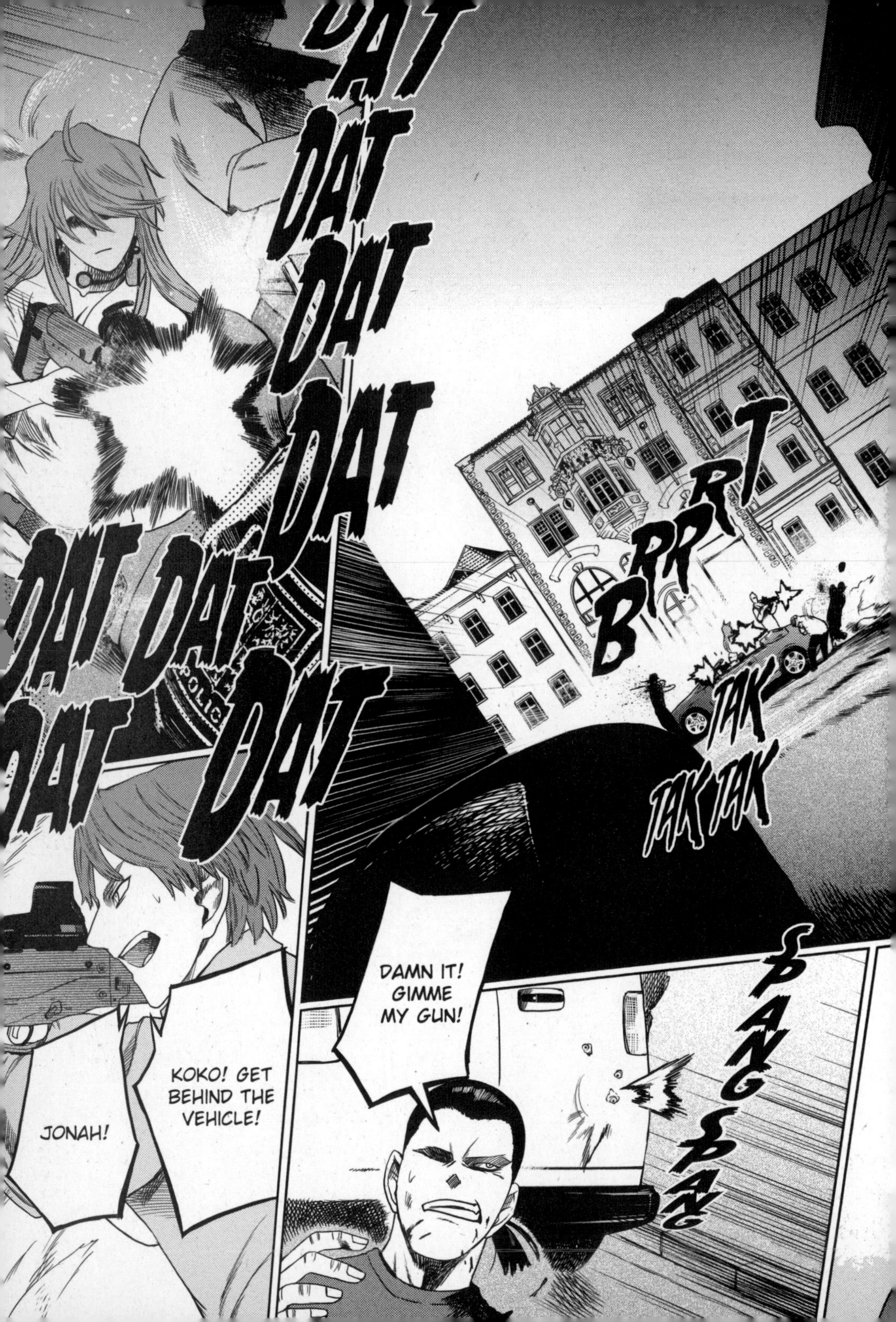
BRRRT
TAK TAK TAK
DAT DAT DAT DAT DAT DAT
DAT DAT DAT
DAT
SPANG SPANG
DAMN IT! GIMME MY GUN!
KOKO! GET BEHIND THE VEHICLE!
JONAH!

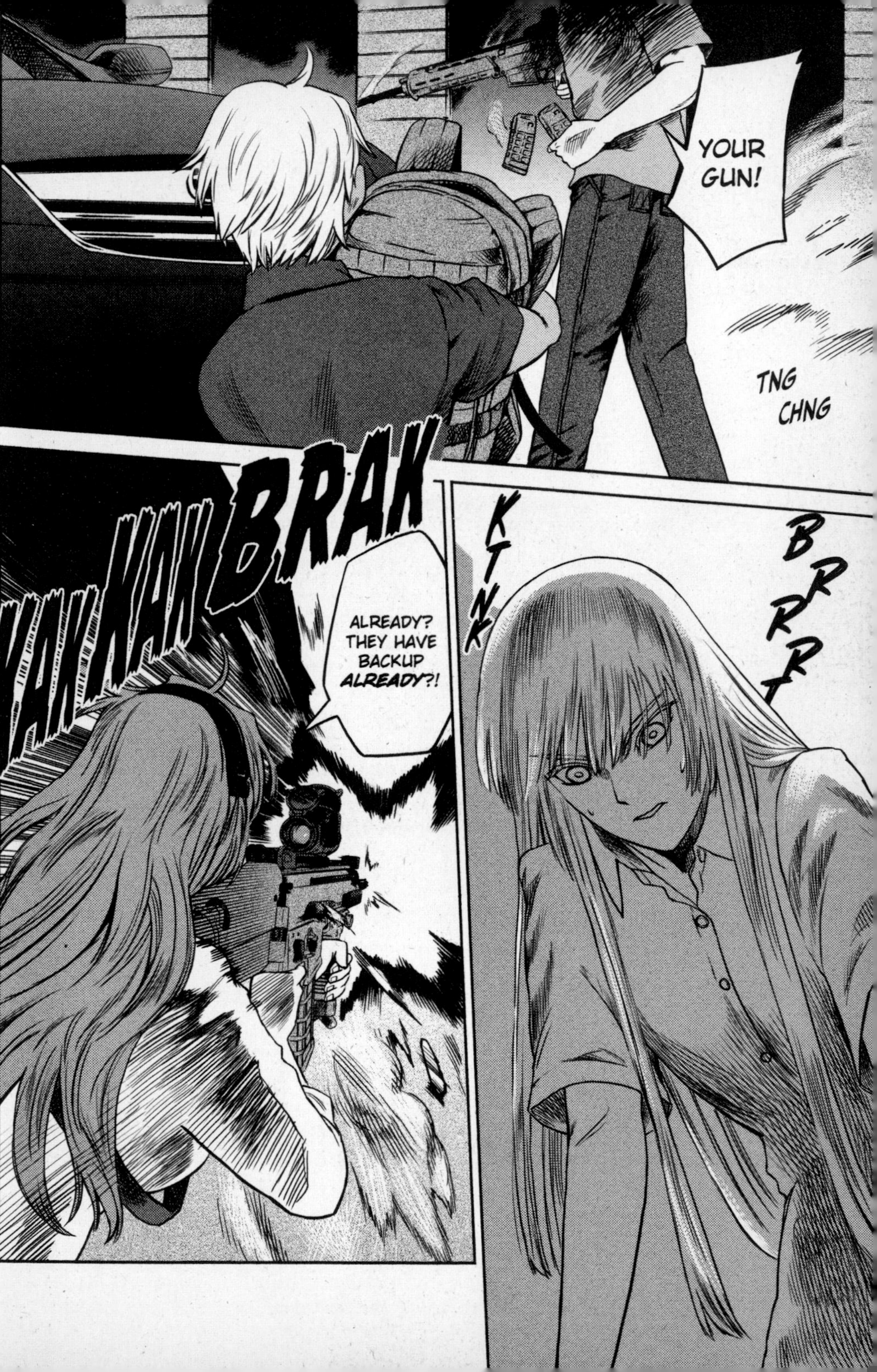
YOUR GUN!
TNG CHNG
KTNK
BRRRT
BRAK
WAK WAK WAK
ALREADY? THEY HAVE BACKUP ALREADY?!

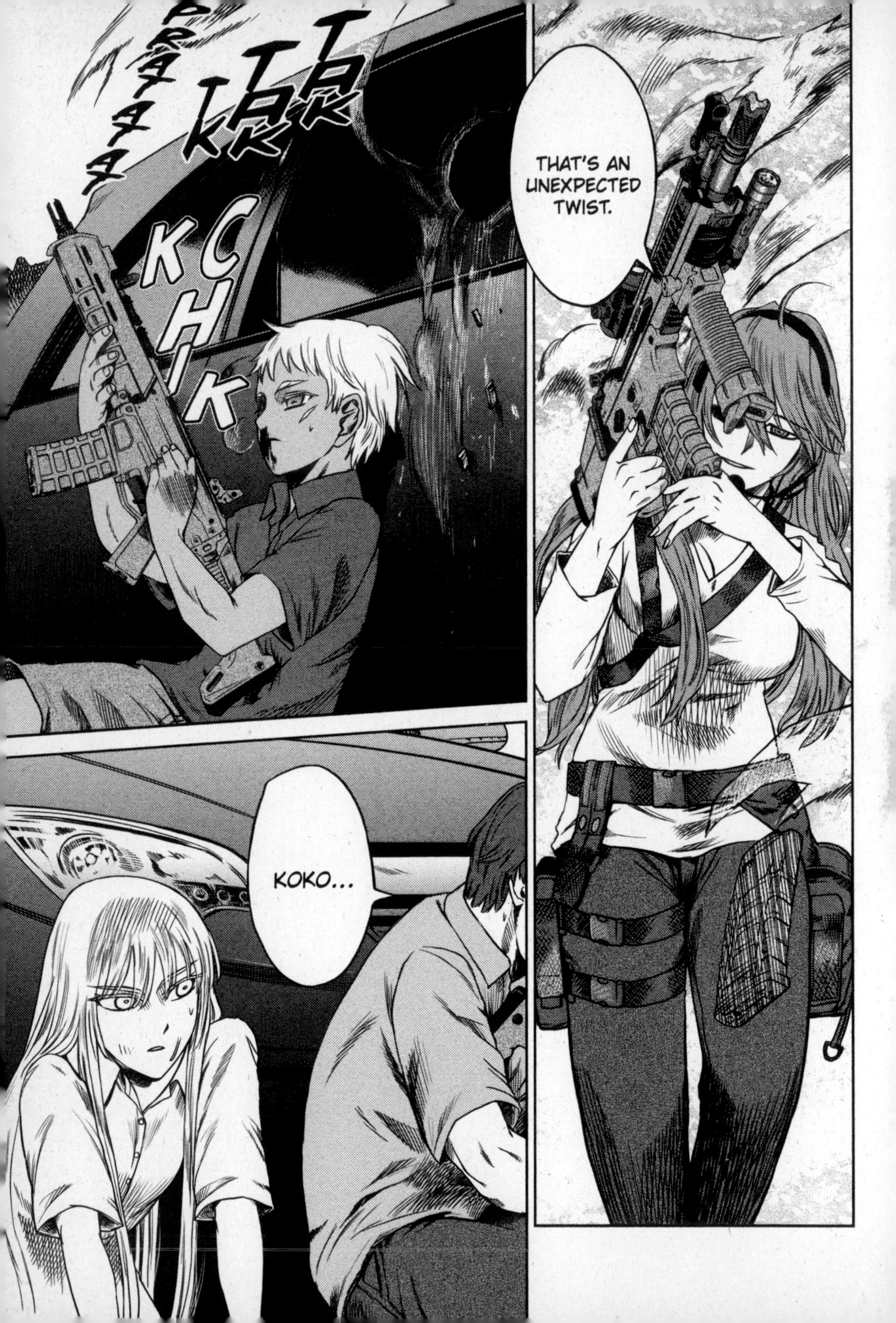
THAT'S AN UNEXPECTED TWIST.
TRR
TRR
TK
PRATATATA
KCHIK
KOKO...

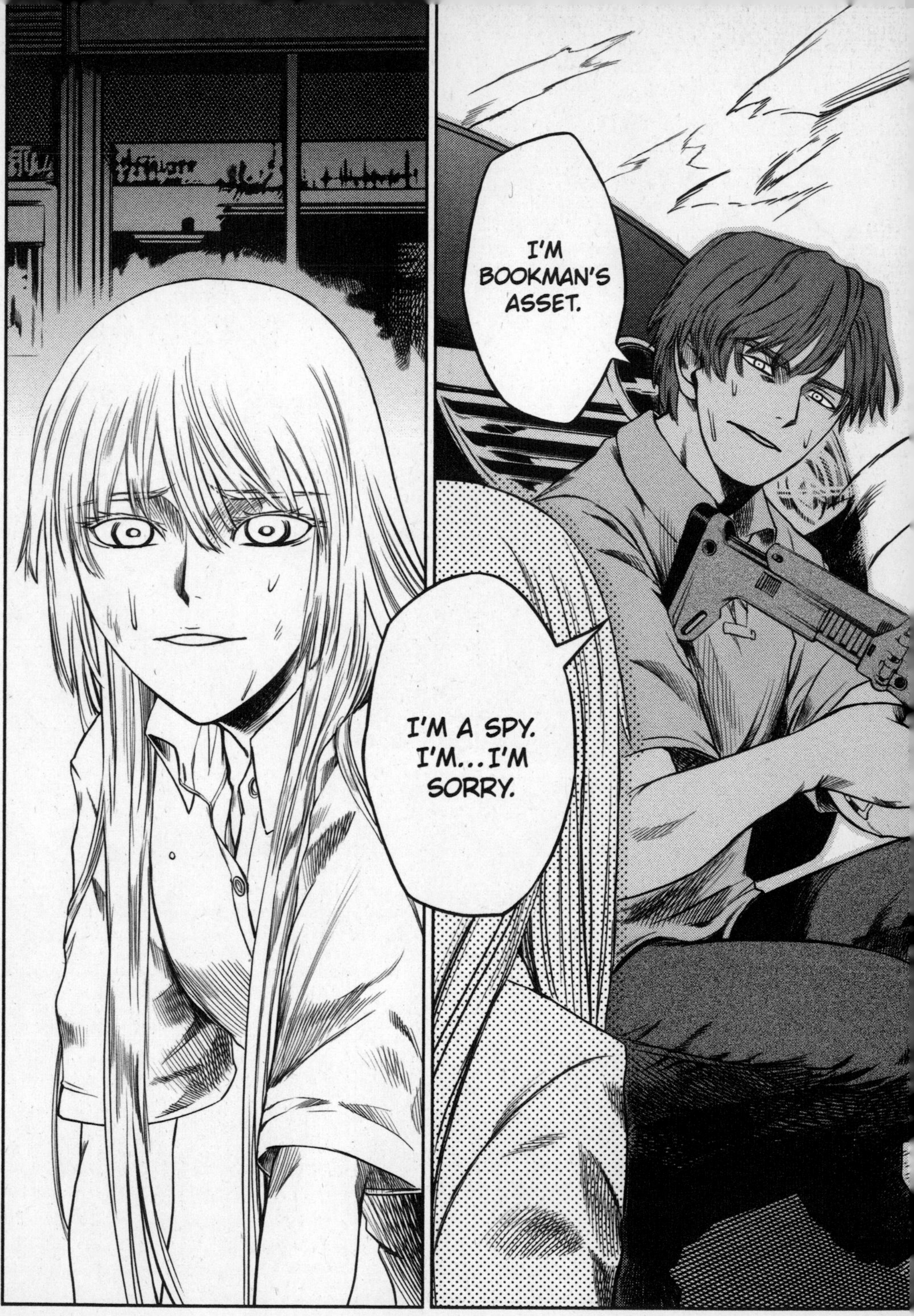
I'M BOOKMAN'S ASSET.
I'M A SPY. I'M...I'M SORRY.

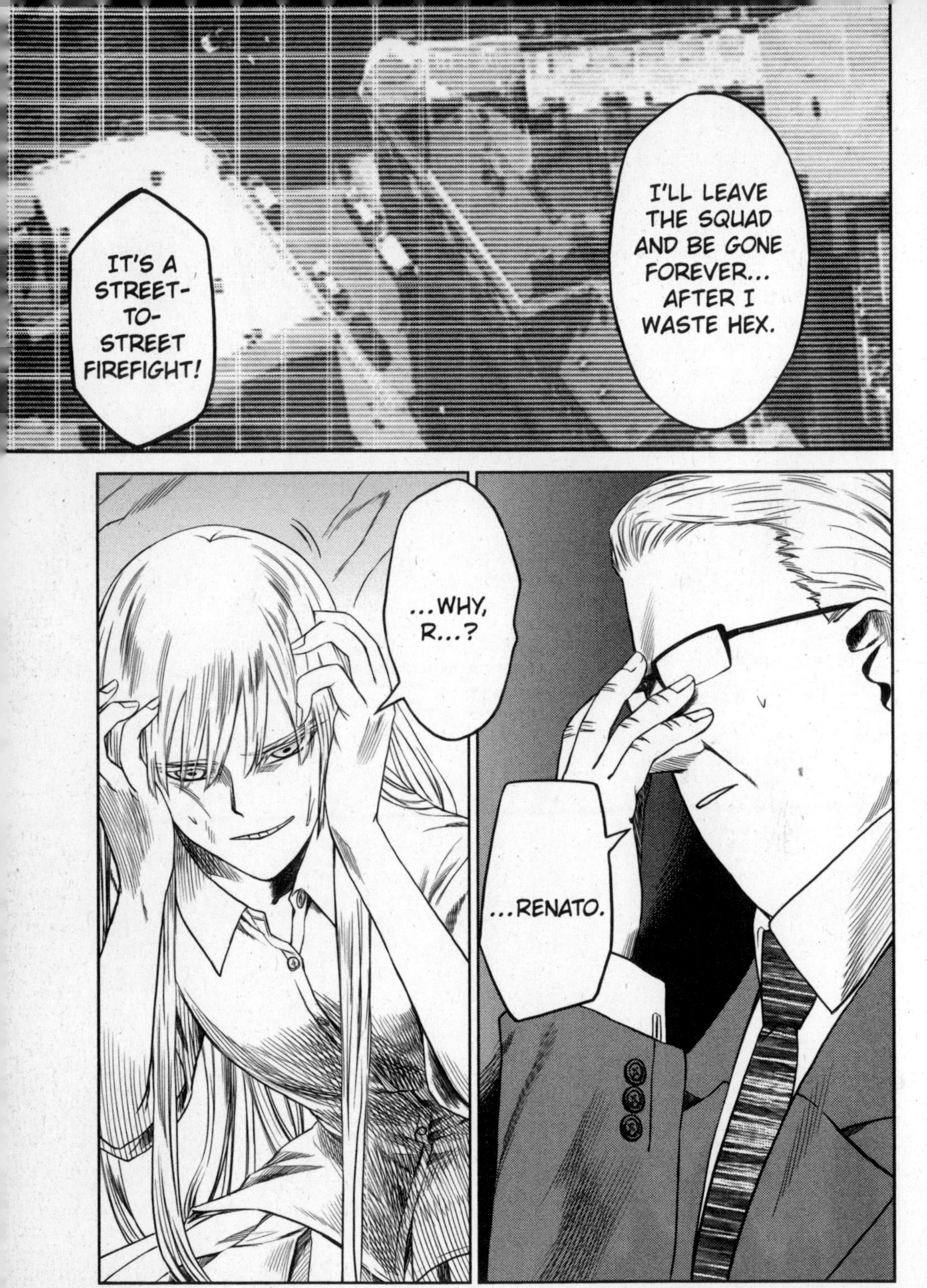
I'LL LEAVE THE SQUAD AND BE GONE FOREVER... AFTER I WASTE HEX.
IT'S A STREET-TO-STREET FIREFIGHT!
...RENATO.
...WHY, R...?

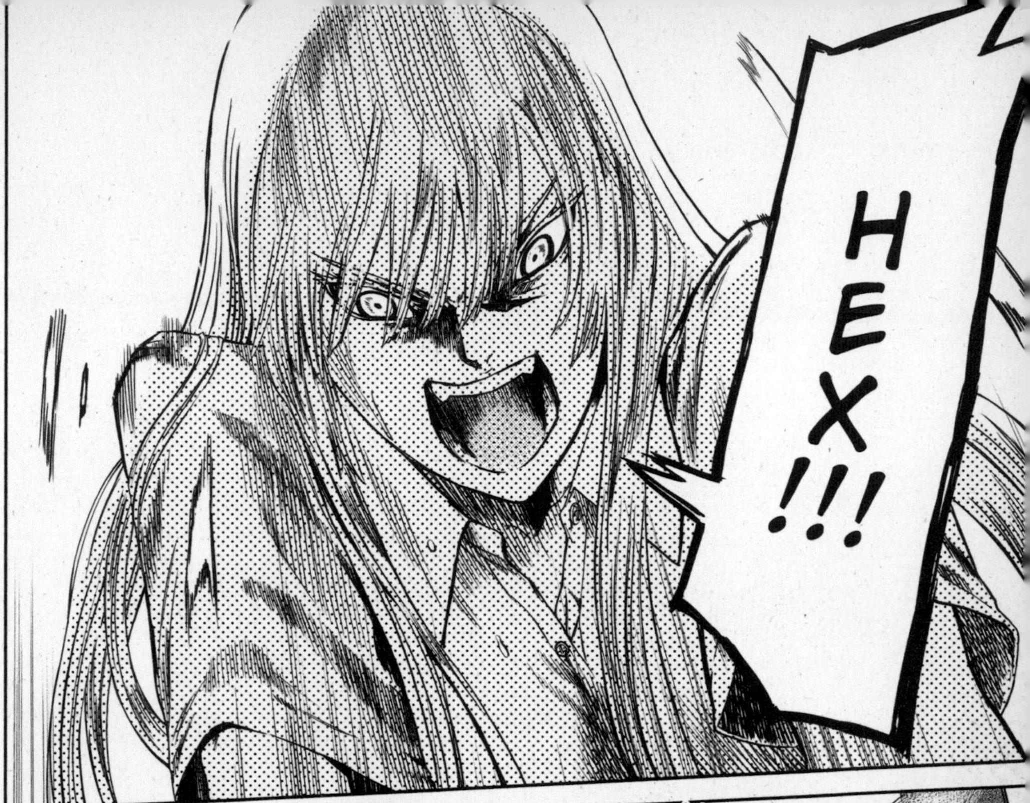
HEX!!!
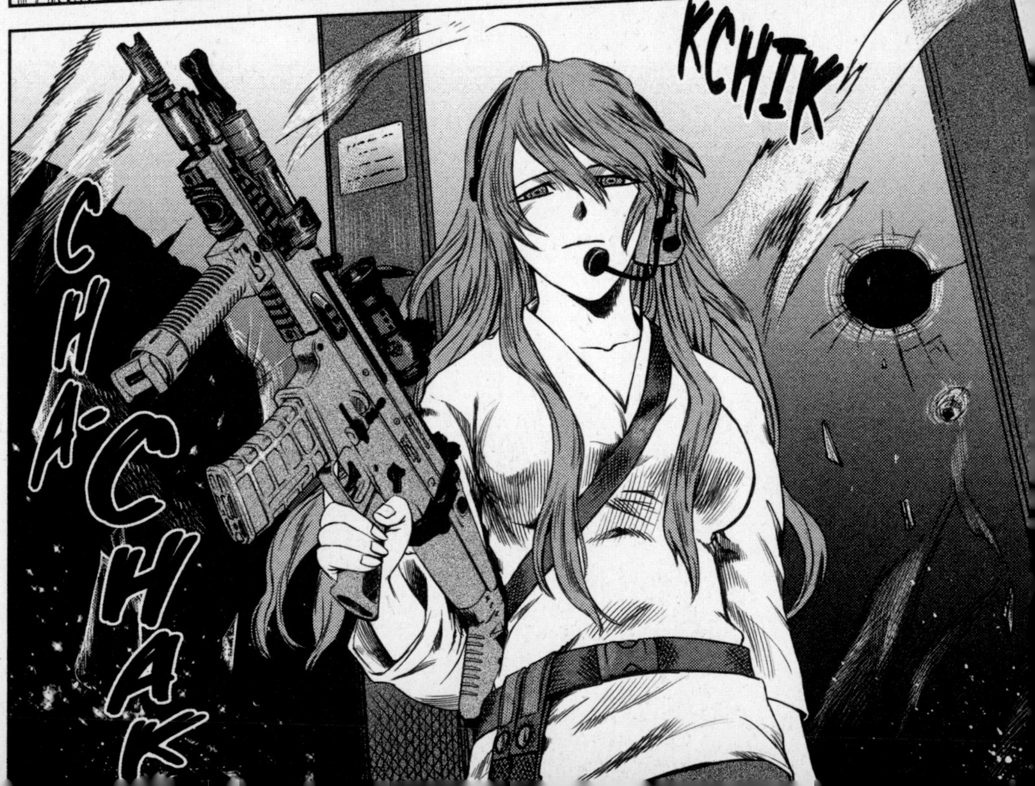
KCHIK
CHA-CHAK

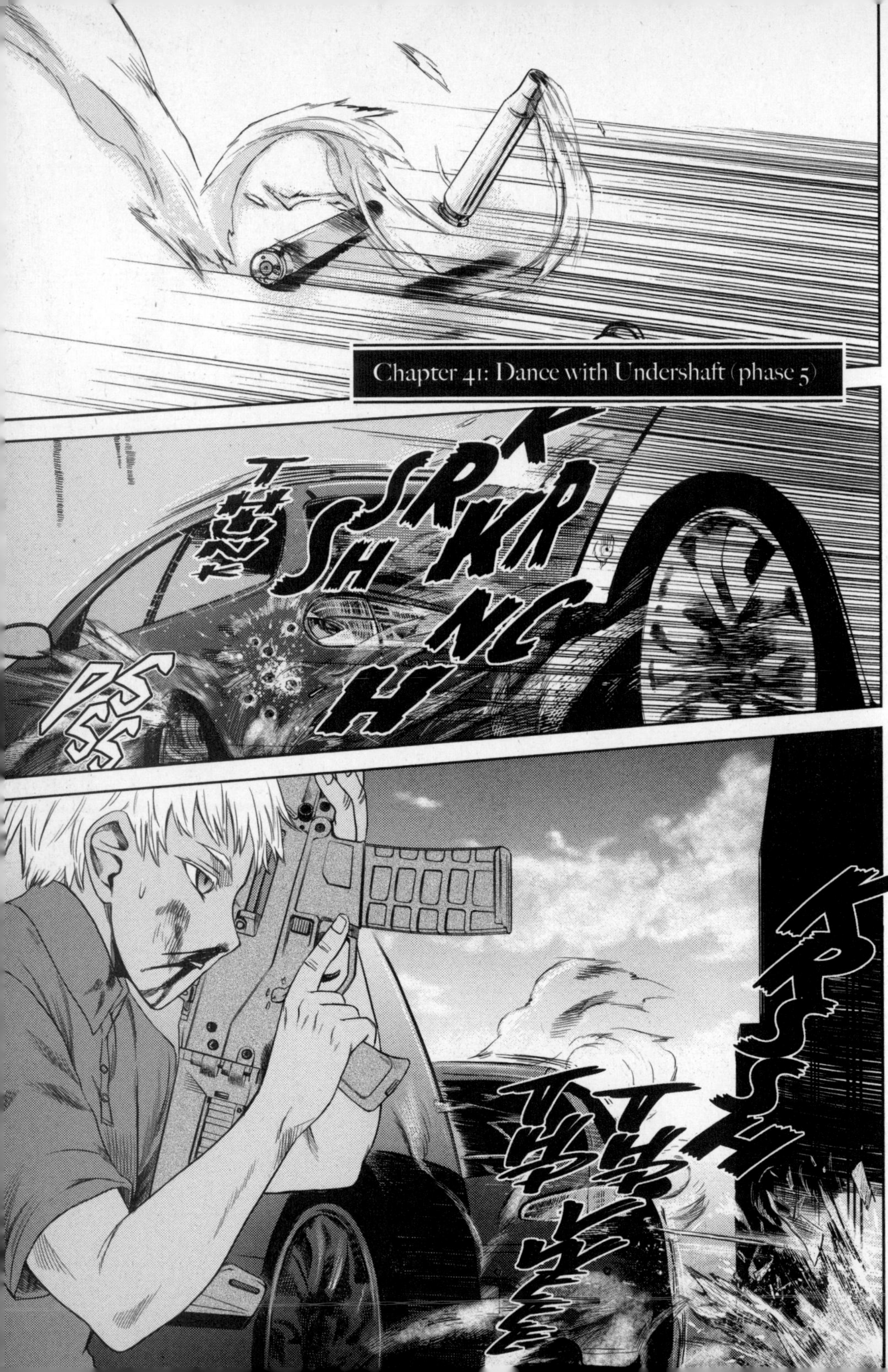
Chapter 41: Dance with Undershaft (phase 5)

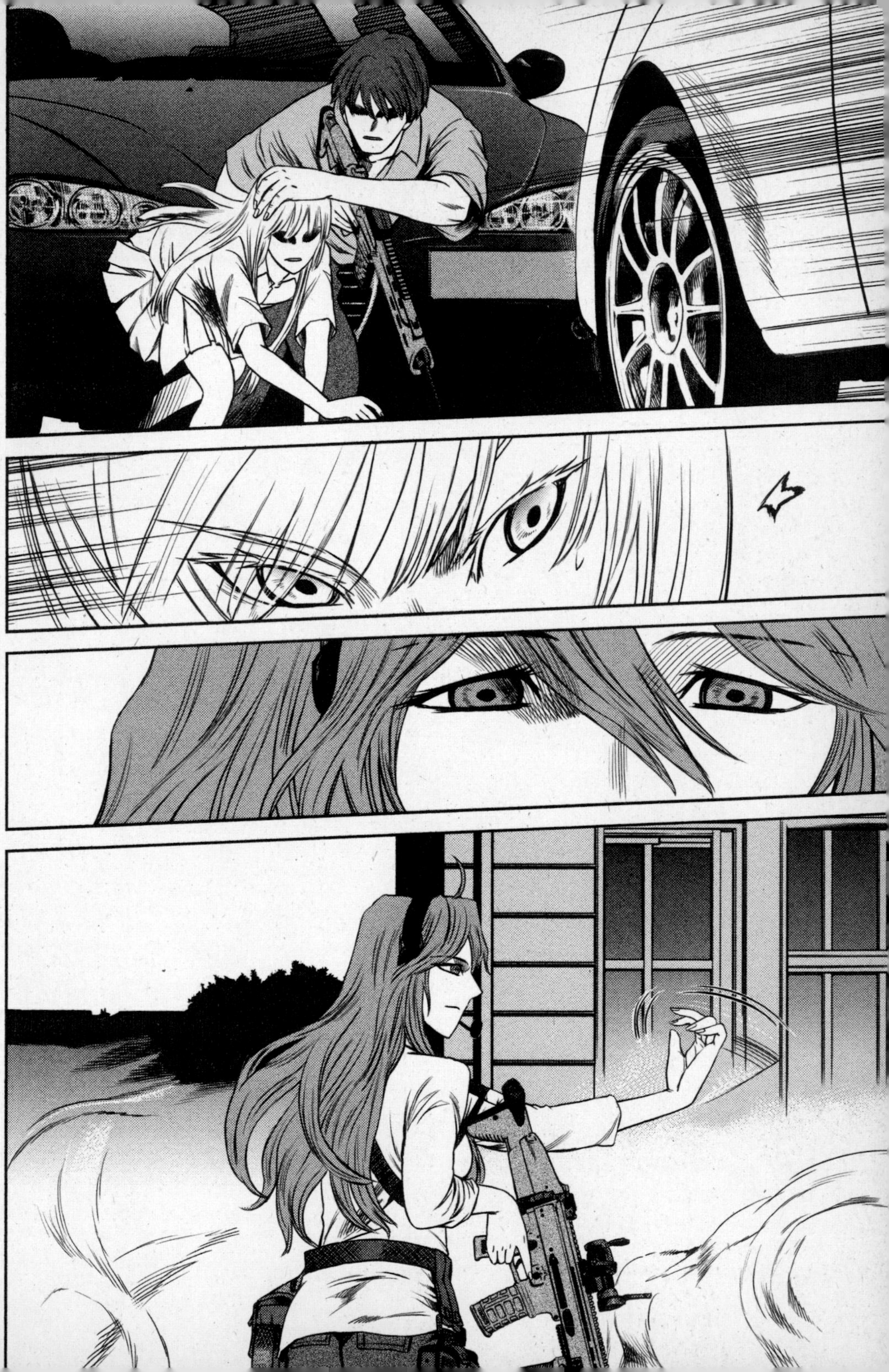

Chapter 41: Dance with Undershaft (phase 5)

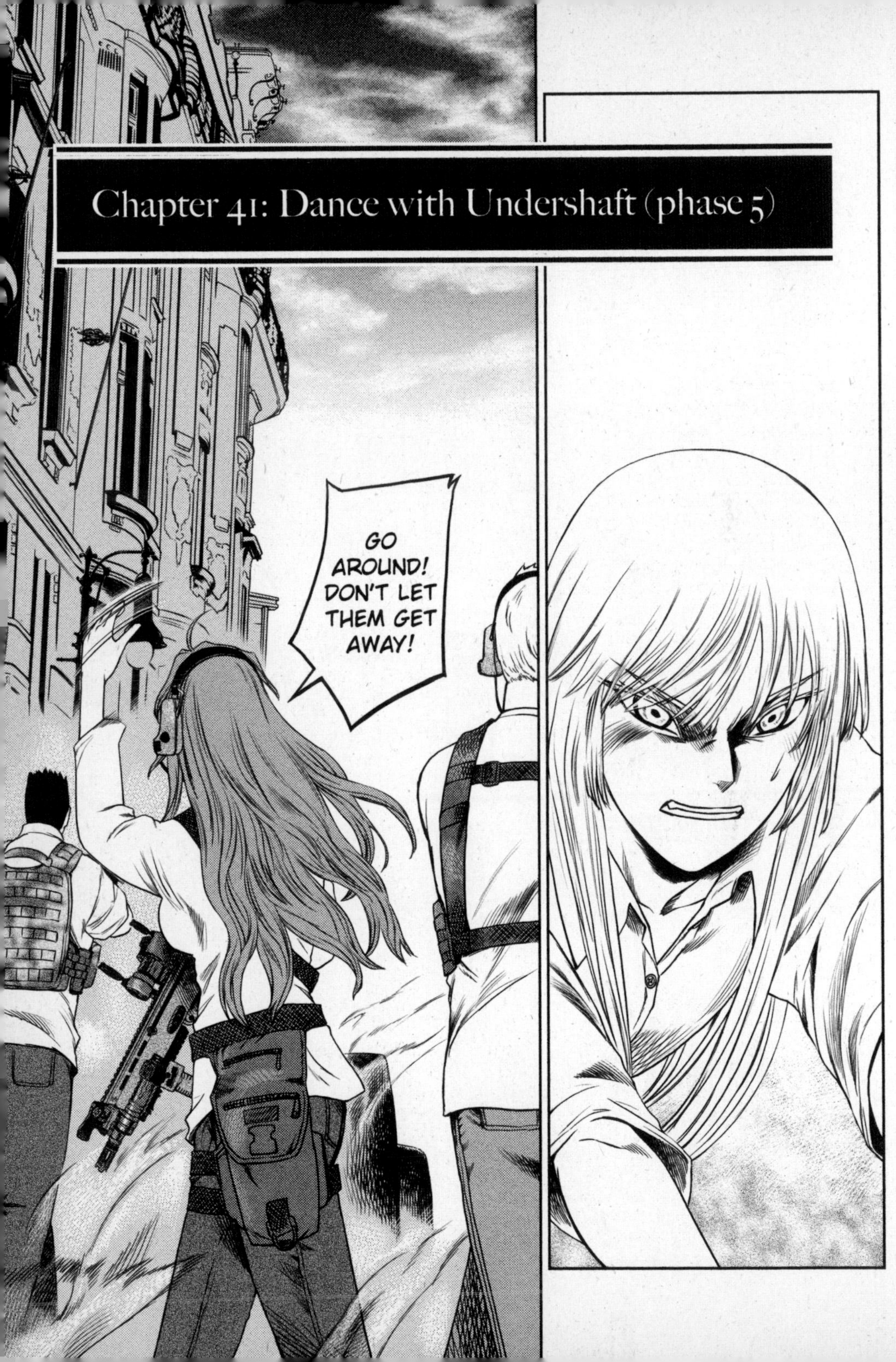
GO AROUND! DON'T LET THEM GET AWAY!

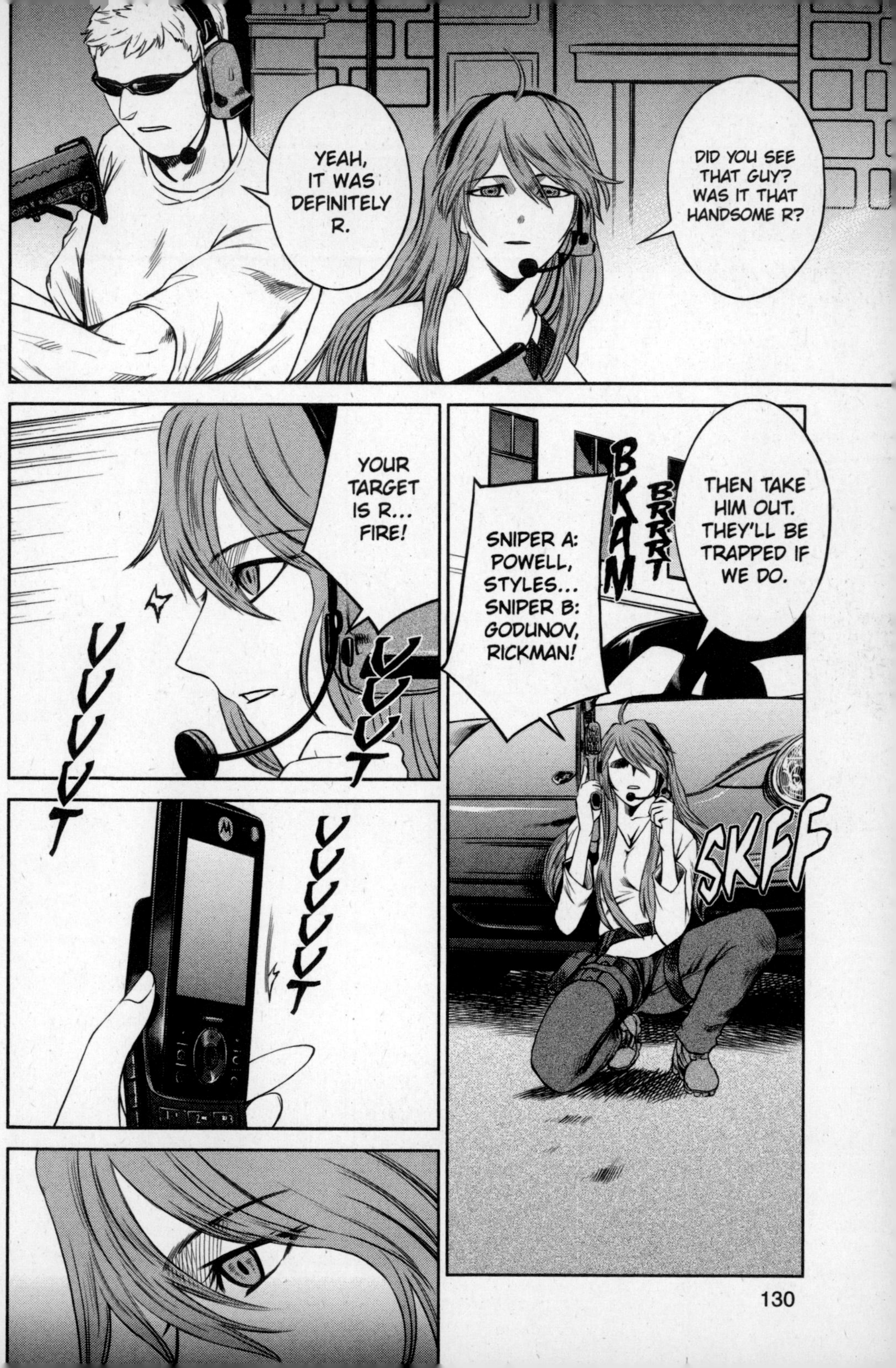
DID YOU SEE THAT GUY? WAS IT THAT HANDSOME R?
YEAH, IT WAS DEFINITELY R.
THEN TAKE HIM OUT. THEY'LL BE TRAPPED IF WE DO.
BKAM
BRRRT
SNIPER A: POWELL, STYLES... SNIPER B: GODUNOV, RICKMAN!
SKFF
YOUR TARGET IS R... FIRE!
VVVT
VVVVVT
VVVVVVVT

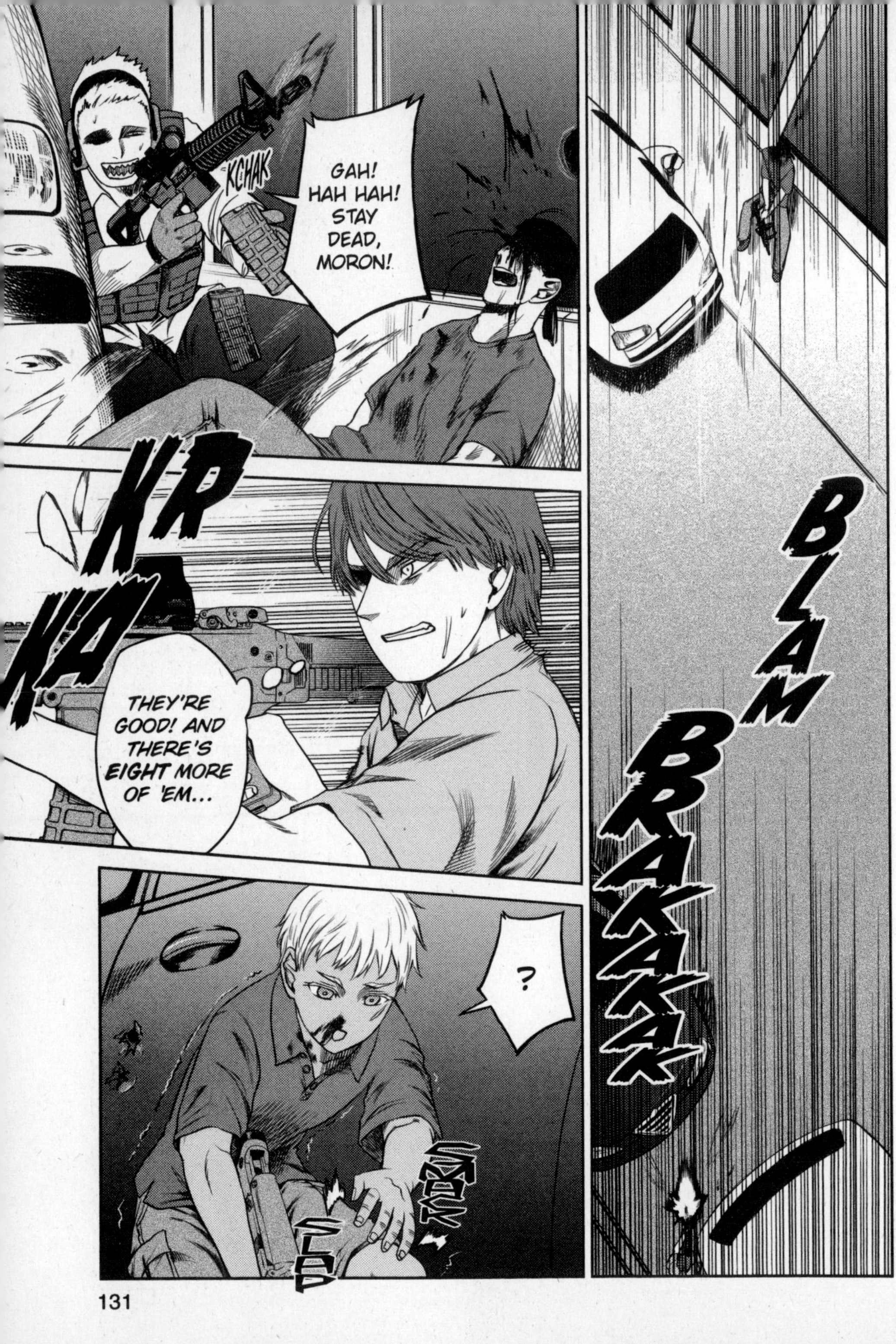
BLAM
BRAKAKAK
KCHAK
GAH! HAH HAH! STAY DEAD, MORON!
KR
THEY'RE GOOD! AND THERE'S EIGHT MORE OF 'EM...
?
SLAP

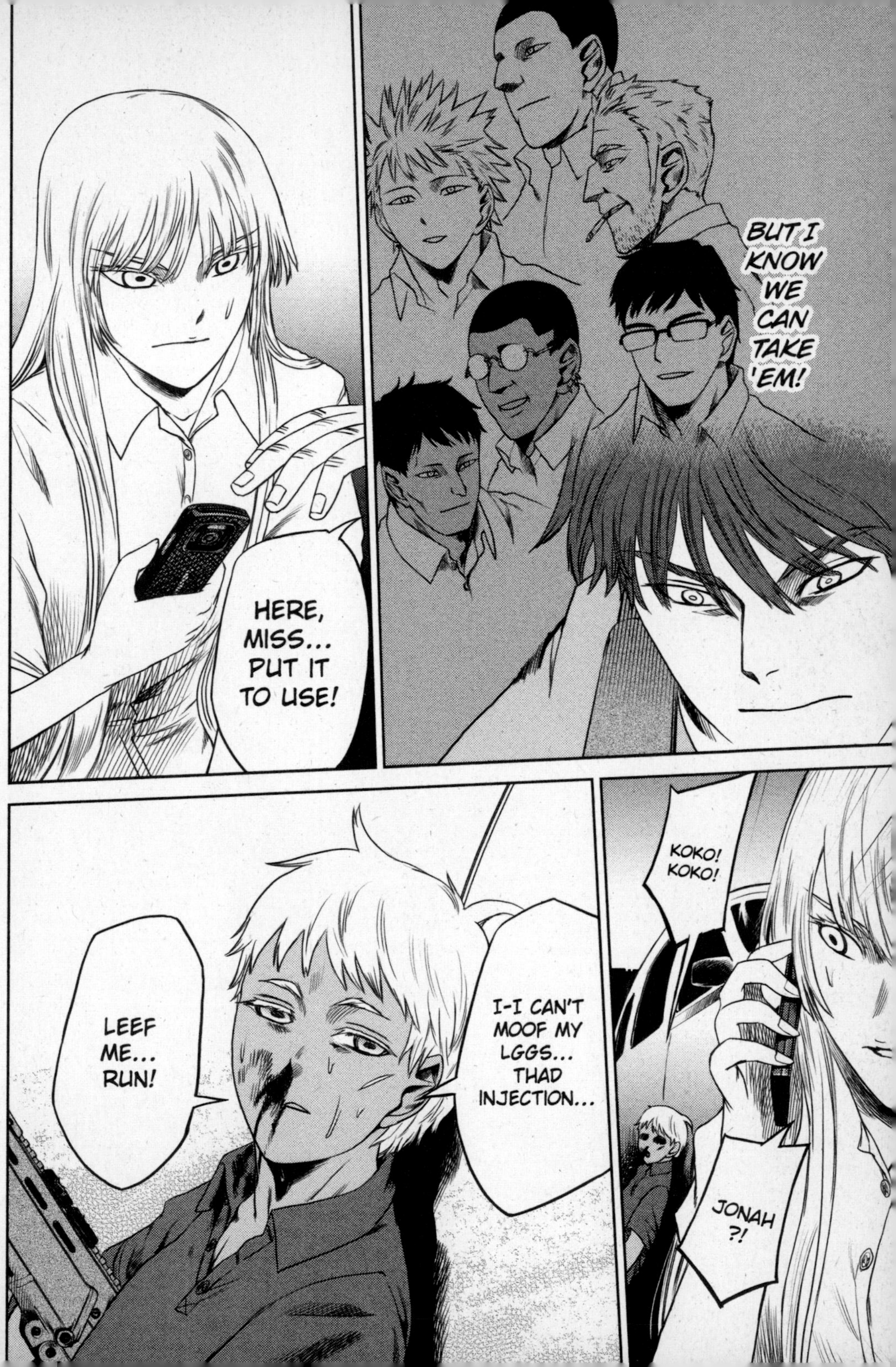
BUT I KNOW WE CAN TAKE 'EM!
HERE, MISS... PUT IT TO USE!
KOKO! KOKO!
JONAH ?!
I-I CAN'T MOOF MY LGGS... THAD INJECTION...
LEEF ME... RUN!

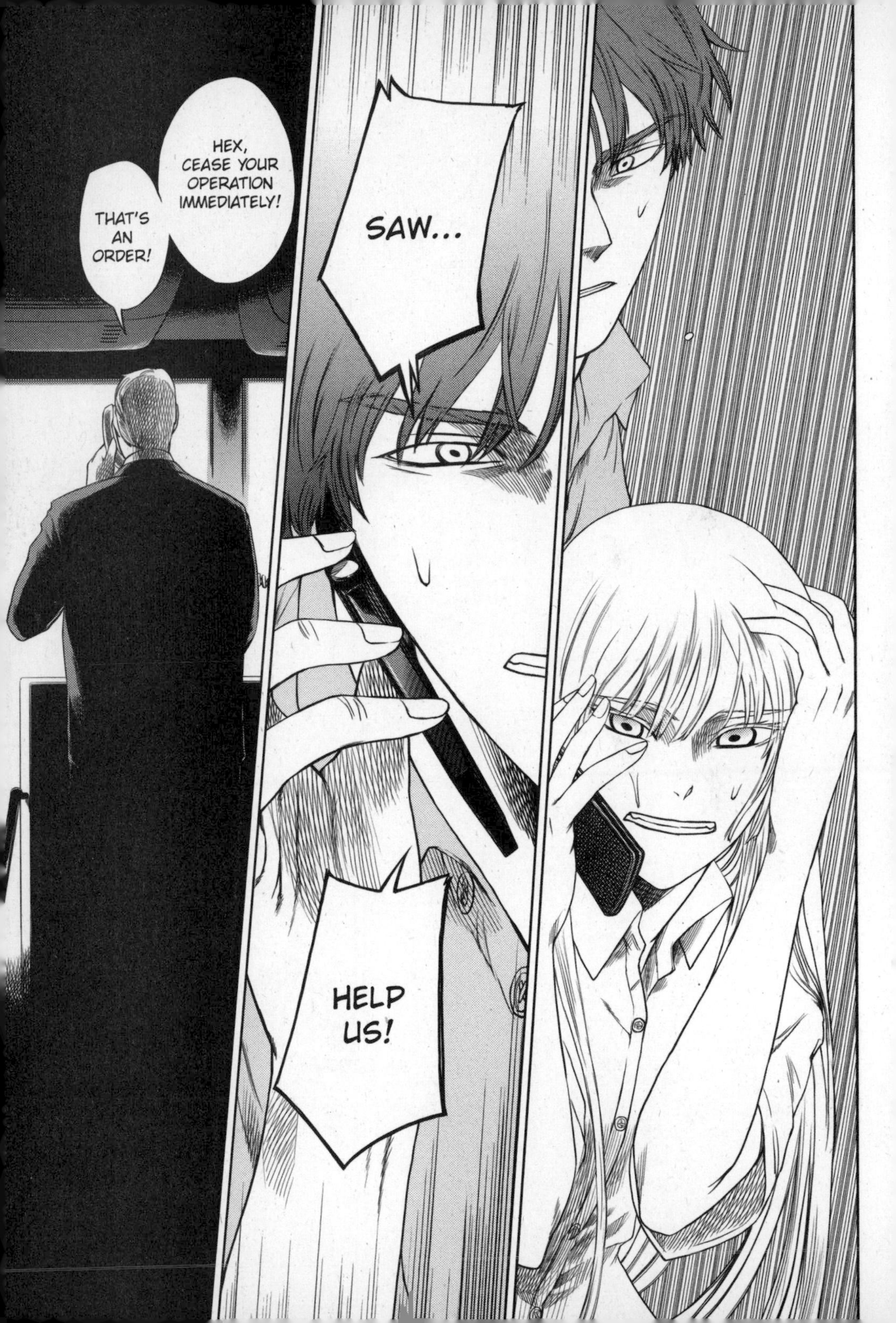

SAW...
HELP US!
HEX, CEASE YOUR OPERATION IMMEDIATELY!
THAT'S AN ORDER!

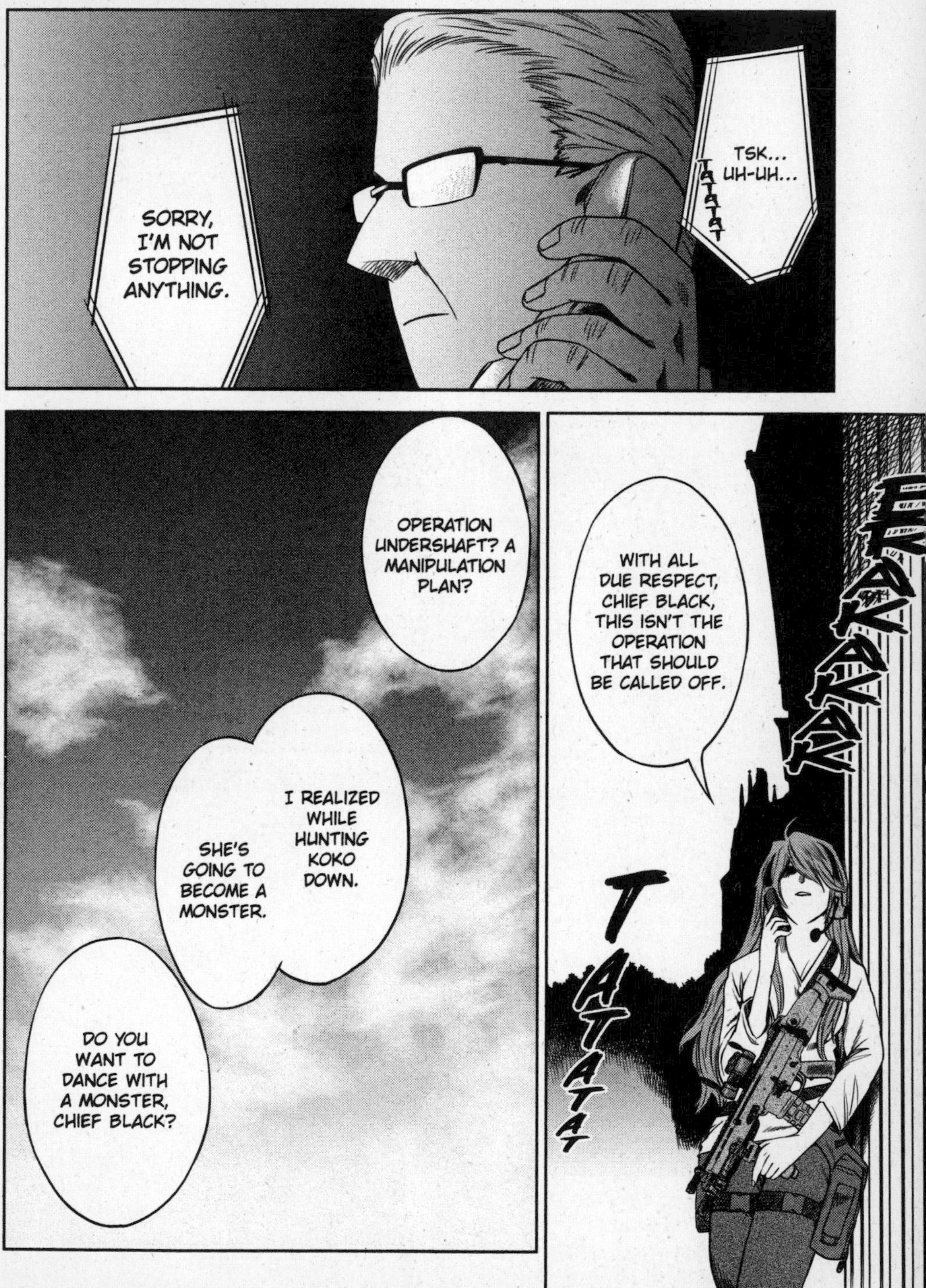
TSK... UH-UH...
TATATAT
SORRY, I'M NOT STOPPING ANYTHING.
WITH ALL DUE RESPECT, CHIEF BLACK, THIS ISN'T THE OPERATION THAT SHOULD BE CALLED OFF.
TATATAT
OPERATION UNDERSHAFT? A MANIPULATION PLAN?
I REALIZED WHILE HUNTING KOKO DOWN.
SHE'S GOING TO BECOME A MONSTER.
DO YOU WANT TO DANCE WITH A MONSTER, CHIEF BLACK?

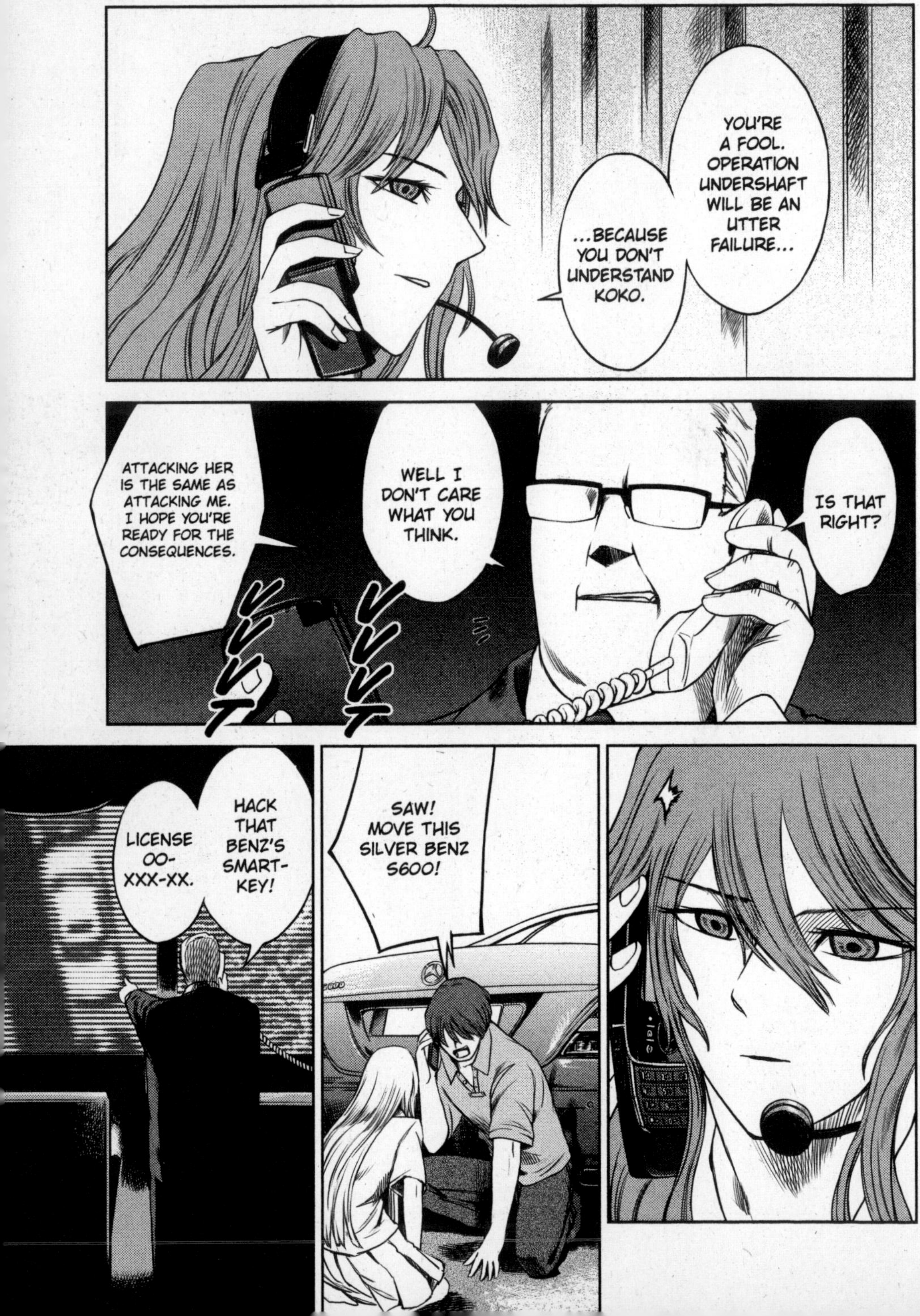
YOU'RE A FOOL. OPERATION UNDERSHAFT WILL BE AN UTTER FAILURE...
...BECAUSE YOU DON'T UNDERSTAND KOKO.
IS THAT RIGHT?
WELL I DON'T CARE WHAT YOU THINK.
VVVVT
ATTACKING HER IS THE SAME AS ATTACKING ME. I HOPE YOU'RE READY FOR THE CONSEQUENCES.
VVVVT
SAW! MOVE THIS SILVER BENZ S600!
HACK THAT BENZ'S SMART-KEY!
LICENSE OO-XXX-XX.

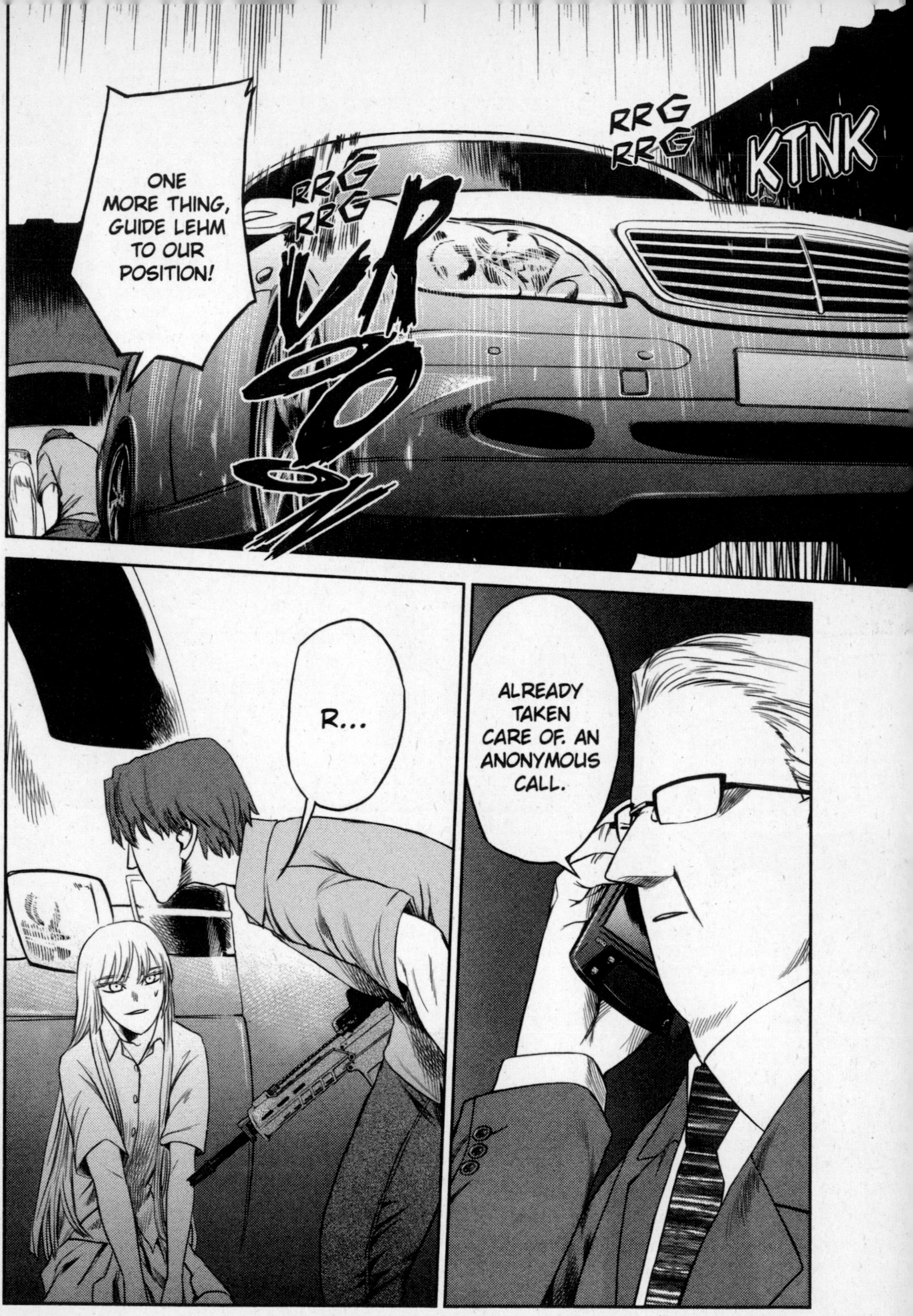
KTNK
RRG RRG
RRG RRG
VROOOM
ONE MORE THING, GUIDE LEHM TO OUR POSITION!
ALREADY TAKEN CARE OF. AN ANONYMOUS CALL.
R...

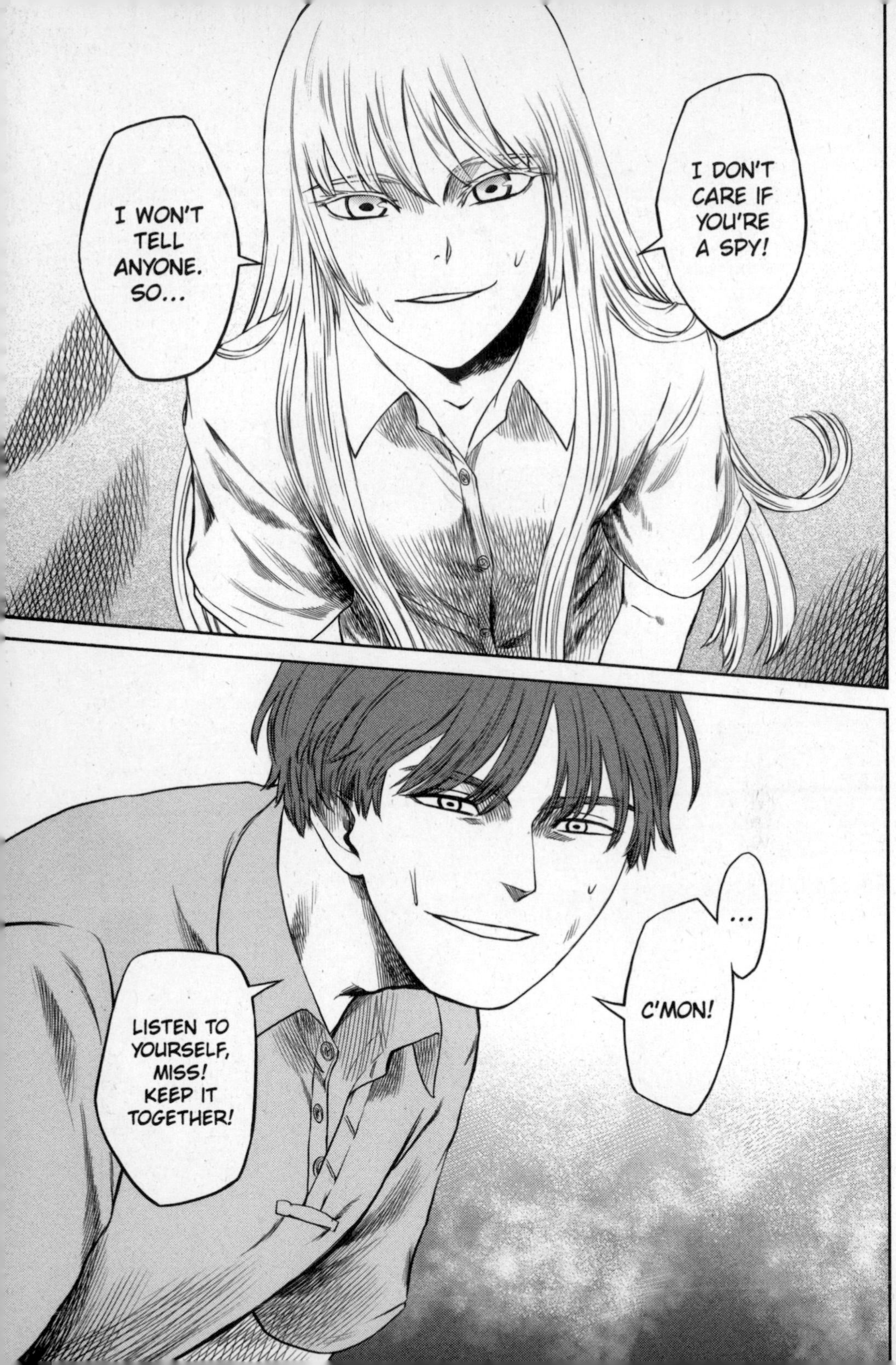
I DON'T CARE IF YOU'RE A SPY!
I WON'T TELL ANYONE. SO...
...
C'MON!
LISTEN TO YOURSELF, MISS! KEEP IT TOGETHER!

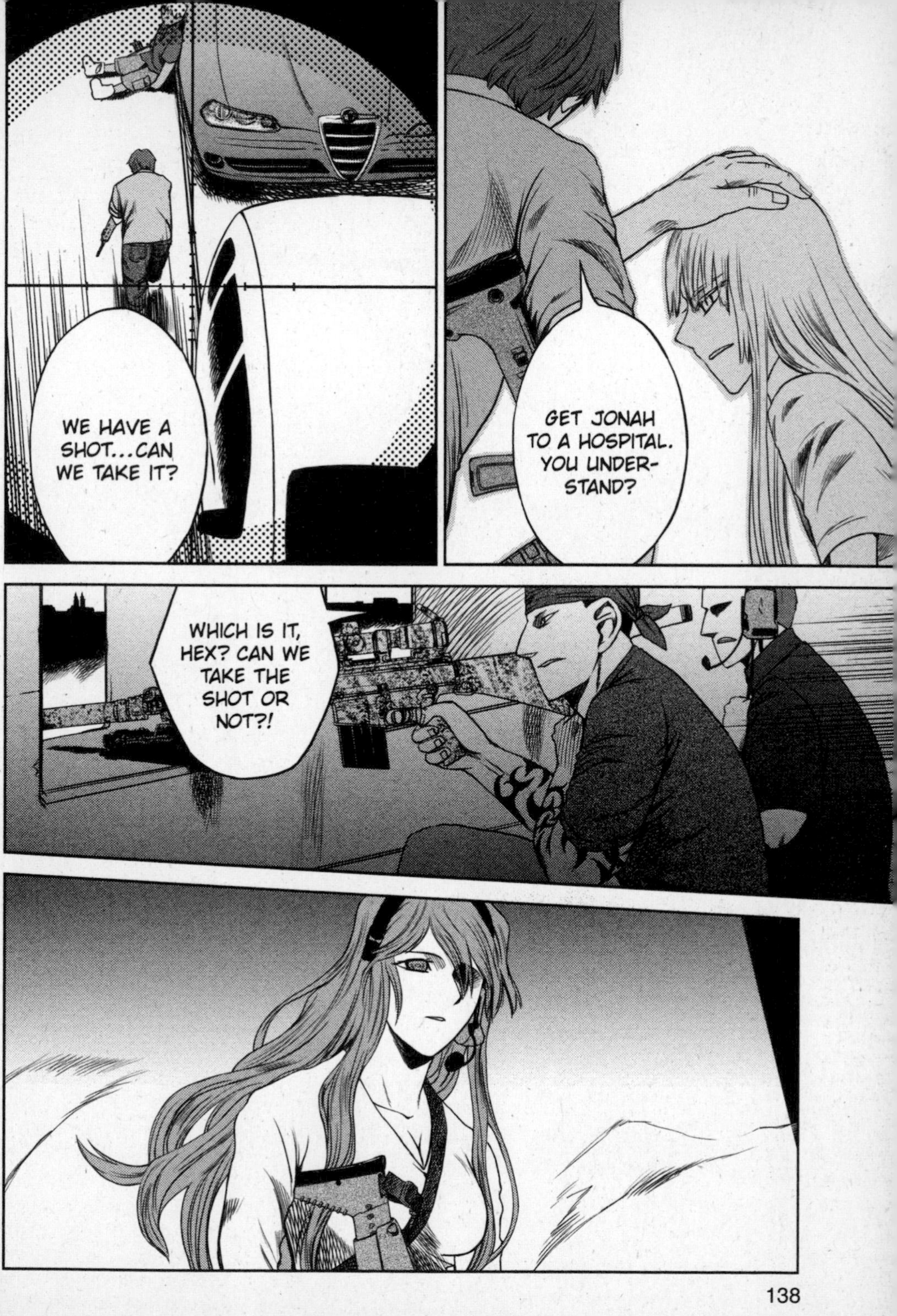
GET JONAH TO A HOSPITAL. YOU UNDER-STAND?
WE HAVE A SHOT...CAN WE TAKE IT?
WHICH IS IT, HEX? CAN WE TAKE THE SHOT OR NOT?!

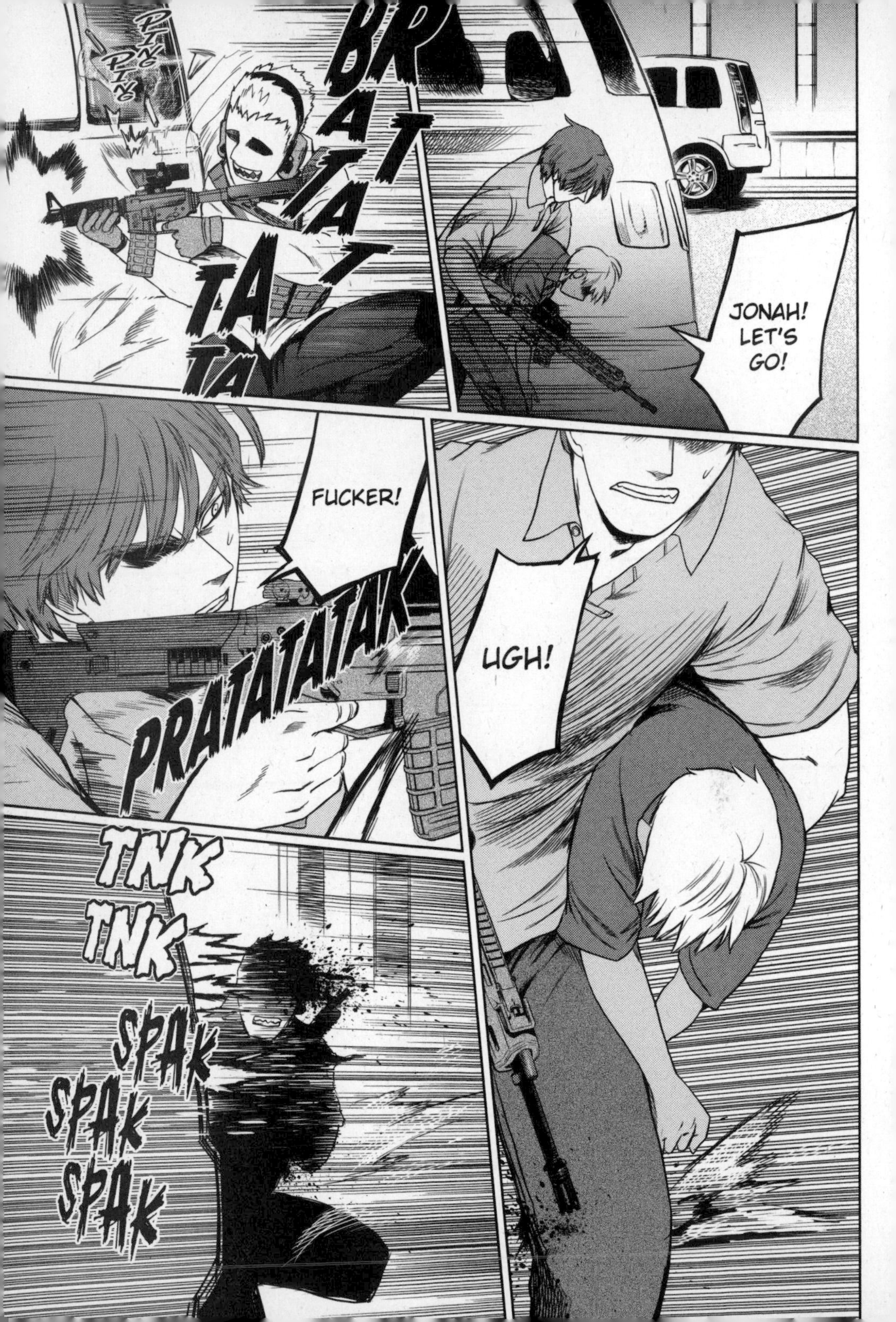
JONAH! LET'S GO!
BRATATATATA
PING PING
UGH!
FUCKER!
PRATATATAK
TNK TNK
SPAK SPAK SPAK

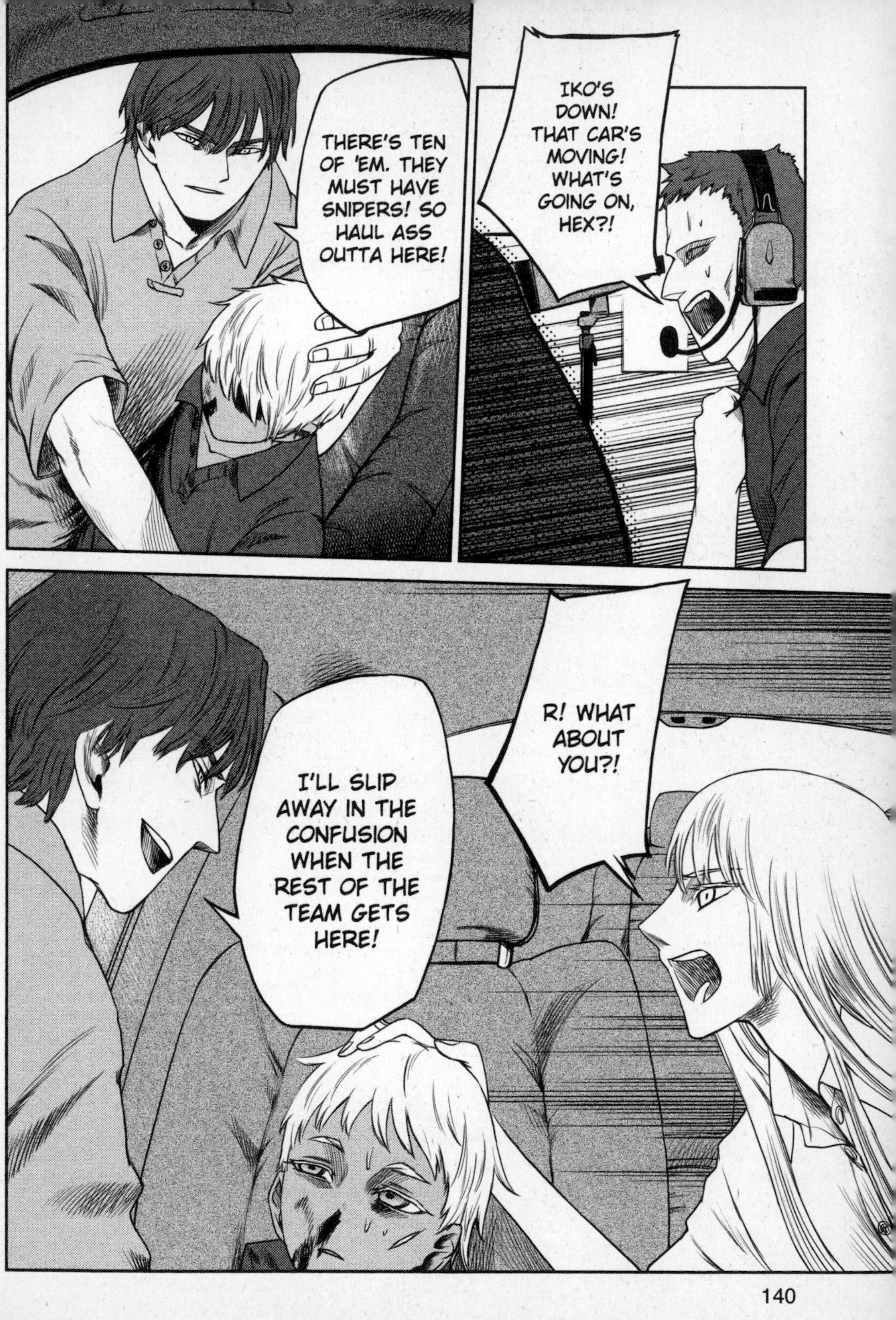
IKO'S DOWN! THAT CAR'S MOVING! WHAT'S GOING ON, HEX?!
THERE'S TEN OF 'EM. THEY MUST HAVE SNIPERS! SO HAUL ASS OUTTA HERE!
R! WHAT ABOUT YOU?!
I'LL SLIP AWAY IN THE CONFUSION WHEN THE REST OF THE TEAM GETS HERE!

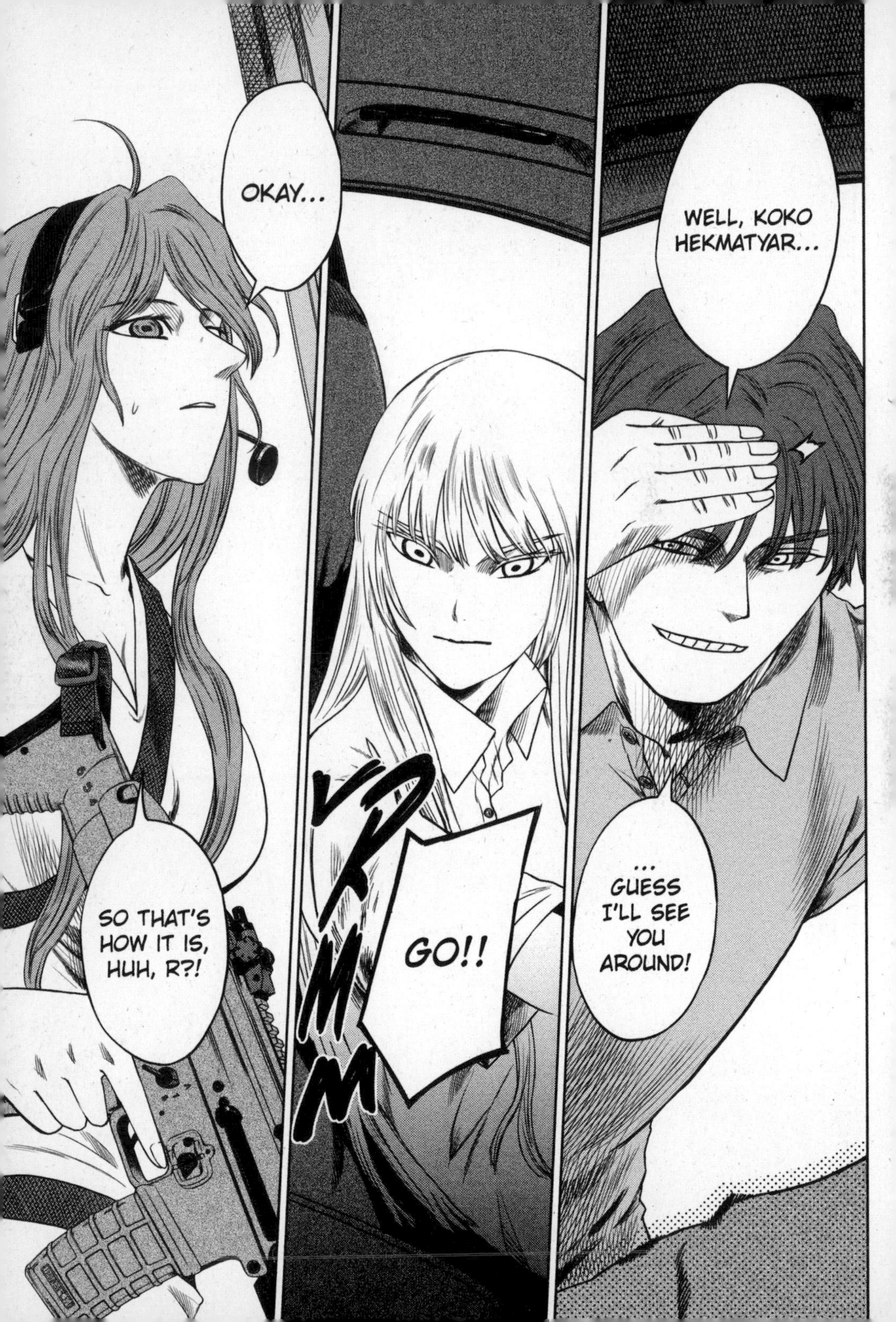
WELL, KOKO HEKMATYAR...
...GUESS I'LL SEE YOU AROUND!
GO!!
VRMM
OKAY...
SO THAT'S HOW IT IS, HUH, R?!

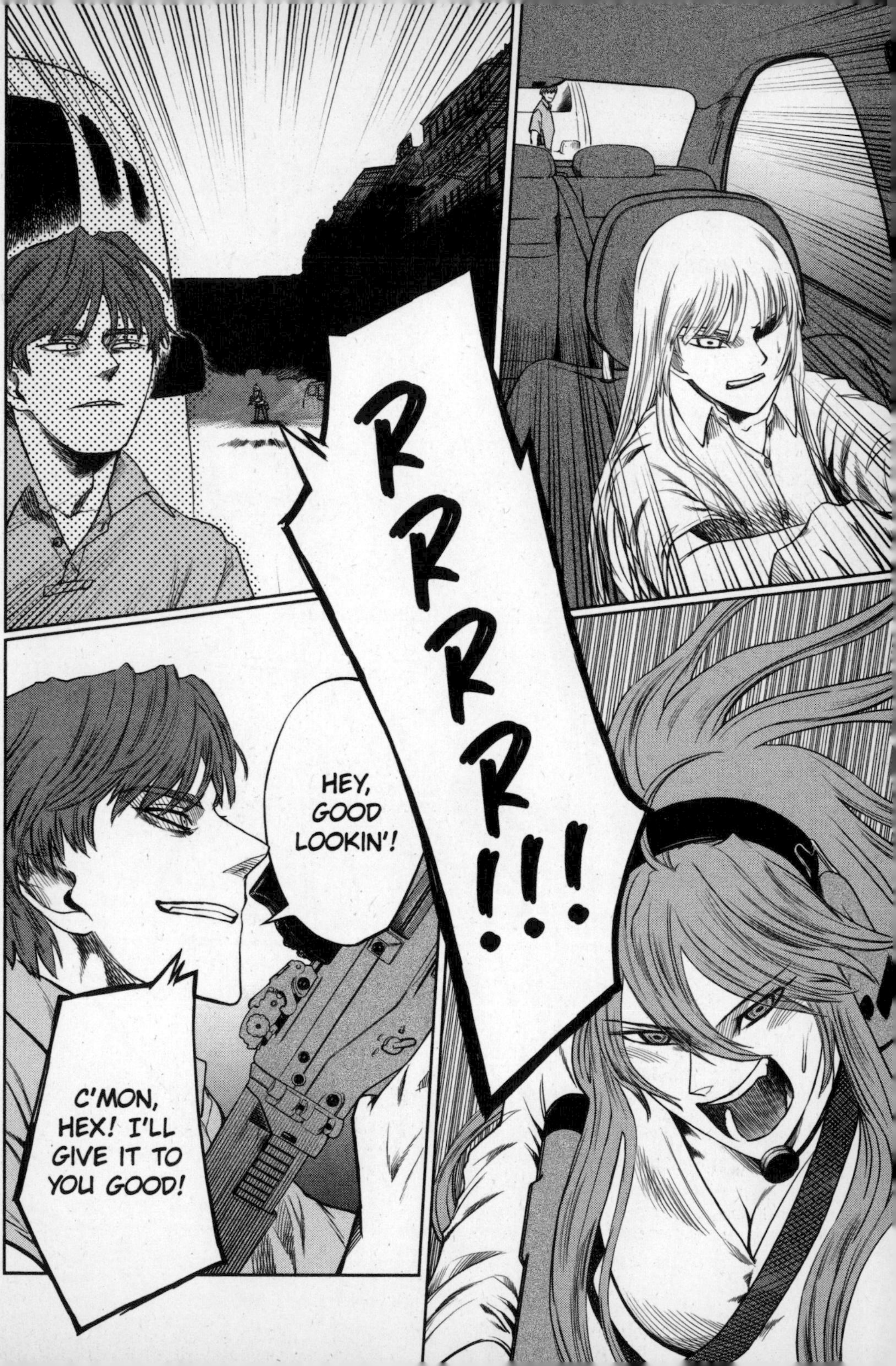
RRRRR!!!
HEY, GOOD LOOKIN'!
C'MON, HEX! I'LL GIVE IT TO YOU GOOD!

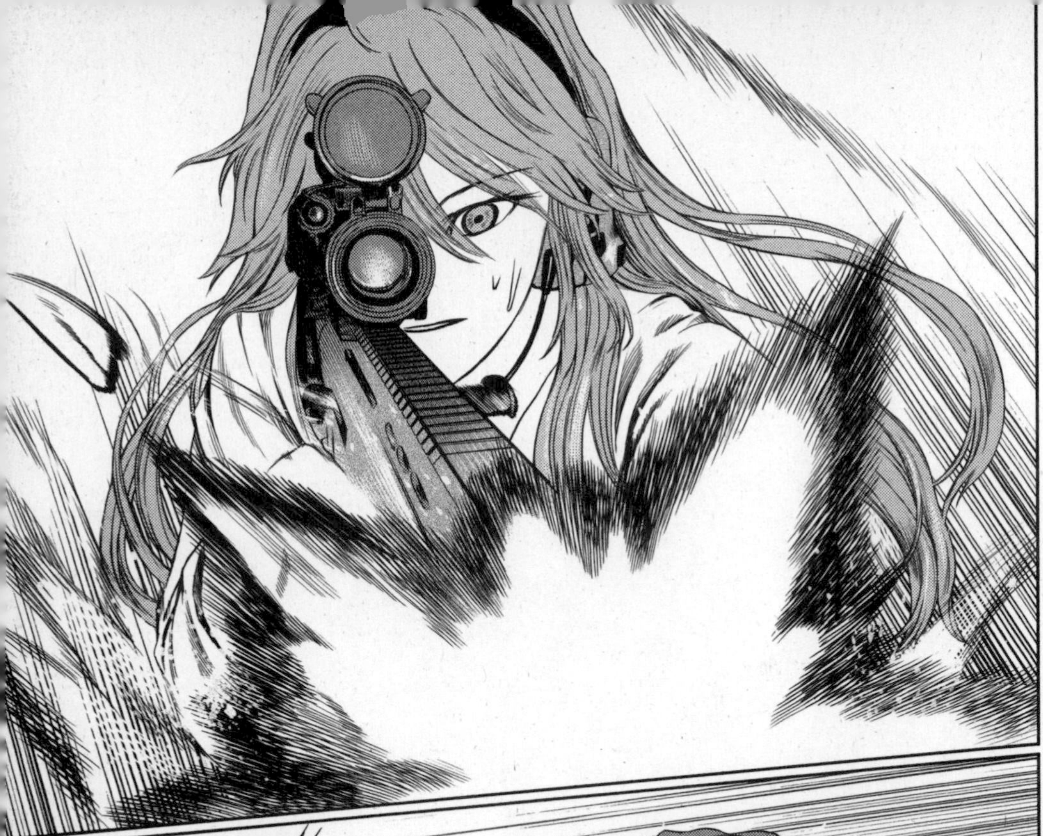
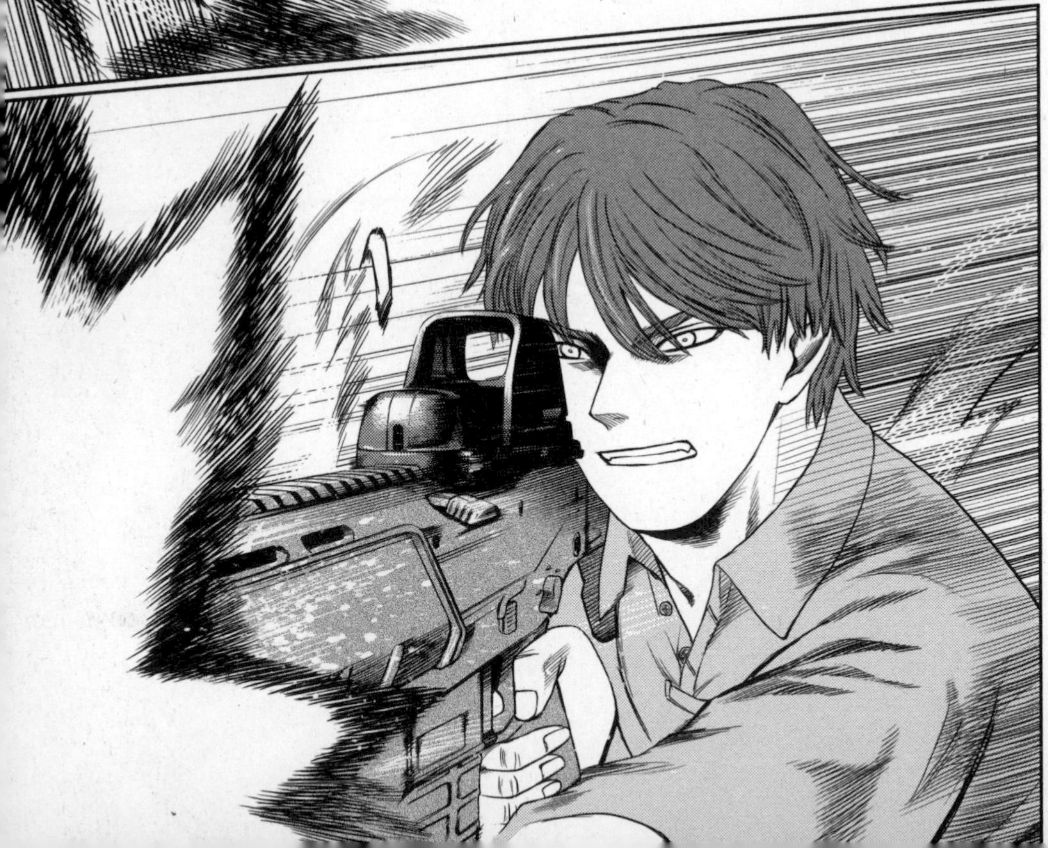

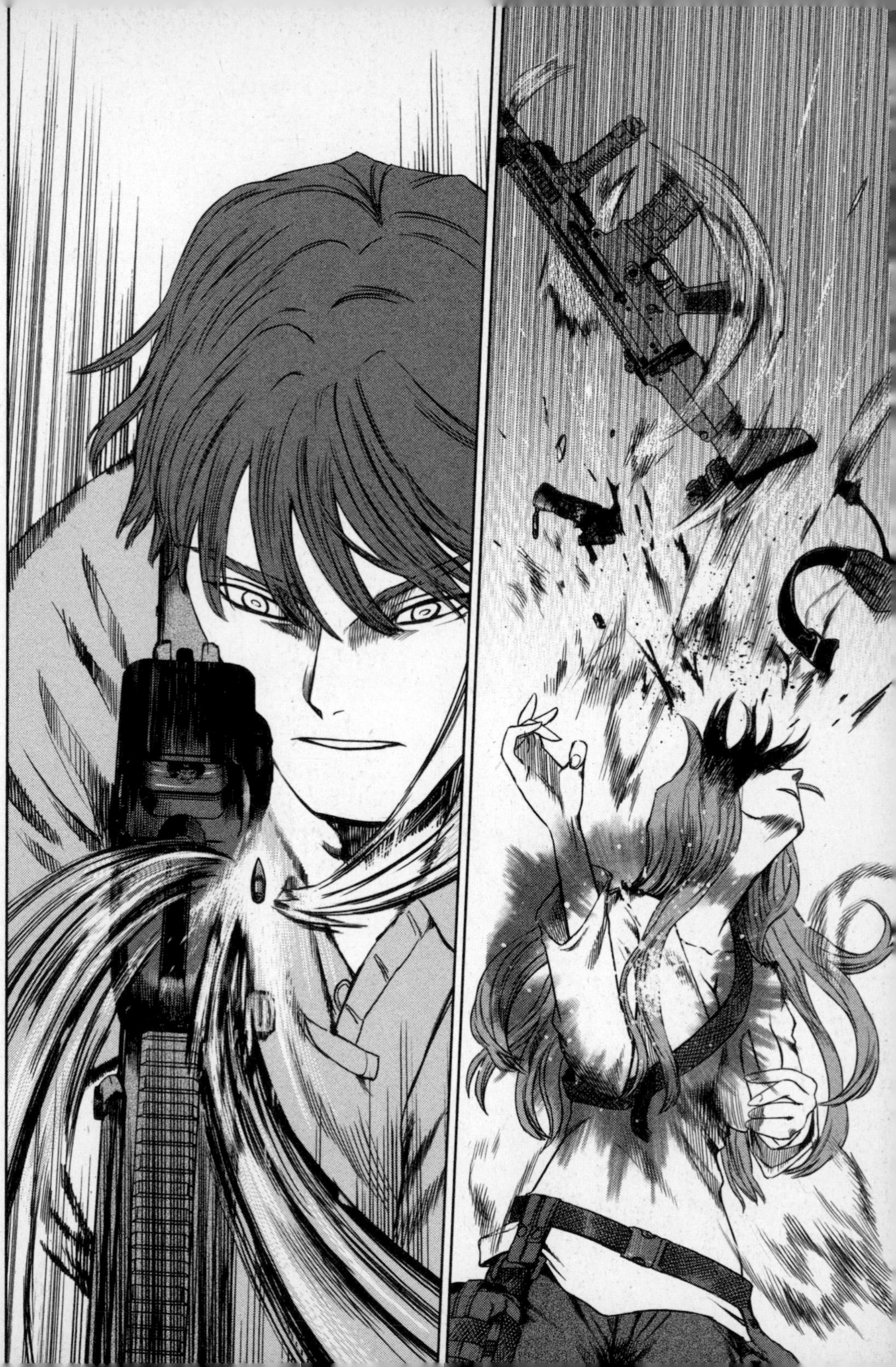

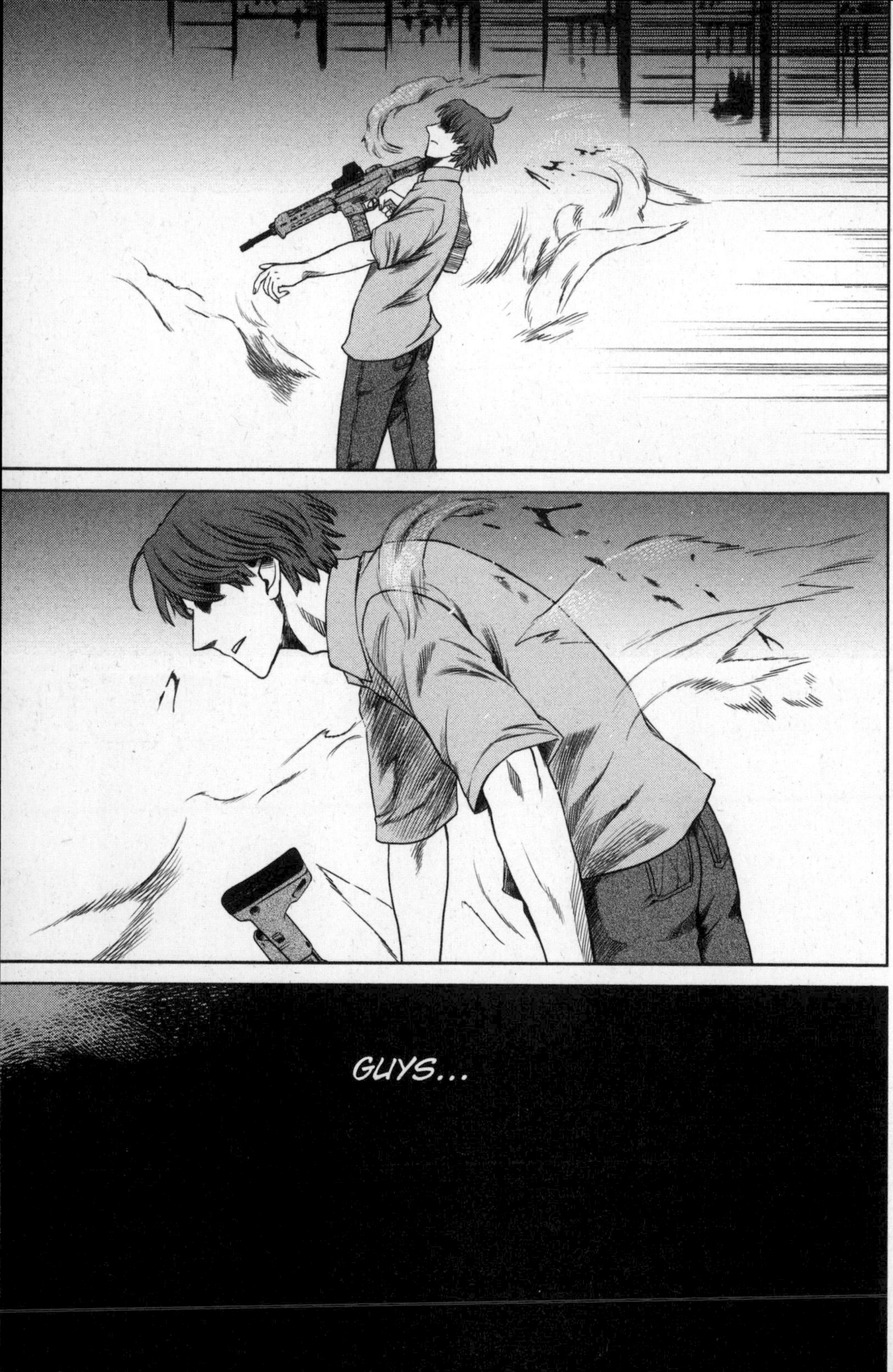
GUYS...

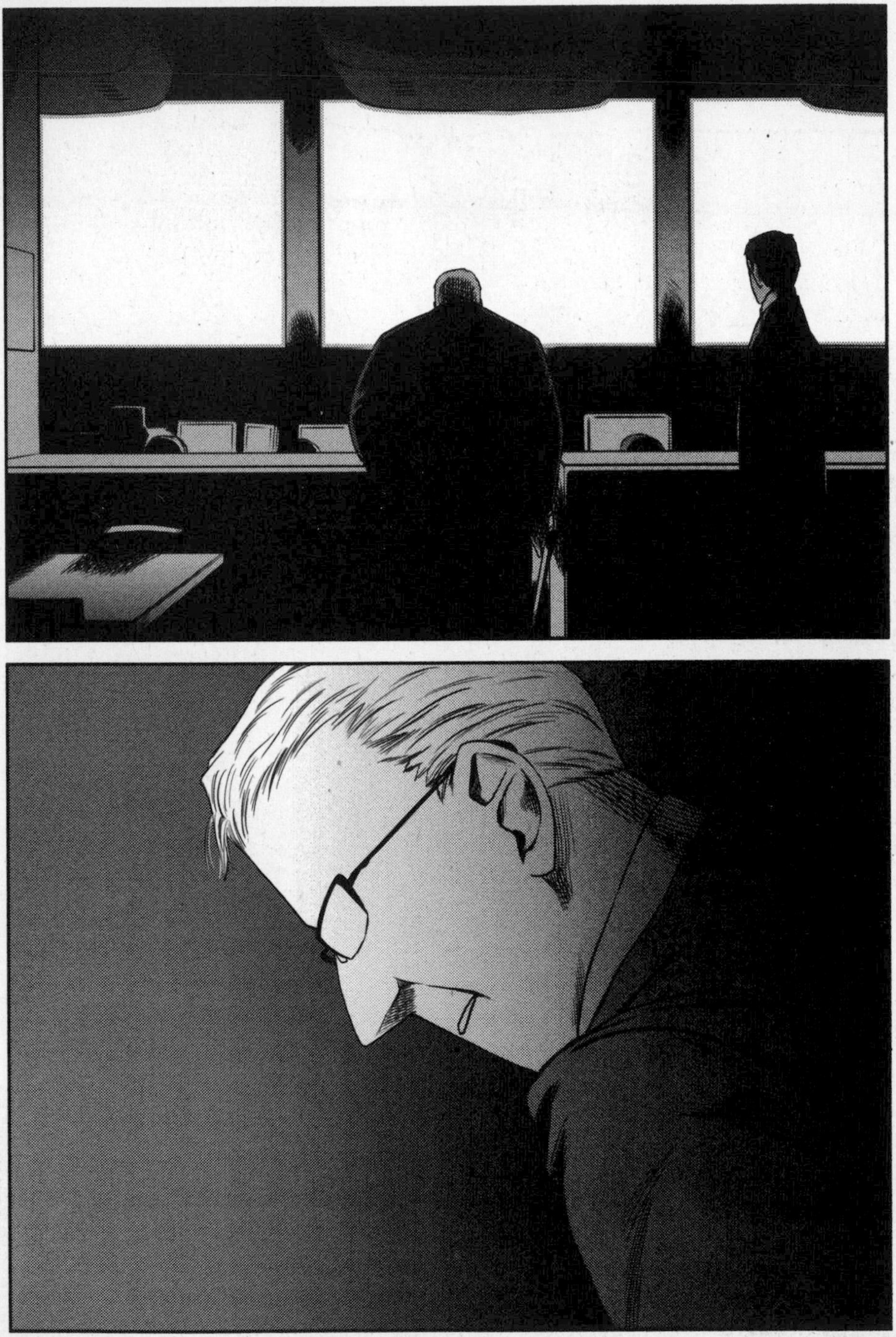

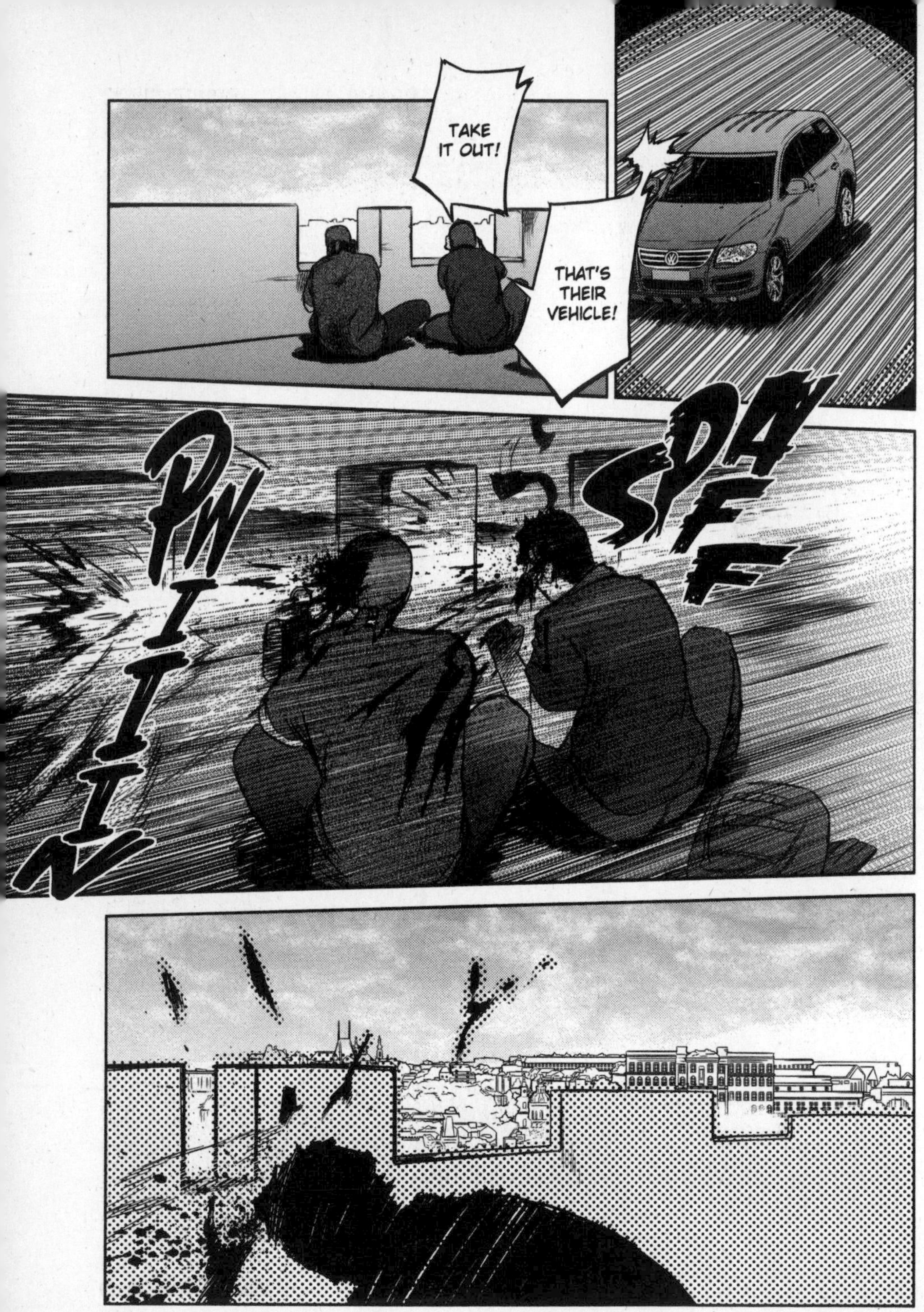
THAT'S THEIR VEHICLE!
TAKE IT OUT!
SPAFF
PWIIIN

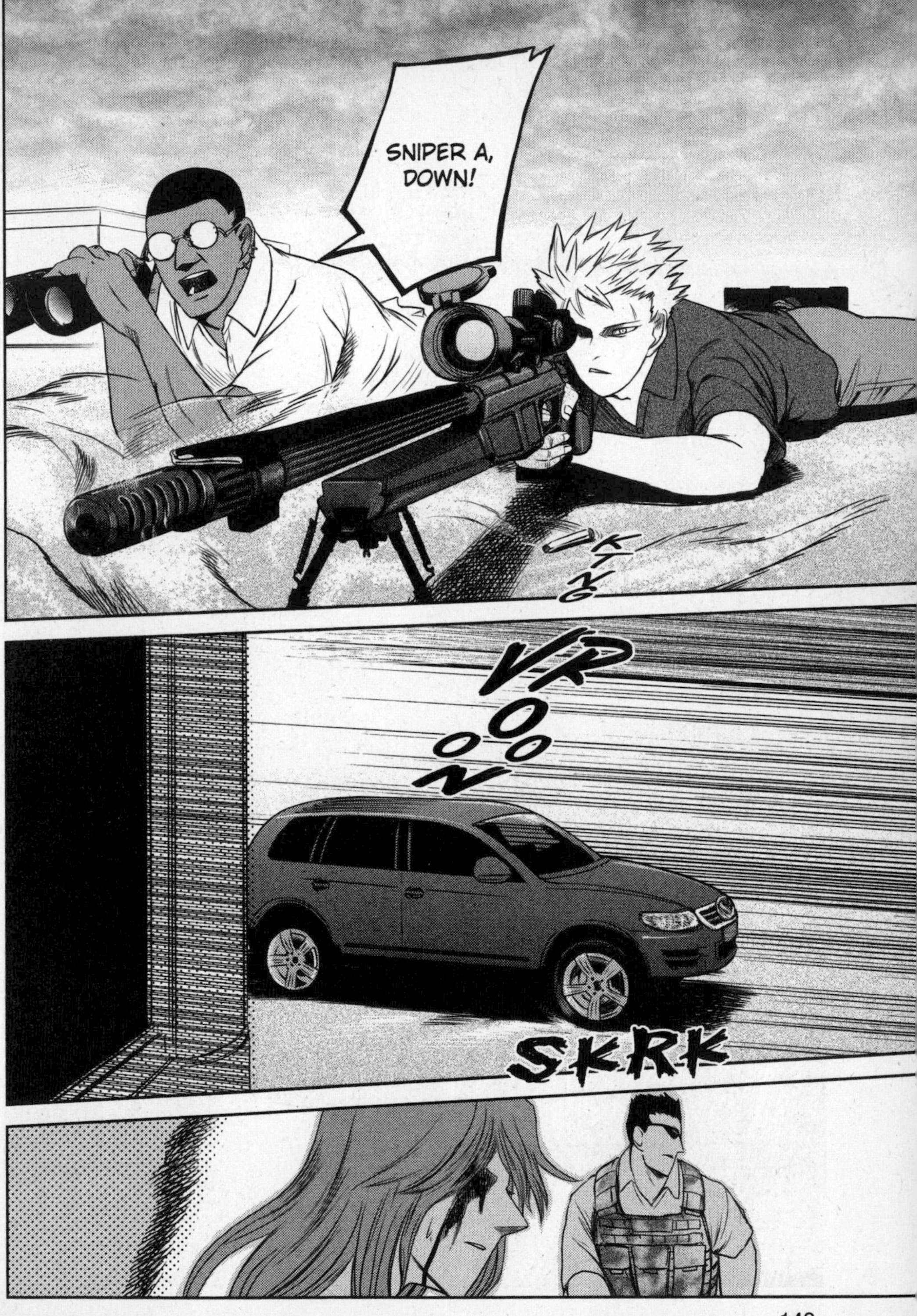
SNIPER A, DOWN!
KTING
VROOOON
SKRK

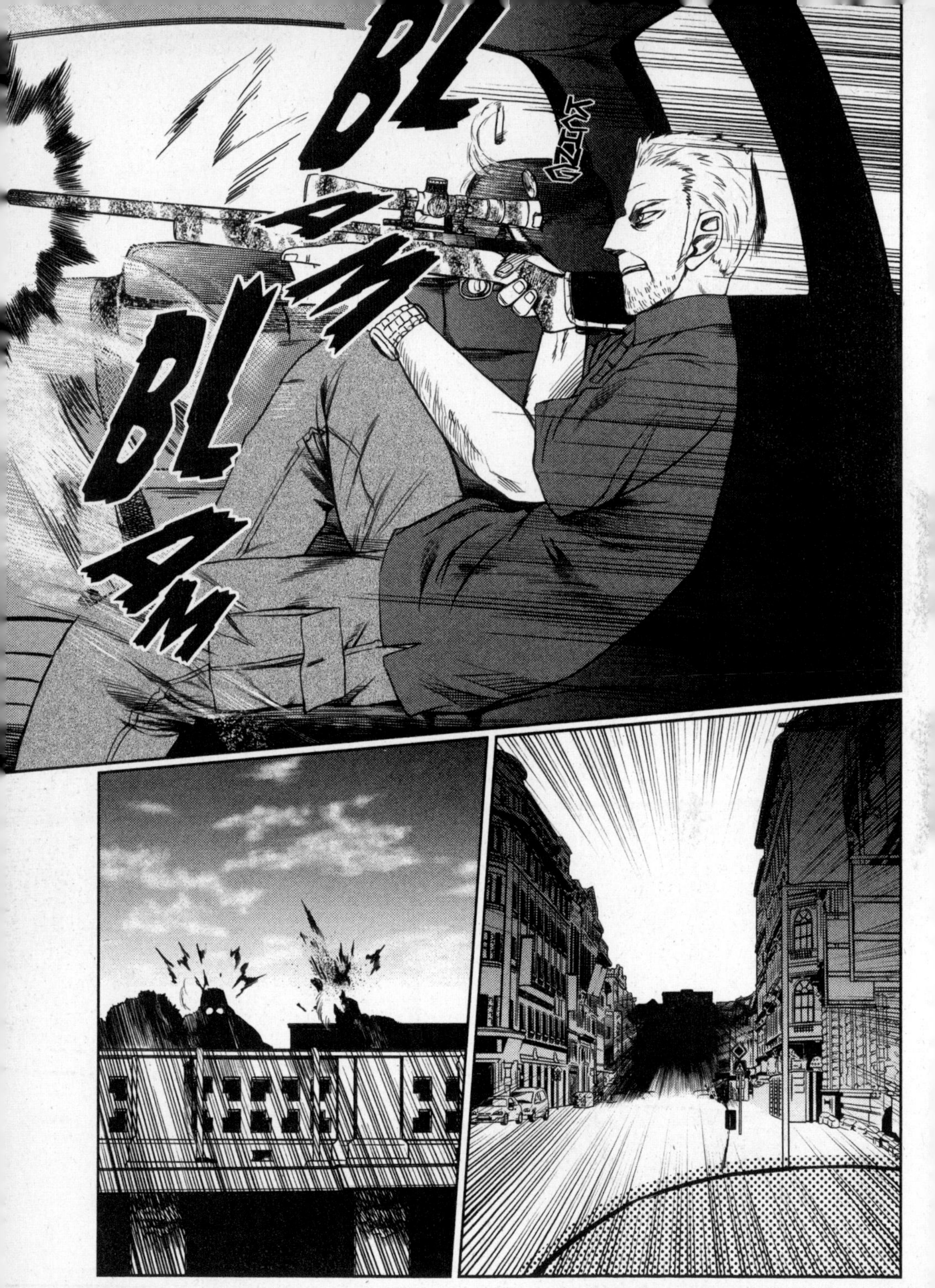
BLAM
BLAM
KCHING

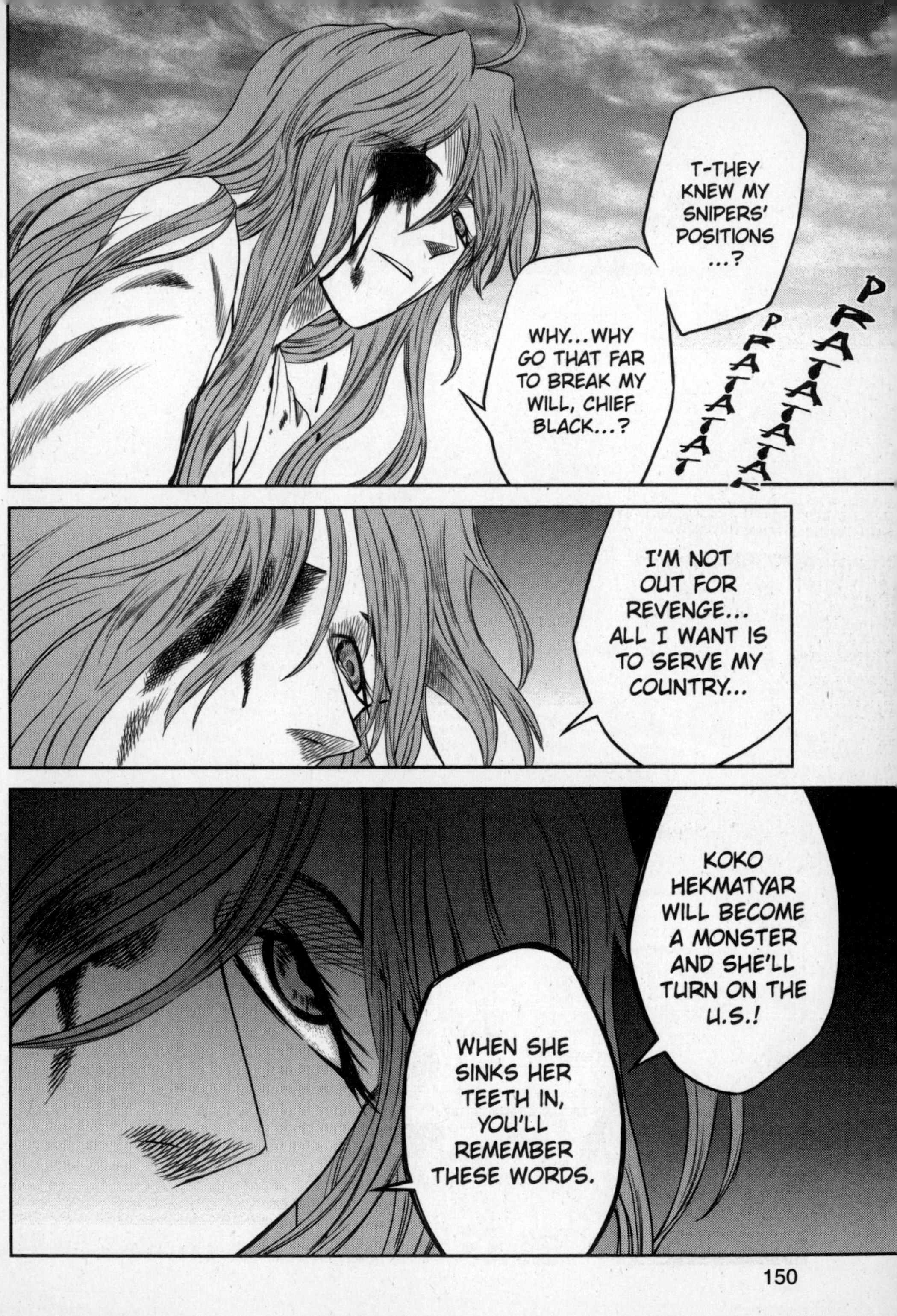
T-THEY KNEW MY SNIPERS' POSITIONS ...?
WHY...WHY GO THAT FAR TO BREAK MY WILL, CHIEF BLACK...?
PRATATATAT
PRATATAT
I'M NOT OUT FOR REVENGE... ALL I WANT IS TO SERVE MY COUNTRY...
KOKO HEKMATYAR WILL BECOME A MONSTER AND SHE'LL TURN ON THE U.S.!
WHEN SHE SINKS HER TEETH IN, YOU'LL REMEMBER THESE WORDS.

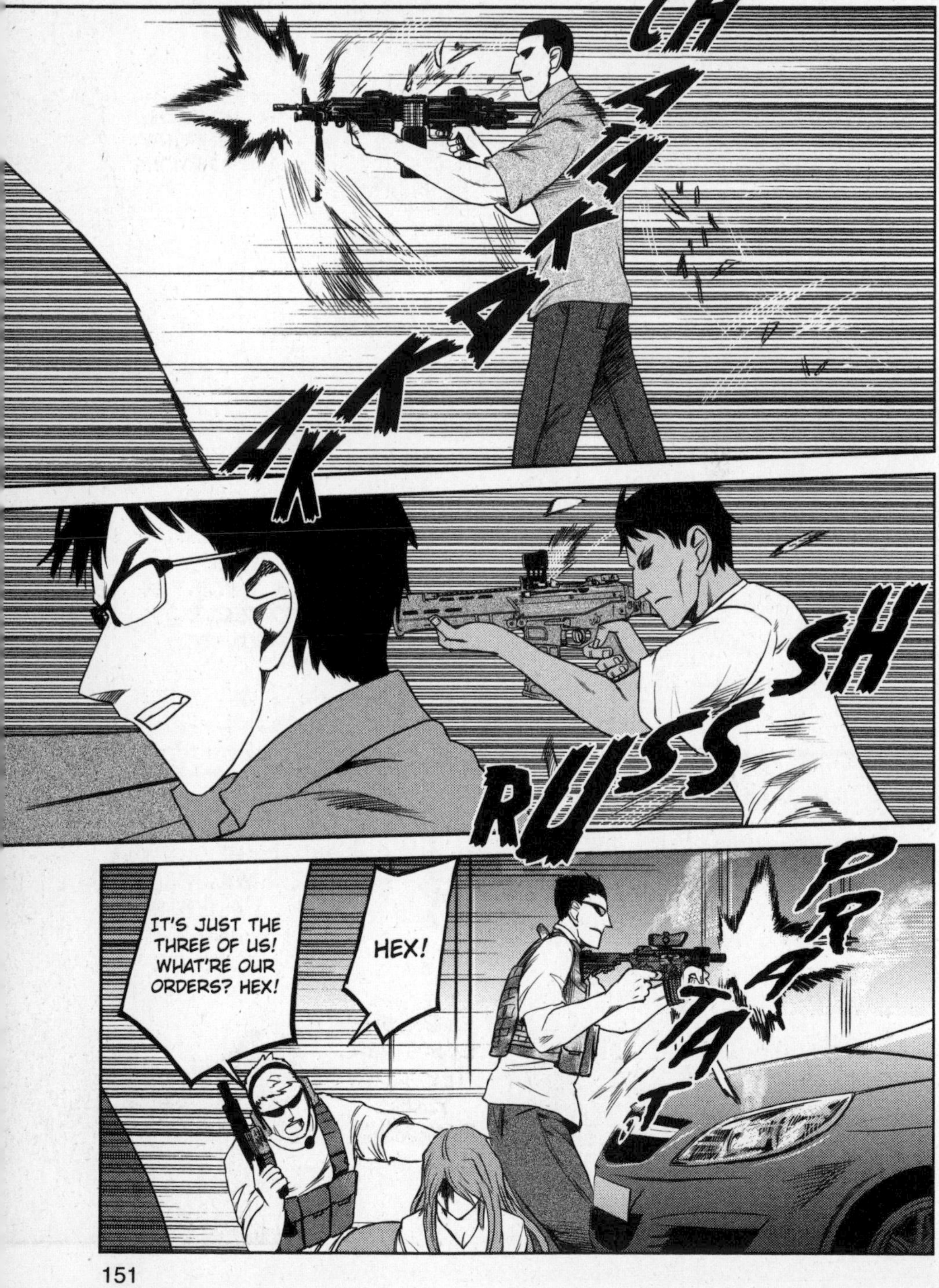
CHATAKAKAK
RUSSSH
PRATAT
HEX!
IT'S JUST THE THREE OF US! WHAT'RE OUR ORDERS? HEX!

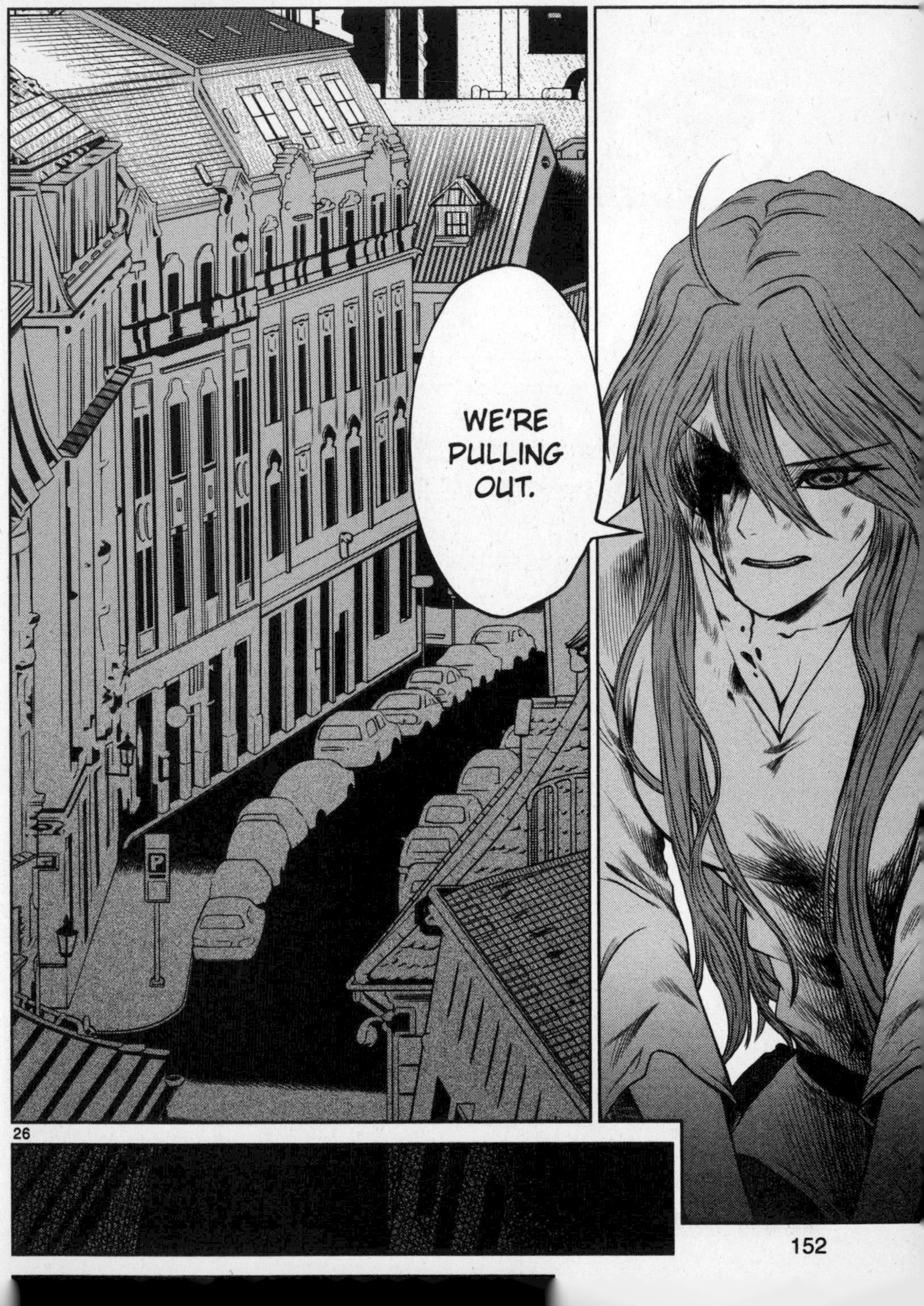
WE'RE PULLING OUT.

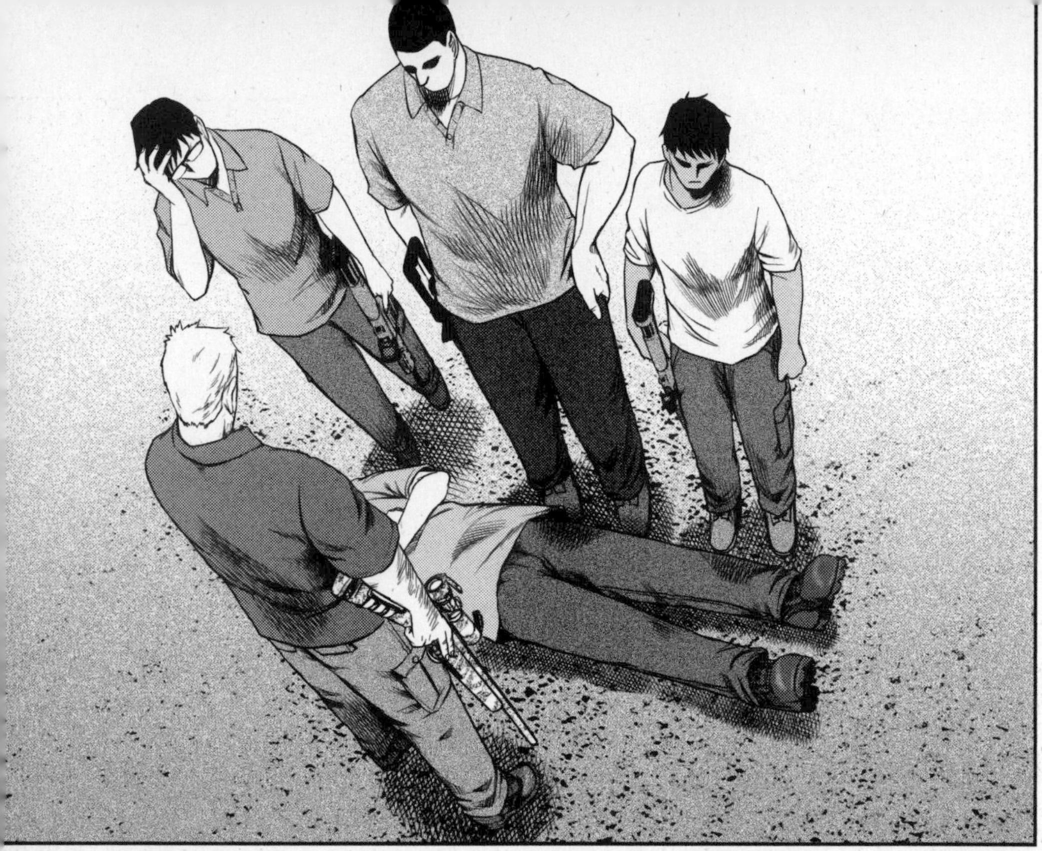

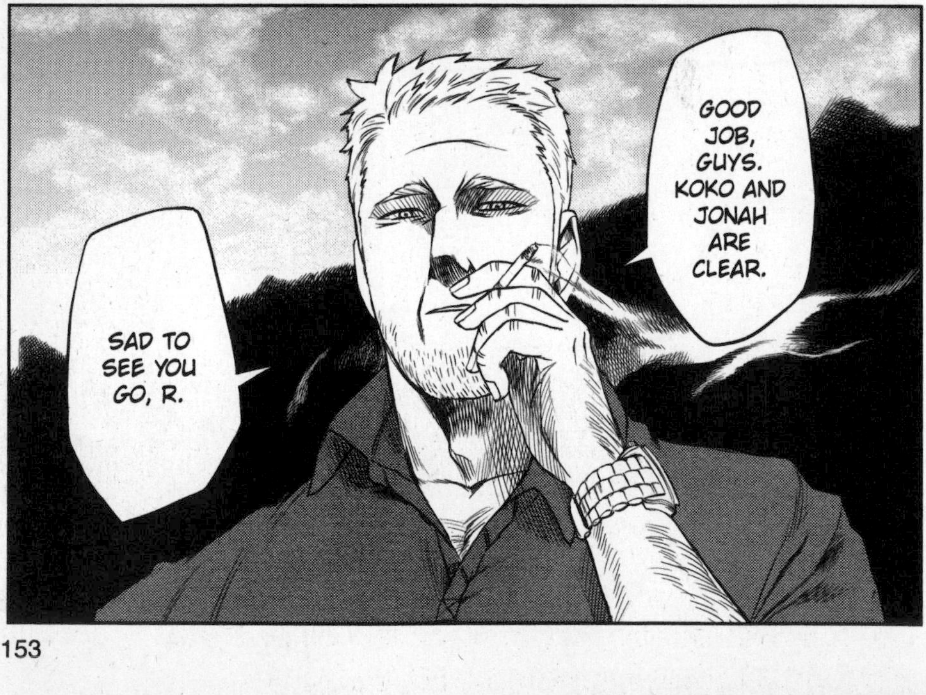
GOOD JOB, GUYS. KOKO AND JONAH ARE CLEAR.
SAD TO SEE YOU GO, R.

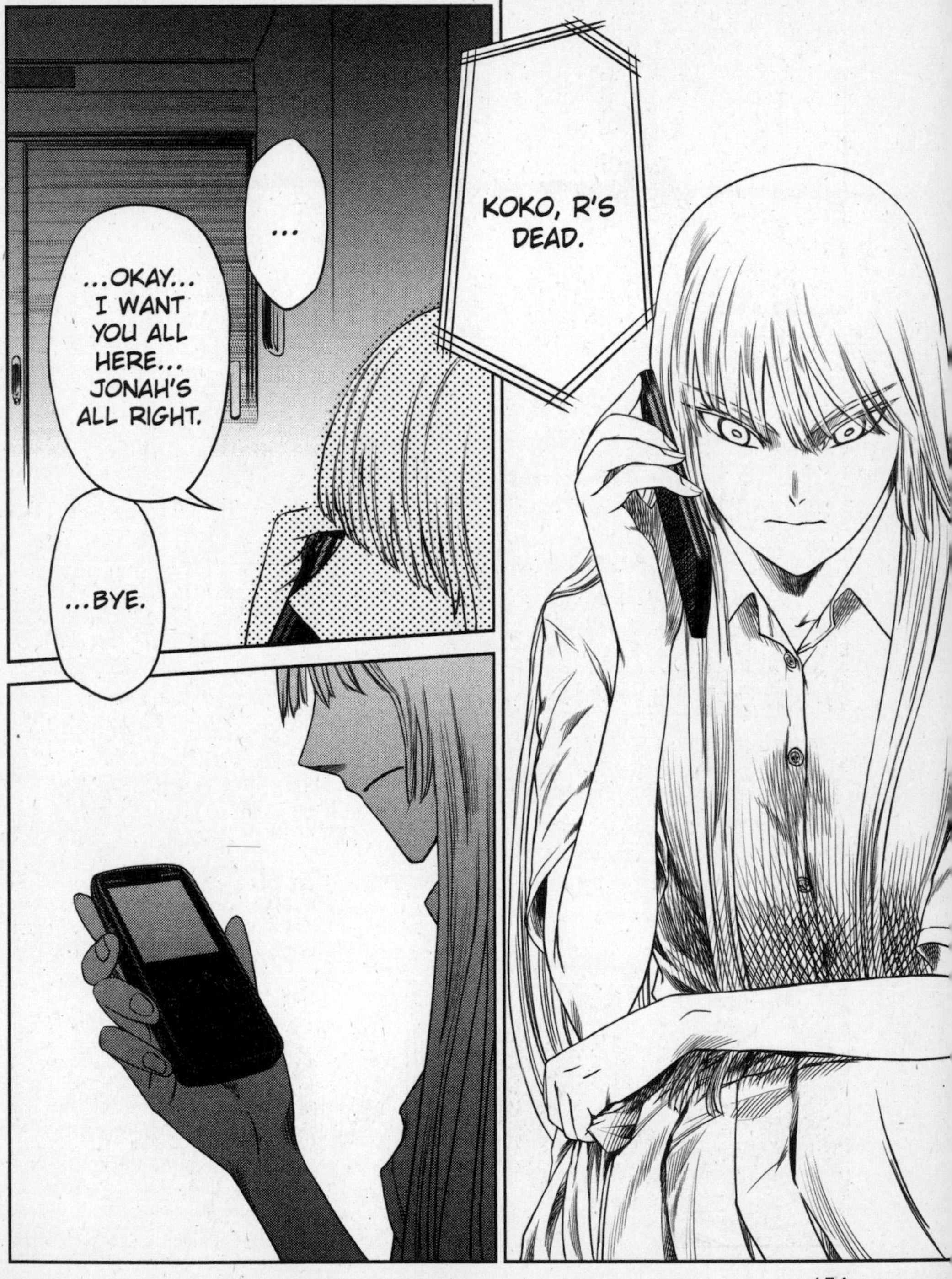
KOKO, R'S DEAD.
...
...OKAY... I WANT YOU ALL HERE... JONAH'S ALL RIGHT.
...BYE.

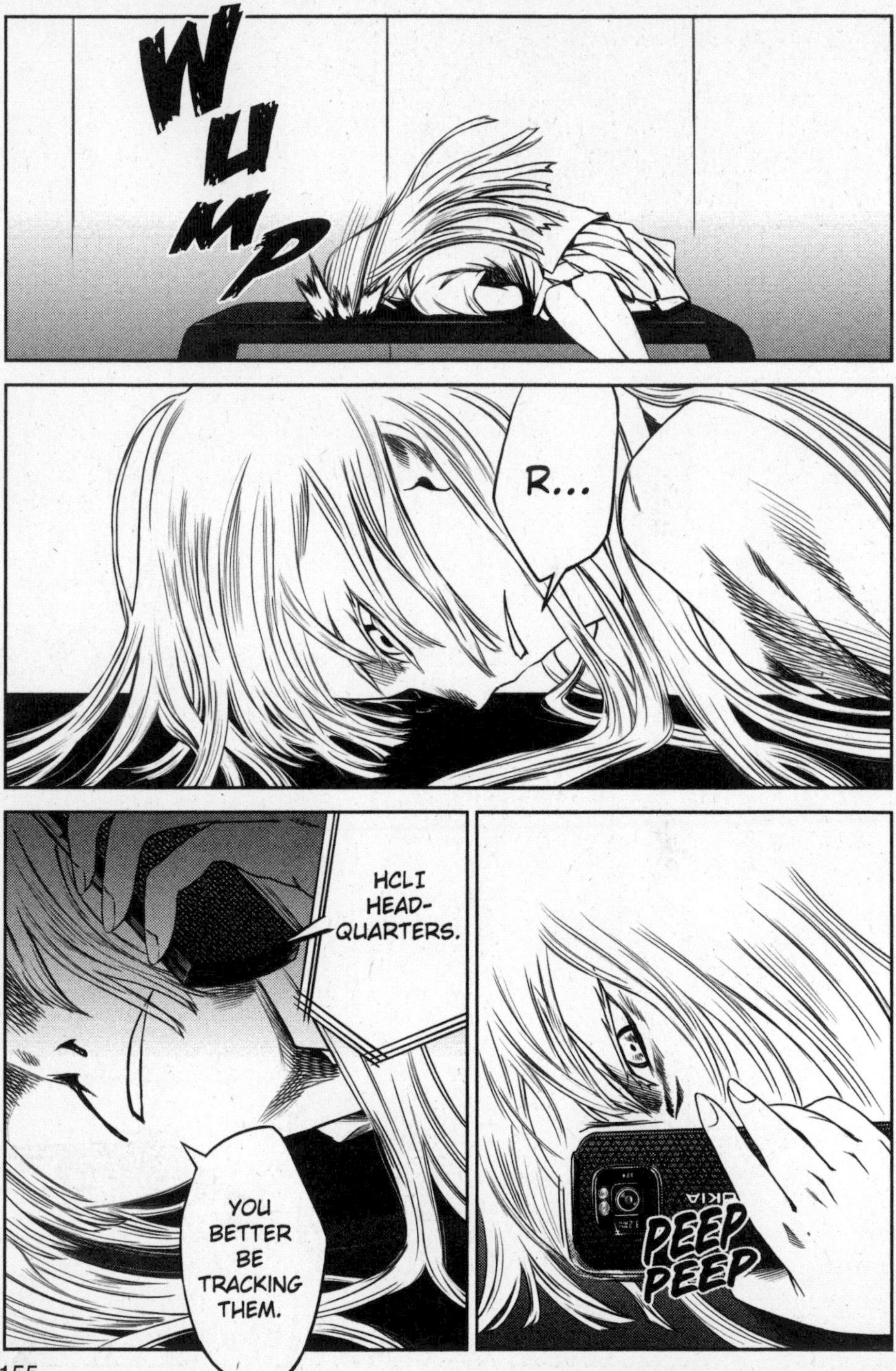
WUMP
R...
PEEP PEEP
HCLI HEAD-QUARTERS.
YOU BETTER BE TRACKING THEM.

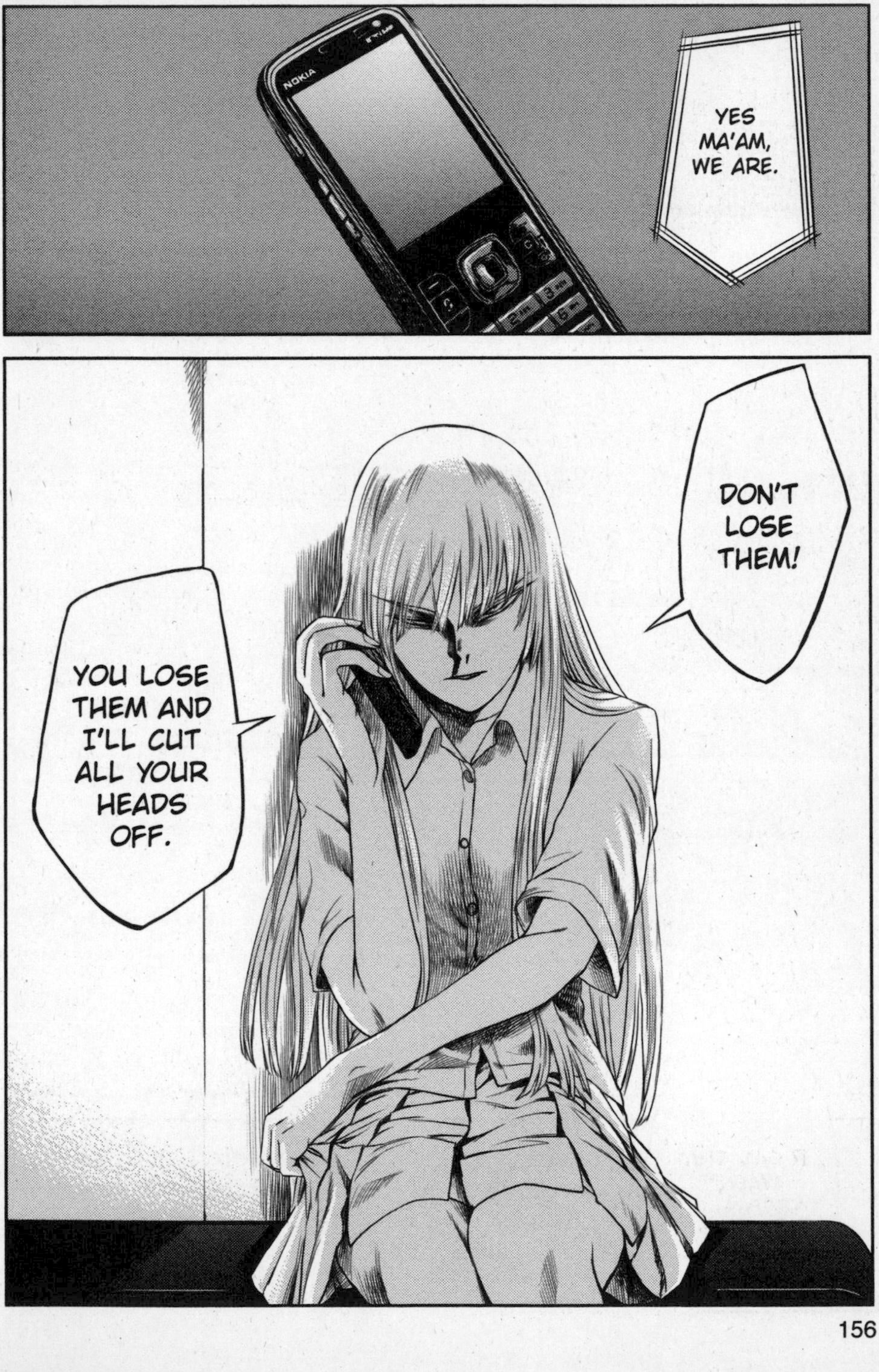
YES MA'AM, WE ARE.
DON'T LOSE THEM!
YOU LOSE THEM AND I'LL CUT ALL YOUR HEADS OFF.

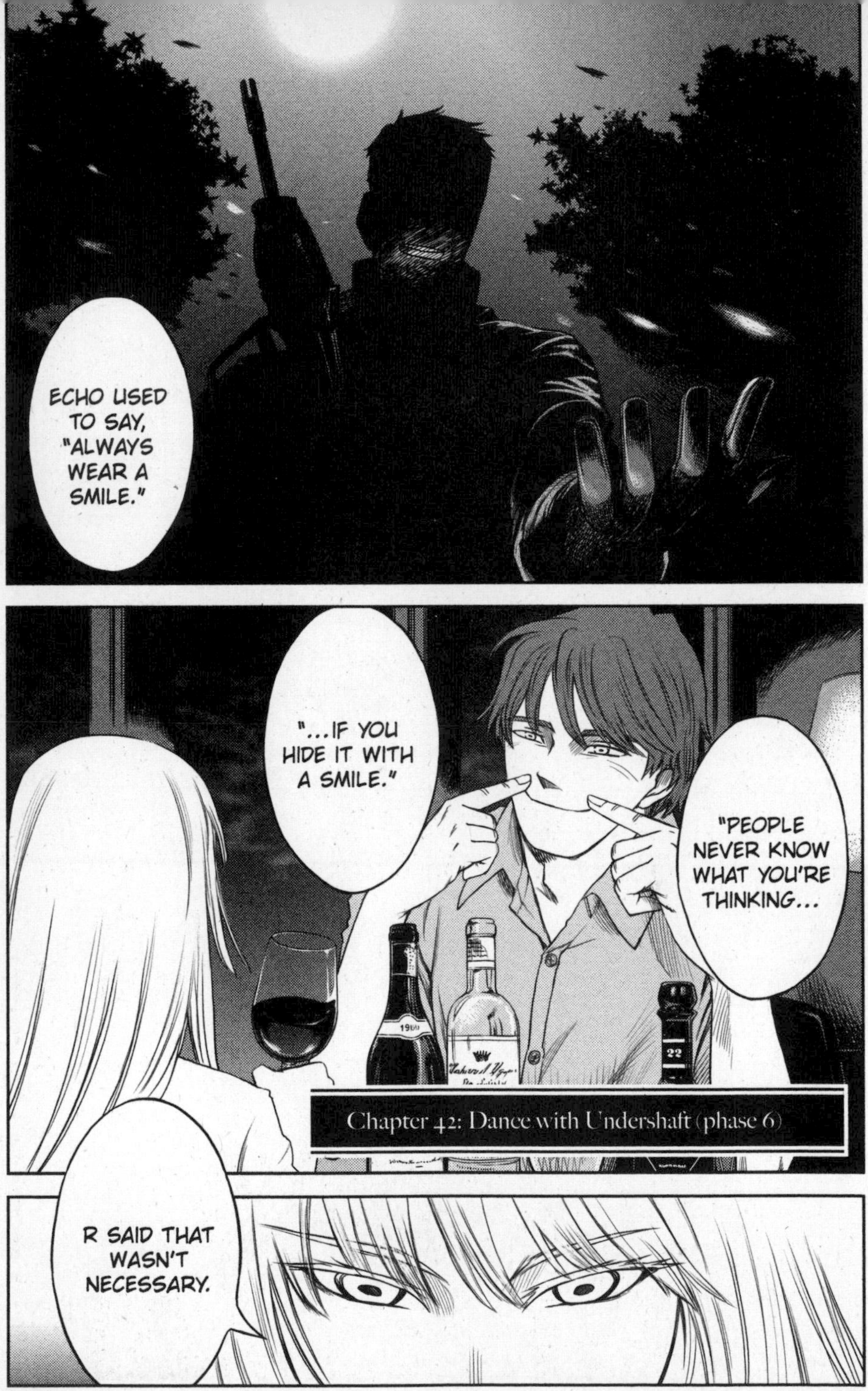
ECHO USED TO SAY, "ALWAYS WEAR A SMILE."
"PEOPLE NEVER KNOW WHAT YOU'RE THINKING...
"...IF YOU HIDE IT WITH A SMILE."
Chapter 42: Dance with Undershaft (phase 6)
R SAID THAT WASN'T NECESSARY.

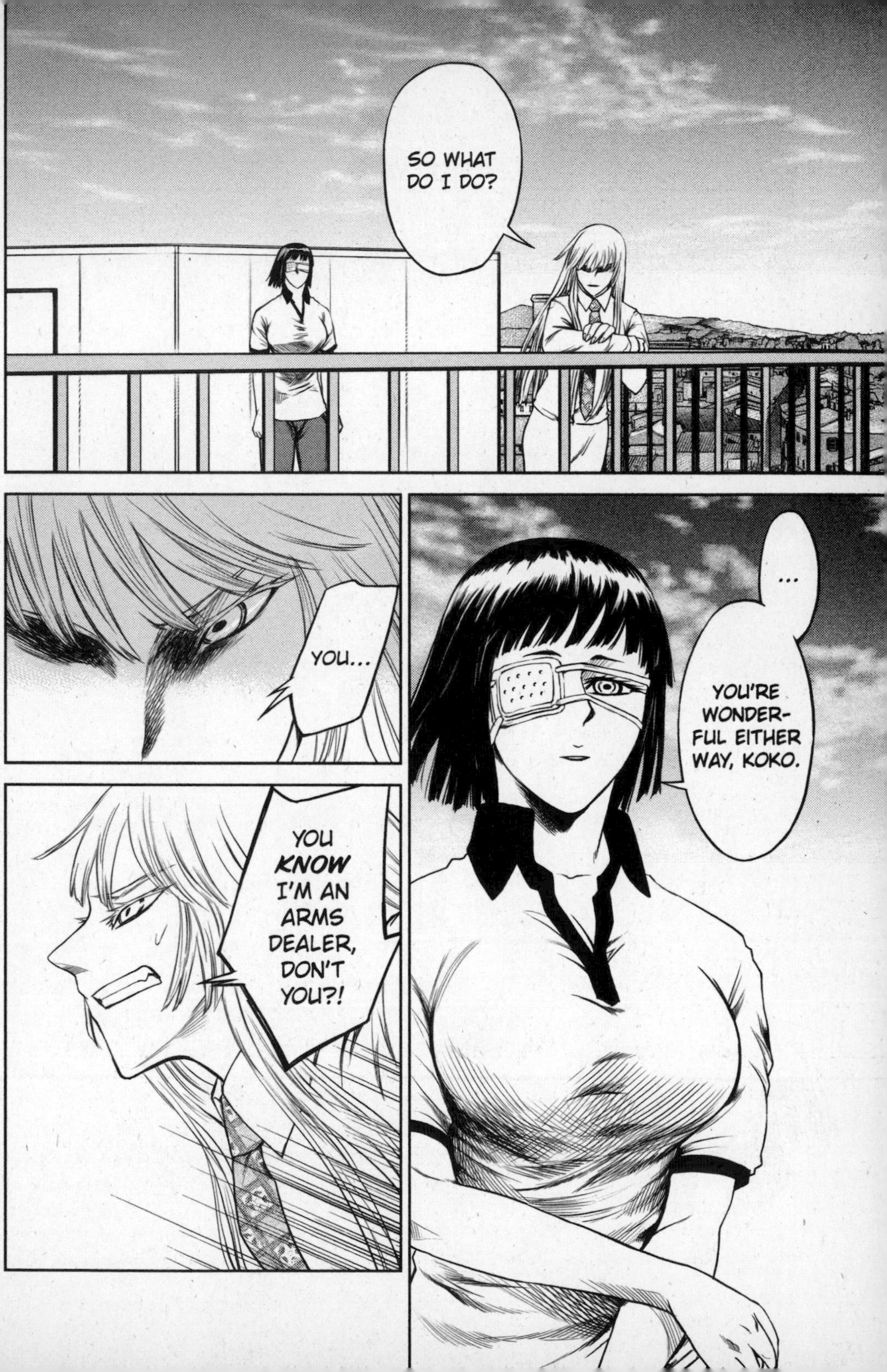
SO WHAT DO I DO?
...
YOU'RE WONDERFUL EITHER WAY, KOKO.
YOU...
YOU **KNOW** I'M AN ARMS DEALER, DON'T YOU?!

Chapter 42: Dance with Undershaft (phase 6)

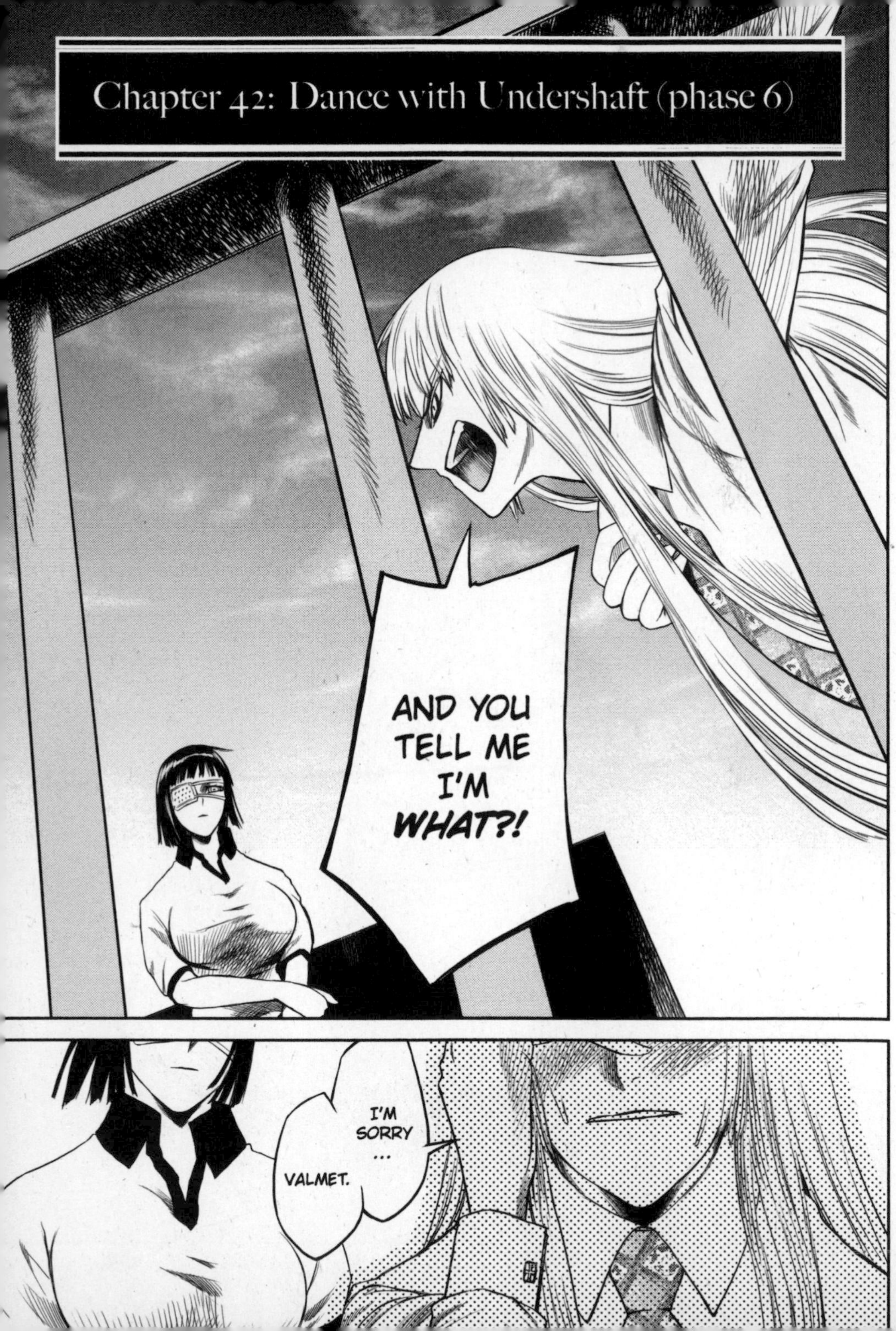
AND YOU TELL ME I'M *WHAT?!*
I'M SORRY ... VALMET.

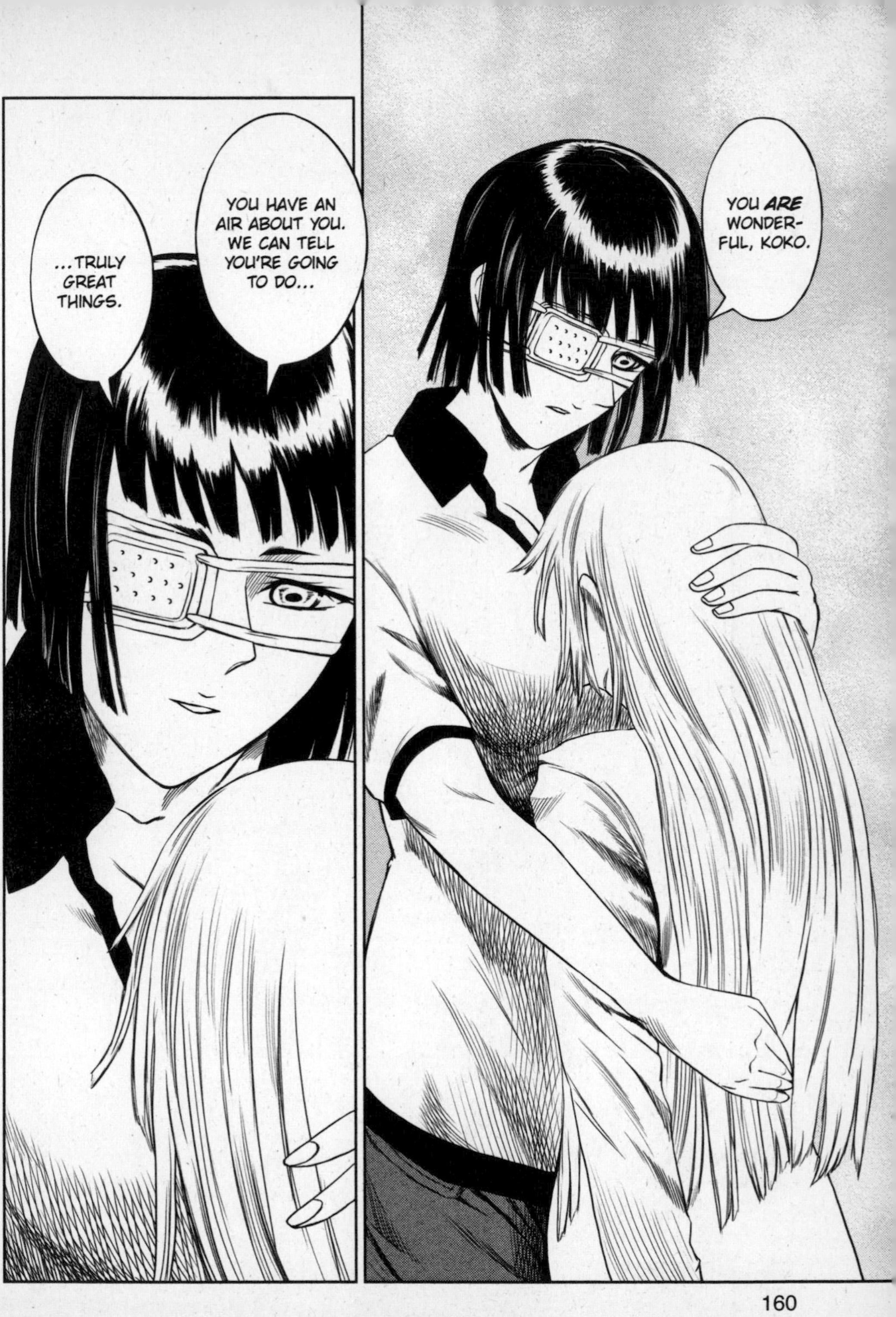
YOU **ARE** WONDER-FUL, KOKO.
YOU HAVE AN AIR ABOUT YOU. WE CAN TELL YOU'RE GOING TO DO...
...TRULY GREAT THINGS.

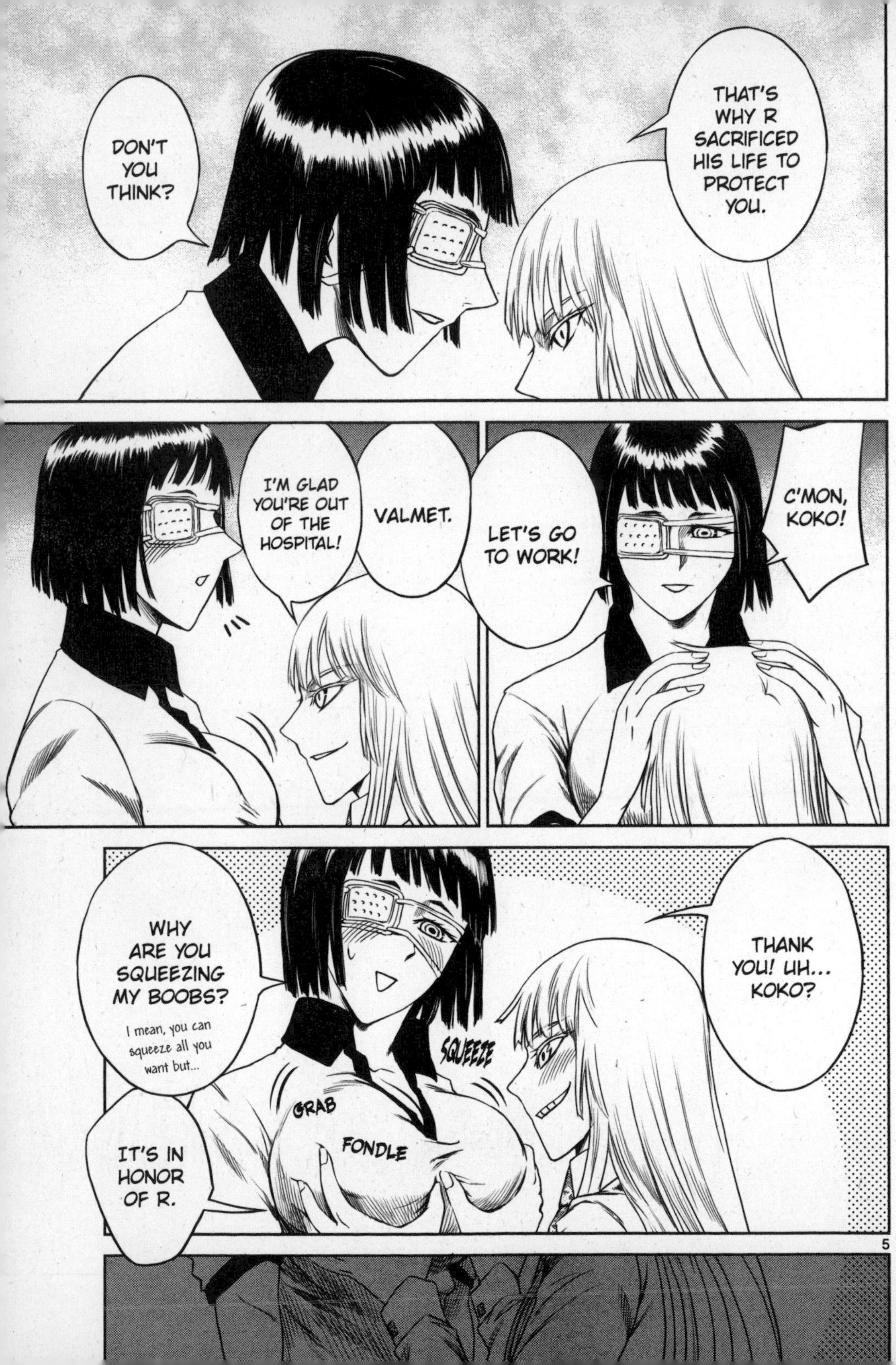
THAT'S WHY R SACRIFICED HIS LIFE TO PROTECT YOU.
DON'T YOU THINK?
C'MON, KOKO!
LET'S GO TO WORK!
VALMET.
I'M GLAD YOU'RE OUT OF THE HOSPITAL!
THANK YOU! UH... KOKO?
WHY ARE YOU SQUEEZING MY BOOBS?
I mean, you can squeeze all you want but...
SQUEEZE
GRAB
FONDLE
IT'S IN HONOR OF R.

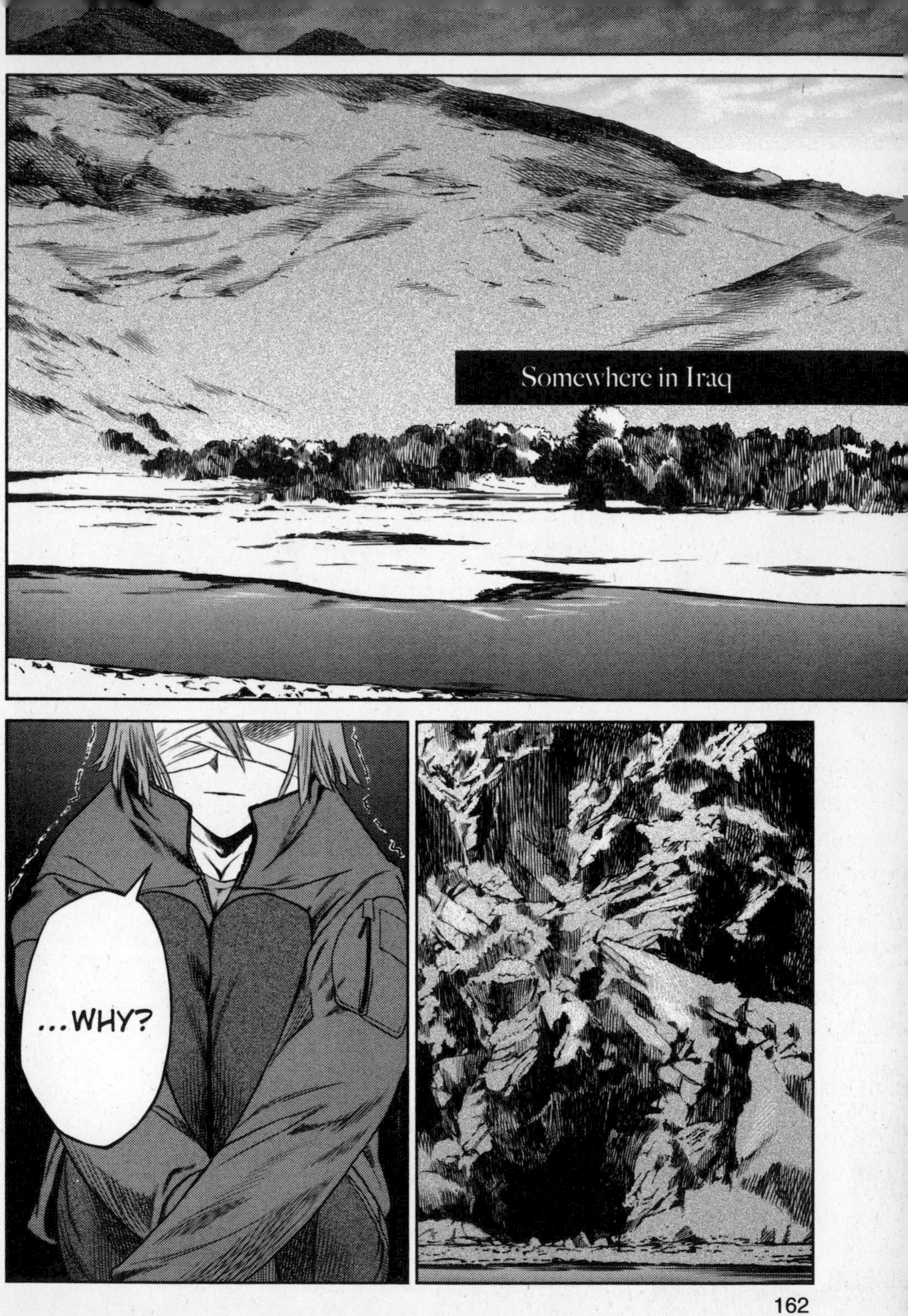
Somewhere in Iraq
...WHY?

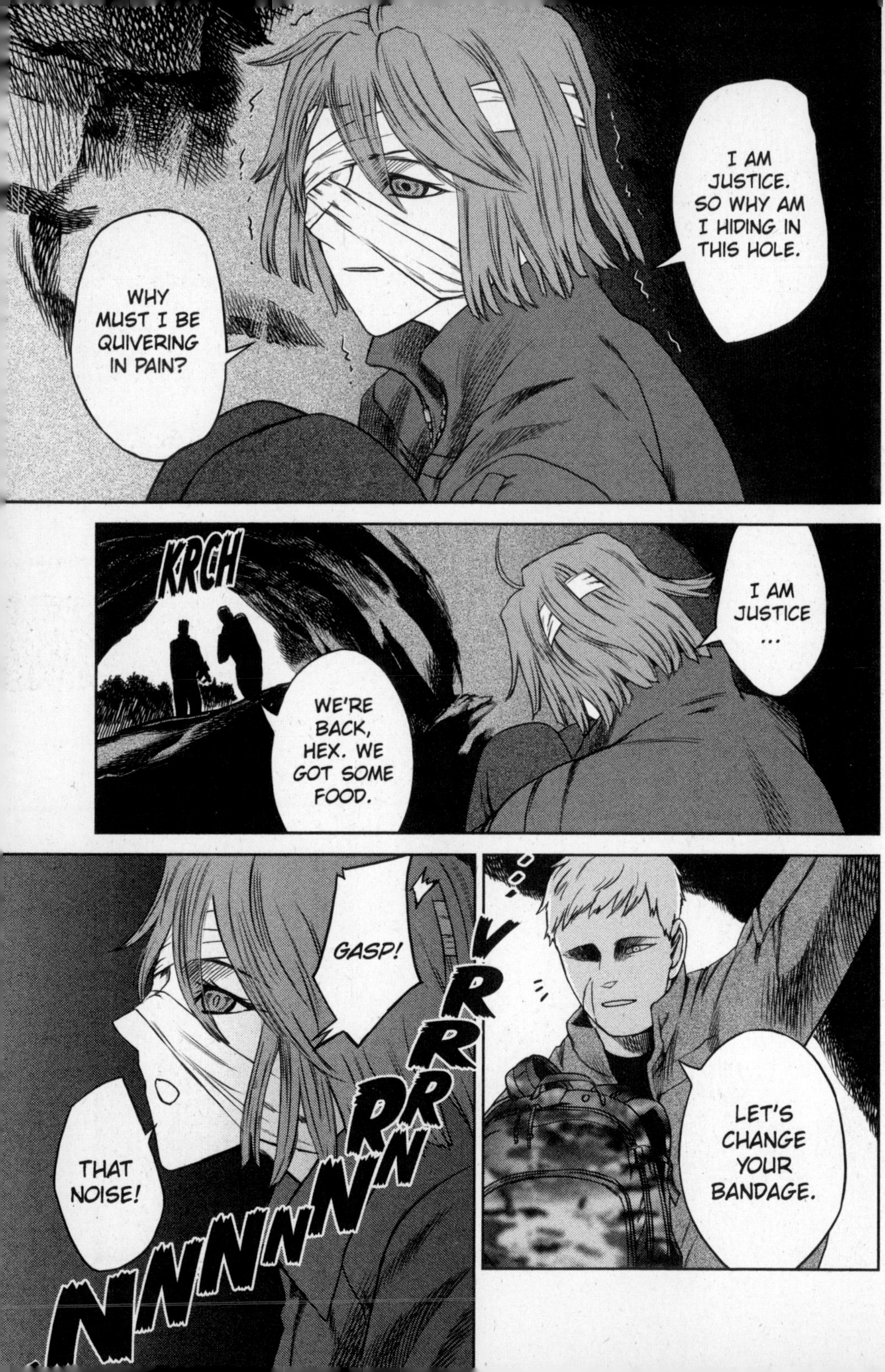
I AM JUSTICE. SO WHY AM I HIDING IN THIS HOLE.
WHY MUST I BE QUIVERING IN PAIN?
I AM JUSTICE ...
KRCH
WE'RE BACK, HEX. WE GOT SOME FOOD.
...
LET'S CHANGE YOUR BANDAGE.
VRRRRNNNNNNNN
GASP!
THAT NOISE!

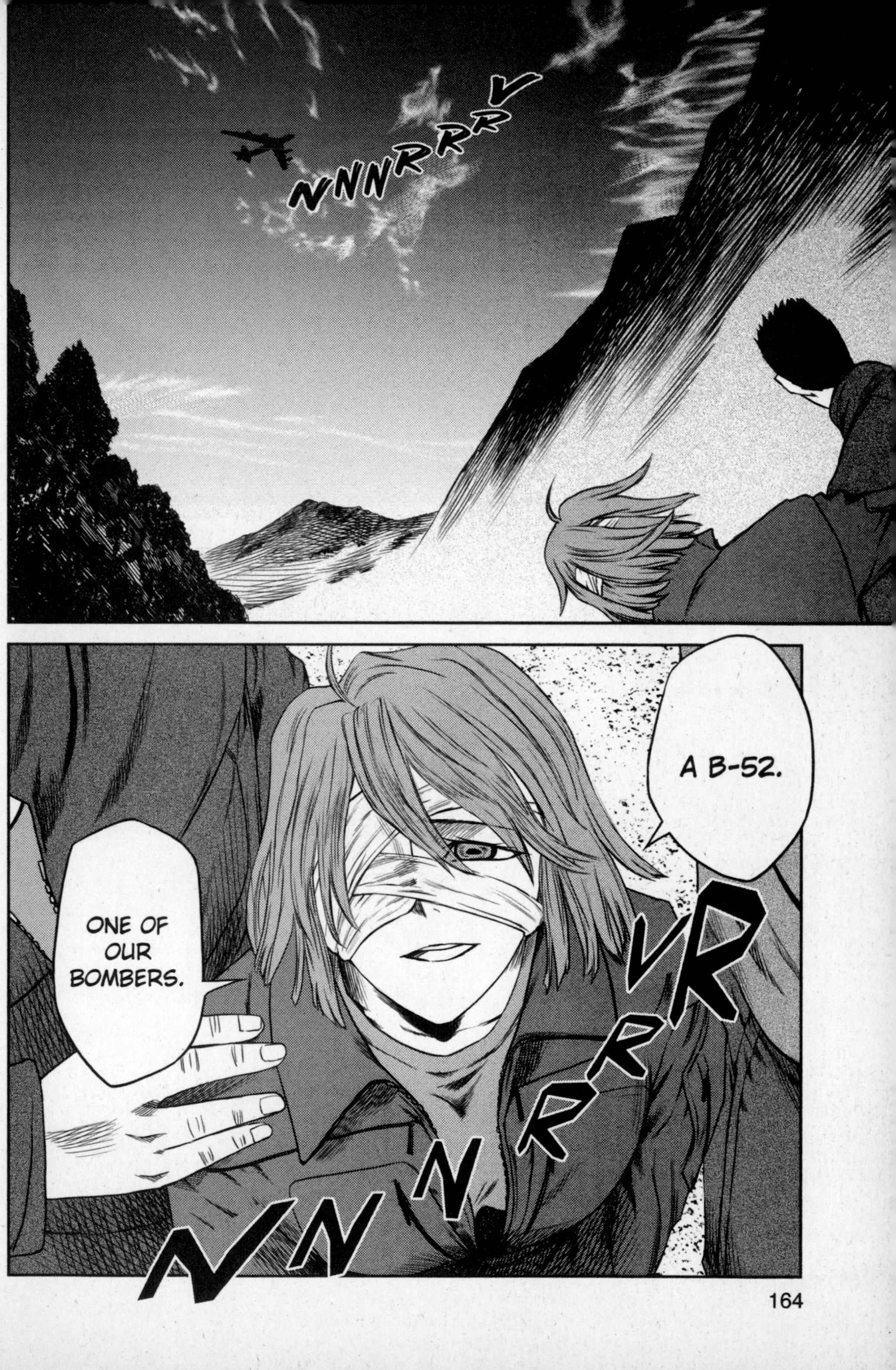
NNNRRRV
A B-52.
ONE OF OUR BOMBERS.
NNNRRRVR

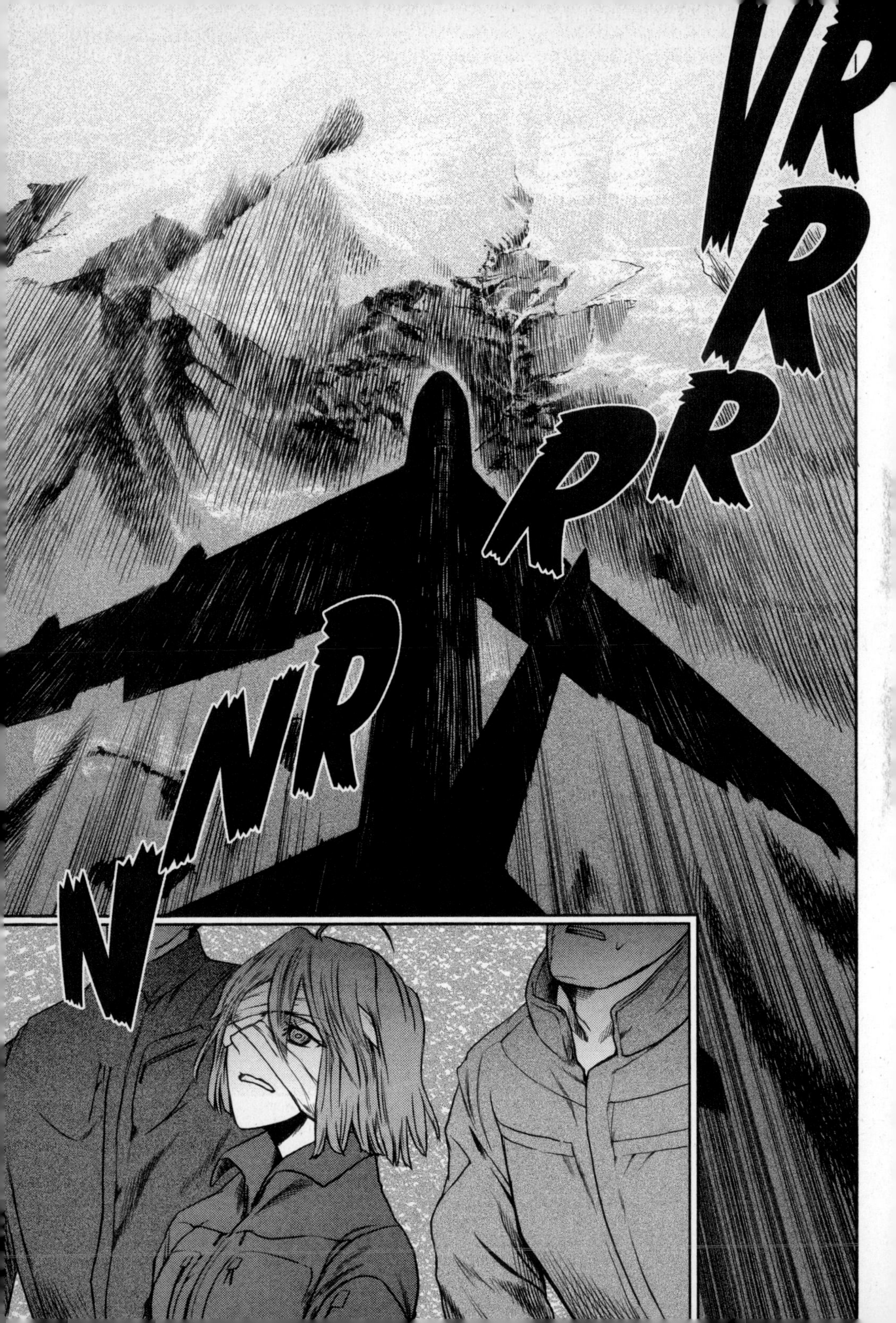
VR R R RR R NR N N

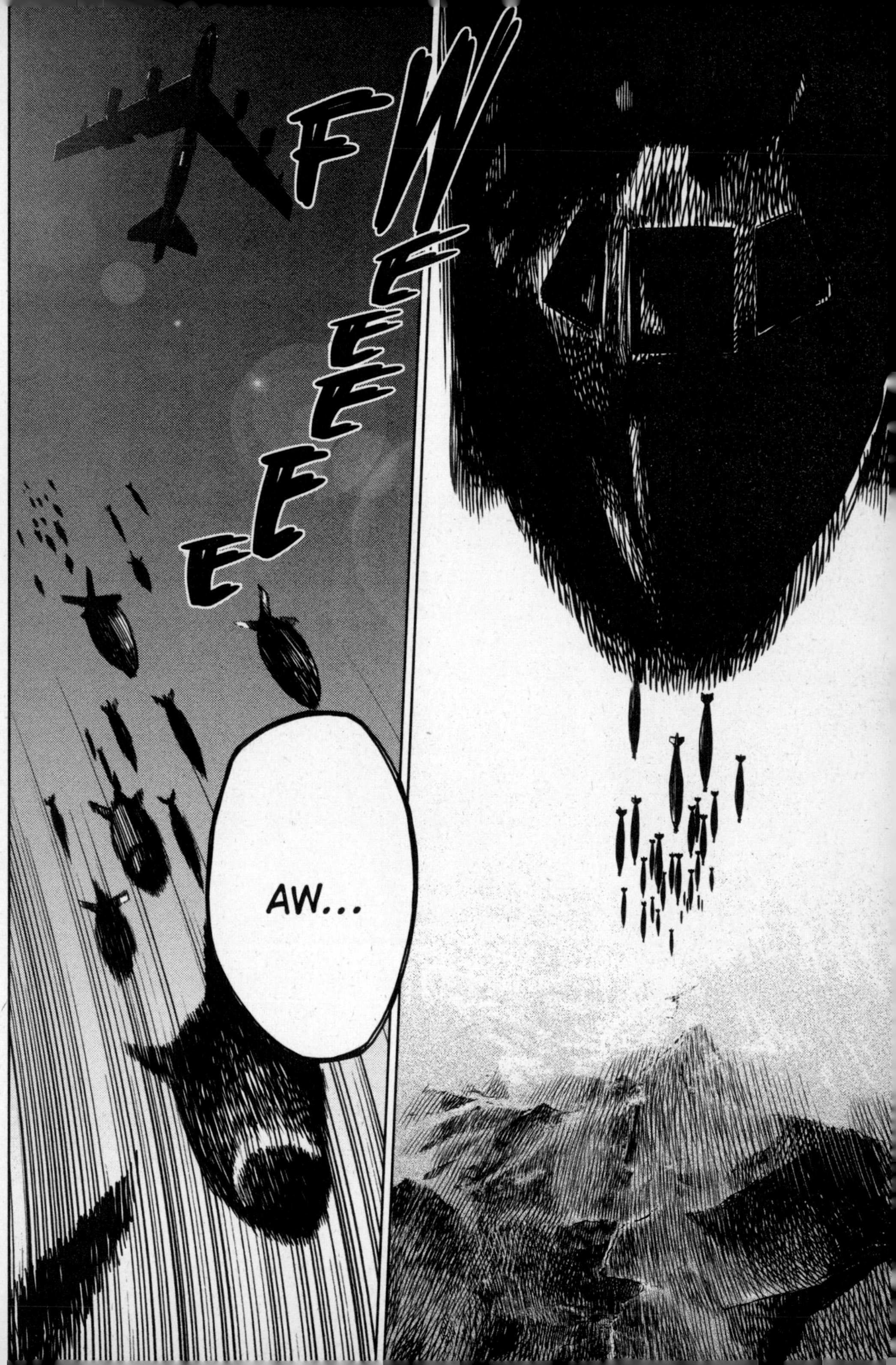
FWEEEEE
AW...

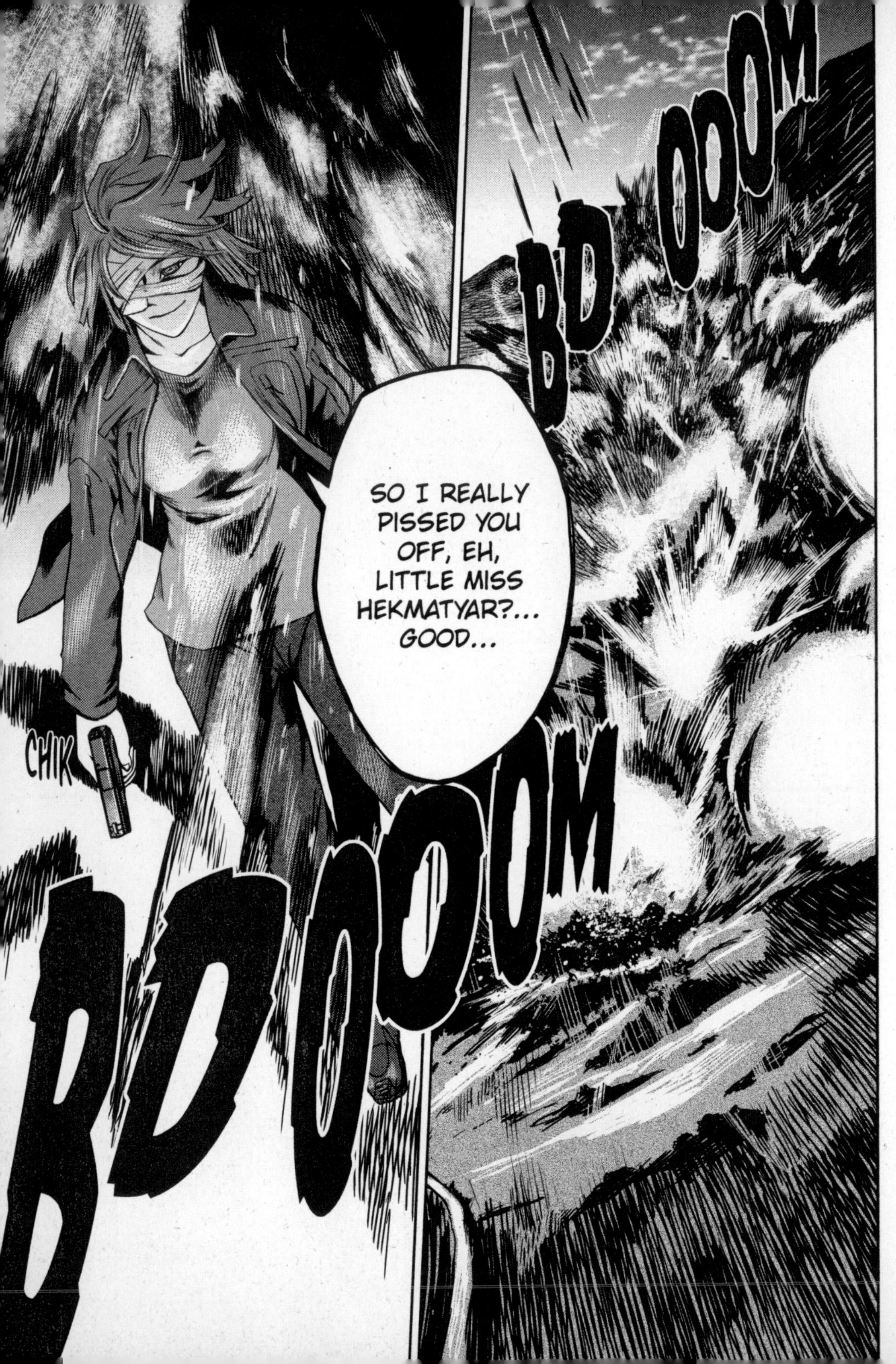
BD OOOM
SO I REALLY PISSED YOU OFF, EH, LITTLE MISS HEKMATYAR?... GOOD...
CHIK
BDOOOOM

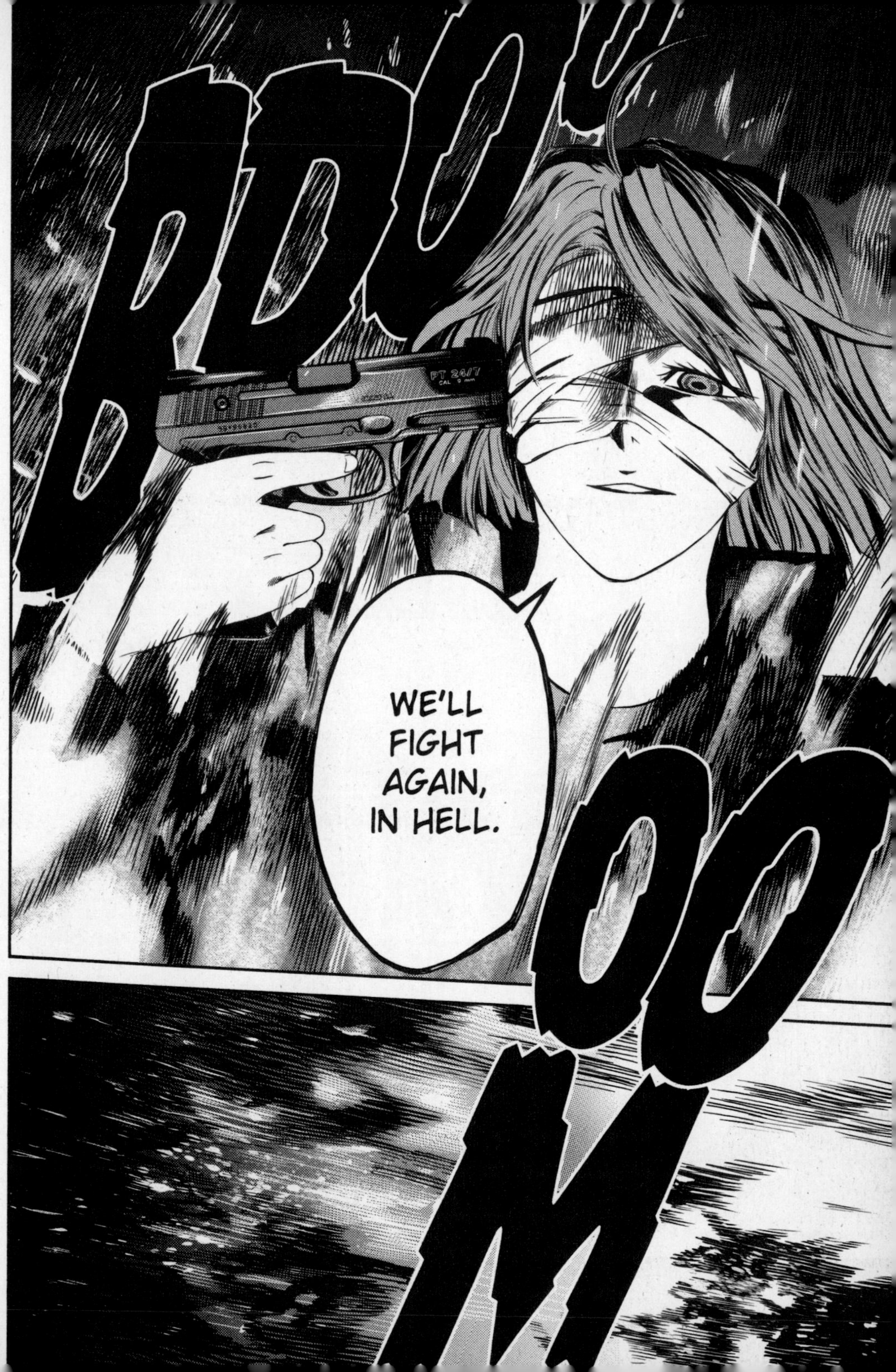
BDOOOOM
WE'LL FIGHT AGAIN, IN HELL.
PT 24/7 CAL 9 mm

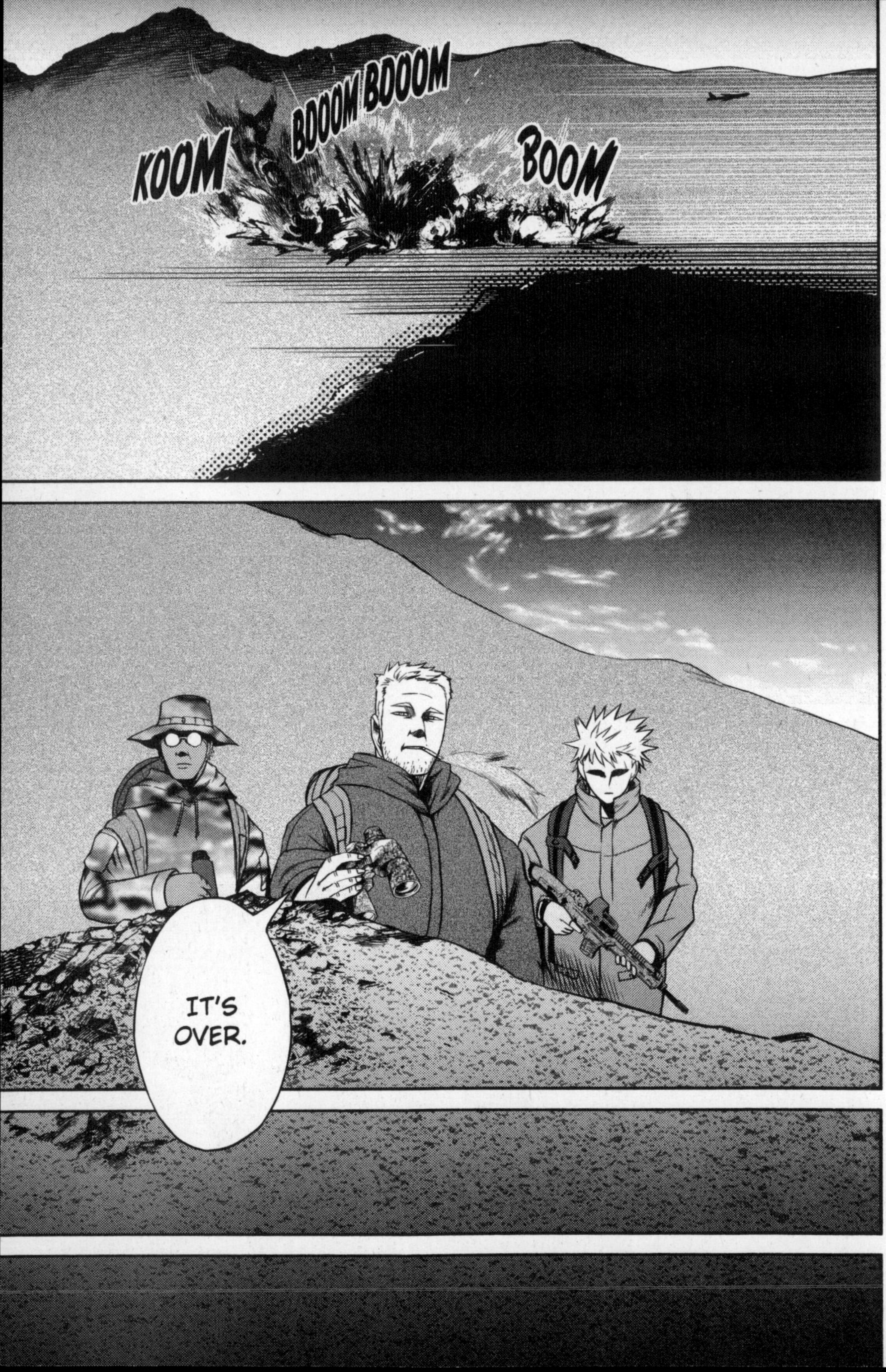
BOOM
BDOOM BDOOM
KOOM
IT'S OVER.

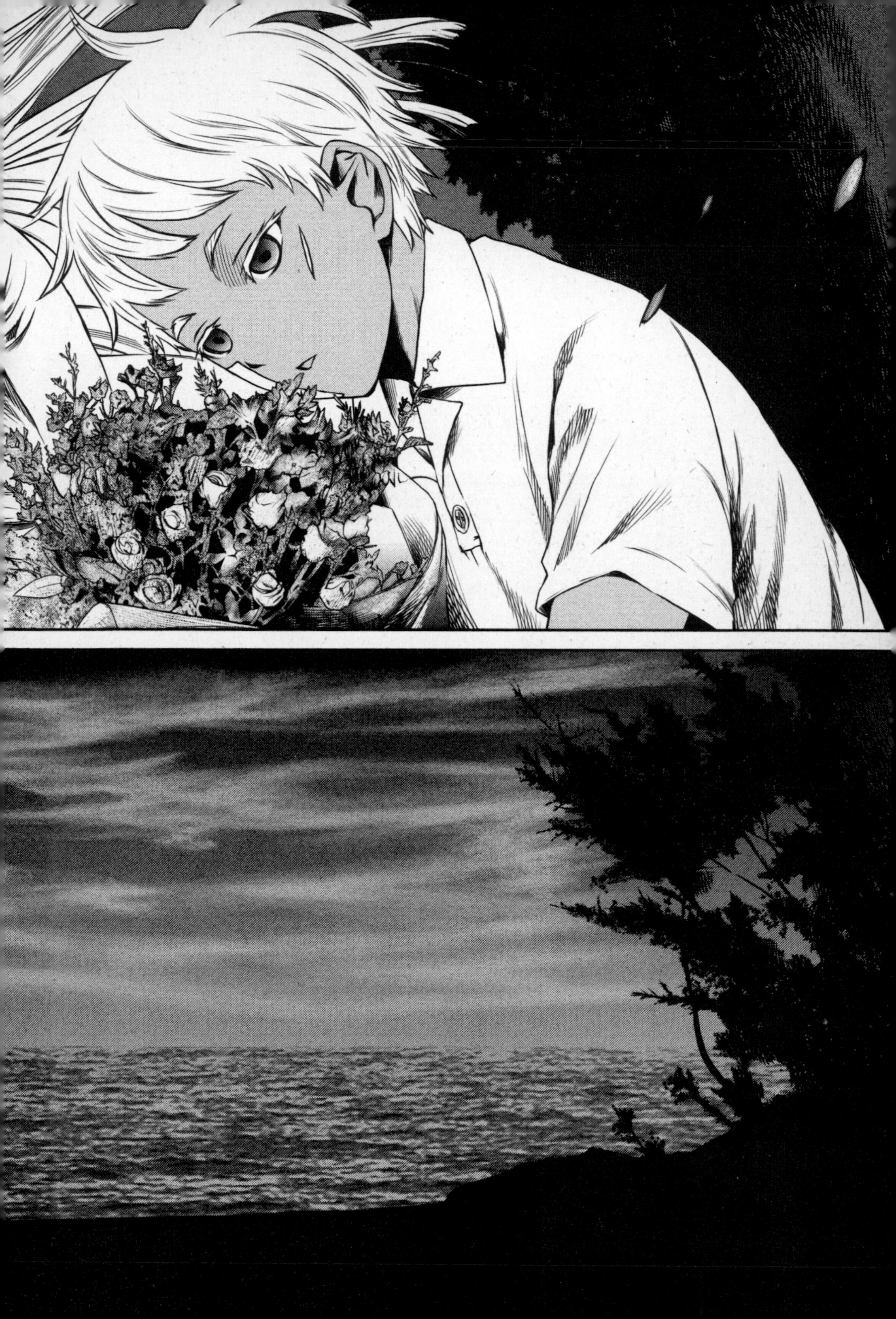

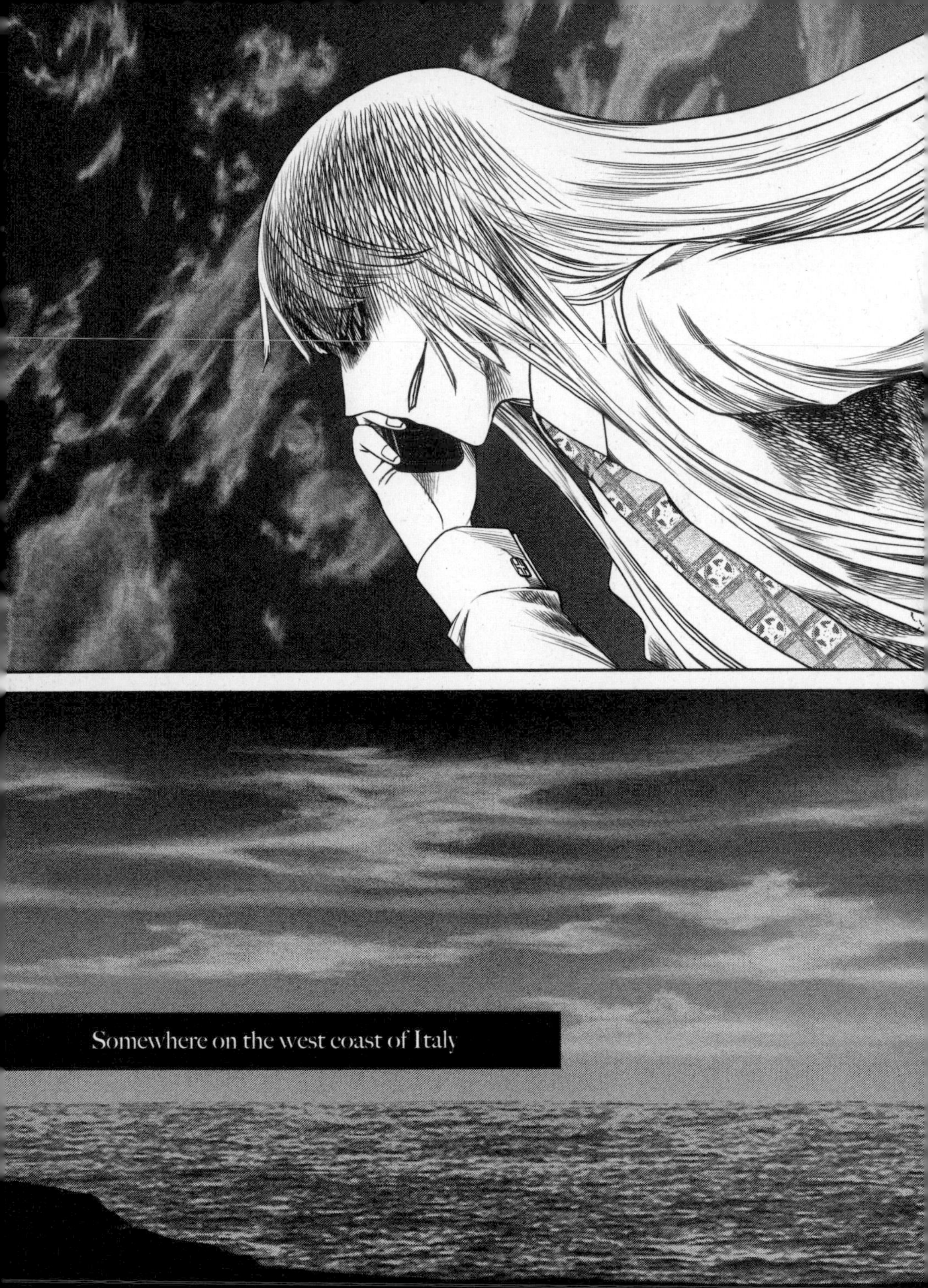
Somewhere on the west coast of Italy

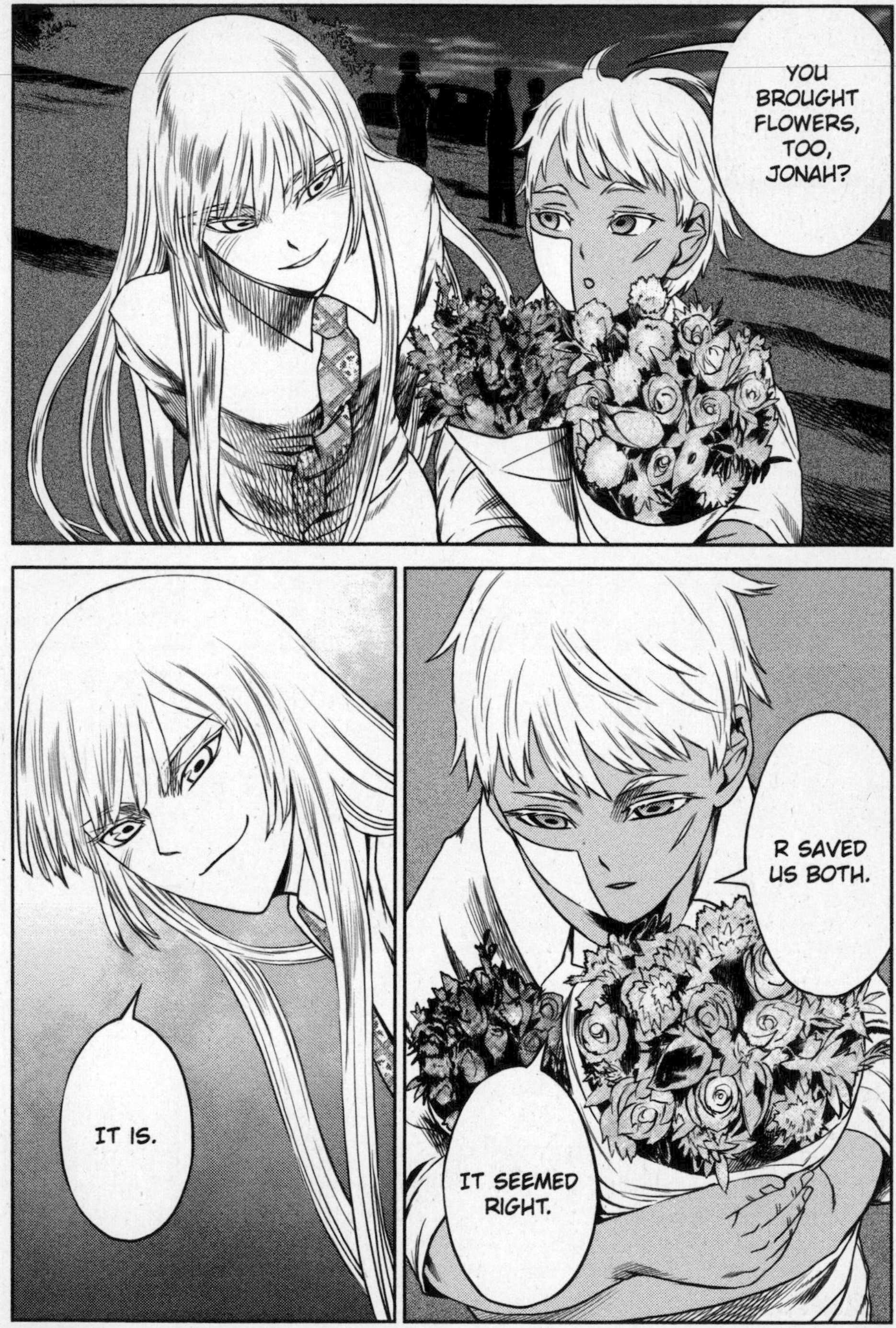
YOU BROUGHT FLOWERS, TOO, JONAH?
R SAVED US BOTH.
IT SEEMED RIGHT.
IT IS.

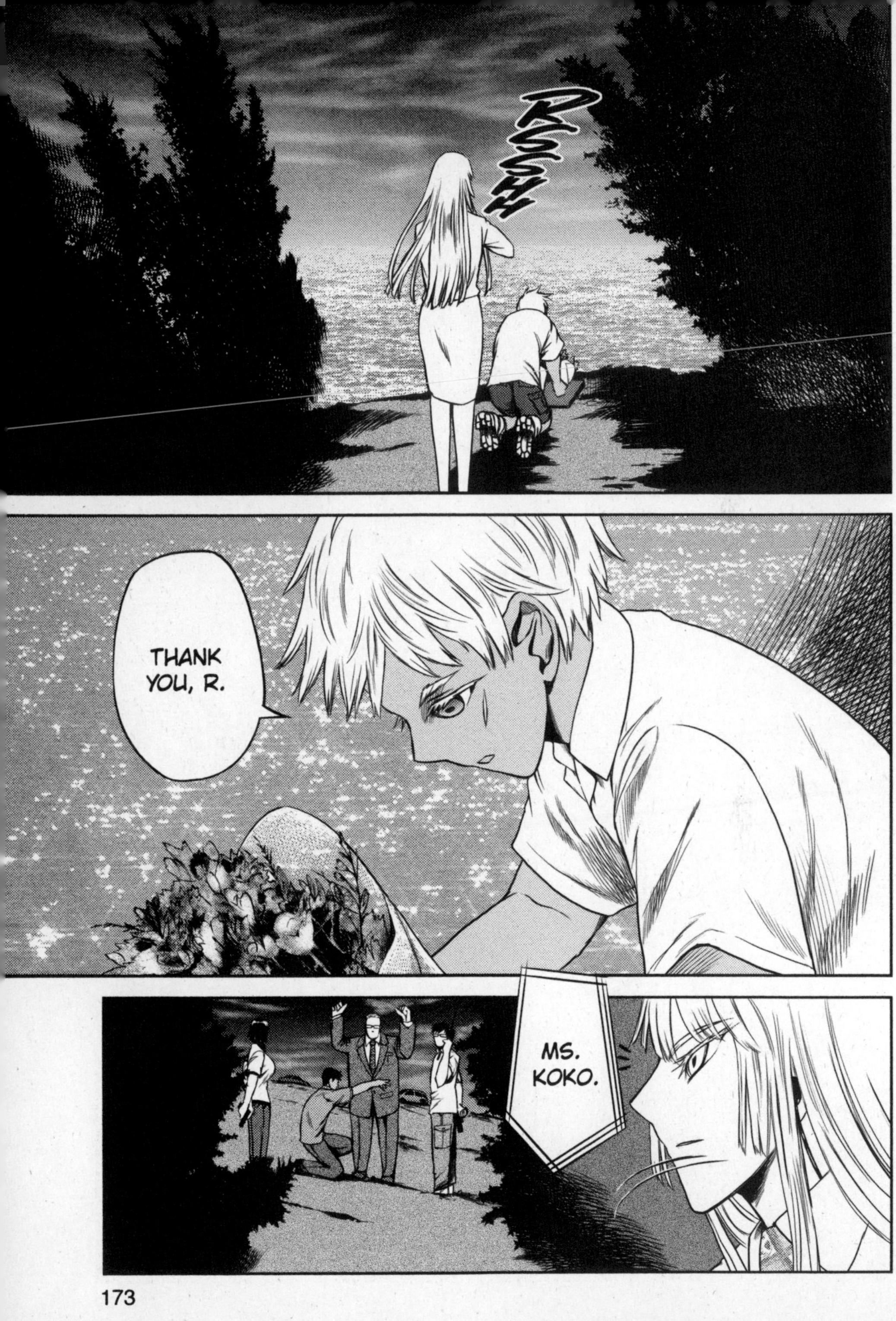
RSSHH
THANK YOU, R.
MS. KOKO.

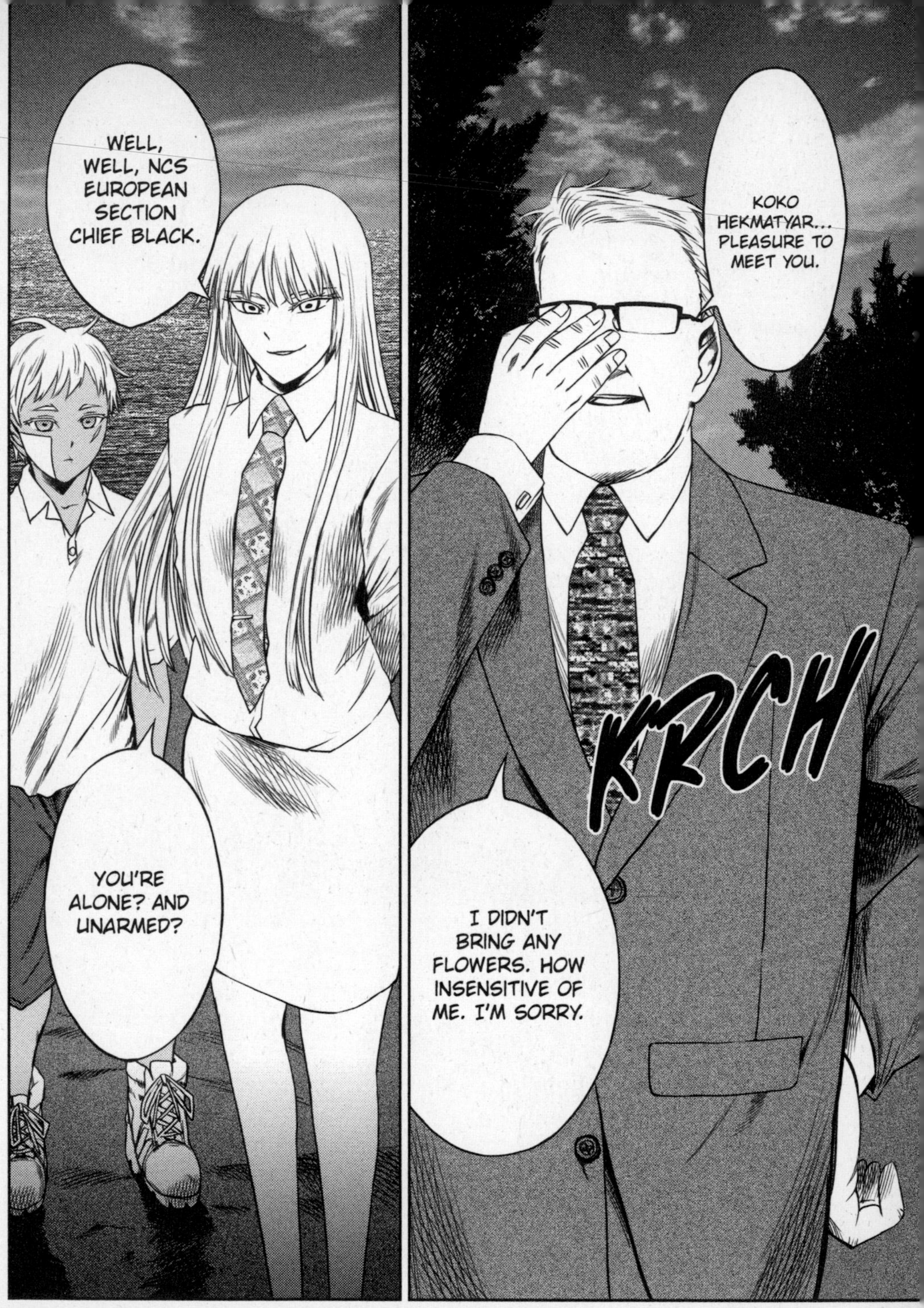
WELL, WELL, NCS EUROPEAN SECTION CHIEF BLACK.
YOU'RE ALONE? AND UNARMED?
KOKO HEKMATYAR... PLEASURE TO MEET YOU.
KRCH
I DIDN'T BRING ANY FLOWERS. HOW INSENSITIVE OF ME. I'M SORRY.

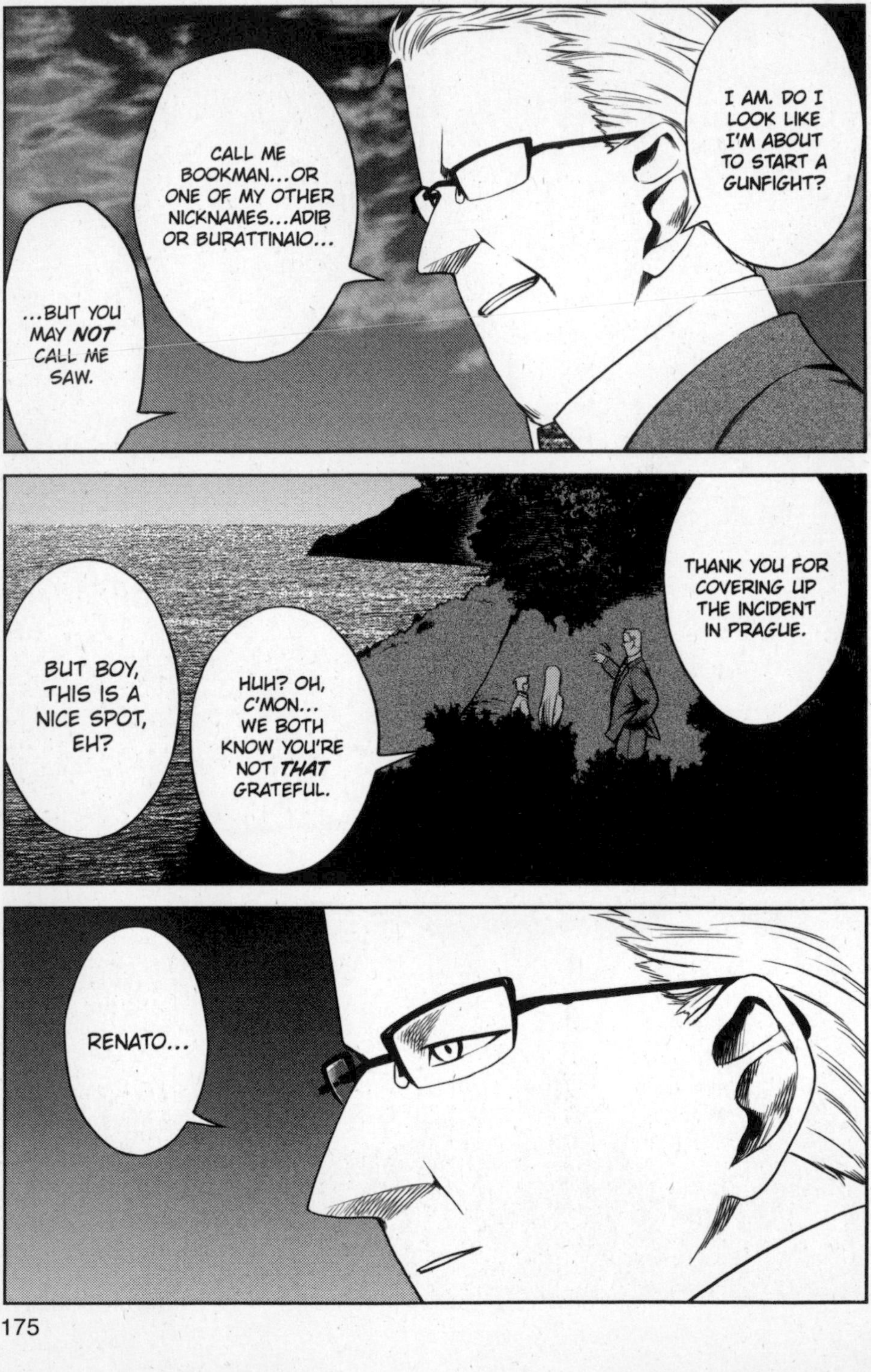
I AM. DO I LOOK LIKE I'M ABOUT TO START A GUNFIGHT?
CALL ME BOOKMAN...OR ONE OF MY OTHER NICKNAMES...ADIB OR BURATTINAIO...
...BUT YOU MAY ***NOT*** CALL ME SAW.
THANK YOU FOR COVERING UP THE INCIDENT IN PRAGUE.
HUH? OH, C'MON... WE BOTH KNOW YOU'RE NOT ***THAT*** GRATEFUL.
BUT BOY, THIS IS A NICE SPOT, EH?
RENATO...

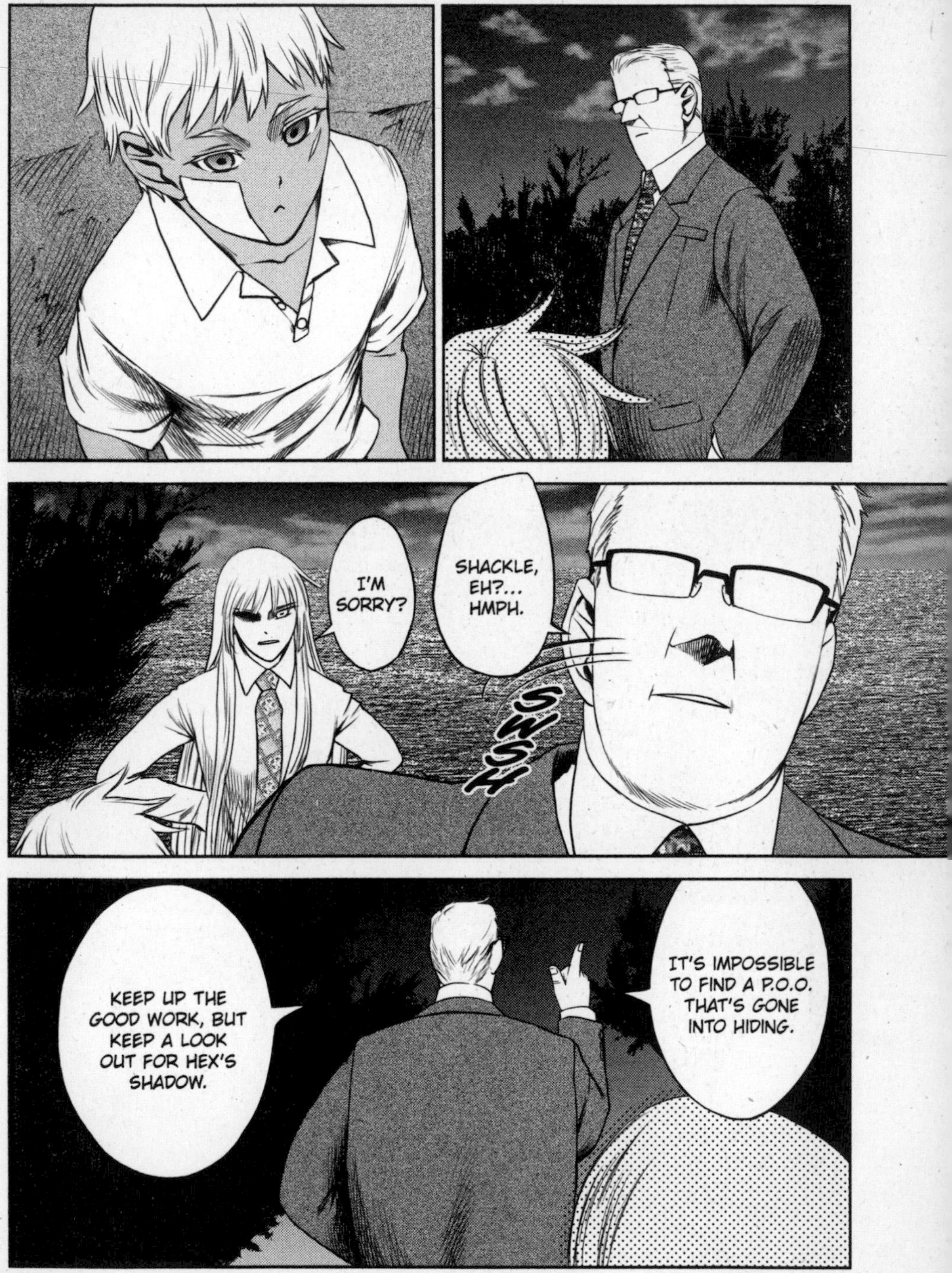
SHACKLE, EH?... HMPH.
I'M SORRY?
SWSH
IT'S IMPOSSIBLE TO FIND A P.O.O. THAT'S GONE INTO HIDING.
KEEP UP THE GOOD WORK, BUT KEEP A LOOK OUT FOR HEX'S SHADOW.

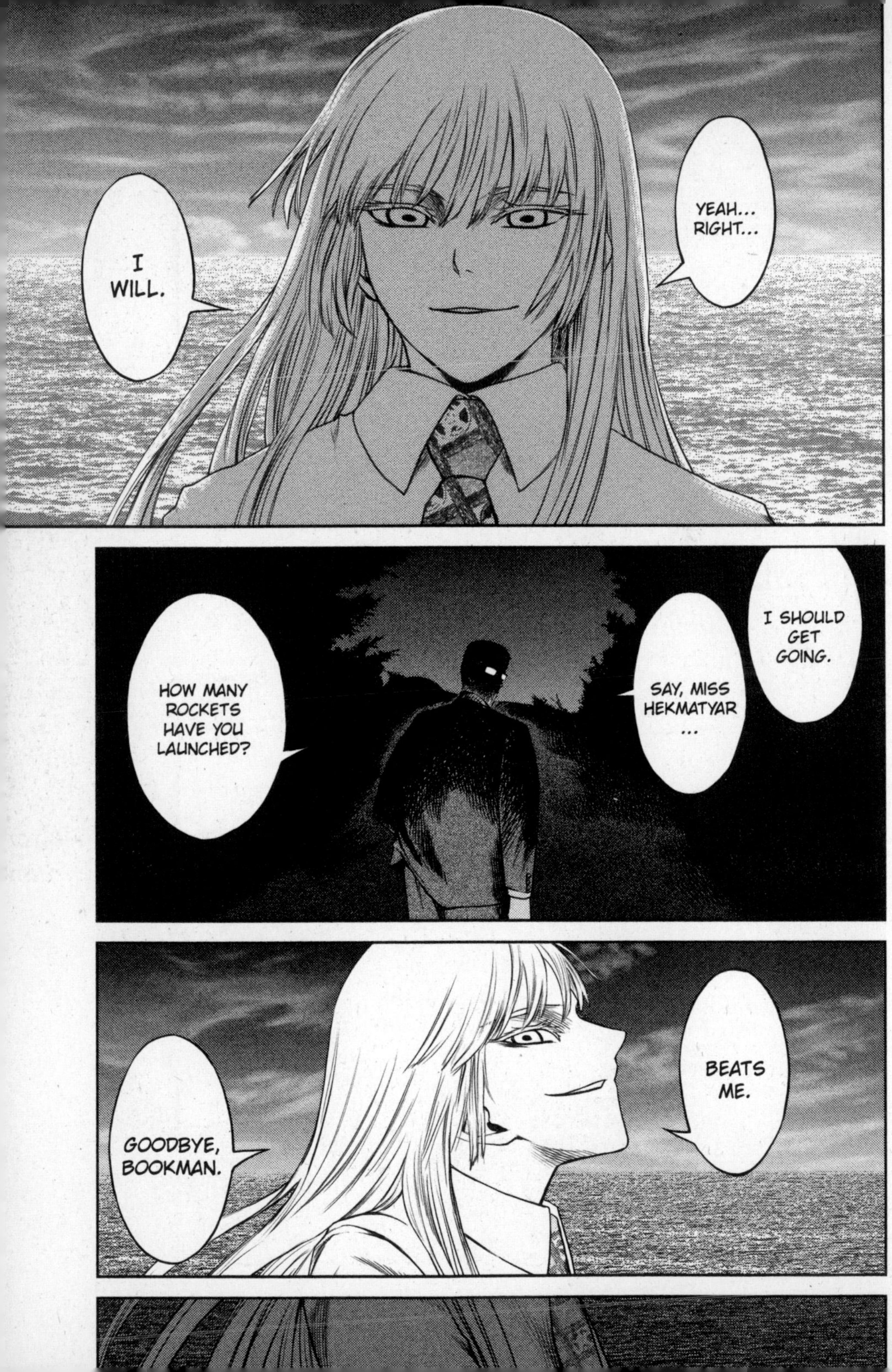
YEAH... RIGHT...
I WILL.
I SHOULD GET GOING.
SAY, MISS HEKMATYAR ...
HOW MANY ROCKETS HAVE YOU LAUNCHED?
BEATS ME.
GOODBYE, BOOKMAN.

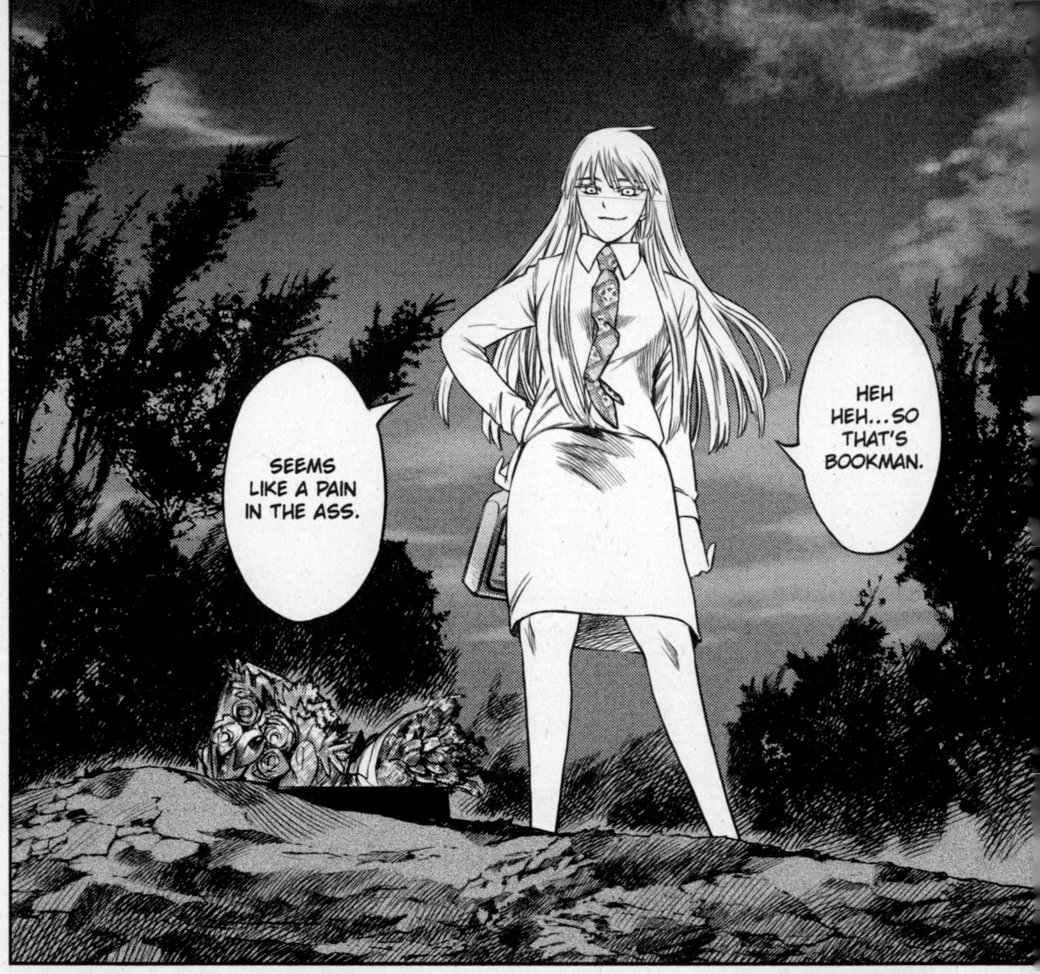
HEH HEH...SO THAT'S BOOKMAN.
SEEMS LIKE A PAIN IN THE ASS.
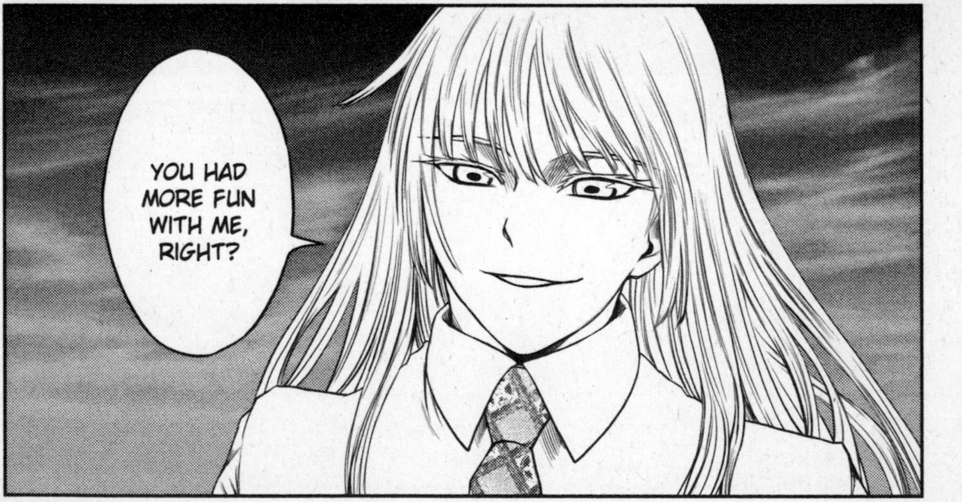
YOU HAD MORE FUN WITH ME, RIGHT?

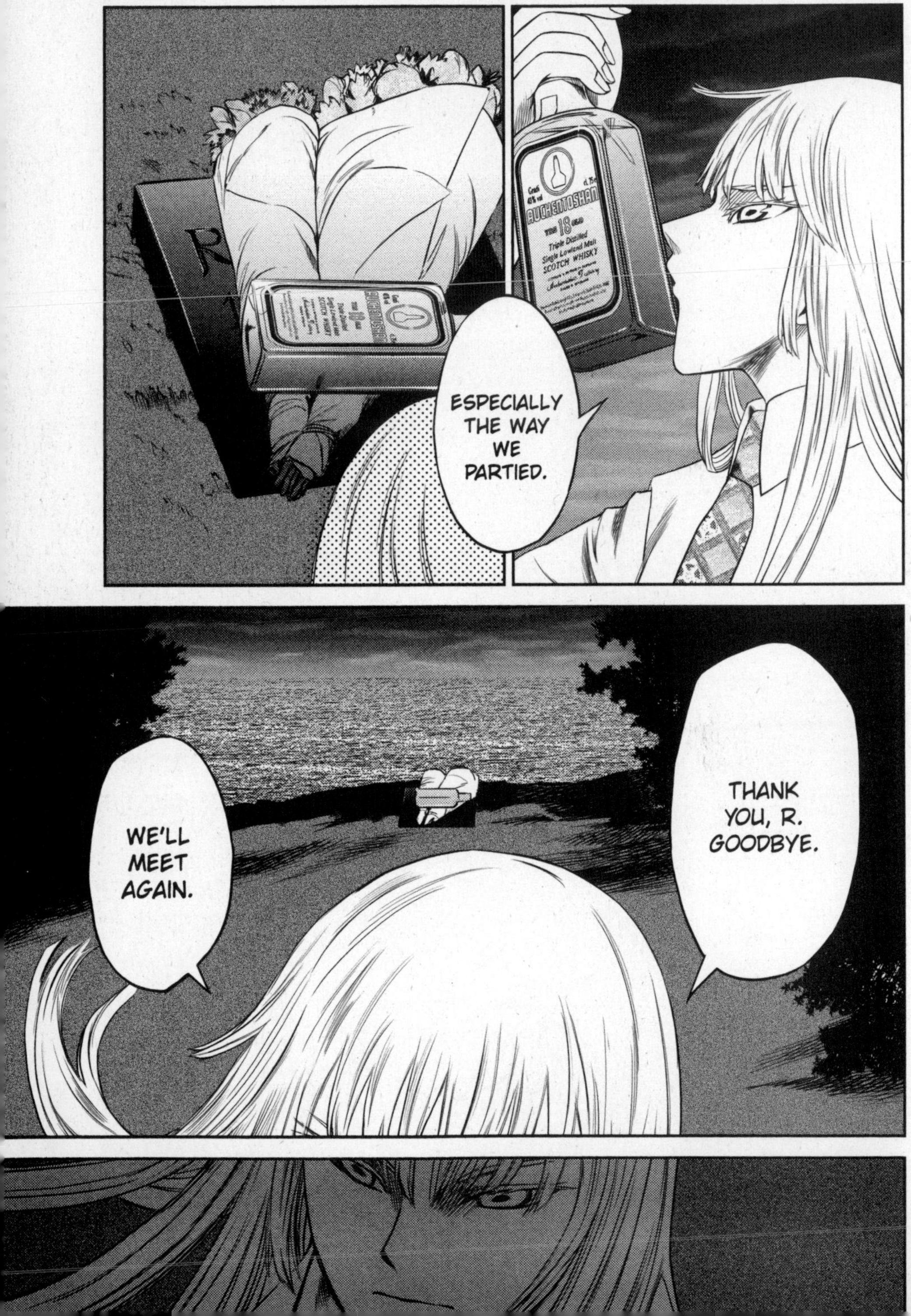
AUCHENTOSHAN
18
Triple Distilled
Single Lowland Malt
SCOTCH WHISKY
ESPECIALLY THE WAY WE PARTIED.
THANK YOU, R. GOODBYE.
WE'LL MEET AGAIN.

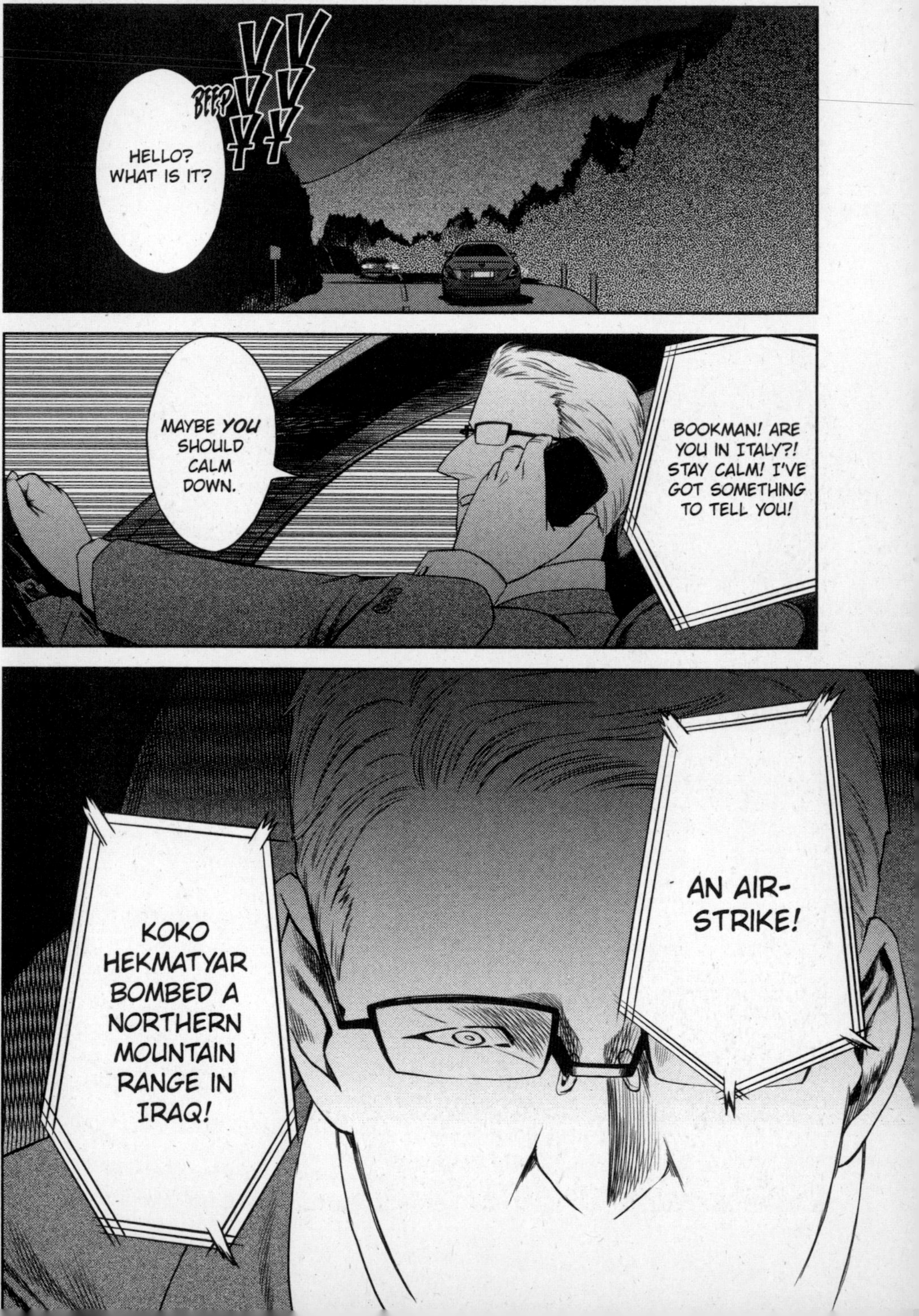
BEEP
HELLO? WHAT IS IT?
BOOKMAN! ARE YOU IN ITALY?! STAY CALM! I'VE GOT SOMETHING TO TELL YOU!
MAYBE *YOU* SHOULD CALM DOWN.
AN AIR-STRIKE!
KOKO HEKMATYAR BOMBED A NORTHERN MOUNTAIN RANGE IN IRAQ!

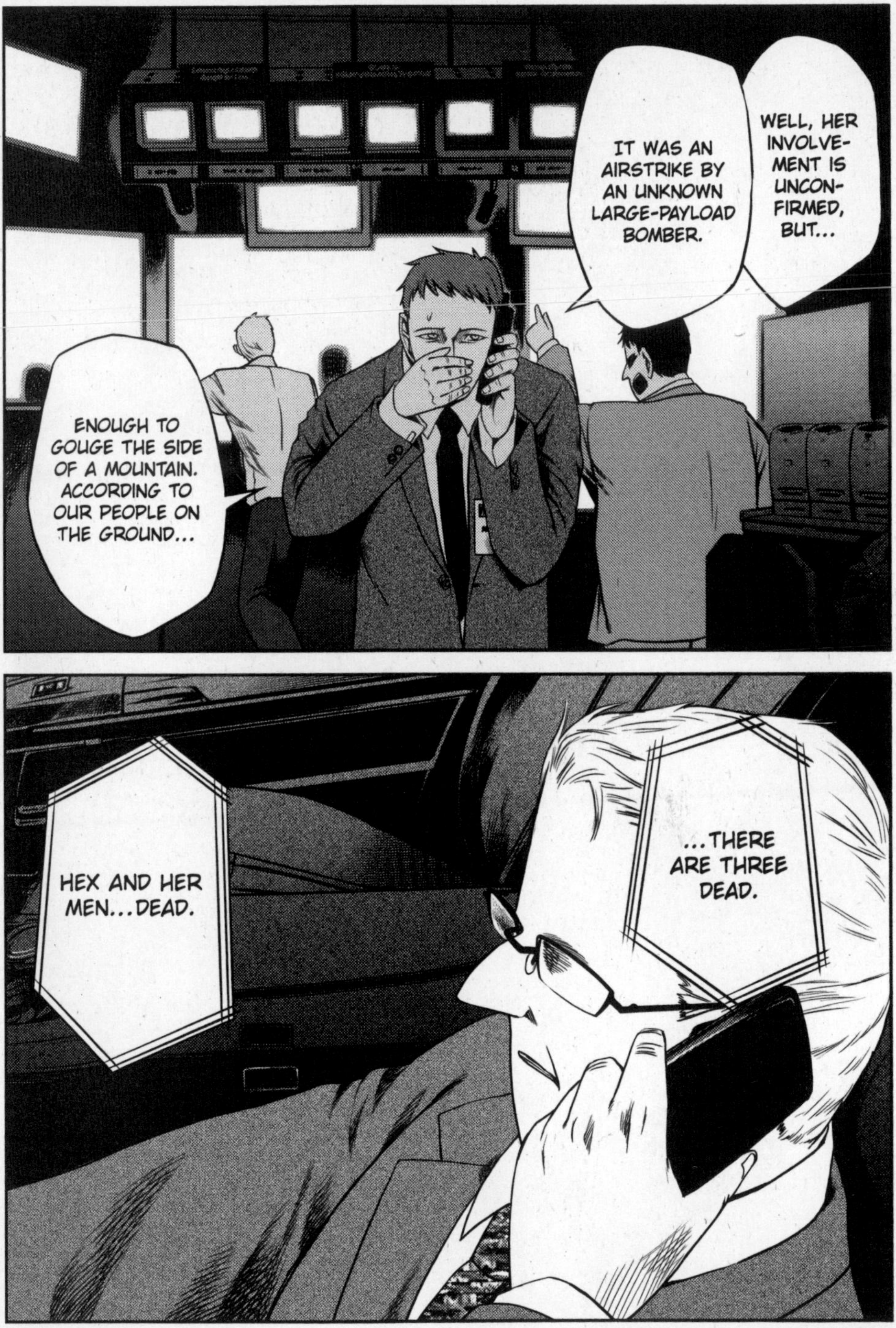
WELL, HER INVOLVEMENT IS UNCONFIRMED, BUT...
IT WAS AN AIRSTRIKE BY AN UNKNOWN LARGE-PAYLOAD BOMBER.
ENOUGH TO GOUGE THE SIDE OF A MOUNTAIN. ACCORDING TO OUR PEOPLE ON THE GROUND...
...THERE ARE THREE DEAD.
HEX AND HER MEN...DEAD.

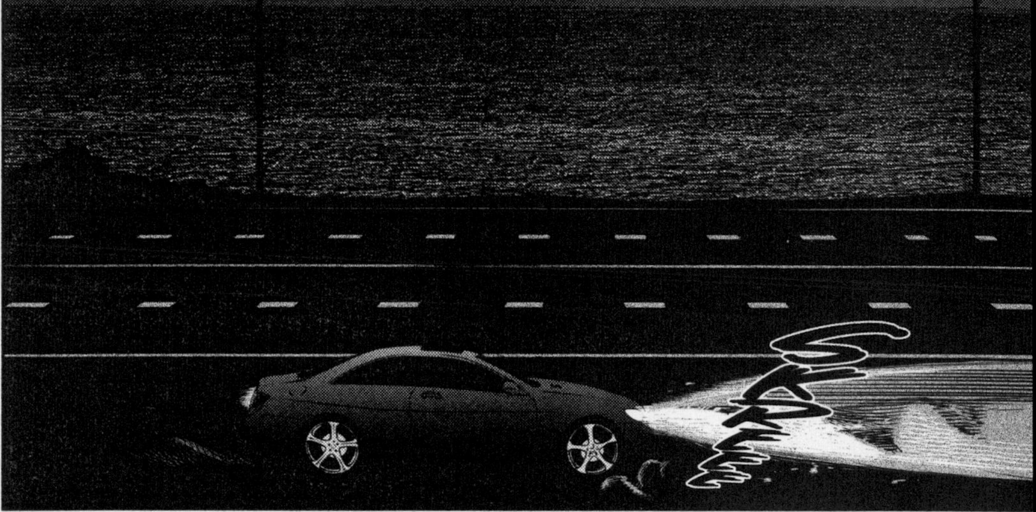
SKREEE

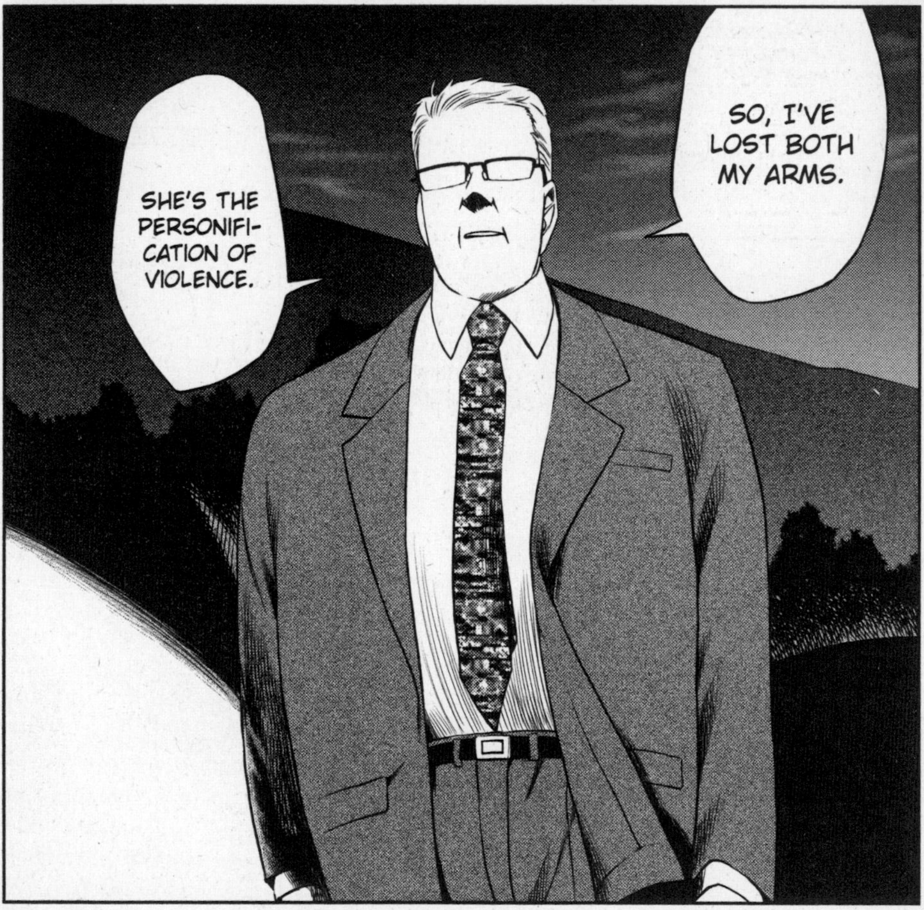
SO, I'VE LOST BOTH MY ARMS.
SHE'S THE PERSONIFICATION OF VIOLENCE.

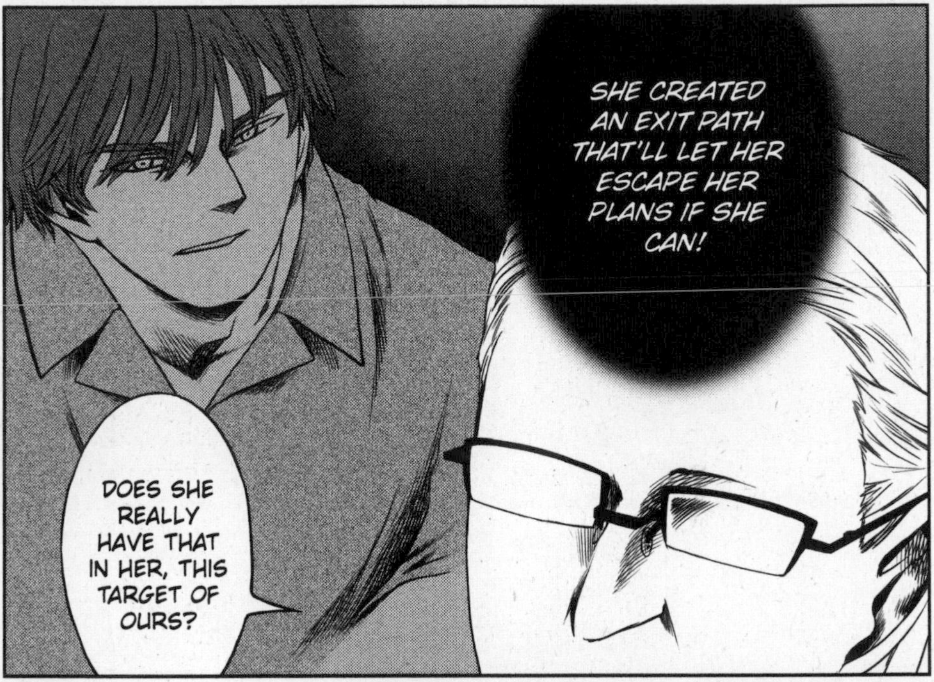
SHE CREATED AN EXIT PATH THAT'LL LET HER ESCAPE HER PLANS IF SHE CAN!
DOES SHE REALLY HAVE THAT IN HER, THIS TARGET OF OURS?

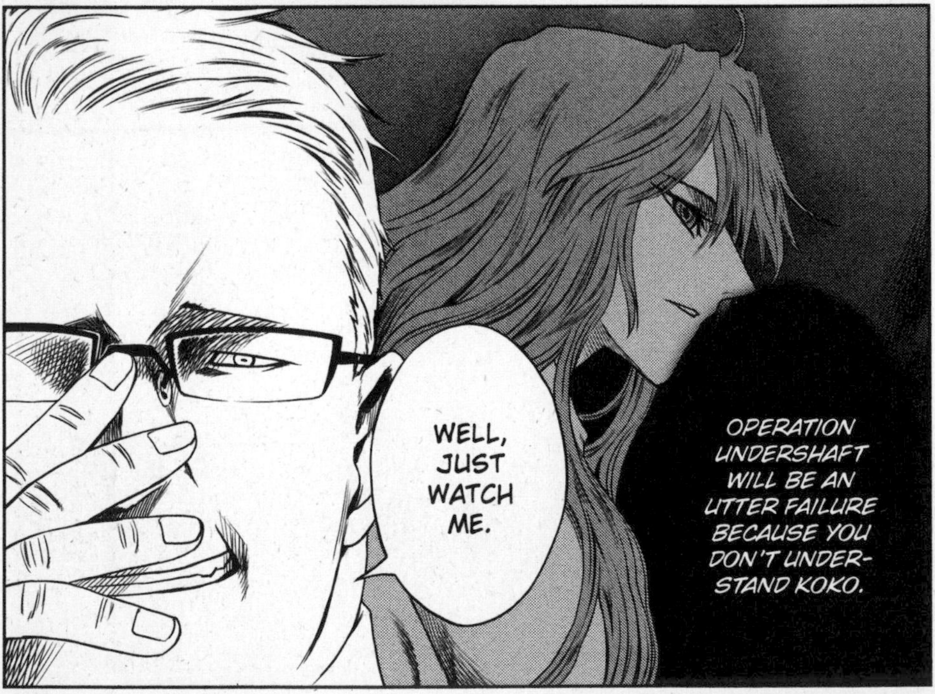
OPERATION UNDERSHAFT WILL BE AN UTTER FAILURE BECAUSE YOU DON'T UNDER-STAND KOKO.
WELL, JUST WATCH ME.

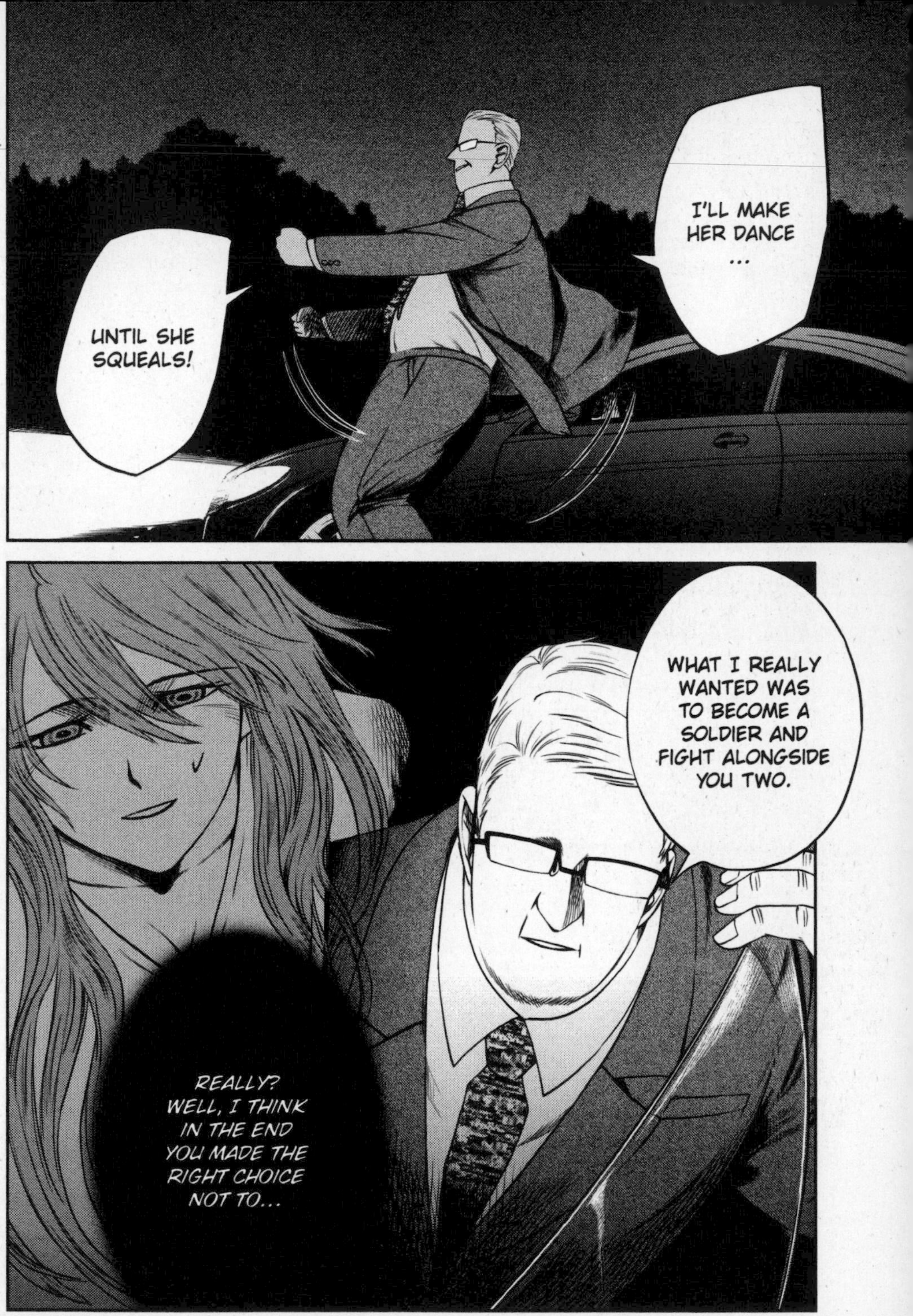
I'LL MAKE HER DANCE ...
UNTIL SHE SQUEALS!
WHAT I REALLY WANTED WAS TO BECOME A SOLDIER AND FIGHT ALONGSIDE YOU TWO.
REALLY? WELL, I THINK IN THE END YOU MADE THE RIGHT CHOICE NOT TO...

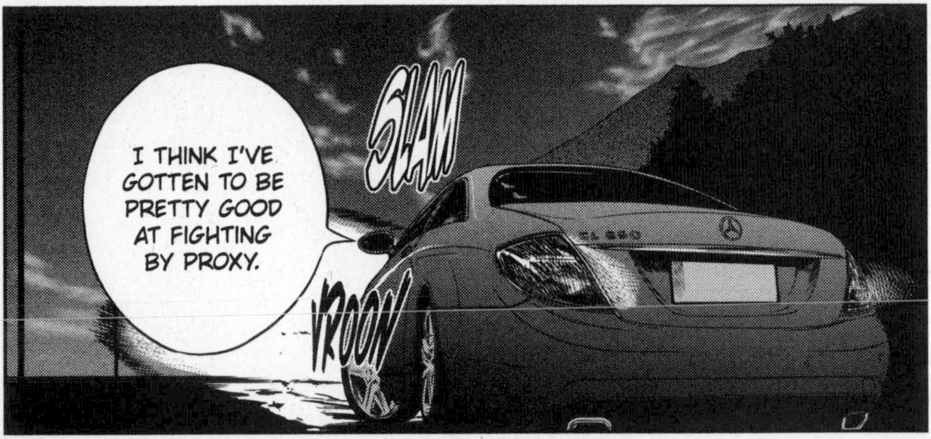
I THINK I'VE GOTTEN TO BE PRETTY GOOD AT FIGHTING BY PROXY.
SLAM
VROOM

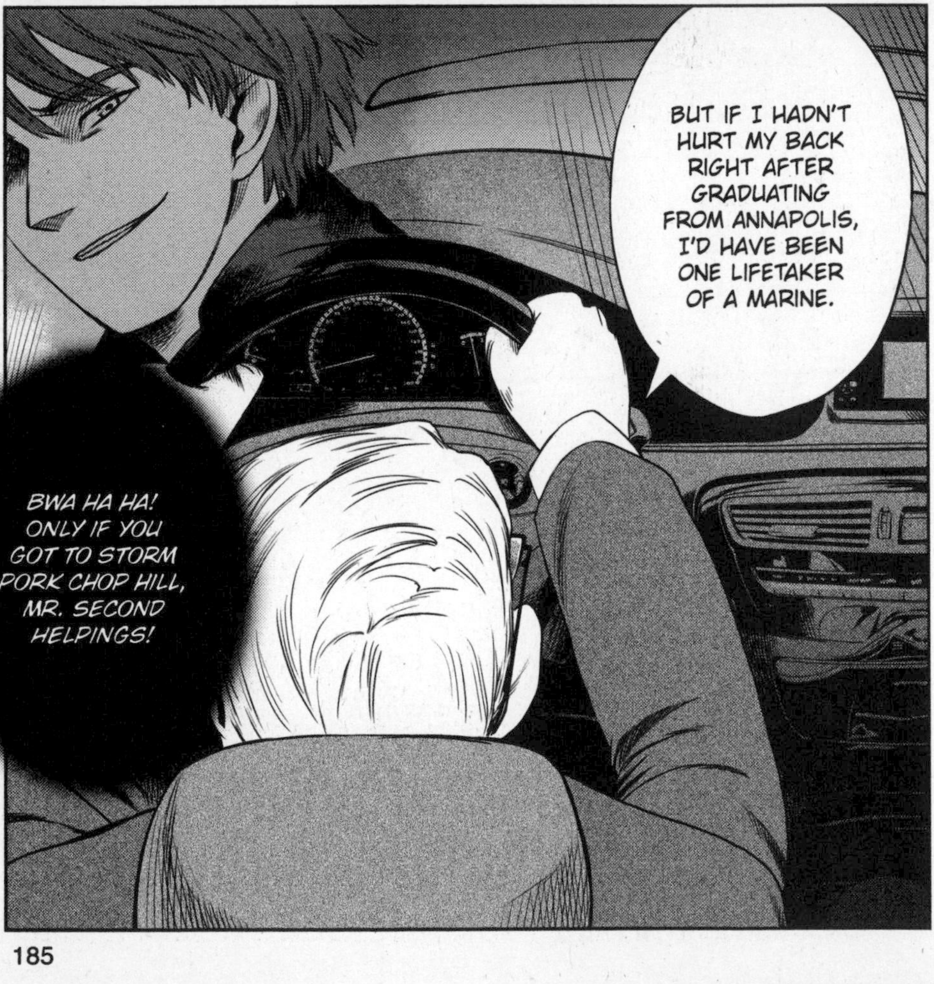
BUT IF I HADN'T HURT MY BACK RIGHT AFTER GRADUATING FROM ANNAPOLIS, I'D HAVE BEEN ONE LIFETAKER OF A MARINE.
BWA HA HA! ONLY IF YOU GOT TO STORM PORK CHOP HILL, MR. SECOND HELPINGS!

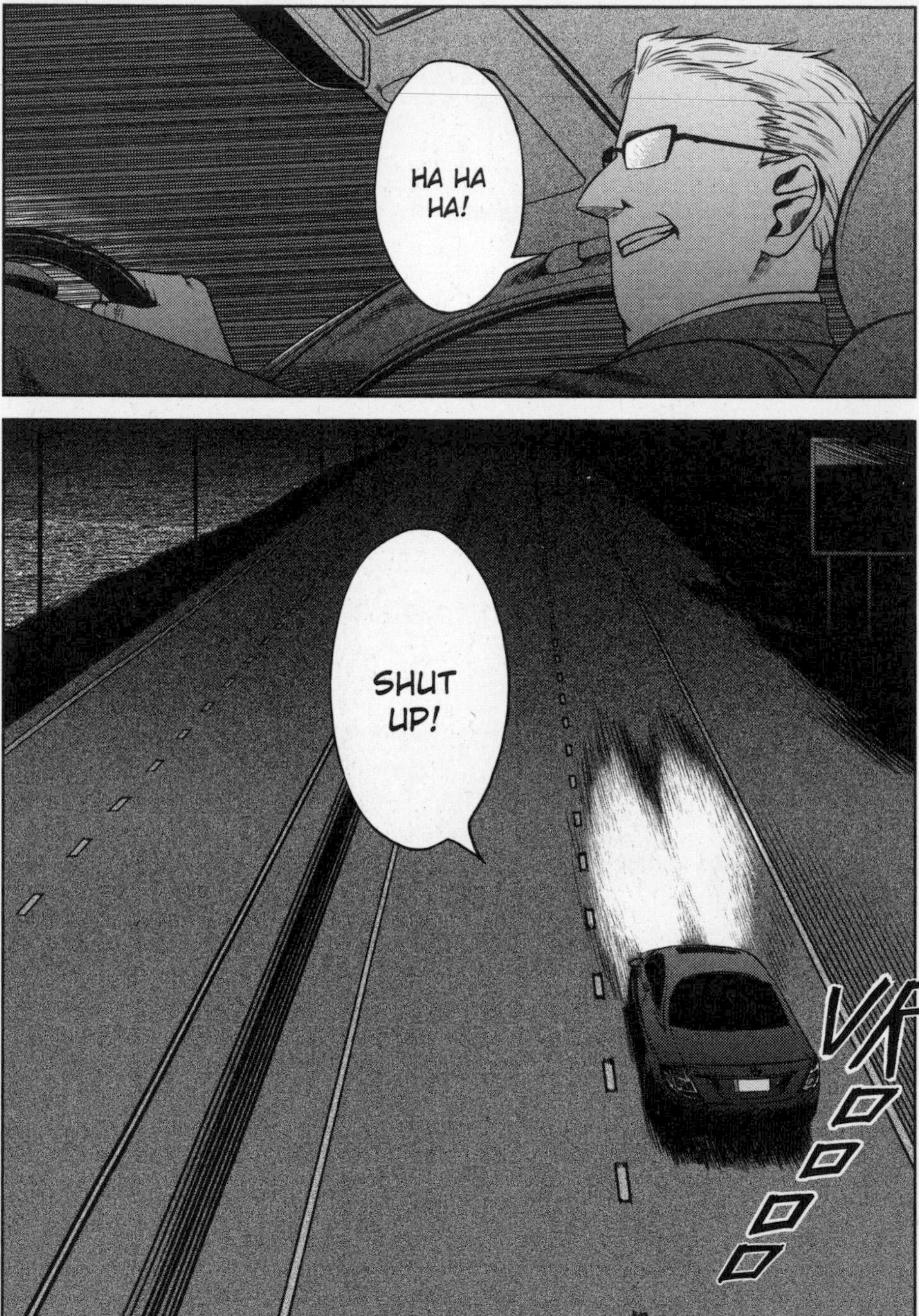
HA HA HA!
SHUT UP!
VROOOOO

JORMUNGAND VOLUME 7 – END –

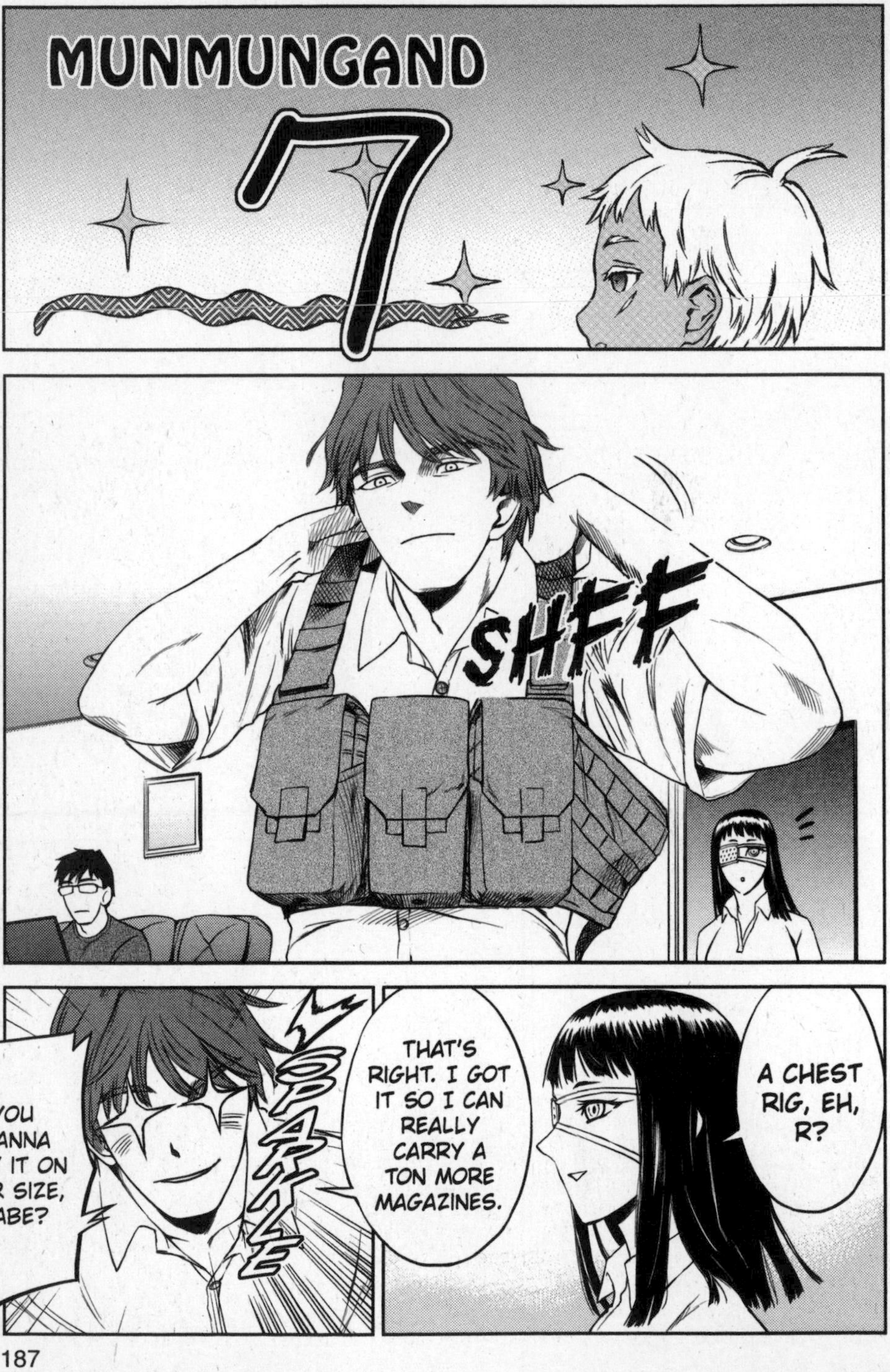
MUNMUNGAND
7
SHFF
A CHEST RIG, EH, R?
THAT'S RIGHT. I GOT IT SO I CAN REALLY CARRY A TON MORE MAGAZINES.
SPARKLE
YOU WANNA TRY IT ON FOR SIZE, BABE?

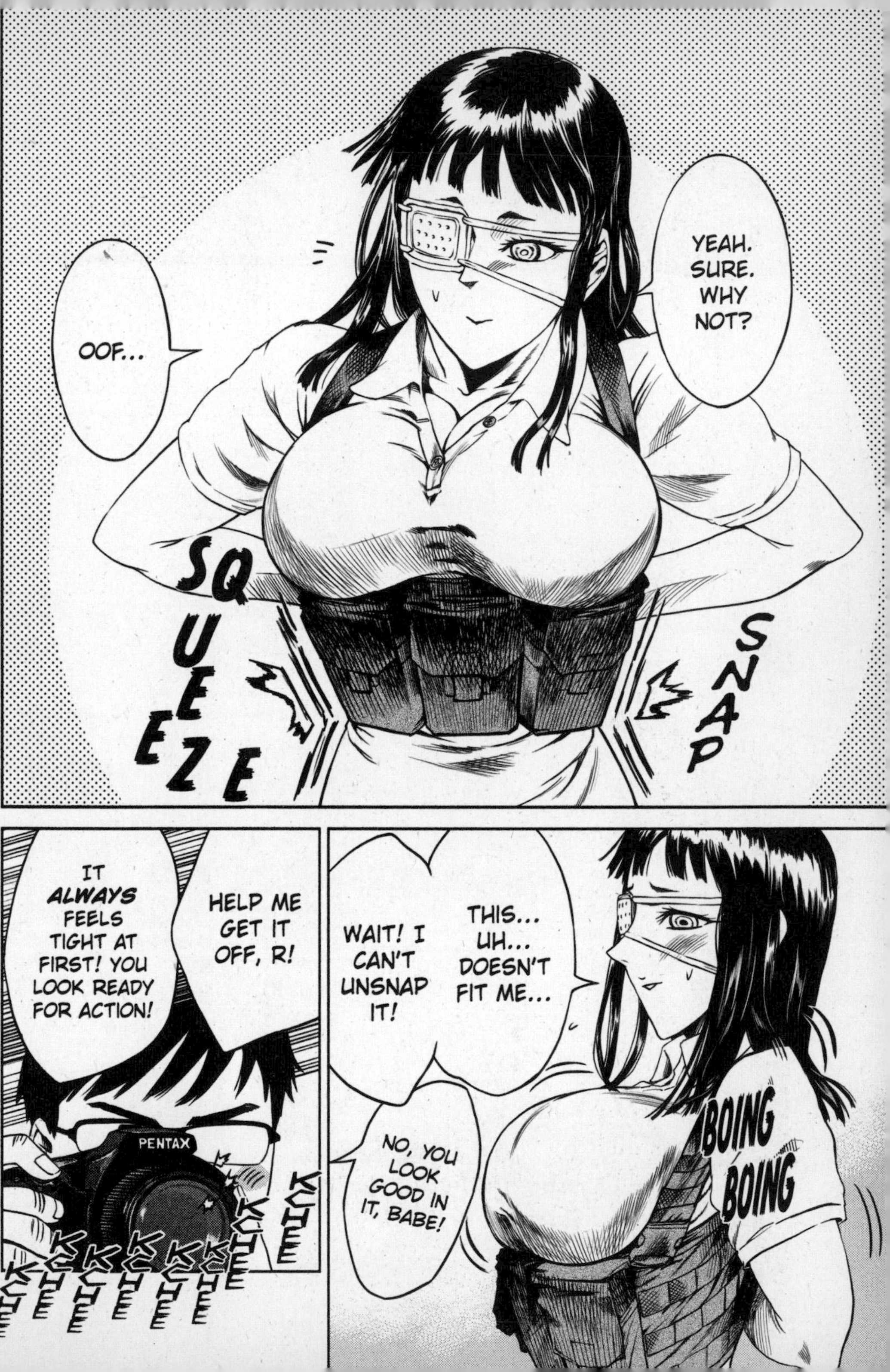
YEAH. SURE. WHY NOT?
OOF...
SNAP
SQUEEZE
THIS... UH... DOESN'T FIT ME...
WAIT! I CAN'T UNSNAP IT!
BOING BOING
NO, YOU LOOK GOOD IN IT, BABE!
HELP ME GET IT OFF, R!
IT *ALWAYS* FEELS TIGHT AT FIRST! YOU LOOK READY FOR ACTION!
PENTAX
KCHE KCHE KCHE KCHE KCHE KCHE KCHE

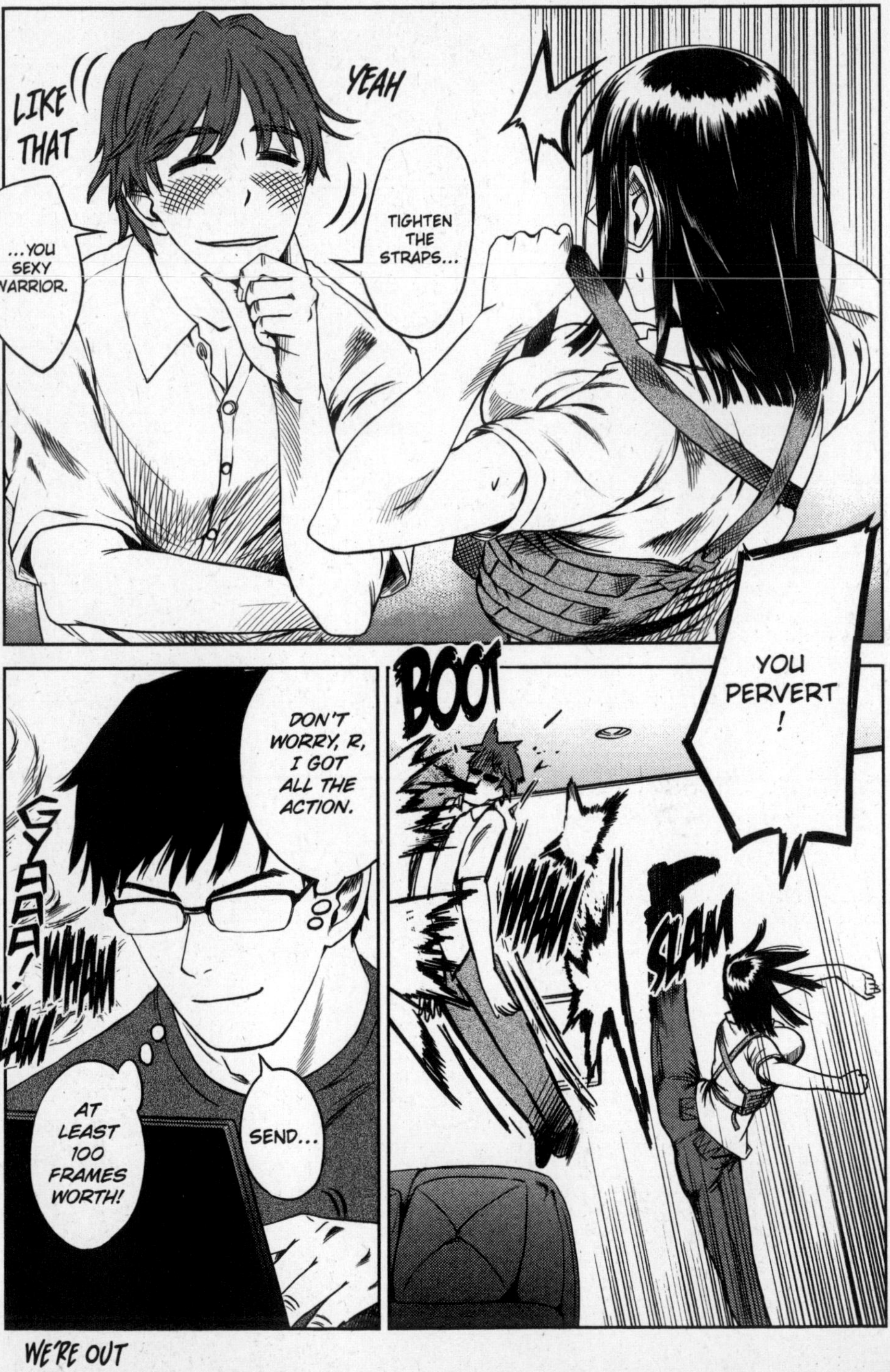
YEAH
TIGHTEN THE STRAPS...
LIKE THAT
...YOU SEXY WARRIOR.
YOU PERVERT!
BOOT
WHAM
SLAM
DON'T WORRY, R, I GOT ALL THE ACTION.
GYAAAA!
WHAM
SLAM
SEND...
AT LEAST 100 FRAMES WORTH!
WE'RE OUT

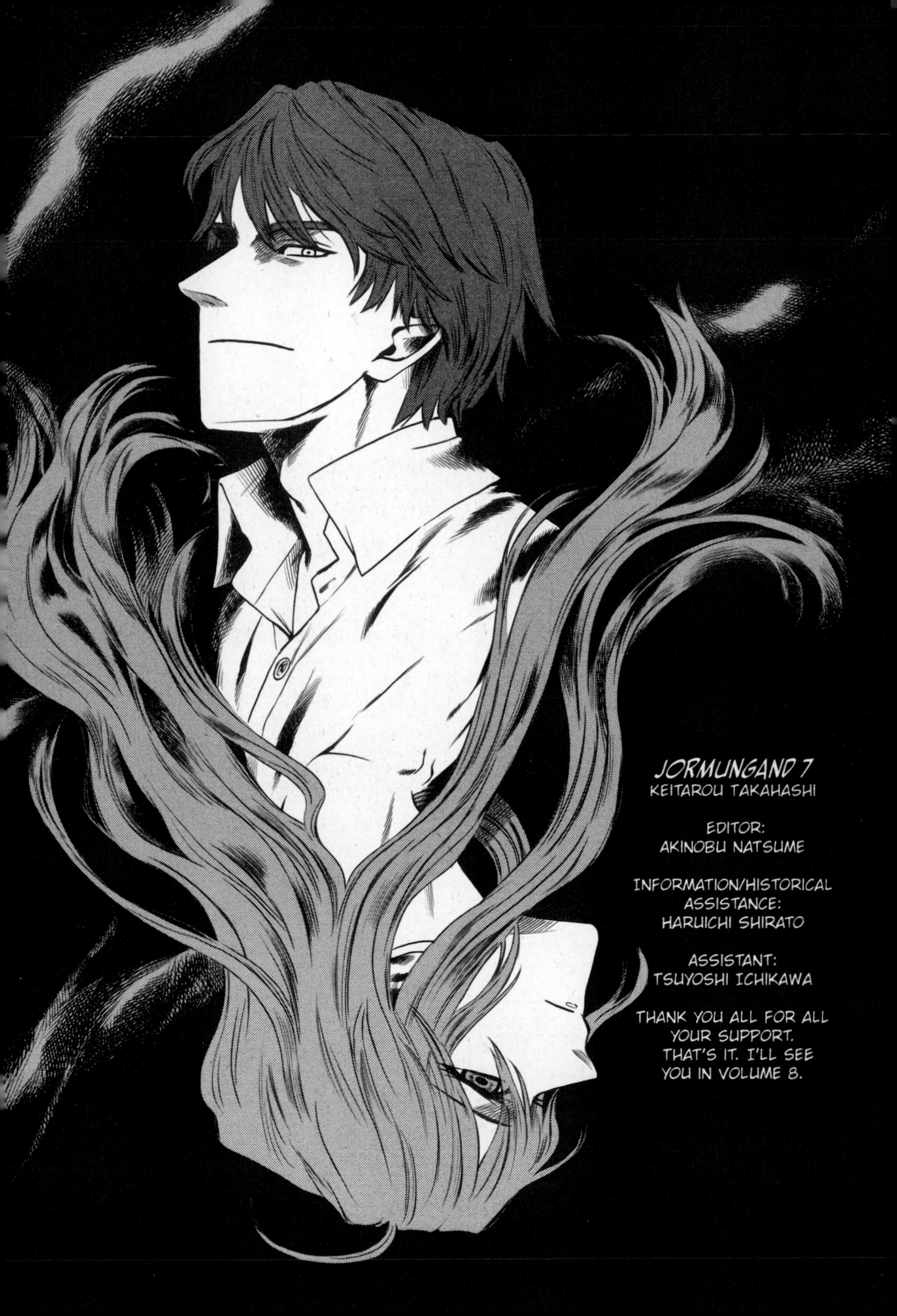

JORMUNGAND 7
KEITAROU TAKAHASHI

EDITOR:
AKINOBU NATSUME

INFORMATION/HISTORICAL
ASSISTANCE:
HARUICHI SHIRATO

ASSISTANT:
TSUYOSHI ICHIKAWA

THANK YOU ALL FOR ALL
YOUR SUPPORT.
THAT'S IT. I'LL SEE
YOU IN VOLUME 8.

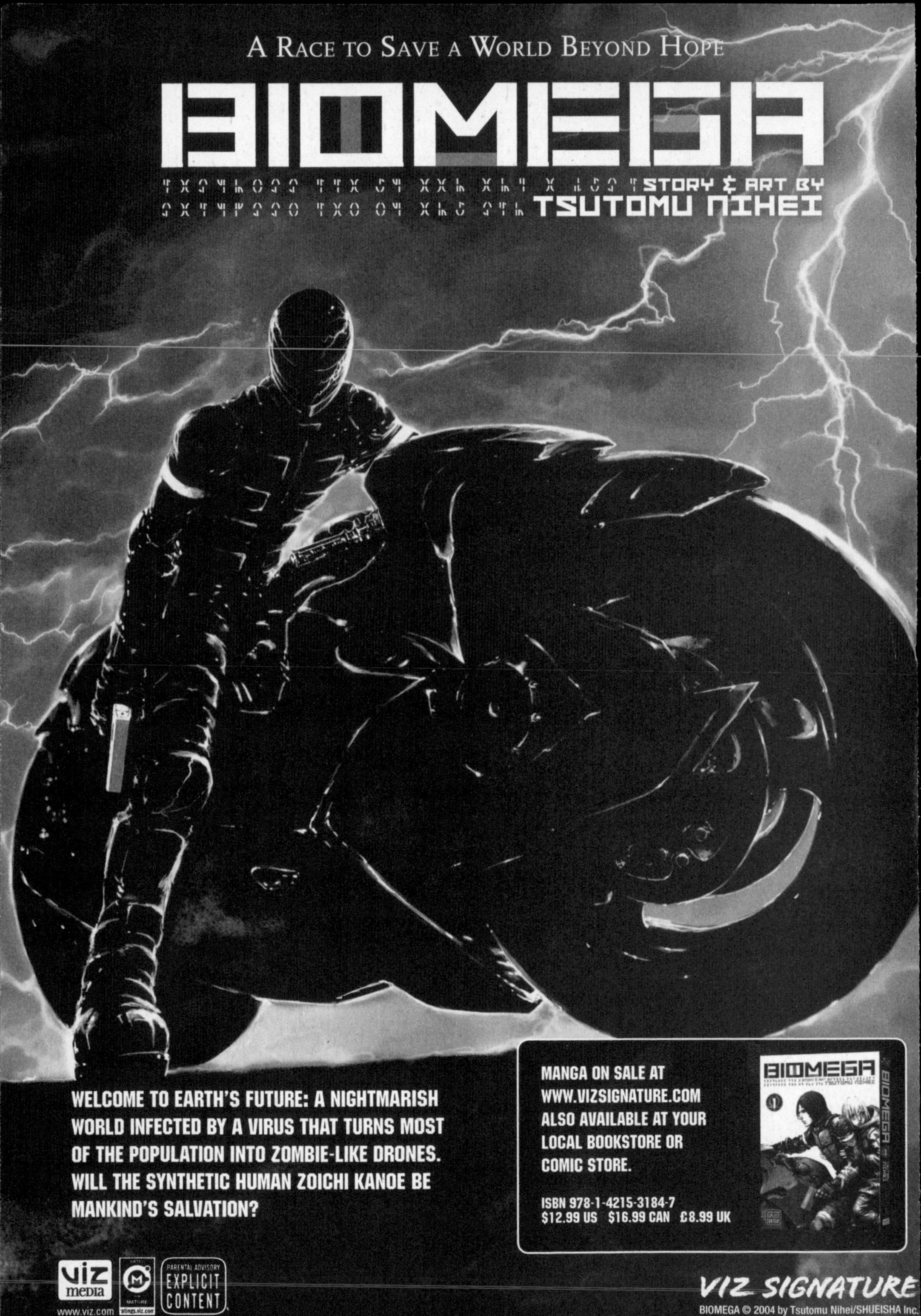
A RACE TO SAVE A WORLD BEYOND HOPE
BIOMEGA
STORY & ART BY
TSUTOMU NIHEI
WELCOME TO EARTH'S FUTURE: A NIGHTMARISH WORLD INFECTED BY A VIRUS THAT TURNS MOST OF THE POPULATION INTO ZOMBIE-LIKE DRONES. WILL THE SYNTHETIC HUMAN ZOICHI KANOE BE MANKIND'S SALVATION?
MANGA ON SALE AT WWW.VIZSIGNATURE.COM
ALSO AVAILABLE AT YOUR LOCAL BOOKSTORE OR COMIC STORE.
ISBN 978-1-4215-3184-7
$12.99 US $16.99 CAN £8.99 UK
BIOMEGA
viz media
www.viz.com
PARENTAL ADVISORY EXPLICIT CONTENT
VIZ SIGNATURE
BIOMEGA © 2004 by Tsutomu Nihei/SHUEISHA Inc.

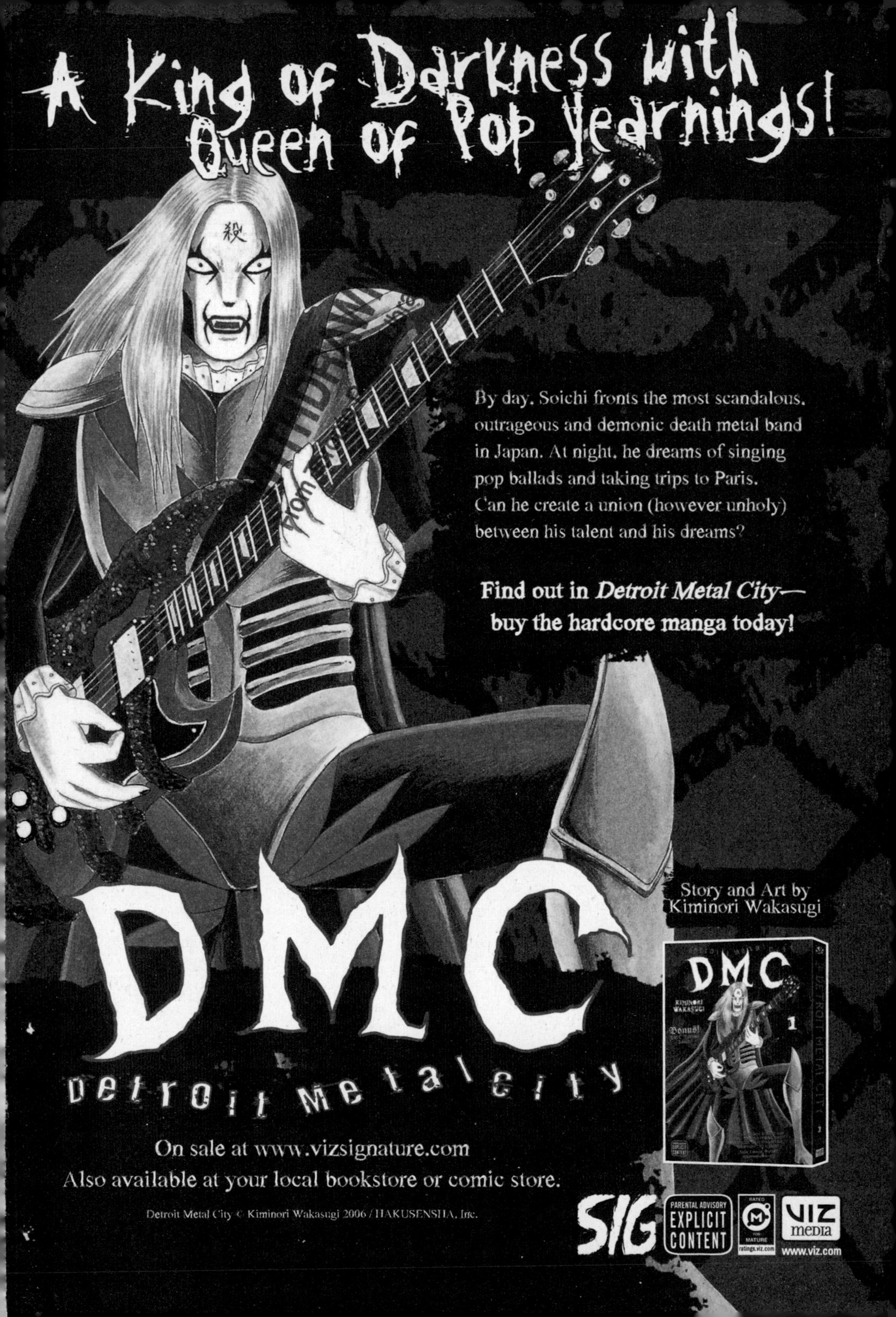
A King of Darkness with Queen of Pop Yearnings!
By day, Soichi fronts the most scandalous, outrageous and demonic death metal band in Japan. At night, he dreams of singing pop ballads and taking trips to Paris. Can he create a union (however unholy) between his talent and his dreams?
Find out in Detroit Metal City— buy the hardcore manga today!
Story and Art by Kiminori Wakasugi
DMC
Detroit Metal City
On sale at www.vizsignature.com
Also available at your local bookstore or comic store.
Detroit Metal City © Kiminori Wakasugi 2006 / HAKUSENSHA, Inc.
SIG
PARENTAL ADVISORY EXPLICIT CONTENT
RATED M FOR MATURE ratings.viz.com
VIZ media
www.viz.com